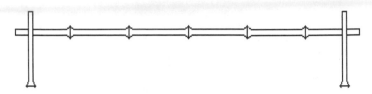

Living in China

A Guide to Teaching and Studying in China Including Taiwan

Rebecca Weiner
Margaret Murphy
Albert Li

CHINA BOOKS & PERIODICALS, INC. • SAN FRANCISCO

Cover design by Robbin Henderson
Text design by Robbin Henderson

Library of Congress Catalog Card Number: 91-73126

ISBN 0-8351-2480-0

Printed in the United States of America by CHINA
BOOKS
& Periodicals, Inc.

This book is dedicated to our parents:

Midge and Herb
Peg and Joe
Shu-Zhen and Yong-An

Table of Contents

v

INTRODUCTION

So You Want To Go To China . . .

You're a student of Chinese, or acupuncture, or calligraphy. You're a teacher of English, or Western culture, or physics. You're a retiree and want to get back in the classroom. You're just starting out and want an interesting first job. You plan a career in Asian business or law or journalism and want to teach or study as an entree to the East. You've just heard how interesting China is, and you want to go live there for a while.

You want to go to China.

This book was written for you.

The *Guide* is for people heading off to China as students, teachers, or researchers. The book will help you choose where to go and how to get there, what to bring and how to make the most of your time once you've arrived. Other books exist for specialized China experts on high-level exchanges (two of our favorites are *Chinabound*, and the *Teaching in China Preparation Series;* see Appendix B for details). Those books teem with suggestions on dealing with officials at the Ministry of Education and the Bureau of Foreign Experts, on how to get books published in China and how to get access to specialized research libraries. This book doesn't re-cross that same ground. Instead, this book is about the nitty-gritty of heading off to China on your own, whether individually or through an exchange organization. It will tell you which foods you can get in China, and how to buy a train ticket, how to combine teaching or studying with travel and how to take advantage of China's freemarkets. It's about real life in China for foreigners without the support provided by high-level exchanges—foreigners who won't be assigned interpreters and guides.

Structurally, the book falls into two parts. Part I runs chronologically through your China experience, from choosing a school to choosing a route home. Part II contains directories of schools and sending organizations. The book is both a reference work for deciding where to go in China and planning how to get there, and a manual on how to make the most of your experiences once you've arrived.

The authors have all been both teachers and students in China. This book contains our views as "insiders" on how life in China really works. We've also bolstered our own experiences by sending out surveys to foreign teachers and students at 552 Chinese institutions, asking about their experiences. Both text and directories have been greatly enhanced by the results of those surveys.

The authors would like to thank the following individuals and institutions without whose help this work would not have been possible. Where the book succeeds much of the praise is theirs; where it fails, the blame is ours: the National Committee on U.S.-China Relations, and in particular Jan Berris and Elizabeth Kurz; the U.S.-China People's Friendship Association, and in particular Judy Manton and Jo Croom; the Australia-China Chamber of Commerce, and in particular Robert Cousland; the Canadian-Chinese Friendship Association; the Washington, D.C. Embassy of New Zealand, and in particular Lesley Jackman; the British Council's Washington, D.C. liaison, and in particular Margaret Lynch; the National TESOL Organization, and in particular Helen Kornblum; the Council on International Educational Exchange, and in particular Suzanne Fox; AFS Intercultural Programs, and in particular Carol Byrne; Virginia Walden of Sister-Cities International; Jacklyn Levine of the University of Rochester's Study Abroad Office; and the Institute of International Education, and in particular Peggy Blumenthal, Dulcie L. Schackman and Ed Battle. These people and organizations individually and collectively represent phenomenal wisdom about foreign teaching and study, and about China. They were instrumental in directing us to sources of information. IIE deserves special kudos, for their excellent international guides to *Teaching Abroad, Vacation Study Abroad,* and *Semester Programs Abroad* (which are updated yearly) provided the format and starting information for the surveys which grew into our Directories of Sending Organizations. Dr. Beatrice Bartlett, Steve Carlin, Dr. Jo Ellen Green, Dr. Brett Hinsch, Lillian Hreljac, Dr. David Kaiser, Dr. Murray Levith, Sr. Anne Phibbs, Barbara Rosenberg, and Paul Williams were extremely generous with their time and helpful with their comments, talking and reading through numerous drafts. Paul Williams was our resident computer wizard. Many Chinese friends (best not named) made possible the gargantuan task of sending out envelopes full of surveys to 552 schools in the P.R.C. Adam Aronson, David Bogart, Jeff Davis, Dan Gaiser, Mary-Ann Hill, Linda

G., Carolyn Matthews, and Harlan and Bonnie Seyfer gathered voluminous and invaluable information on Beijing schools on a very tight schedule. Editor Charles Wang and Senior Editor Bob Schildgen at China Books & Periodicals were constantly supportive and inspiring, and the entire China Books staff approached the project with an enthusiasm that reinfected us through the draft #47 blues.

The authors wish to thank all the individuals at sending organizations for teachers and students going to China who took the time to fill out our surveys, allowing us the most up-to-date possible information for our directories. We also thank the following respondents to our survey of teachers and students in the mainland who agreed to be listed in our acknowledgments, as well as the many others who asked not to be listed, but whose thoughtful responses have so enriched our text. These men and women out in the trenches in China's educational system are the real "insiders," and their ideas are as central to this book as our own: Michael Angelusto, Adam L. Aronson, Elmah Baines, Don Barnett, David Bedell, Bernadette Brennan, Ramona and Richard Boyle, Cao Shuang-lin, Molly Deatherage, Keith Dede, Carol DeGrange, Harry and Mo Disney, Laurie Elsen, Sharon Flynn, Patricia Foster, Kevin Gambrel, Erin Gregory, Guo Xian-ting, Ellen Hauser, David Kellogg, Miles Lozinsky, A.S. Maclean-Bristol, Richard Mann, Henri Marcel, Paul Maynard, Heidi Myer, Mik Moses, Jenny Presland, Isabelle Pryor, David Silverglade, Shen Jun-cai, Sun Hong-guang, Judith Valois, Jim Vining, Jon Weston, and Zhang Zhao Xiang.

Finally, we would like to thank our students and teachers in China. In the hopes of sending more and better-prepared foreign teachers and students to China, this book was written also for them.

Note on Transliteration Style and Terminology: Rather than make a political statement by our choice of romanization style, the authors have transliterated all Chinese proper names using the spelling most common in the place discussed. Thus all mainland Chinese names are romanized in Hanyu Pinyin, and all Taiwan names in Wade-Giles. All Chinese phrases are transliterated in Pinyin. See Appendix A for pronunciation guides in both systems.

Throughout the text, the terms "PRC" and "mainland" refer to the People's Republic of China, while Taiwan is called Taiwan. Unless otherwise indicated, the terms "China" and "Chinese" refer to both.

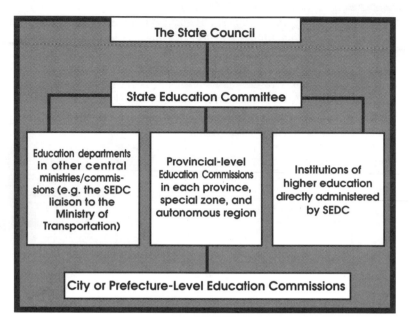

FIGURE 1:   OVERALL STRUCTURE OF CHINA'S EDUCATIONAL
BUREAUCRACY

1

The Big Picture

CHINA'S EDUCATIONAL SYSTEM

Education, like most things in China, is a top-down affair. The State Education Commission (SEDC), primary arbiter of educational policy, fits directly under the State Council in China's Governmental hierarchy. This position reflects both the emphasis China places on education, and the need felt by China's leadership for strict central control.

The SEDC carries out State Council policy through a network of education commissions and officers (see Fig.1). At any one school, teachers (both Chinese and foreign) may be inspected by officials from school-local-provincial-and national-level education commissions, and by SEDC officials from other ministries related to the school's academic focus (such as railway officials at a School of Transportation Engineering). As might be expected, demands are varied and complex. Chinese schools of significant size hire innumerable vice presidents, and assign at least one to full-time liaison duty with the SEDC.

China mandates 9 years of public education, from ages 6 through 14, or through middle school (for an international reference chart comparing systems of grade numbering, see Fig. 2). In rural areas, where almost 75% of China's people live, the majority of students make do with those 9 years. In cities and more well-to-do rural areas, however, many students begin kindergarten at age 3 or 4 and continue on after middle school. At age 14 students take a municipal or regional exam. Many students then go on to general high schools. Others are tracked into specialized high schools, depending on their exam results (see Fig. 3). Specialized high

1

Grade Levels	Grade Levels	Grade Levels	Grade Levels	Grade Levels	Grade Levels
17	12	Gao 3 (Great Exam)	Form 7 (College Exam)	Form 7 (College Exam)	Upper 6 (A Levels)
16	11	Gao 2	Form 6	Form 6	Lower 6
15	10	Gao 1	Form 5 (Nat'l Exam)	Form 5	Form 5 (O Levels)
14	9	Zhong 3 (Nat'l Exam)	Form 4	Form 4 (Nat'l Exam)	Form 4
13	8	Zhong 2	Form 3	Form 3	Form 3
12	7	Zhong 1	Form 2	Form 2	Form 2
11	6	Xiao 6	Form 1	Form 1	Form 1
10	5	Xiao 5	Primary 6	Primus 5	Primus 6
9	4	Xiao 4	Primary 5	Primus 4	Primus 5
8	3	Xiao 3	Primary 4	Primus 3	Primus 4
7	2	Xiao 2	Primary 3	Primus2	Primus 3
6	1	Xiao 1	Primary 2	Primus 1	Primus2
5	Kindergarten	Kindergarten	Primary 1	Kindergarten	Primus 1
4	Preschool	Preschool	Kindergarten	Playschool	Kindergarten
3	Preschool	Preschool	Playschool	Playschool	Preschool
Approx. Age	US/Canada	Chinese System	New Zealand	Australia	United Kingdom

FIGURE 2:   COMPARATIVE CHART OF ELEMENTARY/SECONDARY GRADES

schools include: college preparatory comprehensive schools, secondary professional schools (for training to be nurses, technicians, paralegals, and the like), and secondary vocational schools (for training in electronic assembly, auto mechanics, and the like). Students in general or college preparatory high schools compete 3 years later in the grueling 3-day "College Exam," (*gaokao:* 高考).   Based on Gaokao results, students will be accepted into the colleges of their choice, tracked into other colleges, rejected outright, or tracked into tertiary vocational or professional schools. Students in B.A. programs then face a final "Graduation Exam" before receiving their degree, and foreign instructors must teach students what they need to know for this exam. Taiwan's system is structurally identical, except all 12 years are mandatory.

All mainland schools and all departments within schools must have a Communist "Party Secretary" (*danwei shuji:* 单位书记), whose full-time job consists of implementing and monitoring "Communist Education and Morality." Until several years ago Taiwan had "Security Secretaries" (*danwei mishu:* 单位秘书) from the Kuomingtang party filling comparable roles. Party secretaries form a "dual hierarchy" paralleling the academic hierarchy of department heads and presidents. As might be expected, in some cases the two hierarchies work together well, and in others they bicker constantly. When department heads and departmental party secretaries lock horns, little gets accomplished within the department. Even at its best many Chinese decry the system as wasteful. Deng Xiao-ping's 1980s reforms promised a gradual phase out of the dual system. However, in the aftermath of the 1989 Democracy Movement central control of education has once again come to the fore. For the foreseeable future, foreigners in Chinese schools can expect to keep negotiating between political and academic hierarchies.

Departments appoint a class monitor for each classroom, a student responsible for liaison duty with the department head and party secretary. At larger schools, class monitor functions may be divided among several students, or even a whole class council, with some students responsible for recreation, some for distributing meal tickets, some for attendance records, and so on. At small schools, one student may fill all these roles. The class monitor responsible for political liaison is called a *tuanwei* (团委), a reference to membership in the Party Youth Corp; all other class monitors are called *banzhang* (班长). The tuanwei's duties include bringing all classroom materials in for departmental review, and reporting on any untoward classroom discussion, including any "indiscretions" of teachers or classmates. Westerners tend to abhor these "class spies," but they are a fundamental part of the Chinese system, and have been since long before Communism; Taiwan has them too, though their political function has declined in recent years.

All mainland schools through secondary level, and nearly all colleges and universities, are publically funded. A few small colleges, such as Xiamen's Overseas Chinese University, are privately funded, but are still administered by SEDC policy. On Taiwan many schools at all levels are privately funded and administered, but the R.O.C. Ministry of Education retains veto rights over curricula and teaching. On the mainland, the SEDC, like most nations' Ministries of Education (although unlike the U.S. or Canadian Departments of Education), sets detailed national educational policy. At the elementary and secondary levels this control extends to commission and selection of individual textbooks and course curricula. At the tertiary level schools and teachers have more leeway. Nevertheless, all teaching materials and methods are subject to SEDC approval. Foreigners working in China need to understand this hierarchy. The teacher who refuses to assign certain materials to foreign students may be following central mandates. Meanwhile, foreign teachers who assign illicit materials to Chinese students mark those students for questioning and suspicion.

The goals of State Council educational policy are best expressed in the inimicable style of the SEDC itself: "China lays special emphasis on

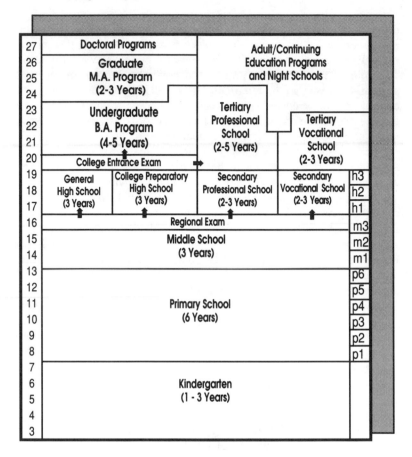

27	Doctoral Programs		Adult/Continuing Education Programs and Night Schools			
26	Graduate M.A. Program (2-3 Years)					
25						
24						
23	Undergraduate B.A. Program (4-5 Years)		Tertiary Professional School (2-5 Years)	Tertiary Vocational School (2-3 Years)		
22						
21						
20	College Entrance Exam ➡					
19	General High School (3 Years)	College Preparatory High School (3 Years)	Secondary Professional School (2-3 Years)	Secondary Vocational School (2-3 Years)		h3
18						h2
17						h1
16	Regional Exam					m3
15	Middle School (3 Years)					m2
14						m1
13	Primary School (6 Years)					p6
12						p5
11						p4
10						p3
9						p2
8						p1
7	Kindergarten (1 - 3 Years)					
6						
5						
4						
3						

FIGURE 3:   OVERALL STRUCTURE OF CHINA'S EDUCATIONAL SYSTEM

making students develop morally, intellectually and physically, on culti-
vating in them a devoted and hardworking spirit for the welfare of the
country and people, on having ideals, morality, culture, discipline, love
for the socialist motherland and construction, and on having a scientific
attitude and unswerving will of pursuing new knowledge and bravely
creating new things on the basis of seeking truth from facts and independent thinking." (*Study in China: A Guide for Foreign Students, Foreign
Student Administration Society* [Beijing Languages Institute Press, 1987],
p. 7.)

In other words, academic content is only one part of what the SEDC hopes to impart to Chinese students (certainly no one stresses the evil of run-on sentences). Many Chinese students have begun to oppose these agendas, and to laugh along with foreigners at SEDC "goals." But even these students must take part in non-academic activities. Typical study programs include political study sessions, physical training, military training, inculcation of "moral values," and participation in community projects aimed at "socialist reconstruction" on top of an academic course load. While foreigners are excused from participation in this "other education," both foreign teachers and foreign students should be aware of the demands it makes on their Chinese counterparts.

In this book we lump together all foreigners who teach in China as foreign teachers, small "f," small "t." The Chinese government divides foreigners into Foreign Teachers and Foreign Experts. This distinction means little once your contract is signed (see Chapter 5); Foreign Experts and Foreign Teachers generally live in the same dorms and teach much the same sort of classes. But Foreign Experts receive substantially better salary and benefits than Foreign Teachers. Judging from our surveys, most Foreign Teachers earn between 600 and 900Y/month RMB, and may or may not receive FEC. Foreign Experts generally start at around 1100Y/month, and almost certainly are eligible for some FEC, usually 30%.

Try if at all possible to be classed as a Foreign Expert. You'll have substantially better leverage in contract negotiations, and may get first crack at the best dorm rooms and most interesting classes. According to the SEDC's brochure "Information on the Recruitment of Foreign Experts," language teachers who wish to be classed as Experts:

1. Should have a relatively high attainment in their own language and literature.

2. Should have been engaged in regular language teaching or the teaching of literature at the college level, or should have been regular language or literature teachers for 5 years or more in senior high schools, and possess a senior high school teacher's certificate.

3. Should have obtained an MA or higher degree. As practically applied, these regulations generally mean that anyone with a masters or higher and 2 or more years' teaching experience can generally expect Expert status. Clever negotiators have also wrangled Expert status with only the degree or the experience.

Following is a breakdown of China's post–high-school educational institutions, the sort most foreigners are likely to become involved with:

1. LIBERAL ARTS COLLEGES/UNIVERSITIES: These are large institutions granting 4-year baccalaureate degrees and/or graduate degrees. Most have broad ranging academic departments, from the familiar Chemistry, History, and Music to such uniquely Chinese disciplines as "History of the Chinese Communist Party" and "Central Economic Planning." Most colleges and universities accept foreign students capable of studying in Chinese into all departments, and foreign teachers in many departments; many also provide specialized programs taught in English specifically for foreigners. The central government has designated approximately 100 of China's universities as "Key Universities," with special funding and materials. From Beijing University to Guangzhou's Sun Yat Sen University, virtually all of China's most famous schools are Key Universities.

2. TERTIARY PROFESSIONAL SCHOOLS: As in many nations (although unlike in the U.S. and Canada), most professional schools in China, from law and medicine to fine arts and normal (teacher preparatory) schools, accept candidates directly from high school. Tertiary professional schools cover a wide range of topics, but are not as broadly focused as the liberal arts colleges and universities. Most tertiary professional schools accept foreigners as both teachers and students. The largest number of students from developing nations on Chinese government scholarships attend professional schools in development-related areas such as Medicine and Engineering. Other students who arrange individual study programs in less conventional disciplines such as acupuncture or Beijing Opera often find professional schools more flexible about their needs than the great universities. In China's educational hierarchy the tertiary professional schools sit below the liberal arts schools. However, as politics plays such a great role in school selection, students at the professional schools are not necessarily less qualified than those at the universities, just less well connected.

3. TERTIARY TECHNICAL/VOCATIONAL SCHOOLS: China has hundreds of post-high-school vocational schools, teaching everything from textile manufacture to electronics. Many, such as the Postal Workers Institutes, are run by government

ministries to prepare workers for their bailiwick; others are run directly by individual factories and workplaces. These institutes accept many foreign teachers, most to train students in English, but some for technical expertise as well. Often these schools offer the best financial packages for foreign teachers. Relatively few technical/vocational schools accept foreigners as students, and those generally only in specially organized programs, such as short-term courses in Chinese banking.

FOREIGNERS IN CHINESE SCHOOLS

The famed Chinese social critic Lu Xun once wrote, "Throughout the ages, we Chinese have had only two ways of looking at foreigners: either up to them as gods or down on them as beasts." Lu Xun may have exaggerated, but some of the attitudes he described still prevail. Foreigners in China live the best and worst of lives. Feted and made into buffoons, welcomed and kept at arm's length, they are both honored individuals and pawns in the struggle of an ancient culture now both embracing and resisting Westernization.

Students and teachers feel these contradictions more keenly than most, for they enter into the deepest social relationship (teacher-student) in Chinese culture other than that of family. Yet they enter as outsiders. The cost is an experience as powerful in its joys as its frustrations. The prize is an understanding closer to the bone of Chinese life than any can claim, be they journalists, businesspeople, or diplomats, who approach China only through official screens.

Whether your time in China is a springboard to a career in Asia, an academic adventure, or just a lark, you are likely to find it an overwhelming experience which changes you, for better or worse, forever. Foreigners who have taught or studied in China tend to love or hate her. Neutrality is rare.

THE UNPLANNED LIFE

The first thing to understand about teaching or studying in China is that however you prepare, including by reading this book, reality will likely turn out quite different from expectation. Conditions in China change rapidly. Then too, few people before they arrive can pin down Chinese institutions on just what they'll study or teach. Those that do often find everything changed on arrival. History lectures become economics seminars, and composition classes conversation classes, often without apparent reason or consideration of your resume.

For many this is the first inkling of the vast unpredictability of life in

China, which will soon extend to the availability of such sundries as electricity, water, and transportation. Chinese cooks rarely plan a menu before they shop; rather they see what they can find in the market, and cook accordingly. Likewise, it is the rare teacher, foreign or Chinese, who can plan a semester's syllabus ahead. Who knows if textbooks will arrive or ditto machines work when they are needed?

It may be unclear why you are at the school. The classes promised for you may not have been arranged. Your room may be without heat or electricity. The school may seem very honored to have foreigners around, but may have done very little to prepare.

Foreigners often become uneasy with this lack of predictability. With time, however, most come to see it as part of a larger pattern. How can anyone you depend on be predictable when the people they depend on are not? In time, you may become less predictable yourself. "The nice thing is," points out survey respondent Jon Weston, "whatever you do here— getting lost, being delayed in travel, etc.—it is interesting and new. Sit back and treat it as a part of a plan."

"GOOD FOR THE STUDENTS" IN WHOSE EYES?

Everything in China can be seen in more than one way. Once courses get going you'll have to find out what the school expects and what your students or teachers expect, all of which may or may not have anything to do with the course description or with what you want. Teachers will need to learn which exams their students are preparing for, and how to help them both prepare for the graduation exams, and learn useful material beyond. At they same time, teachers need to remember that what they consider useful may not seem so to their students, or the department, or the department's party secretary. Students will need to learn what the school expects them to learn, as opposed to the teacher, as opposed to what they hope to get out of their studies.

If you're at a small institution you'll likely become a Jack or Jill of all trades, setting up the library and lecturing on topics you never realized you knew anything about. If you're at a large school you'll become intimate with the Chinese concept of bureaucracy. At either sort of place you'll learn about the complex interplay between politics and expertise in China, between procedure and personality.

Slowly, you'll learn who at your institution has formal power and who has actual power, how they wield it, and how to approach them. You'll learn both official and unwritten rules governing your personal and professional behavior. You'll have freedoms, in travel and in contact with ordinary Chinese people, that no tourist or journalist will ever know. But at the same time you'll be held to a higher standard of behavior. You will probably, if you stay in China long enough, become more subtle in human relationships than you are now.

YOU'RE NOT IN KANSAS ANYMORE

Life in China for many foreigners involves relative physical deprivation, with sporadic water and electricity, and little or no access to cars, stereos, or evening entertainment. You may lose extra pounds you've carried for years, and develop terrific leg muscles. Of course, for the independently wealthy, joint-venture hotels in China's largest cities stock most any convenience a Western heart could desire. But though the average foreign teacher earns 8 to 10 times the salary of her Chinese counterpart, if she wants to live within that salary, stays at the Great Wall Sheraton are out of the question.

Instead you may rediscover a world of simpler pleasures. Depending on what your city has to offer, and what of it is open to foreigners, you may go dancing, or roller-skating, or to the movies. You will likely go with your students, classmates, and teachers on picnics and for walks. You may relearn the arts of conversation and of reading for pleasure. But more perhaps than at any other time in your life you will be thrown back on yourself. You may learn as much about yourself as you do about China, by learning what you can do without, and what you have within.

You will taste objects you never considered edible, from sea slugs to fried bark to dog. You will come to grips with the sights, sounds, and smells of a people far less inhibited than Westerners about bodily odors and functions. You will learn about overcrowding, and life in an economy of scarcity.

You'll be a racial minority among a very insular people. You'll be stared at and pointed at and endlessly interrogated about your age and income. Even overseas Chinese are subject to this scrutiny because their clothing styles and uncalloused hands set them apart from mainlanders. If you speak Chinese well enough, you'll hear yourself called "outlander" (*laowai:* 老外) or even occasionally "barbarian" (*yangguizi:* 洋鬼子) and you'll be pushed to the fronts of lines by some people and resented for it by others. You'll most likely be stung badly sometime, just when you think you've understood the culture: the colleague you thought was a friend will turn out to have been assigned to you by the government; your favorite teacher will be fired; your favorite student will report your indiscretions to the authorities. You may decide you can't hack it and go home.

If you stick it out you'll make your own peace with that mixture of ignorance and vainglory in the Chinese mind which both is and is not racism. You'll learn to forgive, and to understand. You'll appreciate quiet powers of the spirit, and you'll make a few friendships which run very deep.

"I am now 62," writes survey respondent Mik Moses from her teaching post in Shanghai, "and have lived a not uneventful life, but my years in China have been among the most interesting. Teaching in [my home country] had become predictable, the students predictably disinterested and the curriculum predictably unrelated to their needs. After one year here I decided that I would rather work in China. . . . Here, I learn something every day, and absolutely nothing is predictable." If you stay long enough, you'll most likely end up with China under the skin, a part of you and a place you'll want to return to time and again.

MAINLAND CHINA SINCE TIANANMEN: TO GO OR NOT TO GO

"I can't imagine your motivation," fulminated one survey respondent who preferred anonymity, "to sell China to foreigners now given the present situation. Have you all no shame?" For anyone who cares about China and the Chinese, the tragic events of the spring and summer of 1989, and the aftermath which continues today, are horrifying beyond words. The question is, what should a concerned person do? The indignant respondent quoted above wrote us from China, where he continues to teach; and therein, for us, lies the answer.

Teachers and students from the West bring new ideas to China. This inescapable fact lies at the heart of the ambivalence with which the government views foreigners. Western language skills, teaching methods, technological expertise, and currency are valued, but China's government views with alarm the openness foreigners bring to China's academic process as well as ideas about everything from political democracy to religion to taste in music. Class monitors in Westerners' classrooms are specially instructed to look out for signs of subversive teaching, and teaching materials are carefully screened. Only the foolish foreign teacher would use openly anticommunist teaching materials or language in the classroom. But new ways of thinking get transmitted unavoidably, in informal discussions and ways of talking and living.

It would be foolish to overemphasize the role of Westerners in the "Beijing Spring" democracy movement. The uprising was Chinese in root and leaf, looking back more to the May 4th movement of 1919 than to the Mayflower. Nevertheless, Western influence was present, from the Statue of Liberty–esque "Goddess of Democracy" to the medical students from foreign countries who helped tend wounded after June 4. Westerners provided moral and practical support of many kinds, and in many instances were able to protect Chinese around them from retribution. "Distant water won't put out a near fire," goes the old Chinese saying about the importance of neighbors. Foreign teachers and students enraged at seeing China in flames were in the best position of anyone to do something about it.

For foreigners to boycott China now, we believe, would be to abandon rather than support the people and goals involved in the democracy movement. China's government has demonstrated time and again its tenacity in the face of isolation. As a Chinese friend puts it, "if the West cuts off economic and cultural contacts now, all that will happen is that China's people will be poorer and more ignorant of the West." If the sad truth be told, the events of 1989 were hardly unique in Chinese history. Westerners in China before Tiananmen always worked in the shadow of "rectification" campaigns from the Hundred Flowers to Spiritual Pollution—and much earlier ones as well. Remember the Boxers? And the crushing of the largest civil war in human history, the Taiping Tianguo Movement in the 1850s and 1860s? Long before communism arrived on the scene China had a highly centralized and totalitarian government, and through the centuries, including our own sad one, that government has perpetrated bloody campaigns that make Tiananmen pale by comparison.

Rarely have foreigners ever gone to China to admire her enlightened government. Instead foreigners go today as they have always gone, intrigued by the warm people, astonishing landscapes, and fascinating culture of the Middle Kingdom. Those things haven't changed.

Nor are foreigners in any way unsafe in China today. Even at the height of the 1989 movement foreigners who appeared in the wrong places were spirited away to their hotels or dorms, and perhaps questioned, but not threatened. China's government, ever practical, is too aware of its need for Western businesspeople, teachers, students, and travelers to scare them away permanently. Quite the contrary, a number of survey respondents who have worked in China for several years mentioned that their more recent treatment is better than ever, as the Chinese government attempts to return to "normalcy" even while trials of 1989 protestors go on.

In terms of numbers, teachers and students are entering China about as fast as ever. According to a November 1990 Institute of International Education (IIE) report on the "Current Status of Academic and Cultural Exchanges Between US and PRC Institutions a Year After Tiananmen," after some falling off in the 1989–1990 academic year, most programs are now at or above their pre-1989 levels.

Data on Westerners heading to China is somewhat more anecdotal. In our survey of sending organizations we asked the number of students sent in each of the last 3 years. Most programs showed a sharp drop in 1989 but an increase in 1990 up to or above the 1988 level. Among our teacher and student surveys, many respondents mentioned that the number of foreigners at their institutions was as high as ever, and only the one quoted above expressed opposition to new teachers and students arriving. "It is a terrible and wonderful thing that has happened," wrote one teacher who has lived in an interior city for 3 years. "People can be killed, but ideas cannot be killed." We believe that for those who care about China, there is no better time to go.

One last concern arises, however, in the special problems of living in China soon after a political campaign. Contact with Westerners and their "Spiritual Pollution" has repeatedly been used against Chinese people during political campaigns. As a result, during times of political stress Chinese people tend to withdraw from foreigners. Some Westerners, concerned that contact with foreigners could make their Chinese friends into political targets, question the morality of ever seeking out intimate friendships with mainland Chinese. We don't support this view, but do note that in politically turbulent times, foreigners do tend to feel cut off.

Many foreigners who lived in China during and immediately after the "Campaign Against Spiritual Pollution" in 1983–1984 reported feeling isolated. "In a year in Nanjing," admits one student of that time with some bitterness, "I was never once invited to a Chinese person's house, or on a picnic. I never even went for a walk with just one Chinese person." In the years just before Tiananmen, almost the opposite was true. Both Margaret and Rebecca found that invitations to dinners, picnics, dances, and parties with Chinese friends came so thick and fast some had to be refused to leave any time for work.

The impact of Tiananmen in these areas is less clear. China's government does seem committed to as swift a return to normalcy as possible, and there has been no repeat of the "Spiritual Pollution" slogans, no organized effort to discourage contact. Still, the spectacle of television trials has cast something of a chill over relationships. As one foreign teacher still in China who has been teaching since 1987 puts it, "nothing has changed that I could really put my finger on, but everything is a bit more formal." As time goes on no doubt more relaxed relations will develop again. In the meantime, the best advice is to follow the cues of the Chinese people around you. They know better than anyone what degree of friendliness is safe.

Choosing:
Mainland or Taiwan

In mainland China old men trundle through neighborhoods on tricycle carts shouting *jiu pinzgi!* ("drink bottles!"), as they collect the empties for recycling. On Taiwan the same sort of old men perform the same service, only their tricycle carts are motorized and the *jiu pingzi* blares from a tape recorder.

Taiwan and the mainland are amazingly similar in their "Chineseness." Many mainland visitors attribute this to the effects of communism phenomena that appear as well in Taiwan, and which are far more Chinese than communist. Both Taiwan and mainland China claim to be the legitimate heir to Chinese culture. Taiwan is wealthier, more urbane, more international, and more high-tech in daily life than the mainland. Her population includes vast aboriginal and native Taiwanese populations with unique cultural heritages. But Chinese culture as brought to Taiwan by the Nationalists in 1948–1949 still dominates the island's government and much of daily life, particularly in the large cities.

TAIWAN AND THE MAINLAND: AN OVERVIEW

Long lists of similarities link Taiwan and the mainland. Politically, both governments impose order and control. Both have press censorship and political prisoners and essentially one-party rule (opposition parties were illegal in Taiwan until 1987 and remain fragmented). Academically, both Taiwan and the mainland stress centralized educational control, administered by government authorities in the school system. Until recently the Taiwanese had Nationalist Party "security secretaries" in their school system exactly equivalent to the PRC's "Communist party secretaries," and both still have "class spies" in the form of class monitors. (Taiwanese class monitors now have greatly reduced political functions compared with the past, but many Taiwanese students still fear their influence.) Culturally, Taiwanese and mainlanders share language, fine arts, cuisine, and fundamental world view, including the dual idea that foreigners are both gods and beasts which Lu Xun cited. They also share certain features of Chinese culture. Much political and economic corruption stymies both Taiwanese and mainlanders.

The fact that Taiwan—the richest of Asia's Four Little Dragons of Commerce and the 13th largest trading power in the world—boasts a thriving capitalistic economy is what most sets it apart from the mainland and makes it an easier place for Westerners to adjust to. You can buy Cadbury Fruit 'n Nut bars at 11:00 p.m. in Taiwan, sample Italian pasta, French haute cuisine, Korean barbecue, and other international fare at all times of day and night. Taiwan's cities suffer no shortage of entertainment. In Taiwan you can lead a social life much as you do at home, seeing first-run movies and going out dancing on Saturday nights. You can choose where you want to live, share apartments with Chinese roommates, and apply for jobs after you arrive. In short, you can have a much more "normal" lifestyle in Western industrialized terms than on the mainland.

There is of course a downside to life in Taiwan. Despite Taipei's claim to cultural legitimacy, Taiwanese culture has been heavily influenced by both Japan and the U.S. as well as by the native Taiwanese heritage. Taiwan does boast some fabulous cultural treasures, from the Palace Museum in Taipei to the temples of Hualien Gorge. In addition, Taiwan's Chinese language schools concentrate on traditional complex written characters, crucial for study of Chinese history, literature, and traditional culture. Mainland schools focus on simplified characters, and offer the traditional characters only in special classes. However, Taiwan's very wealth and cosmopolitanism tend to break up the weight of Chinese tradition so omnipresent on the mainland. Taiwan offers, to some extent, Chinese culture in diluted form. In addition, Taiwanese cities are urban nightmares, with terrible pollution (silver jewelry will tarnish overnight), constant traffic jams, and motorcycle demons who speed through traffic lights, all of which produce a great deal of stress. It's also a bit too easy in Taiwan to move into a foreign enclave, dine on hamburgers and ice cream and socialize with other expatriates.

There are, in fact, many advantages to studying and working in the mainland. Most of the skills, knowledge, and practices of ancient China remain alive there. Even Taiwanese admit the superiority of most mainland artists; "To master Chinese calligraphy," explained a Taiwanese journalist of our acquaintance, "requires constant practice over years. Who has time for that in Taipei? In the mainland that's all they have to do." More programs in ancient traditions exist for foreigners in the mainland as well. Only 1 medical school in Taiwan, for example, offers courses in traditional Chinese medicine, and it accepts only 2 foreign students per department. In the mainland, every sizeable city has a College of Traditional Medicine, many with large programs for foreigners. The one thing that it is difficult to explore in the mainland is traditional Chinese religion. While it is possible to make private arrangements for study with local monks in the mainland, no mainland schools offer formal study of Buddhist or Taoist traditions, whereas several Taiwanese schools do.

If you want to study acupuncture, practice martial arts, or paint Chinese landscapes, you'll probably learn more in the mainland. If you desire a steady flow of fascinating (albeit sometimes maddening and depressing) experiences, mainland China won't disappoint you. Also, because the mainland lacks the stress which accompanies modern industrialized life, you may find life there very peaceful, allowing you to accomplish more in the way of intellectual or artistic pursuits than you would in Taiwan. Although at times in our mainland years we would have sold our firstborn to see a Western movie or hear live Western music, life there was never dull.

Mainland China is harder to cope with than Taiwan in many ways. Her poverty results in spartan living conditions, little entertainment, and a population made xenophobic by ignorance. Politically, despite similarities, the mainland is also far more repressive than Taiwan. Orchid Island, the Taiwanese gulag, holds dozens of political prisoners as compared with probably tens of thousands in the mainland's Qinghai; and independently owned Taiwanese newspapers print stories daily which would mean death sentences in Beijing. In fact, the only regularly banned topic for today's Taiwanese papers is Taiwanese independence.

But many foreigners find the mainland provides a richer experience of Chinese culture in its purest form. In Taiwan's rural areas the ancient Min-An culture preserves many Chinese and Taiwanese cultural traditions. Even Taiwanese urbanites celebrate Spring Festival with plenty of fireworks and the Mid-autumn Festival with moon cakes. In some ways, particularly in religious traditions, Taiwan's fesivals can be more traditional than the mainland's. Taiwan also boasts specialists in Chinese culture who, owing to the freer flow of information, can produce better research than anyone on the mainland. But to us, the greatest difference lies in the vitality of Chinese tradition on the mainland, whereas in Taiwan, at least in the cities, many Gucci-booted youth seem to be abandoning Chinese tradition for greater participation in the life of the international jet set. Of course, many of our mainland students had grown up without reading ancient Chinese philosophers and poets, many of whom have been banned in various political campaigns. But they all lived lives steeped in tradition; even our class monitors could tell us ghost tales heard from their grandmothers or give us 32 recipes for dumplings. Our Taiwanese students had memorized Li Bai and Mo Zi for the college exams but often knew more about the television serials "Dallas" or "Dynasty" than about the *I Ching* or acupuncture. Our mainland students took us on hillside picnics in the shadows of temples. Our Taiwanese students were more likely to take us to discos and give us hot stock-market tips.

GENERAL INFORMATION ABOUT TAIWAN

Information on Taiwan appears throughout this book, and we have pointed out in each section which topics refer only to the mainland, which to Taiwan, and which to both. This overview introduces some statistical bases for comparison, as well as broad ways in which foreigners' working lives differ on the "Two Sides of the Ocean Abyss." Taiwan's population hovers around 20 million; the mainland at last official census reported 1.13 billion and climbing. The actual population of the mainland may be considerably higher. Per capita income in Taiwan is first-world level, US$8,000 per year of reported income, and actually considerably higher due to additional incomes in a large underground economy which go unreported. Mainland per capita income is US$300 per year and falling. Taiwan is less than 200 miles long, and less than 40 miles wide at her widest point; the mainland has the fourth largest land mass of any nation. Taiwan's climate is subtropical and heat and humidity can be intense during the summer months. The mainland ranges from the subtropical to the subarctic. Taiwan's countryside is lush and beautiful; the major cities, however, are extremely polluted and crowded, and expensive. The mainland ranges from lush countryside to desert; its cities are as crowded as Taiwan's, but are less polluted due to lower industrialization (though they're still hardly clean). Average families in Taiwan have 1.7 children, and as of 1989 the Taiwanese owned 1 car for every 8 people, and 1 motorcycle for every 2.5 people. Average mainlanders may or may not own a bicycle. Mainland families by official policy have 1 child in cities and 1 or 2 in the countryside, though many in the countryside circumvent these rules. Overpopulation remains the most serious problem on the mainland, a matter of profound concern to people across the political spectrum.

The PRC maintains diplomatic relations with most natons. Taiwan's official diplomatic relations are few, but her trade partners are numerous. In most major countries, Taiwan, though barred from maintaining formal embassies and consulates, posts government representatives in offices marked with cryptic names. In the U.S., Taiwan government offices are called "Coordination Councils for North American Affairs."

In Taiwan, as on the mainland, foreign teachers and students flock to the largest cities; according to one official, over 75% of all foreign students and teachers in mainland China live in Beijing, Nanjing, Shanghai, and Guangzhou. In Taiwan well over half of all foreigners live in Taipei. More daring foreigners (who often report the most lively experiences) scatter to smaller cities throughout both areas—in Taiwan largely to Taichung in the central region, or to Tainan or Kaohsiung in the south.

Standards of living are lower in the mainland, but expenses are also much lower. Housing and insurance is generally free for mainland teachers and students. Teachers instructing Chinese people on the mainland rarely earn enough to save anything (grade-school teachers in the mainland's International Schools generally earn more than Ph.D.'s teaching in mainland universities). But because prices are so low, mainland salaries generally allow significant travel around China, and the purchase of many fine handicrafts and consumer goods.

Taiwanese salaries are competitive internationally, but the cost of living has soared. Years ago Taipei was the destination of choice for Westerners backpacking through Asia in need of a pit stop to reline their wallets. Not today; with Taiwan's booming economy, even after the stock market crash of 1989 housing and food prices have increased vastly since the mid-1980s while foreign teachers' salaries have remained steady. Many foreign teachers report more difficulty living within their means in Taiwan than in the mainland. Because mainland schools assign free housing for teachers and subsidized dorms for students, while the Taiwan-bound fend for themselves in a housing market dizzy with speculation, you may just be able to afford more comfortable quarters in Beijing than in Taipei.

Because Taiwan is more urbane and international than the mainland, it is relatively easy to mingle and develop friendships with the Taiwanese. There is, in fact, quite a bit of dating between Westerners and Taiwanese. While discouraged by many Taiwanese parents ("you're dating a barbarian?!"), mixing with foreigners in Taiwan carries none of the fear of political retribution so weighty in the mainland. For this reason many young single people prefer Taiwan; the mainland can be a lonely place.

Teaching

The mainland accepts foreign teachers only in formal posts at tertiary schools which must be arranged before arrival. Taiwan offers formal, pre-arranged posts at colleges, universities, and technical institutes as well. These "real school" positions generally require solid teaching credentials, are best applied for in advance, and are fundamentally similar to mainland teaching posts; see Chapters 1, 3, and 6 for details.

Taiwan's more open system, however, allows several other levels of more "entrepreneurial" teaching as well: many small, private, for-profit English Language Institutes; agencies which arrange on-site teaching to employees of foreign subsidiaries; and *buxiban* (补习班) ("study-cramming institutes") dot Taiwan and all will hire foreigners and permit a range of part-time as well as full-time opportunities.

Because of the high turnover in Taiwan's foreign population, you can generally arrive at any time of year and find a job soon. Winter is still the slow season. The easiest time to find a buxiban job is right after the schools recess for summer vacation when many students take summer English classes. Tote your resume and transcripts, particularly if you have advanced degrees, and look up "English Teaching" in Taipei's English-language Yellow Pages, or buxiban in the Chinese Yellow Pages in other cities. The better English Language Institutes and teaching agencies require a BA and prefer some teaching experience. The buxibans vary; many require only that foreigners walk, talk, and speak English, and end up with some astoundingly bad teachers. Be careful, though; some unscrupulous buxibans rope in unwary foreigners just off the plane to slave-labor contracts offering dorm rooms, cafeteria board, and some Chinese tutoring in return for unconscionable amounts of teaching. Don't sign anything till you've had a few days to get on your feet and have a look around.

Many foreigners also privately tutor well-to-do Taiwanese in return for cash and/or room and board; look for signs seeking tutors on buxiban bulletin boards, or ask other foreigners. As with buxibans, be careful. No-shows for classes are common. Try to get payment in advance, and be clear that lessons must be paid for even if not attended. If you get a room-and-board arrangement, make sure that outside a reasonable number of tutoring hours your time is your own. Wealthy Taiwanese may enjoy having foreign live-in maids, but you just may not want to be one.

Studying

Foreign students proficient enough in Chinese to study in it can apply to any degree program in Taiwan. Foreign degree candidates must be high-school graduates. Many schools also have special English-language programs for foreigners. Application for admission should be sent directly to the dean of studies of the host institution.

Taiwan has 5 government-accredited Chinese Language Programs, at National Taiwan Normal University, Fu Jen University, Feng Chia University, Tunghai University, and National Cheng Kung University. There are also major, highly respected Chinese-language training programs at Taiwan University's Interuniversity Program (formerly called the Stanford Center), at the Taipei Language Institute, and the Kuoyu Jipao newspaper. Students wanting to study Chinese at these institutions should submit 2 copies of their application form, official transcripts, 2 letters of recommendation from teachers, a health certificate (including proof of no infectious diseases), and a study plan.

There are also numerous other language training programs and programs offered through private colleges and universities. The tuition per semester at private universities ranges from NT$17,740 to NT$24,590 (at current exchange US$1 = NT$27.1); at public universities tuition runs from approximately NT$4,120 to NT$5,350 (based on 1990 Taiwanese government figures). Evening schools charge approximately NT$580 per credit hour. These schools vary greatly: some are merely visa mills, and discourage serious study.

Our Directory #1 lists all major schools in Taiwan after the listing of schools for the mainland. Our Directories #2 and #3 list programs sending teachers and students to Taiwan. For more information and prospects to look for, see Chapter 3.

Accommodations

Mainland schools provide free or cheap housing for foreign teachers and students. On Taiwan, "real school" study programs or posts may include dorm accommodations, but more likely the school will simply assist foreigners in locating housing, and less formal posts involve no housing assistance at all.

When you first arrive in Taiwan you may need to stay in a hostel or hotel until you locate a room or apartment. Relatively cheap places include the YMCA/YWCA dorms and International Youth Hostel dorms which dot the island. Four relatively cheap hostels in Taipei are:

1. The International House, 18 Hsin Yi Rd., Section 3, Taipei, Taiwan (Phone [02] 703-3151).

2. YMCA, 19 Hsu Chang St., Taipei, Taiwan (Phone [02] 311-3201).

3. YWCA, 7 Tsing Tao West Rd., Taipei, Taiwan (Phone [02]

371-4493).
4. The Travel Stop Hostel, 3rd Floor, #35-4, Lane 36, Chungshan N. Rd., Section 2, Taipei, Taiwan (Phone [02] 561-8560).

Get a tourist guidebook for other cities (see Appendix B for suggestions). Just outside Taipei the Academica Sinica runs a longer-term hostel called the "Taipei International Youth Activities Center" (Huodong zhongxin) which offers single rooms for around US$400 per month, very reasonable by Taipei standards. Be sure to write in advance for reservations, as they dislike unexpected arrivals. Write to Academica Sinica, 128 Yanjiuyuan Rd., Langang District, Taipei, Taiwan (Phone [02] 782-2120), or to the Activities Center at 30 Hsin Hai Rd., Section 3, Taipei, Taiwan (Phone [02] 362-1170).

For the longer term, should your school not offer dorms and you do not care to stay in a hostel, you'll have to arrange homestay with a Taiwanese family or rent a room or apartment. Some homestays are commercial and arranged through schools; others are free or in return for English tutoring. Check buxiban bulletin boards and talk with other foreigners for information. Bulletin boards and word of mouth are among the best sources to find what passes for cheap rents in Taiwan. For those who read Chinese, red rental signs posted on telephone poles are often the only advertising for most apartments. Walking around the rental area of choice can turn up bargains. Also, leases are flexible at taofung (studio apartments) in red-light districts. Buildings are filled with prostitutes, but the areas are not dangerous. For those who want short-term leases (by the week), this is a tolerable alternative. Of course your Taiwanese friends might be shocked and/or fascinated when you reveal your address. As in the West, most apartments advertised in the papers tend to be expensive. As of this writing a 1-room efficiency in downtown Taipei averaged US$700 per month, and climbing. Many foreigners rent rooms and kitchen privileges from families in such outlying areas as Yung-ho or Pan-ch'iao; these generally start at around US$350 per month.

3

Planning:
Your Institution
and How to Get There

Your institution in China will shape your Chinese life; choose it carefully. Chapter 5 explains in detail the Chinese *danwei,* or "work unit." For now, suffice it to say that your school in mainland China controls not just the classes you teach or study, but also everything from your sleeping quarters to your transport. Beyond that, China's regions, less homogenized by television and rapid transit than their Western counterparts, offer fundamental differences in culture, language, and custom as well as geography and climate. City and country in China are different worlds. Going independently also creates a different experience than going through an institution. Spend some time thinking carefully about where you want to be in China and how you want to get there. Read on for suggestions on the kinds of questions to ask, then flip through our directories to help you choose where you want to be.

THE INSTITUTION

Before considering specific schools, decide what you want to accomplish in China. Do you want to work in the capital, making contacts at elite universities with the children of power? Do you want to live in a region rich with historical and architectural finds for you to explore? Do you want to learn Mandarin? Learn Cantonese? Climb mountains? Study minorities? Keep your overall goals in mind when you make more specific choices. More than one eager student of Mandarin has chosen a school in Guangzhou, where only the elite speak standard Mandarin. Don't let it happen to you!

Aside from your overall goals, 3 basic considerations should shape your choice of a school: the region of China you want to live in, the choice of big versus small cities and schools, and the services and facilities available at the school itself.

Region

China's regions range from the howling, desolate deserts of Xinjiang, whose people speak a language related to Arabic and pray toward Mecca 6 times daily, to the bustling markets of Guangzhou, where girls in heavy make-up and boys in tight jeans dance to the latest hits from Hong Kong. Space prohibits detailed descriptions of cities here. Our directory gives overviews of each region. But for details, sit down with an atlas and a good tourist guidebook (see Appendix B for suggestions) and make some choices about the kind of region you want to call your Chinese home. Here are some factors to keep in mind:

1. CLIMATE. Chinese live more exposed to the elements than Westerners. Other than in joint-venture hotels, only the Northern provinces allow heating, and only the deep south has air-conditioning. Much of daily life, from exercises to cooking to socializing, takes place outdoors due to lack of space. If you suffer in the cold, think south; never assume you can just crank up the thermostat in your Chinese apartment. If you can't stand heat, think north and far west. If you like rain, think south or southeast; for deserts think north central and northwest. Wherever you go, bring adequate clothing for the climate; see suggestions in Chapter 4.

2. GEOGRAPHY. Transportation in China is complicated and slow. You'll relearn the (considerable) joys of walking or bicycling to the places you want to go. However, you'll have to give up the joys of hopping in your car and zipping to the mountains for the weekend or the seaside for the afternoon. Live where you want to be in China, otherwise you'll have trouble getting there. China offers the world's highest mountains and the world's deepest desert basin, huge lakes, miles of shoreline, rivers, jungles, and high plateaus. Which do you like to live in? And how about travel? Will you feel a need to "escape" to Hong Kong once a month for Western-style entertainment? Want to visit Beijing often? Unless you'll tote heaps of cash for plane fares, live near the places you'll want to see often.

3. HISTORICAL, ARCHITECTURAL, AND ARCHAEOLOGICAL
   RESOURCES. In the jungles of Xishuangbanna ancient Dai
   temples shine out among the banyan trees. In the dusty
   plains of central Henan centuries of Buddhists have carved
   images in sandstone. Qingdao on the coast combines
   traditional fishing villages with the Bavarian architecture of
   the German occupation. Foreign residents with special
   interests in art, archaeology, architecture, or religion can
   gain unparalleled access to their region's cultural treasures.
   Do you want to study Yellow Lamaist scripture on
   weekends with a local monk? Live in Inner Mongolia,
   Qinghai, or Tibet. Do you want to learn the needlepoint arts
   of the Shani, Dai, or Hmong? Live in Yunnan. If you have
   special interests in any area of Chinese culture, live in the
   areas richest with those resources.

4. LANGUAGE. Dialect varies tremendously between regions.
   Many "dialects" of Mandarin, such as Hunanese, are so
   thick as to be opaque. In the Shandong dialect, for example,
   wo ("I") becomes *an*, and *rou* ("meat") becomes *yo*.
   Cantonese, Fujianese, and Shanghainese are distinct languages from Mandarin, while Tibetan, Inner Mongolian,
   and many other minority languages come from wholly different linguistic groups. If you want to speak relatively pure
   Mandarin on the streets, north central or northeast China is
   the place to go. For Cantonese, stick to Guangzhou; for
   Fujianese to Fujian, for Shanghainese to Shanghai, and so
   forth. Mandarin is the official language, and in all areas
   you'll find fluent speakers with the purest tones. But the
   man and woman on the street speak local dialects, and if
   language study is your chief focus, this should be a concern.

Big City, Small City; Big School, Small School

In general, the larger and more coastal the city, the more Westernized it
will be. The larger and more famous the school, the more competition
there will be both among Chinese students and among foreigners. The
trade-off is a choice between one type of China experience and another—
between big ponds and little ponds, of course, but also between making
contacts with the known and learning about the new.

BIG CITY, SMALL CITY

Bigger cities offer more formal cultural entertainments—more movies,
theater, operas, museums, dance halls, sports events—than their smaller

cousins. Guangzhou and Shenzhen are just subdued versions of Hong Kong, where bars and discos stay open till dawn. Beijing is stodgier, but still offers at least one major performance a night. When the Bolshoi Ballet or the Milan Opera tours China their tours include only the largest cities. While cultural offerings in Beijing or Shanghai may seem tame compared with London or New York, they far outweigh those available in the interior towns. Markets are also better in bigger cities, and goods geared towards Western tastes, from cheese and Western liquors to stylish clothing, are generally available only in the largest cities.

Big cities also house large foreign populations, which provide plenty of opportunities to chat about the nature of the universe with unshaven expats in grimy teahouses. Because China's foreign populations are truly international (the Chinese government offers scholarships to needy students from many developing nations), living in Beijing or Wuhan you'll be as likely to learn about Sri Lanka or Zaire as about China.

Small towns offer none of these things, and if you can't face living where the sidewalks roll up at dusk, stick with the large cities. For the self-reliant, however, small towns offer much greater access to the rhythms of daily Chinese life than the metropolis. Foreigners are special in small towns, and get invited regularly to private homes, even to special events like weddings and birth ceremonies. The Levith family of Saratoga Springs, New York, (Dr. Murray and Tina, and their sons Nathaniel and Willy) spent a year in Qufu, a dusty village in central Shandong famous only as the birthplace of Confucius. But so welcomed were they into village life that they felt they "couldn't have had a richer experience anywhere else." The young boys of the family got interested in stamp and coin collecting, and were showered with the hoarded treasures of local families, including centuries-old coins and rare stamps from the birth of the People's Republic. Their father, a Shakespearian scholar, was able to mobilize the full resources of the college to contact Chinese Shakespeare scholars across the nation.

A note of caution, however: being special also means foreigners in small towns get far more attention than they like. "When I first came to Yan'an," wrote one respondent, "I was the only foreigner, not just at the University, but in the whole city of Yan'an. Thus I came to be a sort of celebrity, or at least an object of great interest." This "zoo" effect appears throughout China, especially in small towns. If you can't stand this sort of scrutiny, best retreat to the relative anonymity of the large city.

BIG SCHOOL, SMALL SCHOOL

As in the West, universities in China fall into an unofficial hierarchy, with schools like Beijing University, Fudan University, and Qinghua University being the Chinese Harvard, Yale, and Stanford. If your time in

China is a springboard to a career in Sinology, a time to look good on your resume, a time to make contacts with the political elite, by all means apply to these schools. Be forewarned, however—many foreigners share these goals, and competition for teaching or research posts at the top schools can be fierce. Also, the schools often block foreigners together in foreigners-only compounds, leading to a sense of isolation and what respondent David Silverglade called the "foreigners-in-a-cage syndrome." If he had to do it over, Silverglade avowed, he would "enroll in a Chinese school which was small and liberal."

If you care less about your resume than about the content of what you learn, the elite schools may not necessarily be best for you. To be sure, the top schools get a disproportionate share of funding and resources, and great numbers of excellent faculty and students. However, appointments and acceptances in China are more political than in Western universities, even depending on such elements as family history, friendship, and the ever-present *guanxi* ("connections"—for more on this topic, see Chapter 6). As a result, a great deal of well-connected driftwood occupies slots at China's top schools. One New York lawyer described his frustrations in teaching a Western law class at Beijing University which included the son of an important Communist Party leader. The student did no homework, made noise and fell asleep in class, openly mocked the teacher and disrupted other students' work. When the teacher threatened the boy with a failing grade, he simply yawned. "If you fail me, next semester I'll take a make-up exam administered by a Chinese teacher. Do you think any of them would dare fail me?"

Many of China's finest scholars are scattered throughout the smaller schools, unable or unwilling to make the political connections necessary for appointments at the great universities. If you particularly want to study with an individual scholar, find out where he or she works, and go there. Also, because Chinese are not free to live where they like, China has not seen the general drift of talented people in and out of academia to the great cities typical of the West. Beijing in the '90s is not Paris in the '20s. The greatest of China's poets, painters, and playwrights are scattered throughout the country in places like Chengdu, Kaifeng, and Harbin as much as in Beijing or Shanghai. If you are interested in organizing conferences, editing magazines, and otherwise bringing together talented people and their ideas, you're much more likely to get material and emotional support at a small school where you're one of 5 foreigners than at a great university where you're one of 500.

The School

China has some 8,000 post-secondary learning institutions, ranging from huge to tiny, from broad-based universities, to technical and vocational schools, to training centers within work units. Some 550 of these institutions accept foreigners as students and/or teachers, and those schools are listed in our Directory #1. Once you've chosen a region and a size of school, spend some time flipping through the directory to decide on individual schools. Notice that the directory is arranged by province or region and city, with Key Universities starred, and schools divided by category in each list, e.g., University, Minorities/Politics/Law, Art/Music, etc. This directory represents the most complete information ever compiled in English about Chinese schools, and we have tried to standardize information in each listing. We sent surveys to each school and consulted all existing directories in both English and Chinese. Nevertheless, complete information for each school was not always available. Where any information you need is missing, we suggest you write to the individual school and ask for it. Here are some factors to keep in mind while you flip through the directory:

1. TYPE OF SCHOOL. If you want to be at a big, academically focused university, with all its advantages and disadvantages (see above under "Big School, Small"), consider one of the "Key Universities" starred throughout the directory. Many of the smaller Key Universities, such as Shandong University in Jinan or Sichuan Academy of Science and Technology in Chengdu, can offer the benefits of the most elite universities without the fierce competition and politicization. Key Universities generally attract the brainiest students in their province or region and have more funding and better facilities than non-Key schools.

   If you don't care about being at a Key School, but would like to work with highly motivated students or teachers, consider a Normal School, School of Politics and Law, or Medical College. The teaching, medical, and legal professions are poorly paid in China, but nonetheless are extremely difficult to train for, and therefore tend to attract dedicated personnel who believe in what they are doing for its own sake. Some of our happiest comments came from teachers at China's Normal Schools and Medical schools.

   Foreigners who wish to study or teach a technical subject may do best at a technical, vocational, or single-subject school. Many schools of Chinese Music, for example, have better performance departments than the Key Universities, with their focus on a general liberal education. Meanwhile, foreigners who would like to

contribute to China's technical development will have a
freer hand at designing courses at, say, a school of
Minerals and Mining than at Qinghua University. Special-
ized schools in China include schools of Architecture, Art,
Chinese Medicine, Chinese Music, Engineering, Industrial
Chemistry, Materials Handling and Packaging, Medicine,
Minerals and Mining, Music, Police and Army, Post and
Telecommunications, Textiles, and Transportation.

2. PROGRAMS AND FACILITIES. Within each type of university,
   specific programs vary by institution. Our directory lists departments. If you'd like to teach Electrical Engineering,
   don't choose a school without an Engineering department. If
   you'd like to study the *erhu,* choose a school with a music
   department. Best of all, choose a school where the specific
   program you want has already been set up. Someone else
   has done the dirty work, and you won't have to run around
   for weeks getting books and classrooms lined up.

   Consider the limits of available facilities. How highly is
   the library rated in our directory? What about computer
   facilities? Are there secretaries to help you prepare
   classroom materials? Of course, you can always bring
   books and computers and copiers with you, but there's a
   limit to the patience of the airlines, and if a school's
   current facilities are totally unsuited to what you hope to
   do there, best choose another school. Remember, there'll
   be no photocopy shops on the corner.

3. ACCOMMODATIONS AND TRANSPORT. Most students and teachers headed for China are prepared for some discomfort, but
   there are matters of degree. Whether you're given 2 rooms
   or 3 shouldn't be the deciding factor in your choice between
   schools, but if everything else checks out, why not go for
   comfort? Also, school choices on accommodations can af-
   fect your work. Some schools are notorious for refusing
   Chinese students access to foreign teachers' dorms, which
   cuts down on your time with your students and lessens your
   abilities as a teacher. Given the difficulty of transport in
   China, the willingness of the school to give access to school
   vehicles can also be important. If you live 90 kilometers
   from the isolated Buddhist grottoes you hope to study, willingness of the school to let you either get a Chinese driver's
   license and borrow their car or use a car and driver 3 times a
   week can make a big difference in your research.

4. FINANCIAL ARRANGEMENTS AND BENEFITS. Again, no teacher
   or student goes to China to get rich. But all else being equal,
   an 800-yuan monthly salary or $1,000 semester's tuition
   will allow a more comfortable life than a 500-yuan monthly
   salary or $2,500 tuition. But consider the whole package.
   Will you be charged for your room? For health insurance?
   What will board cost? What about travel allowances or shipping allowances? Many independent teachers or students
   will settle these details after arrival (see Chapter 5). But the
   history in our directory gives a base for comparison.

SENDING ORGANIZATIONS AND INDIVIDUALS

Judging from our survey responses, about 40% of foreign students and
teachers in China arrange their stay through some form of sending
organization. These range from Sister City programs and university-to-
university exchanges to missionary organizations and programs for
seniors. The other 60% go as individuals, making arrangements directly
with the Chinese institution, the Ministry of Education, or the Ministry of
Foreign Affairs.

To Solo or Not to Solo

Sending organizations offer stability, experience, and institutional backing should conflicts arise. Most sending organizations also provide
financial compensation, travel bonuses, and training. Individual travel
offers greater flexibility in choice of institution and negotiations over
program. Going individually also avoids conflicts over organizational
philosophy, rules, and regulations. Here are some factors to keep in mind
when making your choice:

1. EXPERIENCE. Sending organizations offer experience. Many
   have been sending teachers and students to China for decades, and are familiar with the politics and culture of
   China. Often these organizations deal year after year with
   the same Chinese institutions, and know all the internal politics of their Chinese partners. Virtually all sending organizations arrange some pretravel training for participants; many
   provide midsemester conferences as well. Most also help in
   contract negotiations. While a few organizations emphasize
   voluntarism, and therefore arrange minimal compensation
   for participants, most engage in solid financial negotiations.
   Unless you're very experienced at business talks, you'll almost certainly get a better financial deal going through an
   organization than as an individual.

2. ORGANIZATIONAL BACKING. Chinese society functions better
   at the group than the individual level. Your Chinese institution will feel happier in discussions with a sending organization representing 20 teachers than in 20 discussions with individual teachers. Should conflicts arise, foreigners who
   represent a sending organization also generally have greater
   leverage than individuals. Finally, organizations can provide
   substantial material and professional support, in the form of
   shipping allowances, teaching materials, and other goodies
   available to individuals only at their own expense. Also, student sending organizations can generally easily arrange
   transfer of credit to your home institution, a process which
   can be agonizing if you go as an independent.

3. AVAILABLE PROGRAMS AND INSTITUTIONS. Most sending organizations deal with a finite set of Chinese institutions and
   programs. The Chinese institution of your dreams may host
   no exchange programs, leaving you no choice but to apply
   as an individual. You may also wish to design a program not
   offered by any sending organization. Most student sending
   organizations arrange classes in Chinese language, culture,
   and perhaps business/management. For anything else, from
   Chinese music to minority medicine, you'll likely need to
   go it alone. Teachers also find more flexibility on their own,
   particularly when combining teaching and studying. One enterprising man in Kunming arranged to study acupuncture
   and Chinese music while teaching English and U.S. history.
   Such an individually tailored program will generally require
   going it alone.

4. RULES AND REPRESENTATION. Every organization has rules
   and regulations for participants, and you should consider
   what sort you want to deal with. You represent your sending
   organization and they you. If you're uncomfortable with the
   organization's image, don't get involved; your Chinese institution won't consider You apart from Them. If you hate
   the organization's rulebook, stay away; you'll only cause
   confusion trying to bend rules on the sly. Certain religious
   sending organizations, for example, enforce dress and behavior codes on participants. Some university exchange programs forbid participants to teach or study outside the formal program arranged with the Chinese institution. If you're
   the rugged individual type, uncomfortable with organiza-

tional restraint or eager to be dealt with on your own terms, go on your own.

5. ORGANIZATIONAL PHILOSOPHY. Beyond the rule book, be aware of the sending organization's underlying philosophy. Many sending organizations have specific religious or political agendas. Be sure these goals agree with or complement your own. You'll be very far from Kansas in China, and you won't want people whose basic ideals you detest to have power over your life.

MAKING CONTACT

Once you've made your choice, it's time to make initial contact.

1. CONTACTING SENDING ORGANIZATIONS. Our Directories #2 and #3 offer the most complete list ever compiled in English of student and teacher sending organizations dealing with China. We have tried to collect the most up-to-date information possible on sites in China, subjects taught, eligibility, credits granted, available positions, and other information needed for an educated choice. We've also included any ratings of each sending organization given by respondents to our survey, and any information we had on each program's special focus or affiliations. Write or call the organizations directly for more detailed information and for application materials.

2. MAKING CONTACT AS AN INDEPENDENT—USE PERSONAL CONTACTS. Our Directory #1 lists addresses and phone numbers of all schools in mainland China that accept foreigners as teachers and/or students, and all major schools in Taiwan. Once you've chosen a school, write to it directly. However, your first challenge will be getting the Chinese institution to write back to you. Chinese people dislike dealing with strangers and prefer introductions. Chinese institutions are no different. Institutions that receive blind letters and resumes often have no idea what to do with them or how to evaluate them, and more than one such letter is gathering dust on a shelf while a fine position goes begging.

If possible, get yourself an introduction to the institution from someone whose name will be familiar. If you know anyone who has worked with a Chinese institution, ask for a recommendation. Try asking at your local community college if anyone has been to China on a speaking tour.

Write your local Chamber of Commerce or your local chapter of one of the China-related resource organizations listed in Appendix C.

If you or anyone you know will be going to China, stop in at a school there. Meeting in person can break the ice in ways a resume and cover letter can't.

Try meeting representatives of Chinese institutions in the U.S. Check with your local college or community college to ask about visiting scholars, speakers, or exchange students you might hook up with. One Chinese exchange student in Maine has arranged several placements for American teachers and students simply by writing letters of recommendation to his, his wife's, and his friends' alma maters.

Try also attending a conference of the Teachers of English to Speakers of Other Languages (TESOL) Association (write National TESOL Association, 1600 Cameron Street, Suite 300, Alexandria, VA 22314, Phone [703] 836-0774, for a schedule). Many Chinese institutions send representatives to regional TESOL conferences, and every national conference boasts 15 or 20 different institutional representatives. Visit the Educational and Cultural Section of the mainland Chinese Embassy or Consulate or of Taiwan's government representative nearest you. Helpfulness of staff varies, but they can probably direct you to a number of institutions in China, and may even help with applications. Appendix C lists Chinese Embassies and Consulates, and Coordinating Councils for Taiwan.

If you can't get any sort of introduction, try applying through the Foreign Expert's Bureau of the Ministry of Education (get an application from a Chinese Embassy or Consulate, or write P.O. Box 300, Friendship Hotel, Room 71633, Beijing 100088 PRC. Phone 86-1-849-8888). The Bureau will keep your application on file and offer it to Chinese institutions seeking teachers or students.

As a last resort, write blind letters to the institutions listed in our directory. But leave plenty of time and send as much information as possible. A detailed, descriptive Curriculum Vitae, for example, works better with Chinese institutions than a resume, whose terseness reads to them as opaque. Send photographs, copies of diplomas and

awards of merit, anything that will help establish a
personal relationship. Be patient, and if necessary write
several times. Just remember, if you start to get frustrated,
it'll make great tales for the grandkids.

Choosing a Route; Saving on Tickets; Exotic Routes

If you're going through a sending organization, or if your Chinese
institution buys your ticket, you'll likely have little choice of route. If you
go on your own, however, you'll probably be looking for bargain airfares.
As of this writing, the cheapest (APEX) regular round-trip airline fares to
China are approximately US$1,700 from the East Coast of the U.S. or US
$1,200 from the West Coast. You can get much cheaper rates by flying
through Hong Kong. If your school is very far north or west, however, the
savings might not be worth the trouble. Much cheaper fares are available
through "overbooking agencies," which specialize in buying up blocks of
tickets and reselling them at a discount. These fares run as low as US
$1,000 East Coast or US $800 West Coast to the mainland, and even
cheaper for Taiwan. Chinese-language newspapers and magazines are the
best places to find ads for overbooking agencies that deal with China. Be
careful, though, as many of these tickets have stringent limitations. In
general, avoid "fixed tickets" (tickets which must be used for the flight
indicated, so that if you miss the flight you forfeit the fare), or "open
tickets" good for less than one year. Try to purchase round trip, or have
someone at home make return arrangements. In most PRC cities, buying
international tickets is nightmarish, and because of exchange rates,
buying tickes in Taiwan is far more expensive than buying them at home.

Note that Taiwan visas are good for a maximum of 6 months (minimum
of 2 months). Travelers to Taiwan must leave the island at least 1 week out
of every 6 months, and might therefore find it cheaper to buy their ticket
through to another destination (Boston-Taipei-Bangkok round trip, for
example). This makes the 6-month visa trip abroad far cheaper. For
example, you could fly Boston to Taipei in August; then fly Taipei to
Bangkok round trip in February for a visa trip and vacation; and then
return to the U.S. from Taipei in July.

If you have some time, you might also want to consider a more exotic
route. Foreigners have entered China via the Trans-Siberian Railroad
from Moscow; the Karakoram Highway from Pakistan; the Friendship
Road through Tibet from Nepal; and the Mekong River. Get a good tourist
guidebook geared toward independent travel (see suggestions, Appendix
B) for ideas.

Packing:
Psychological, Personal, and Professional Baggage

You've decided on an institution and chosen a route there. Now's your time to prepare your baggage, both the kind you'll lug with your arms and the kind you'll tote in your head. Remember as you do that China is another world, in both material standards of living and cultural norms. You should consider both mental preparation and physical needs, as well as your professional requirements as teacher, student, or researcher. The following are tips on what to bring— and what not to bring—to help make your adjustment to China as painless and joyful as possible.

PSYCHOLOGICAL BAGGAGE

One of our survey questions asked teachers and students how they'd prepare differently if they went to China again. Over 90% answered they'd *"learn more about China before going."* This goes for Taiwan as well as for the mainland, for while Taiwan's material standards of living are closer to the West's, her culture is not. You can *never* overprepare yourself for China, read too many books, see too many movies, nor talk with too many people who've been there. Forewarned, as the saying goes, is forearmed.

Cultural pride compels prearrival study. Considering China's rank as the world's most populous nation with the world's longest uninterrupted cultural heritage, most Westerners remain woefully ignorant of her history, economy, geography, and traditions. Chinese people feel this ignorance keenly. Some resent it, some are depressed by it, and some use it for intellectual one-upsmanship ("My favorite American authors are

Faulkner, Wilder, and Twain. Which Chinese authors do you prefer?").
Immerse yourself in Chinese culture before you go. Knowing China will earn you respect from students, teachers, and colleagues and help break the ice with Chinese friends. After all, imagine a "Visiting Scholar" from China lecturing as an expert at a university in the UK, and suddenly asking the name of the current prime minister, or whether Dublin was next to Dorset. Wouldn't such basic ignorance raise questions in your mind about the scholar's competence and level of concern about Britain and British students? Foreigners who can't separate Zhou En-lai from Zhao Zi-yang, or who wonder which province Shanghai is in open themselves to the same suspicions.

Every language student knows the raptures Chinese people pour forth on hearing Westerners attempt their tongue, even a word as simple as *ni hao* ("hello"). Deeper interest reaps even greater rewards. One student in Kunming wrote of asking a Bai minority classmate about Bai wedding customs, and getting an invitation to the classmate's sister's tribal wedding, a three-day affair which was the height of the student's China stay. Quote a passage from the poet Li Bai, and Chinese friends will fête you with the ultimate compliment for a Westerner in China, calling you a *zhongguo tong* (中国通 : "China Hand").

1. LANGUAGE. Despite great stress in recent years on English education, very few Chinese have got beyond "hello." Speaking even a few words of pidgin Chinese will open new worlds of communication and possible friendships for you. Attaining fluency in Chinese presents many hurdles. A chasm divides Chinese from all Western linguistic groups; remembering characters is fiendishly difficult (native speakers often forget the more obscure ones); thousands of regional dialects confuse even the locals; and the infamous "tones," by which words take on different meanings depending on their musical pitch, terrorize many a learner.

   Survival Chinese, on the other hand, can be learned remarkably quickly. Several factors simplify learning basic Chinese. First, Chinese grammar ranks among the world's simplest. No verbs conjugate, nor do nouns decline. Adding particles like *le* and *yao* magically transports sentences to past or future tense. Compared with English (ever try to list all possible forms of *to be?*) this simplicity is sublime. While few cognates (words with related pronunciation) link Chinese to Western languages, Chinese uses phonemes (building blocks of pronunciation)

virtually identical to English; see the pronunciation guide
in Appendix A for details. A few cognates exist as well to
cheer the learner's way; even the most dispirited students
recognize *ka-fei* as "coffee" and *han-bao-bao* as "ham-
burger." Consider a semester or two of language before
you go. For the time-pressed, many schools offer intensive
summer courses packing a year's worth of Chinese into 8
or 10 weeks. Even if you're heading to China to study
language, consider studying some beforehand. Any
language learning proceeds faster from a base; you can
build that base more comfortably with the teaching
methods of your homeland than with the Chinese equivalents; and you'll sidestep dealing with regional dialects at
the same time as you struggle with your first words of the
language. In addition, many PRC programs are very poor,
with presence in China being the main draw. Taiwanese
language programs are generally (though not always)
better, but require learning *bo po mo fo*. Most Chinese-
language semester and summer programs in your home
country offer college credit and financial aid. See Appendix A for a list of programs, and write individual schools
for detailed information and applications.

Nonstudents might try self-study courses, using one of
the fine book/tape series available (see our list of suggestions in Appendix B). Even without formal study you can
pick up a little Chinese. Try calling your local college or
university International Students Association and offering
to help Chinese exchange students with their homework in
exchange for tutoring in Chinese. Failing that, tote your
Berlitz guide. Even a few words of Chinese can make the
difference between dependency and independence in Asia.

2. READING, LOOKING, AND LISTENING. Hundreds of books,
    movies, and tapes published in English explore every aspect
    of China's culture, history, and peoples. Appendix B con-
    tains an annotated bibliography of our favorite suggestions,
    divided by category. Don't neglect the videos; images give a
    visceral reality to your understanding missing from even the
    best books.

    Also, talk to people who have been to China, as tourists,
    teachers, students, or businesspeople. Learn what they
    thought and felt, regretted bringing or leaving behind, or
    found difficult to adjust to. Ask how they suggest you

prepare. Find the best advice you can, and take it. You'll
need it. "This place," swore one respondent, "can be
heaven or hell." Learn everything you can to improve your
odds.

3. CROSS-CULTURAL AWARENESS. A cultural gulf separates
China from the West. Some thought on cross-cultural communication and conflict can save much pain. Any number of
books have come out full of advice on coping with culture
shock and understanding cultural differences. You may find
some of these books useful; Appendix B contains a suggested list.

But the most important preparation for cross-cultural
sensitivity occurs in the mind. Take some time to consider
life in a wholly different culture, and how you'll react to it.
In many ways, Chinese etiquette and cultural values are
opposite the Western. How will you adjust to Chinese
values, or not adjust to them? For example, when meeting
for the first time, many Chinese people ask about age,
income, and marital status. These questions, considered
frightfully personal in the West, are in China a common
way of expressing friendly interest in another person,
regardless of nationality. Will you answer these questions
(literally hundreds of times, as you'll meet many strangers
during your stay)? Will you explain the Western reserve
regarding these topics, and ask that Chinese people respect
your privacy—also hundreds of times? Will you follow the
example of one teacher in Yunnan, who had a T-shirt
printed with his name and all relevant details, and wore it
incessantly to avoid being asked?

Planning a strategy for coping with cultural conflict
saves much hair-pulling and allows a happier, more
productive stay. Only you know which approach will work
for you. Just remember, Chinese culture will not change,
nor should it change, simply because it makes you
uncomfortable. The Chinese themselves say *ruxiang suisu,*
(when you enter a village, follow its customs), a rough
equivalent of "When in Rome. . . ". Whether you should
imitate Chinese custom in China or politely explain your
preference for your own ways depends on your character
and tolerance for adjustment. But preparing yourself
mentally to recognize cultural differences and develop a
conscious strategy for coping with them works better than

yelling at people whose manners make you uncomfortable, or sniggering at them behind their backs.

Recognize also that mental preparation has its limits. No doubt, whatever resolve you make to politely answer the questions listed above each time asked, one day on an unvented train steaming through the jungles of Guizhou the poor soul who happens to be the 40th to ask your income that afternoon will trigger an explosion. Prepare yourself mentally for that day as well. Recognize that you are human. Screaming at the poor soul in Guizhou is hardly noble, and will do little to improve the image some Chinese hold of foreigners as not quite civilized. But it's understandable, probably inevitable, and may even have some therapeutic value. If you can recognize your limits of cultural tolerance, and forgive yourself for outbursts when those limits are crossed (while recognizing that little good comes of such outbursts), you can minimize their frequency.

For more on this topic, see Chapter 6: "Adjusting: The Big Seven Hate List of Cross-Cultural Conflicts."

4. SUNDRIES: TOOLS TO PREVENT WESTERN WITHDRAWAL SYNDROME. Despite all best preparations and plans, you'll sometimes feel so frustrated with Chinese culture you could gleefully murder, and other times feel so homesick you could weep. For both of those times, prepare a few treats to help you relax and forget about China.

Think about what you do on days when you really want to relax and get away from it all at home. If your answer is "go for a spin in my Porsche," you're probably out of luck in China. But most people can think of a few favorite activities that revive them after a hard day, and which are portable: listening to music, reading a trash novel, drinking a big mug of hot chocolate, playing the guitar, going for a hike. Whatever it is, and whatever you need to do it, bring it along. When you need it, it'll be there; lock yourself away and enjoy.

PERSONAL BAGGAGE: THE NECESSARIES

Material living standards in China can't compare with the West. Taiwan is coming very close (who knows— if current economic trends continue, Taiwan may soon race past the West). But in the mainland, and particularly in smaller cities, life is spartan, as we have already noted. You can't do much about the plumbing, but you can make choices about material goods. Many products we take for granted are rare or unknown. Other products exist, but not in familiar brands. While international trade with China is developing rapidly, the government limits importation of consumer goods to preserve hard currency. On Taiwan you can buy virtually any import goods, for a price. But in the mainland the U.S. shampoo and Canadian beer and Swiss skin cream available at the supermarket may be sold only in large cities, or not at all.

Obviously, more than a billion people thrive on Chinese products. Very flexible foreigners fascinated with Chinese culture may decide to wear the clothes, eat the foods, and use the toiletries of the natives. But most mortals find a total break from all familiar material goods downright unpleasant. Adjusting to real cultural differences causes enough trouble; making more anxiety by weaning yourself from your favorite shampoo at the same time is pointless.

The following sections suggest which Western products are sold in China, which are unavailable but have reasonable local equivalents, and which you should bring from home. Obviously, bringing a year's supply of every product you use is impractical, and given the many joys of modern travel, you will want to keep your luggage to a minimum. But if you must have Grape Nuts for breakfast, by all means ship 20 boxes of Grape Nuts. Better pay excess baggage charges than go stir-crazy over lack of a breakfast cereal.

Necessary #1: Clothing

Before you stuff your duffle to head for Asia, try a quick experiment. Check the tags on each piece of clothing you've bought in the last 5 years. Chances are much of what you planned to haul to Asia came from there in the first place.

The moral is that China makes very high-quality clothing and sells it at very reasonable prices. Many Chinese-made clothes sold in the West are export only, not officially sold inside China because of their hard-currency earning potential abroad. But many other fine brands are sold in China, particularly in the freemarkets. Even supposedly "export only" brands, with the designer labels sewn in, often find their way to the freemarket stalls. The larger the city, the more variety the local freemarkets yield. We've bought Jordache jeans in China for $4.00, polo shirts for $3.00, and a Pierre Cardin 3-piece wool suit for $50.00, including tailoring. Taiwan sells equally high-quality clothing at only somewhat less modest prices.

Most foreign teachers and students buy clothing in China, so starting out with an overstuffed bag makes little sense. Heavy or very tall people will have trouble finding sizes that fit (though they can have apparel tailored). But most others should pack with the assumption they'll go home with more clothes than they brought. Many foreigners, in fact, bring a favorite outfit which fits well from home and have it copied by Chinese tailors in a variety of fabrics and colors. For more on this topic, see shopping suggestions in Chapter 8.

Obviously, however, you'll want a few changes of clothes to start out with. The Taiwan-bound can bring clothes they'd bring to any Western country, remembering weather conditions and slightly more modest necklines. But the mainland demands special consideration. The following guidelines should help you pack.

"DRESS CODES"

Most mainlanders care less about fashion than Westerners. In the Hong Kong–ized cities, such as Guangzhou (Canton) and Shenzhen, fashion reigns supreme. Many foreigners unfamiliar with the scope of reforms have been shocked to see low-cut dresses and punk hairdos. Yet dress codes even in Guangzhou remain informal. No one looks askance if shoes don't match handbags or socks are the wrong shade of gray.

Chinese in interior cities dress more casually still. The days when foreign journalists mocked China's "blue ants" are long gone and unlamented. Blue cotton "Mao Coats" and "Mao Hats" (the Chinese call them "Sun Yat Sen Coats" *(zhongshanfu)* and "People's Hats" *(renminmao)* remain cheap, durable, and common; during political campaigns everyone dusts them off. But only the rare Chinese now gets through life wearing nothing but monotone cottons. Nevertheless, dress codes are hardly exacting. Plaid skirt, striped shirt, and polka-dotted jacket match just fine in Chinese eyes, so long as they display similar colors.

Bring one nice dress or sports jacket and tie for the banquets you'll inevitably attend. But for everyday wear, so long as your clothing is neat and clean, Chinese won't mind if it's less than fashionable, or notice if it's more. Indeed, foreigners living in depressed areas, such as the mining towns of Northern Shaanxi now hit by heavy unemployment, should avoid expensive clothing and accessories, which could easily raise resentment or scorn.

Three points to bear in mind, however: First, Chinese appreciate neatness. The preppy "unfashions" of the West—the untied Docksiders worn without socks, the holes in the knees of the designer jeans—to most Chinese appear merely slovenly. Second, most Chinese find very bright colors inappropriate for wearers over 40. If you live to wear lime green sweaters and scarlet suits, by all means wear them. You may even strengthen cross-cultural understanding by explaining Western "young at heart" views. But be prepared for puzzled stares from folks on the street who may wonder why you don't "act your age." Third, while the Hong Kong–ized belt is quite permissive, in most of China wearing revealing clothes is still not done. Most Chinese find tight pants, short shorts, micro-bikinis, and low necklines vulgar, and wearers risk reducing their professionalism in the eyes of students, teachers, and colleagues.

PRACTICAL CONSIDERATIONS FOR CLOTHING

Wise packers remember that China is dry and dusty; that many gooey goods get carried throughout her streets without packaging; and that travel by crowded bus is far messier than travel by private car. At the same time, China lacks the abundance of both water and electricity that makes the Western push-button laundry possible. In other words, it's a lot easier to dirty your clothes in China than in the West, and a lot harder to clean them; this is largely true in Taiwan as well as the mainland. Your very best clothes should stay at home, lest they get stained forever with chicken blood from the freemarket butcher or axle grease from your bike. Clothes you bring should be sturdy and easily washable; cotton-synthetic blends, for example, clean easier than pure cotton. Depending on accommodations, you may have to wash your clothes with a scrub board and lye soap. Even if you've access to a washing machine it'll be Chinese style: fill it from the tap, let it swish, haul out the clothes wet, and put them through the wringer. Take it from us: you may enjoy your burgeoning biceps, but you'll want no clothing one iota harder to clean than necessary.

Leave the dry-clean–onlies at home. Outside joint-venture hotels mainlanders dry-clean with kerosene, which leaves a stench that lasts for days and may stain fine fabrics.

Bring a good variety of warm and cool clothes. China's chronic energy shortages leave her people far more exposed to the elements than Westerners. Warm clothes for winter and breezy for summer are essential. Even on Taiwan, you should have sweaters and jackets for winters, which can be surprisingly cold and damp. The Chinese make lovely and warm, if rather shapeless, padded trousers and jackets. The fashion conscious should bring thermal undies from home.

Shoes, particularly women's shoes, can be a problem; most Chinese versions qualify as arch-crushing torture instruments. Bring all the shoes you'll need, particularly athletic or hiking shoes.

Necessary #2: Food

China's cuisine is as varied as it is ancient. From the spicy stews of Sichuan to the tangy garlic sauces of Shandong to the sweet gooey treats of Guangzhou, Chinese food offers an endless, mouthwatering array. You'll likely fall in love with many a delicacy, and probably even lose weight and lower your cholesterol in the process, for the Chinese diet emphasizes plenty of grains, fish, and fresh vegetables. Many foreigners never miss their native cooking and feel no need to carry any foods from home.

Most foreigners, though, need some familiar foods to eat happily. You may or may not have a kitchen, but much can be done on a hotplate, or even with just thermoses of hot water. Shops in Taiwan's cities (and to some extent even rural areas) hawk any Western food you could want, and though you may not be able to afford it on a teacher's salary, splurging there is still probably cheaper than shipping from home. But the mainland is another story.

The following chart suggests foods available and unavailable in the PRC. Pack any unavailables you'd feel happier tasting now and again. Strictly speaking, food imports are controlled, but most officials won't bother about small amounts. A familiar meal can help you relax after a tough day, and few of the agonies of cultural withdrawal are as poignant as craving a hot chocolate and knowing the nearest cocoa powder is 8,000 miles away.

Few Whole Grains

Chinese people prefer highly refined flour and rice. Western preferences for brown rice and whole wheat flour seem inexplicable; the Chinese eat them only when they can't afford finely milled versions. If you insist, your schoolmates will search out a place to buy whole-grain staples, but they may gain you a strange reputation.

Herbs and Spices Hints

Many Western herbs and spices aren't sold as food, but as medicine. Bring the list of herbs and spices, with translations in Appendix A, to any Chinese herbal medicine store. Unlisted seasonings aren't sold in China, and neither are non-Chinese spice mixes such as curry powder or garam marsala; bring your own. The larger Friendship stores hawk a few tins of Spice Islands seasonings, but they're outrageously priced and usually stale.

Dairy Hard to Find

Chinese people detest most dairy products. One Chinese word for "cheese" is *qise*, a transliteration which literally means "the color of anger." Many Chinese lack lactase, the enzyme necessary to digest the lactose in milk, so dairy foods give them stomachaches. Additionally, much as many Chinese delicacies seem repulsive to foreigners (would you believe sea slug and fish maw soup?), Chinese find Western love of cheese faintly horrifying. Look at cheese as an outsider: moldy milk so curdled it's gone solid.

As a result, few Chinese stores sell dairy products. Friendship stores stock a full range; many a foreigner has lugged a wheel of cheese on the train from Beijing or Shanghai back to their school. Mongolians and Tibetans like dairy products, so in Inner Mongolia and Tibet you can eat hearty—though yak butter and powdered goat cheese may take some getting used to. But elsewhere in China your dairy choices are limited to three: yoghurt, powdered milk, and ice cream. Chinese yoghurt (*suannai:* 酸 奶) is runnier than Western, but delicious and widely sold in plain and fruit flavors. Powdered milk is also easily available; our polls indicate Anchor Steam Brand from Australia tops most foreigner's lists (in a few cities fresh milk is also sold through a central distributor). Chinese love ice cream, but be warned that Chinese like far less milkfat than Westerners; you'll taste more ice than cream.

BRING COFFEE IF YOU NEED IT

Real perk coffee exists only in joint venture hotels, which sell it only by the cup. Fresh-roast addicts should bring a drip pot with a year's supply of filters and beans (a re-usable Melitta-style filter is best). They will guarantee popularity with the expatriate crowd, but don't be surprised if your Chinese friends can't tell the difference between your best Columbian roast and Maxwell House. Just imagine how they feel when you prefer Orange Pekoe to a prizewinning Oolong or Longjing.

LIQUORS AND WINES

Friendship Stores sell many Western liquors at steep but not outrageous prices, though for fine brandies or cognacs you'll have to try Hong Kong. China also sells a few indigenous "brandies," which are quite tasty but very unbrandy-like; more like a cross between Southern Comfort and Old Thunderbird. Most Chinese wines taste like Manischewitz with added sugar, but a few palatable varieties exist; China's first varietal vintage winery, Huadong Winery in Shandong province, produces a lovely Riesling and a Chardonnay whose 1986 vintage took a Silver Medal at bordeaux. Traditional Chinese liquors, such as Shao-Xing, Mao Tai, and Lao Jiao, take some getting used to. Most pack a punch, as much as 180 proof. Experiment, however. You may develop a taste for them.

Necessary #3: Personal and Health-Care Products

Chinese use most toiletries Westerners use, though often less liberally. On Taiwan virtually any product is available, though again often at inflated prices (at last check a 5-ounce tub of Nivea Brand skin cream sold for US$15 in Taipei). See Chart 2 for suggestions of what is available in the mainland.

PRODUCT	READILY AVAILABLE	LARGE CITIES ONLY	EASY TO FIND GOOD SUBSTITUTES	UNAVAILABLE
Staples				
MEATS, FISH	✕			
GRAINS	✕ *: also see Note 1*			
FRUITS, VEGETABLES	✕ *: in North, in cold months, choices can be very limited*			
FLATBREAD, BUNS	✕			
YEAST, YEAST BREADS		✕		
SOFT NOODLES	✕			
HARD DURUM PASTA		✕		
CHINESE SPICES	✕			
OTHER SPICES: SEE NOTE 2				
DAIRY: SEE NOTE 3				
Beverages				
CHINESE TEAS	✕			
WESTERN TEAS		✕	✕	
INSTANT COFFEE	✕			
FRESH-BREWED COFFEE: SEE NOTE 4				
NON-DAIRY CREAMER	✕			
DRINKABLE TAP WATER				✕
BOILED WATER	✕: *thermoses in every room*			
COKE, PEPSI, FANTA	✕: *but not in diet incarnations*			
OTHER SOFT DRINKS	✕: *but many Chinese sodas are very sweet*			
PURE FRUIT JUICE		✕: *except the kind in the fruit*		
GOOD COCOA POWDER	*(Chinese brands would insult dishwater)*			✕
BEER	✕: *Tsingdao Brand is the best, but experiment*			
LIQUOR AND WINE: SEE NOTE 5				
Other				
CONVIENCE FOODS	✕: *Chinese*			✕: *Western*
CANDY	✕			
WAXY CHOCOLATE	✕			
GOOD CHOCOLATE				✕

Chart 1:   AVAILABLE FOODS

TAMPONS

Amusingly, because Chinese remain conservative about premarital sex and the preservation of the hymen, until recently some tampons in China were sold with a warning on the box against use by unmarried women!

PRESCRIPTION DRUGS: BRING FULL YEAR'S SUPPLY

Be sure to bring a full supply of all prescription drugs. Most foreigners get the best care that China's medical system offers, but nevertheless, especially in rural areas, quality varies. Then too, quite aside from practitioners' qualifications, many Chinese generic medicines have chemical compositions slightly different from their Western equivalents, enough to cause problems. If you are prone to respiratory or digestive troubles be sure to ask your doctor for preventatives and remedies, as China's dry air and lax hygiene attack those two systems with particular vigor. See "Medical Preparations" below for required shots.

RECREATIONAL DRUGS?

The answer is, *DON'T*. The Chinese have a deep-rooted racial horror of the influence of foreign drug users dating back to the Opium War. Nothing, with the possible exception of rape, raises such fury as a foreigner providing illegal drugs to a Chinese. Nor will any other activity, including underground political activism, be as likely to land you in jail. If you have a drug problem, keep it out of China. Period.

Necessary #4: Professional Supplies

Mainland teachers and students rely much less than Westerners on professional presentations. Everything you might need, from art supplies to computers, is available, but not always in the quality you might be used to. See Chart 3 for details (unless otherwise noted, all items are available on Taiwan).

PHOTOCOPYING DIFFICULT

Most Chinese schools have photocopiers, but restrict their use because of expense (China needs to import toner). Instead materials are dittoed. If you want to assign large sections from books be sure your school has a thermal transfer machine to create ditto masters from photocopies. Otherwise everything will have to be retyped. A sad comment on Chinese wage structures appeared from this fact. When Rebecca's school's thermal transfer machine broke down, the school hired a typist to retype book sections Rebecca wanted to assign onto ditto masters: the typist's wage cost the school less than the difference between dittos and photocopies. If you intend to produce your own materials, remember only wide-carriage typewriters hold Chinese ditto masters.

PRODUCT	READILY AVAILABLE	LARGE CITIES ONLY	EASY TO FIND GOOD SUBSTITUIES	UNAVAILABLE
Toiletries				
SHAMPOO, CONDITIONER	✗	✗ Western Brands		
MOUSSES, GELS, SPRAY				✗
HAIR COLORING	✗ (black only)	✗ Western Brands		
SOAPS	✗ Zest, Lux, other imports—also many good Chinese brands			
PERFUMES, COLOGNES		✗ (Chinese brands very sweet)		
MAKE-UP		✗ (some easy-to-find Chinese brands OK)		
MOISTURIZERS		✗ (you'll need them in the North or West)		
LIP BALM	✗ we recommend Double Horses Brand			
Feminine Care				
TAMPONS	✗ See note 1			
PADS	✗			
PMS/CRAMPING MEDICATION				✗
Contraceptives				
CONDOMS/FOAM	✗ (though selling to foreigners may cause giggles)			
DIAPHRAGMS/JELLY				✗
IUDs				✗
PILLS	✗ (but Chinese doctors often prescribe very high doses)			
Eye Care				
EYEGLASSES	✗ simple correctional lenses, nice frames (complex lenses can be difficult, best bring extras)			
CONTACT LENSES		✗		
CLEANING SOLUTIONS	✗			
Skin Care				
FIRST-AID NEEDS	✗			
INSECT REPELLENTS				✗
SUN-TAN LOTIONS		✗		
Medicines				
VITAMINS	✗ synthetic	✗ naturally derived		
ASPIRIN	✗			
IBUPROFEN-BASED PAINKILLERS				✗
COLD MEDICINES	✗ Chinese	✗ Western	✗ herbal	
PRESCRIPTION DRUGS: SEE NOTE 2				
RECREATIONAL DRUGS: SEE NOTE 3				
Cleaning and Maintenace Supplies				
DISH SOAP	✗			
LAUNDRY SOAP	✗			
BLEACH, FABRIC SOFTENERS		✗		
SPECIAL SOAP FOR FINE WASHABLES				✗
CLEANING TOOLS	✗			

Chart 2:   PERSONAL AND HEALTH-CARE PRODUCTS

ABOUT COMPUTERS

China makes several personal computers; best is the Langchao, an IBM PC clone (rumored, in fact, to be pirated from IBM technology, but that's another story). It's hellish to buy in China (export only), but many schools have them available for foreign teachers. Should you bring your own computer, your students, teachers, and friends will crowd into your quarters at any opportunity to fiddle with it. Most larger cities have stores selling moderately good computer paper in standard sizes, a few sizes of ribbon cartridges, 5.25" (very occasionally also 3.5") floppy disks, and software. But given China's spotty record with intellectual property rights, any software you buy in China may be subject to confiscation back home (equally true on Taiwan, and computer viruses are rampant in pirated Taiwanese software).

Computer users must use a current stabilizer and a surge protector in addition to the step-down converter (see below). In the case of 3, 6, or 9 volt laptops, an AC/DC adaptor is also required. Many computer stores sell international current adaptor/surge protector/stabilizer kits in one box, with hefty price tags; or just buy components. Bring the surge protector and adaptor from home; Chinese stores sell bulky but excellent current stabilizers for about $15. The order of plug-in, from the wall out, should be: stabilizer, surge protector (and any grounding wires necessary for the surge protector), step-down converter, AC/DC adaptor (if necessary), computer. The experts say China's erratic electricity will still wear down your computer faster than use in the West, but we used ours for 2 1/2 years with no noticeable ill effects.

OTHER ELECTRONIC GADGETS

Both mainland and Taiwan electrical systems feed 220 or 240 volts AC into wall sockets. U.S./Canadian travelers bringing their own appliances will need a simple step-down converter changing 220/240 into 110/120. Buy a converter with a variety of plug adaptors, as Chinese wall sockets vary widely. Radio Shack sells a converter/plug adaptor set in a carrying case for $10.95. Walkman-style tape recorders also require conversion from 110 volts AC to 3, 6, or 9 volts DC. Bring both the step-down converter and an AC/DC current adaptor from home; in China, from the wall out, plug in the step-down converter, the adaptor, and the recorder. Chinese stores sell AC/DC adaptors which convert 220 volts AC directly to 3, 6, or 9 volts DC, but the plugs often don't fit tape recorders made for sale in the West.

Very few foreigners bring televisions, as most schools provide televisions in foreigners' quarters. Should you insist, however, ask an expert at your local electronics store for advice. Hz cycles in China's electrical

Product	Readily Available	Large Cities Only	Easy to Find Good Substitutes	Unavailable
Art/Display Supplies				
CHINESE ART GOODS	X *(inkstones, silk, rice paper, ink, Chinese brushes, etc.)*			
WESTERN ART GOODS	X *(standard goods—premixed pigments, premade canvases, etc.)*			
HIGH-QUALITY/NONSTANDARD WESTERN ART SUPPLIES			X	
EASELS	X			
FLIPCHARTS/DISPLAY PAPER		X		
LIGHTWEIGHT PAPER	X *all colors/styles, but all flimsy*			
HEAVY DUTY PAPER/CONSTRUCTION PAPER	X			
HIGH-QUALITY CRAYONS/MARKERS				X
Writing Materials/Desk Supplies				
PENCILS, PENS	X			
SCISSORS, GLUE	X			
STAPLERS, RULERS	X			
PAPER CLIPS	X			
EASY-TO-USE CLEAR STICK TAPE	*(the Chinese kind sticks to itself)* X			
CARDS, POSTCARDS	X			
HIGH-QUALITY STATIONERY		X		
MANUAL TYPEWRITERS	X			
STANDARD RIBBONS	X			
GOOD ELECTRIC TYPEWRITERS, NON-STANDARD RIBBONS				X
DITTO MACHINES	X			
DITTO MASTERS	X			
PHOTOCOPIERS: SEE NOTE 1				
COMPUTERS: SEE NOTE 2				
ELECTRICITY: SEE NOTE 3				
Audio-visual Supplies				
TAPE RECORDERS	X *(but pocket-sized portable recorders are rare)*			
CASSETTE TAPES	X *(blank and prerecorded)*			
VCRs: MOST SCHOOLS HAVE, BUT MAY BE NTSC FORMAT—ASK AHEAD				
VIDEOTAPES		X *(or through school supply office)*		
SLIDE PROJECTORS: ASK AHEAD IF YOUR SCHOOL HAS ONE				
SLIDE FILM/SLIDE FILM PROCESSING				X
OVERHEAD PROJECTORS: ASK AHEAD IF YOUR SCHOOL HAS ONE				
TRANSPARENCIES		X	X *(acetate sheets)*	
RECORD PLAYERS		X		
LPs		X		

Chart 3:   PROFESSIONAL SUPPLIES

current may disrupt TVs made for sale in the West, and TV conversion requirements differ.

PROFESSIONAL BAGGAGE

The Taiwan-bound may not even know where they'll teach or study, let alone what. The mainland-bound will know school, but should take any prearrival advice regarding courseload with a grain of salt, regardless of how definite and specific it sounds. Many people hold sway over foreigners in China, responsible ministries are frightfully slow giving or forbidding consent to curriculum planners, and bureaucrats nurture jealous rivalries, so that whatever A approves B forbids. Chinese officials are often far too enthusiastic about their students'or teachers' abilities. People who give you course lists are probably acting in good faith. But they assume foreigners understand the unpredictability of Chinese life, and this results in much rancor.

Think of any prearrival course lists as guidelines, rather than specific courses. If the list reads, "Seminar in Grammar Development, 2d level; Seminar in Fiction Writing, 4th level; Lecture in British Literature, 1st Year Graduate," assume you'll be teaching a grammar course, a writing course, and a literature course, but assume nothing else. Don't bother preparing a syllabus or planning classes; your work is too likely for naught.

What this means for teachers is that you must bring a library of materials on each of the subjects you'll teach, materials designed for different levels, class sizes, interests, and goals. What this means for students is that you must bring supplementary materials and study aids for topics, rather than classes. On Taiwan foreign-language bookstores have selections of language study and reference books, and photocopying for students is readily available. As a result, Taiwan-bound teachers needn't bother bringing books, unless they have particular favorites. But even there students will want some materials of their own.

As much as possible, continue to politely press your Chinese contacts for specifics on your course load. Recognize that too much pressure may encourage false advice of the sort detailed above. But quiet, courteous, continuous prodding may encourage openness regarding the behind-the-scenes negotiations. You may learn, for example, that you'll definitely teach a conversation course, though the level hasn't been settled.

At the same time, ask for a list of last year's courses. The courses taught or studied by foreigners at each institution differ little from year to year. Narrowing your possibilities reduces the professional materials you must pay excess baggage charges for.

Keep contacting your institute's representatives about your expectations. Teachers can sketch a draft syllabus or sample readings to send over. Students can send lists of topics they hope to cover, or ask for suggested prearrival reading lists. Chinese are often puzzled over what foreigners want, and find waiting until arrival the easiest course. By getting as much information as you can before you leave you can prepare in your homeland, where familiar facilities are at hand, and avoid wasting your first weeks in China while the institution scrambles to make arrangements.

Students: Becoming Your Own Reference Library

Western students assume both that they can choose their courses and that materials they need for research will be at hand. Chinese students can assume neither of these, partly because government ministries and political policy hold sway over curriculum developers in China, and partly because Chinese universities have severely limited budgets, and their libraries are understocked. Many books in Chinese libraries may also be off-limits, depending on your status and relations with the librarian. Foreign students have many advantages over Chinese students, but these basic facts of Chinese student life restrict foreigners as much as Chinese.

Courses offered can vary based on available staff, space, and political directives. Largely apolitical topics such as language and Chinese medicine are least affected; students of such volatile topics as history and sociology should be prepared for surprises.

Chinese libraries simply haven't the resources, especially in Western languages, taken for granted in Western community colleges, let alone in major research institutions. This is still largely true on Taiwan as well as in the mainland. Taiwan's new National Central Library has a good collection of recent Western books and subscribes to a huge number of English academic and popular periodicals, but outside of Taipei resources are much sparser. Assume there'll be an encyclopedia, a few dictionaries, and a small collection of books on a variety of topics. Specialized books and books on politically controversial topics may simply not exist.

Bring or ship a box full of books related to your topic. If you're interested in acupuncture, bring acupuncture treatises. In China you'll find charts, medical school/acupuncture texts in Chinese, and probably a very sketchy textbook in English written for foreign students. You may also find ancient and wonderful manuscripts stored in the university library, or in a temple nearby, wholly unknown in the West. But basic reference information on background, philosophy, varying methodologies, and interpretations may just not exist. For more on this see Chapter 7.

Teachers: Syllabus ex Nihilo

Because pinpointing course load before arrival verges on the impossible, you'll likely spend your first days in China frantically determining courses and creating syllabi. The following tips should help smooth the process.

First, if you'll be teaching English and have no experience teaching (a common state for many foreign teachers), try to learn some methods before you go. Chapter 7 contains a crash course in EFL teaching; see also the list of suggested EFL texts in Appendix B. If possible, take a course at your local community college in TEFL. If you're thinking about a career in ESL/EFL, consider enrolling in a program. Many schools offer 1-year intensive M.A.-Teaching degrees, which will earn you higher salaries both in China and after. At the very least attend a conference of the TESOL (Teachers of English to Speakers of Other Languages) Association, either a huge international convention or a regional meeting in your area. For information in the U.S., write National TESOL Association, 1600 Cameron St., Suite 300, Alexandria, VA 22314. Phone (703) 836-0774.

Next, try to determine at least the subject you'll be teaching before arrival. At home stock up on texts and supplementary materials on the topic, and have them there when you arrive (for tips on shipping, see below). Chinese university libraries may have a variety of EFL/ESL texts, but resources can be imbalanced, with 40 preparation manuals for the TOEFL (Test of English as a Foreign Language, the dreaded exam used as entrance criterion for foreign exchange students by many U.S. universities), and only 1 grammar guide. The Taiwan-bound should assume a wide variety of texts will be available in stores, but bring your particular favorites anyway.

Try also to tote bundles of supplementary "authentic" materials. Recent ESL/EFL methodology stresses "real world" materials and "communicative competence" over grammatical perfection. Bring menus, magazines (*Sports Illustrated, National Geographic,* and columns from Ann Landers and Miss Manners remain perennial favorites with Chinese students), newspapers, maps, advertisements, packages, music tapes, sheet music, want ads, board games, monopoly money, recorded lectures, videotapes (remember to ask if your school has a VCR), video games— anything in English. Think as you go through your daily life of every type of English material you encounter, and bring samples of all of them. Your students will learn more and have more fun "shopping" in a "supermarket" of empty packages brought from home than reading any textbook lesson about shopping.

Many foreign teachers establish and maintain a "Student Library" of English-language books, tapes, and periodicals. Most official libraries are closed-stack to Chinese students, and can be quite discouraging for unsure learners. Maintaining an easily accessible collection of materials for students to read or listen to on their own encourages self-study and mental expansion. We started a student library at Qingdao University in Shandong which, 4 years later, is being managed and augmented by each year's foreign teachers, and averages dozens of borrowers each day. Good sources of inexpensive materials for such libraries include garage sales, library sales, and neighbors' basements. Try also writing your local paper, college or university library, or Rotary or Elk's Club; or to a publishing conglomerate such as National Geographic or Time-Life, explaining your endeavor. They all responded to us generously, adding to our new library by hundreds of volumes.

By your arrival in China, or shortly before, your course load should be set. Ask if a standard text exists for the course; the answer will generally be yes. In most cases you should use the text even though it may be poorly written, for two reasons. First, the text will contain everything the student will be tested on in the national exams. China's national exams stress grammar and vocabulary, and many who pass with high scores can't communicate in real-world situations. Most teachers hope to teach communicative ability far beyond textbook content. However, your students must pass the national exams to graduate, and if you ignore exam content you do them no service.

Second, the standard texts are available. Chinese texts, whether written locally or pirated from a foreign text (only rarely have copyright licenses been purchased), are printed cheaply and are available to your students at affordable rates. You may find a wonderful text with great illustrations, but your students can't afford it full price, and even if you choose to aid and abet its pirating, you can't get it printed up in time to start class. Using the standard text gives your students something in hand. You can reorder the lessons or add topics as you like. Just make sure to cover all textbook content; then you can copy à la carte from texts you have brought or write your own supplementary materials, remembering that everything must be transferred or typed onto ditto masters.

MISCELLANEOUS PREPARATIONS

Shipping

Shipping to China, mainland or Taiwan, is expensive, inconvenient, and slow. All packages are opened and inspected by Chinese customs, which runs a constant backlog and therefore takes weeks. In addition, many classes of items, from the "pornographic" to the "politically offensive," any of which can be defined at the customs officer's whim, are subject to confiscation. Taiwan is less stringent than the mainland, but still can be difficult to deal with.

When possible, carry everything with you. Your first month's clothing, all prescription medicines, valuables, and texts you will use immediately on arrival must be in your luggage, the last three in your carry-ons.

If you ship, plan ahead. Assume that *any* package shipped surface could take up to *6 months* (occasionally even more), so send materials you'll need in November by May. The cheapest surface rate from the U.S. is through printed-matter "M" bags—ask at your post office for details. Air mail runs faster, but is exceedingly expensive, and still never guarantees delivery under a month. Express mail generally arrives within a week, but occasionally takes several.

Some packing tips: use stout boxes and plenty of filler, and wrap messy items in plastic; Chinese postal workers can be brutal. Make and copy a list of all contents before shipping; keep one copy and paste another in the box. This discourages pilferage and, if theft occurs, can help with reimbursement. Also, the more potentially problematic the material in any box, the slower it will get through. Large amounts of religious material (mainland only); politically controversial texts; anything to do with Tibet, Taiwan independence, or the Democracy movement; anything pornographic or perceivable as pornographic by prudish customs officials (such as drawings of scantily clad women on the covers of pulp novels) will slow down your package by months while everything is read to determine possible offensiveness. When in doubt, customs will confiscate.

Pack necessary and obviously inoffensive materials, such as EFL texts, classic novels, and your backup supply of vitamins separately from anything that could slow up the works. If possible carry video and audio tapes. If not, pack them separately and securely, label them "Video and Audio Materials for Use in Teaching English Language," and label each tape with both name and a brief description (" 'The Music Man,' " "U.S. musical drama," etc.).

We do not recommend shipping or carrying materials which are likely to have been banned, such as the Dalai Lama's memoirs, or a collection of speeches by dissident Fang Li-zhi. If discovered they'll draw attention to you, and to any Chinese people who associate with you. Then too, little purpose is served by bringing them. You and other foreigners can read them at home. Chinese can't read them, for being found with banned texts remains cause for imprisonment. Distributing banned materials in China involves risky and delicate timing best judged by those who make it their life's work. Inexperienced foreigners blundering in generally do more harm than good.

Medical Preparations

Both mainland China and Taiwan have eradicated yellow fever and other epidemic diseases. But hygienic conditions remain below first-world par. All foreigners entering should have a series of vaccine shots against hepatitis B, and should consider a supply of gamma globulin to combat hepatitis A. Foreigners heading toward southern provinces or Taiwan should bring antimalaria pills. Try to avoid getting shots on the mainland, where doctors often reuse needles. Many foreigners bring disposable needles from home; ask your doctor for some along with his or her note explaining your medical need for them so they don't get impounded at customs.

Other recommended shots fluctuate, but may include Japanese encephalitis vaccine, antiparasitics, and others. Ask your doctor or a physician specializing in immunology for further advice.

Money Matters

Taiwan has a complex, modern economy. You can use most major credit cards and all major-bank traveler's checks throughout the island. Taiwan's currency, the National Taiwan Dollar or NT, is fully convertible and can be purchased with hard currency at banks throughout the island at fairly rational rates. You can also set up savings and/or checking accounts at any bank, at current exchange of US$1 to NT$27.1. Foreign teachers in Taiwan are also subject to income tax, at approximately 20% of income, though they are exempt for their first 6 months of residence. U.S. citizens on the mainland are not required to pay Chinese income tax, due to a bilateral treaty, but they must file a U.S. income-tax form. Due to a foreign-earned–income exclusion of up to $70,000, you'll owe no tax on your Chinese salary but you may have to pay Social Security self-employment tax. Other foreigners owe tax to the PRC government at 30% of any earnings over 800 yuan per month, though your *waiban* (see Chapter 5) may or may not enforce this.

Mainland China still has a cash-based economy. Joint-venture hotels accept major credit cards, but most other places don't. Foreign students will be expected to pay their school in cash or traveler's checks, and foreign teachers' wages come in cash. Bring enough cash with you to last a month including set-up costs (no less than US$500), since some schools won't pay the first month's salary up front. Travelers checks are safer than cash, and American Express are the most widely accepted.

The mainland "People's Currency" (*Ren Min Bi* 人民币), or RMB is nonconvertible. Foreign currency can be converted at Bank of China offices to "Foreign Exchange Certificates" (*Wai Hui Quan:* 外汇券), or FEC, which are not technically a currency, but function as one. Both

RMB and FEC are tightly controlled; as a result there are flourishing black markets throughout China trading RMB with FEC and both with foreign currencies. In an attempt to rationalize exchange, the PRC government has devalued the RMB to 5.2 RMB to US$1.00, but the RMB still officially equals 1 yuan FEC. On the street at last report, 1 yuan FEC was worth approximately 1.8 yuan RMB, and US$1.00 was worth approximately 6.5 RMB.

You must reach your own decision regarding participation in black-market currency exchange. Money changing is unequivocably illegal, and punishment can include fines and deportation. Such strict application of the law is, however, extremely rare, and generally appears when Chinese officials wish to punish foreigners for other reasons and find money changing a convenient excuse. It's fair to say that most foreigners change money at least once during their China stays, and those who voice the loudest moral outrage against money changing tend to be those who can most easily afford not to do it. You'll certainly have no lack of opportunities, particularly in large cities, where on every street corner hawkers will besiege you yelling "change money!" Some foreigners even buy pre-printed T-shirts declaring *meiyou wai huiquan* ("I don't have FEC") to escape the onslaught.

You can withdraw cash from most foreign banks through large Bank of China offices using any major international credit card. American Express Card members are entitled to home-country currency withdrawals, though Bank of China officials may be peevish about it. MasterCard, Visa, and Diner's Club allow withdrawal in FEC "equivalents," at exchange rates determined by the Bank of China.

You can set up a savings account at Bank of China; checking accounts are very rare. But read the fine print; interest is generally negligible, and BOC sometimes requires deposits of 6 months before withdrawal. Many foreigners just imitate their Chinese neighbors and "stuff it into the mattress." BOC now issues the Great Wall "credit card" (it actually functions as a debit card), which is widely-enough accepted to be worth having; your waiban can help you apply. But try to get an RMB Great Wall card—otherwise you'll have to deposit FEC.

Visas and Arrival Procedures

Your mainland Chinese school will probably arrange your resident visa and contact the nearest embassy or consulate in your home country. You can then just go in or mail in your passport (certified or registered mail only!) for the visa stamp. In rare or rushed cases you may have to enter on a tourist visa. The easiest way is to fly to Hong Kong and get a 1-month tourist visa there, either in the PRC travel office or at a commercial travel agency. If you enter with a tourist visa be sure your waiban begins the paperwork to convert to a work visa as soon as possible. You must have a valid work visa to get a resident card, which gives you permission to live long term in a Chinese city.

The Taiwan-bound can enter on a 6-month visitor's visa; simply apply at your nearest Taiwanese government representative (see list in Appendix C). Students never need any other documents (though remember to leave Taiwan for 1 week every 6 months to get your renewal!). Students can also get a student resident visa, which requires proof of full-time study (16 credit hours undergrad or 6 grad/semester in degree programs, or 10 hours/week of language classes). Foreign teachers technically require a commercial visa, which is expensive and cumbersome, but few ever get one. Most simply get a 6-month visitor's visa, then register with their local foreign affairs bureau in Taiwan to get a temporary work permit.

Both Taiwan and the mainland have strict health codes, and may require a clean-health inspection, including a negative test for HIV antibodies. Check with your waiban or the local Taiwanese government representative for details. If the Chinese government insists on retesting you for HIV after entry, insist they do so with an unused disposable needle.

The mainland also requires that you fill out a detailed summary of all valuables you carry in, especially electronic goods and jewelry. Keep this list; it will be rechecked on exit. Chinese import duties on electronics and jewelry are steep, and the government strongly discourages foreigners from presenting them as gifts, though overseas Chinese can import goods to the PRC more easily.

Arriving:
Your Danwei,
Your Waiban, *and You*

China hits new arrivals full force. Bleary-eyed and jet-lagged, you'll stumble off your plane to a cacophony of families greeting their returnees. Customs officials will poke through your underwear. Cabbies will shout to cram you and 10 others into a swaybacked cab which belches monoxides as it careens through crowded streets at high speeds. A representative of your institution may or may not greet you, perhaps bearing a contract you'll be urged to sign immediately.

Many foreigners react first to China with an overwhelming urge to flee. Chinese people stand closer to one another than Westerners, talk louder, knock less before opening doors, and use less deodorant. The Chinese construct buildings, streets, hallways, and rooms narrower, shorter, and more crowded than in the West. Claustrophobia can set in.

Your first and best defense remains mental preparation. Before arrival, gear yourself up by packing the mental baggage described in Chapter 4. After arrival, strive to adjust to Chinese culture by finding your own combination of imitation, adaptation, and acceptance. The following sections should help you develop a sense of how things work in China and what will be expected of you, and suggest a few strategies for adjustment.

BOSS/LANDLORD: YOU AND YOUR DANWEI

The Danwei for Chinese People

Chinese people grow up in an interwoven web of mutual responsibility networks. The family, the street association, the neighborhood or village

57

brigade all bond the individual to society through complex ties. Misbehaving children reflect badly on parents, siblings, and even neighbors. A thief shames and potentially brings punishment to co-workers and superiors.

On Taiwan mutual responsibility networks have become attenuated, but in the mainland they flourish. In mainland cities the strongest mutual responsibility group is the work unit, or *danwei* (单位). Village brigades function as rural danwei, but foreigners rarely see them. Danwei range from individual factories, schools, or hospitals to massive national danwei such as the Ministry of Transportation. Each danwei both cares for and controls its workers, managers, and dependents. Omnipotent by comparison with Western employers, the danwei not only assigns work duties, salaries, and benefits, but also arranges housing, health care, transportation, travel benefits, rationing coupons, and internal sales of reduced-priced goods. Danwei can give or deny permission to marry, move, travel, and bear children, and are the front line of the Chinese justice system.

Westerners would find such omnipotence intolerable, but most Chinese find it comforting. If bad feelings develop, danwei leaders can consign workers to hell on earth. But most Chinese get along with their danwei, and enjoy job, housing, and neighborhood stability unknown in the West. Westerners accept social instability and professional insecurity as part of the price of freedom. Chinese accept autarchic control over their lives in return for stability and certainty.

The Danwei for Foreigners

Taiwan has no danwei, and Taiwanese schools function much as do Western equivalents. But mainland-bound foreigners, like it or not, join China's mutual responsibility network from their first day in China till their last. Lacking families in China or membership in neighborhood brigades, foreigners tie in solely through their danwei. This relationship is frequently explained as one between "guests" and "hosts," reflecting the traditional Chinese emphasis on hospitality. The foreign guest is received by a Chinese host danwei responsible for the foreigner's needs and actions.

Guest-host relationships for tourists can be tenuous. Individual tourists issued transit or tourist visas at the border may never see their danwei at all unless they run into trouble, yet all remain guests of the Ministry of Travel and Tourism.

The longer foreigners stay in China, however, and the more they participate in Chinese life, the more aware they become of host danwei and their mutual obligations as guest. Businesspeople negotiate through their host danwei for materials transport, import/export licenses, currency exchange, and inter-danwei contractual agreements. Much has been written on the importance to traders of selecting a suitably influential host danwei.

As a foreign teacher or student you must choose your danwei very carefully indeed, for it controls you very directly. Your danwei has nowhere near the power over you as over your Chinese counterparts. Your danwei is, however, your employer, landlord, health insurer, transport company, food supplier, and many other things, including scapegoat for your indiscretions. Should you break laws during your stay, your danwei will take the rap. In extreme cases, while you may be deported, the danwei member responsible for you could go to jail.

THE WAIBAN

The danwei section directly responsible for foreigners at a school is the Foreign/External Affairs Office (FAO)—*waishi bangongshi* in Chinese, or *waiban* (外办) for short. The waiban has many duties unrelated to foreigners, such as interuniversity contracts and liaison with city govern-ment. But for your purposes, the waiban is your link to the danwei. Depending on danwei size, your waiban may be a single person assigned liaison duties, or a large office responsible for everything from preparing visa extensions to hiring maids to swab the foreign toilets.

Your waiban bears direct responsibility for you, suffers more than anyone else for your indiscretions, and wields great power over your daily life. Not surprisingly, many Westerners, unused to such control, come into conflict with their waiban, most frequently about money. The federal government gives waibans a yearly or monthly allowance per foreign teacher set by geographic region, and determines the amount of student tuition remitted to the school. This money the waiban controls, using part for your salary or stipend; part for room, any board subsidies, medical insurance, travel and shipping allowances, and other benefits; part for banquets and other organized activities, and part for waiban coffers. As might be expected, waibans vary, some using every penny for the foreigners, others reducing foreigners to penurious wages while buying official waiban stereos and official waiban cars. Foreigners too vary, some working long hours and volunteering to coach basketball, others shirking class and whining year-round.

But most waibans, like most foreigners, are reasonably professional, moderately materialistic, and hope to cooperate happily. Work from that base. Strive for cordiality with your waiban, if not warmth, and much happiness can be yours. Your friend the waiban can get you theater tickets, be your guide and cultural interpreter, help you buy artwork and gain you access to research facilities. Most waibans love to be asked for advice by "their" foreigners. By playing up to the Chinese system's paternalistic tendencies you stand to gain.

At all costs avoid becoming mortal enemies with your waiban. Your enemy the waiban can move screaming babies to the room next to yours, start construction projects by your window and order workers to start at 5:00 A.M., arrange for a transfer of your favorite teacher, or refuse to extend your visa or arrange travel permits to restricted areas. Quite aside from these horrors, troubles with your waiban can taint your whole stay. Years down the line you'll have forgotten about the time the waiban didn't keep his promise, but you will remember the time you argued with the waiban and got excluded from every field trip from then on. Better to keep on an even keel.

THE CONTRACT FOR TEACHERS AND STUDENTS

Your contract governs your legal and financial relations with both waiban and danwei. It merits serious attention. This is true on Taiwan as well as in the mainland, though Taiwan contracts deal only with the categories familiar in Western versions. Contracts can be negotiated before or after arrival, depending on whether you and your waiban feel more comfortable negotiating in person or by FAX. Prearrival contracts allow more time for reflection and consultation with friends, but tend to be abstract, as you sign them without knowing details of local conditions. Post-arrival contracts allow inclusion of nitty-gritty details like which building you'll sleep in and whom you'll teach, but can be subject to time pressure; much paperwork can't be completed till you sign, and your waiban may push for speedy negotiations.

Student contracts tend to be straightforward. At long-established programs like the Beijing Foreign Language Institute's Chinese program schools present fixed packages. Newer programs may still be plagued with bugs. One student promised a master's program in Chinese literature arrived to find no curriculum, merely a tutor assigned to meet with her twice per week. Particularly if you're among the first foreign students to attend an institution, be sure the courses to be offered you are clarified on paper; you won't be able either to transfer or to obtain a refund after payment. For this reason you may prefer postarrival contracts and payment, with specifics in writing about classes, teachers, books and materials, access to facilities, and hours of instruction per week.

Be sure also to clarify in writing any arrangements for transcripts and credit, as China has no standardized academic credit system, and you may otherwise have trouble arranging transfer of credit to your home school. See also suggestions on housing and benefits under teacher contracts, below. Otherwise student contracts rarely pose problems.

Teacher contracts, on the other hand, vary across the map, both between and within institutions. Negotiate vigorously. Too many foreigners, starry-eyed about Asia, inexperienced at negotiation, and perhaps succumbing to unscrupulous waiban pressure to sign a contract while still gripped by jet lag, neglect the contract's importance, or sign without careful scrutiny. When later discovering their colleagues teach half the courses for twice the wage they howl and scream, but to no avail.

Such foreigners feel cheated, but they shouldn't. Your contract is a business arrangement in which emotions have no place. Chinese understand this and will give absolutely nothing away in negotiations. Neither should you. You may feel idealistic about contributing to Chinese society; attend to your idealism later. No one will stop you from doing more than required in your contract. If you sign up for 12 class hours per week, then teach 4 more without pay, your commitment and sacrifice will be recognized and appreciated. If you sign up for 16 hours, those 16 are taken for granted, and refusal to do any more appears intransigent. Getting a reasonable set of conditions down on paper protects both you and your waiban.

Space prohibits detailed suggestions here on negotiating with the Chinese, but in any case several fine books cover the subject in detail (see Appendix B). Suffice it to say that patient, reasonable discourse and a clear focus on objectives are key. The following, while by no means cut in stone, show our suggested guidelines for discussion.

Teaching Hours

Most Chinese teachers run 5 to 10 class hours per week. Foreign teachers are expected to hold down 12 to 16 hours per week (more variable on Taiwan). This alone should dispel any guilt you may feel about earning a higher wage than Chinese teachers. We suggest agreeing to no more than 10 hours per week of academic classes (history, literature, culture, etc.) or of composition classes (all those essays!), or no more than 12 to 14 hours per week of straight language classes.

"White Cards"

White Cards (which are now in fact yellow) identify foreigners who work for the mainland government. They allow access to some restricted areas and greater ease in applying for reentry visas, but their chief benefit is financial. For hotels, trains, and many other expenses foreigners are expected to pay in FEC (Chinese pay RMB) at approximately twice the Chinese rate. Thus normal foreigner rate, remembering the street value of FEC, is nearly 4 times Chinese rate. The White Card allows payment in RMB, at or near Chinese rate. Students can get student cards, which allow still greater discounts. Even Taiwan student cards are sometimes accepted for discounts on the mainland. We suggest insisting on a White Card unless you're being paid at least 50% in FEC or a hard currency, and at least 1,000 yuan per month.

Salary Range

Mainland salaries range from 350 yuan RMB per month to upwards of 3,000 yuan RMB per month (even more for technical experts), depending on age, experience, academic background, and subject; 700 to 1,000 yuan is average. Salary may be paid wholly in RMB, or partly in FEC or hard currency. Part hard-currency or FEC payment is desirable even if you have a White Card, as some places won't accept White Cards. Mentally convert all FEC/hard-currency payments to RMB to figure your wage; value FEC: RMB at 1.8:, and US$: RMB at 6.5: 1 (note: these exchanges change rapidly; talk with someone who's visited recently). We suggest teachers with master's degrees or higher and 2 or more years' full-time teaching experience accept no lower than 1,000 yuan RMB per month, while inexperienced teachers with bachelor's degrees only accept no less than 600 yuan RMB per month (students without a B.A. will get less). Taiwan salaries range from NT$300 to NT$550 per hour at buxibans, and up to NT$900 per hour at "real school" posts. We suggest not less than NT$500 per hour for experienced teachers, or NT$350 for new. Salary is generally paid monthly on the mainland. On Taiwan, insist on weekly payment, especially from buxibans: many are literally run by crooks. *Note:* some schools will insist on a 1-month "trial period" at a lower wage. This is acceptable *only* if: a) the contract may be cancelled by either party at the end of the 1-month trial, and b) should both parties choose to continue the relationship, an acceptable wage hike is mandated in writing as of the end of the 1-month period. Also, insist on salary for your entire time teaching, including Spring Festival Break and (if you'll teach 2 consecutive years) Summer Break.

Accommodations

Most mainland teachers get a private bedroom, and 1 or more other rooms which may be shared with other foreigners. Foreign students generally sleep 1 or 2 to a dorm room. Taiwan schools may offer dorms, but most foreigners are on their own; see Chapter 2. Given China's premium on space (Chinese students generally sleep 6 or 8 to a room), we advise against griping about room size. Mainland rent, however, should be negligible or free unless wages are very high. Also, be sure you have heat, hot water, electricity, and other facilities comparable with others on campus. We advise against accepting a room whose electricity or running water "will be hooked up soon." Construction projects drag on forever in China, and "soon" may not arrive till you've left.

Other possible accommodations include a kitchen (much to be desired), furnishings, Western flush (as opposed to Chinese squat) toilets, TV, washing machine, refrigerator, bicycle, tape recorder, space heater, fan, and VCR. No foreigner gets all of these, though the school might buy one of each for all foreigners to share. Again, relative equity matters more than absolutes. Foreigners who agree to substantially poorer facilities than other foreigners become pushovers in Chinese eyes, even if they mean well.

Determine the school's policy on guests. If friends visit, can they stay in your room for free? For a small charge? One school in Sichuan drove away foreign teachers by insisting their visiting boyfriends, mothers, and friends stay in separate rooms at hotel rates. Avoid problems by getting fair policy in print.

Food

Most mainland schools provide foreign teachers with kitchen facilities, and/or the choice of the dining hall or a chef; Taiwan schools rarely arrange board. We suggest the mainland-bound press for a kitchen with cafeteria privileges. You won't always want to cook, but Chinese cafeteria fare is no better than Western institutional food as a steady diet, and chef service is expensive and can be inflexible about timing. Also, freemarkets and cooking are focal points of Chinese life, and you'll miss much insight into the culture if you don't go shopping and invite Chinese friends to dinner.

Should you choose chef service, we suggest agreeing to no more than 15 yuan per day or half your salary, whichever is less, for 3-meal 7-day service. Should you choose to cook yourself, we suggest pressing for grain and meat discount coupons. The discount is negligible, but in times of shortage the discount coupons double as rationing coupons.

International Travel

Most foreign teachers teaching at least 2 full semesters at regular posts in China, mainland or Taiwan, get at least one-way international airfare. We suggest this as a minimum. Because of the cost of airfare to China, you might also consider flexibility on salary in return for a round-trip ticket. Some mainland schools will suggest cash payments in lieu of tickets. If so, get an adequate cash payment mandated in the contract. If cash payment is to be made in RMB, figure at 6:1 for U.S. dollars, and remember that you'll have to pay airfare out of your hard currency savings, using RMB payments for expenses in China.

Domestic Travel

Taiwan schools rarely provide domestic travel benefits. Mainland waiban usually greet foreign teachers on arrival, providing 2 to 5 days of paid sightseeing at the port of entry. Most waibans happily agree to this, as they get to accompany you. Some schools also offer travel bonuses for the Spring Festival Break and/or the Summer Break, ranging from 400 yuan to 2000 yuan per break. We make no suggestions here, but note that those with low salaries may wish to push for a travel bonus.

SHIPPING ALLOWANCE

Some mainland schools give foreigners shipping allowances, either for shipping books to China or for sending belongings home. Cash allowances range from 200 to 1,800 yuan RMB, and kind allowances are generally $1/2$ or 1 cubic meter of door-to-door ocean shipping. Shipping allowances can also be used to boost low-range salaries.

MEDICAL BENEFITS

Most mainland schools enroll teachers in China's national health system; the Taiwan-bound may receive benefits, but otherwise must arrange private health insurance. The mainland system's caregivers vary widely. As in the West, some of the worst care comes from school clinics, often staffed by inexperienced interns. We suggest pressing for rights, in the event of serious illness, to hospitalization in the nearest main city hospital, rather than at the school clinic.

VISA EXTENSIONS, MULTIPLE ENTRIES

These cost your waiban little or no money, though admittedly much paperwork, and would be considerable trouble and expense for you. We suggest asking but not pressing for these services.

CONTRACT REVISIONS

We suggest a clause in the contract stating that it may be revised by either party, providing that all revisions are mutually acceptable to both parties.

To recap, remember the following Golden Rules of contract negotiation:

1. Negotiate patiently and politely, remembering that the contract is a business arrangement in which emotion has no place.
2. Be sure all agreed-upon terms appear on paper. Rely on no oral promises.

3. Should contract revision become necessary, renegotiate with patience and respect, remembering that anger is counterproductive.

4. Once you sign a contract, honor it.

TROUBLES WITH WAIBANS

Despite the best of contracts, some troubles will inevitably arise. Following are the 3 most common "hot spots," and some suggestions on how to keep things cool:

Hot Spot #1: The Ogre

Most mainland schools put foreign teachers and students in special dorms with doorkeepers. These doorkeepers, unfondly known as "ogres," officially protect the foreigners' security and privacy. Practically, ogres also watch who comes in and out, at what times, and how often. Visitors may or may not have to sign in; whether or no, you can be sure their arrival is noted. Ogres also bear responsibility for locking doors after hours and deciding who to let in after lockup.

Try having a frank talk with your waiban and chief ogre soon after arrival regarding your hours and visiting habits. If you want Chinese students to have free access, say so; try to get a waiban promise, in the ogre's presence, that they'll not be interfered with. As to your own hours, be reasonable but firm. Chinese schools impose curfews on their students but have no right to impose them on you. Try to negotiate a key to your building (unlikely), or a promise that you can come home whenever you like and be let in.

To maintain good relations, don't abuse any privileges you gain. Most ogres moonlight at day shifts, and need their beauty sleep after the doors lock at night. If you study Beijing opera with the local diva 8 to 11 each Friday night, by all means let the ogre know you'll be in each Friday after 10:00 P.M. lockup. But waking the ogre 3 times a week so you can spend an extra hour at the local bar is unwise.

Foreign guests should try to be in before lockup, and Chinese visitors should be careful. Never let Chinese friends stay past curfew, especially friends of the opposite sex. Also, very frequent visitors should meet you elsewhere sometimes. Records of constant visits to foreigners go in files and can cause damage should anti-Western campaigns start.

You can also help defuse your ogre by a courteous, responsible manner and the periodic distribution of small gifts.

Hot Spot #2: Friendly and Intimate Relations

How friendly mainland Chinese can be with foreigners changes from year to year. Your waiban must monitor your relations with Chinese people and report anything untoward. Be sensitive to the political climate. Never press Chinese people for more closeness than they solicit. Even when friendships have developed, never initiate politically sensitive discussions. If Chinese initiate these discussions, best hold them outdoors, away from crowds, with people you trust. (Foreigners' rooms have often been bugged.) And never use a Chinese person's real name in a politically sensitive context, even with someone you think of as a friend; it can take years to recognize a snitch.

If you arrive in China at a time of openness, enjoy. Dinner at a Chinese home is an all-evening affair, marked by plenty of good food, drink, and conversation. Bring food, candy, or something from your country or some faraway part of China. Chinese bring cut flowers to funerals, however, so they make inappropriate dinner gifts. Also, never give an older Chinese person a clock; the phrase *song zhong* ("to give a clock") is homophonous with a phrase meaning "to wish death."

Chinese are aware of political conditions, and you can safely follow their lead in matters of friendship. Physical intimacy, however, is a different story. Taiwan is as Westernized in ideas about sex as it is in its banking structure. Mainland Chinese, however, remain conservative about courtship, dating, and sex. Recent surveys indicate changing attitudes among Chinese about premarital sex. But most Chinese still harbor romantic ideals about one true and eternal love. Premarital sex is assumed to be between partners who will soon marry. This cultural background predisposes Chinese to take any physical intimacy as a sign of very strong commitment. Never take romance with a Chinese person lightly. Your abandoned amour may feel deeply wounded and be subject to ridicule and censure, potentially even to punishment. This is especially true of matches between foreign women and Chinese men, a combination still far less accepted than the reverse.

In general, unless you strongly believe you might marry, best not get involved romantically with Chinese people. Should your needs be purely carnal, we suggest you consider other foreigners. Prostitution has returned to some Chinese cities, but liaisons with foreigners open the prostitute to grave political and juridical consequences. Meantime, as Chinese prostitutes still rarely use condoms, the foreigner exposes himself to many a nameless disease.

Should you decide to marry a Chinese person, you'll both need permission from your danwei. Proceed cautiously, particularly if your partner is still a student. Greedy waibans have forced foreigners to cough up huge "release fees" to free Chinese from their danwei. Make sure your plans are set when you approach the waiban, come bearing gifts, and be careful.

Hot Spot #3: Travel and Other Restrictions

Travel to many areas on the mainland requires permits and possibly pre-travel registration of any Chinese people you'll be traveling with and what their relationships are. Many dance clubs, bars, and other social gathering points are closed to foreigners. Drug laws are draconian. Lack of cars limits mobility. Many foreigners fret over these restrictions.

Your waiban bears responsibility for you and will be punished if you break the law. Therefore the job of enforcer falls to the waiban. No doubt you'll resent having to get travel passes from your waiban like a grade-schooler getting permission to go potty, and resent not being able to choose where you want to eat, or drink, or dance. You may even be tempted to flout the rules a bit, sneak onto a train into a restricted area, or into a Chinese discotheque. Our advice is, don't. Just remember, the waiban doesn't make the laws, but does take your punishment when you break them.

Consult with your waiban before traveling, especially together with Chinese people, and take any advice you're given. Don't bother trying to sneak into closed clubs. Long-term good relations are more important than a glimpse at Chinese guys dressed up like John Travolta. If you feel too claustrophobic, try the withdrawal techniques described in Chapter 6, or a weekend in Hong Kong.

Adjusting:
How Not to Be a
Foreign Barbarian

Adjusting to China, rhapsodized respondent Miles Lozinsky, is "like a roller coaster, sometimes up slowly, slowly and then down fast, fast, sometimes it makes you sick to your stomach, sometimes the thrill cannot be beat, and there are always twists and turns where you least expect them."

For most foreigners, adjusting to life in China involves many uncomfortable unfamiliarities along with the excitement. Some are cultural, some political, and some economic. Most in the first 2 categories apply as much to Taiwan as to the mainland. The following sections describe some of the most common annoyances, and some suggestions for coping.

THE BIG 7 HATE LIST OF CROSS-CULTURAL CONFLICTS

Cultural conflicts can be harrowing, since we all have the inbred certainty that the customs of our youth are the right ones. Still, understanding goes a long way toward coping, so the following attempts to describe some of the more common conflicts in terms of Chinese culture.

Conflict #1: The Litany of Tedious Questions

What is your name? Where are you from? How old are you? Is this your first trip to China? Are you married? How much do you earn? Do you have any children? What do you think of Chinese people? Where did you buy your clothes/bag/tape recorder? How much did it cost?

As mentioned earlier, Chinese people on first meeting ask each other these and many similar questions. You too will face several thousand such queries. However much you try to appreciate each questioner as a unique individual, eventually the sheer mass of China's people will make it seem as if you're confronting an unending conveyor belt of interrogators from the ninth circle of Dante's Hell: the dreaded Chinese question torture.

Try to remember that Chinese people mean well by this scrutiny. Such questions reveal their interest in you, and are meant to serve as icebreakers—standard openers for people who want to get acquainted and aren't sure how to start a conversation otherwise. Remembering these things will not always prevent annoyance, but it may help you skirt the edge of outrage, at least till you're alone in a room of your own.

Think about which of such questions to answer. If talking about your age or income would seriously bother you, then don't. Explain instead the Western reticence on those subjects. Or just be Chinese and stonewall, saying "It's not clear"; "It varies"; or "We calculate it differently." Whatever your response, develop a strategy for responding.

When you feel like you've had too much, and your best intentions will not prevent you from snapping at the next person who asks your income, withdraw. Go home, and shut the door. Read a book, listen to some music. Go for a walk in an isolated section of a park (most Chinese parks have isolated sections, as Chinese people prefer togetherness, and tend to crowd into the popular sections). If you're on a bus or train and can't escape, try pretending you're asleep, or curling onto an upper bunk of the sleeping car, or burying your nose in a book or some writing. If all else fails, simply tell your interrogator you don't feel wel, and wish to be left alone.

Conflict #2: Lack of Privacy

Chinese lacks a word for the Western concept of privacy. Related words such as *sishi* or *sichu* all carry overtones of secrecy, loneliness, or misanthropy. Chinese people live, birth to death, in crowded rooms and have developed a culture based on sharing everything; not even bathroom stalls are fully enclosed. To the Chinese the Western need for privacy seems inexplicable. As a result, Chinese tend to assume foreigners want company more than may in fact be true, to show up unannounced and stay long, enter without knocking, peek in windows, and otherwise express friendly curiosity which to the foreigner seems monstrously invasive.

Remember the Chinese world view and remember that such actions, whatever their effect, generally stem from friendly intent. Try explaining these differences to your students, teachers, and friends. You may not fully convince them, but you'll be left alone. If not, by all means lay down rules about anything that makes you uncomfortable. Announce that visitors to your room must knock before entering; if your visitors keep forgetting, install a latch inside and a sign on the door. Hang curtains that fall below the sill to discourage peeking. Prepare a bilingual sign to hang on your door to announce when you don't want company, something along the lines of "Dear Friends: Please excuse me for not entertaining you now. I feel rather tired and wish to be alone. I hope, however, that you will come back another time."

Conflict #3: Staring and Pointing—the Monkey in the Zoo

"The sights of the city are free for the beggars. . . . The temple fairs with their merrymaking crowds, the candy sticks with fluttering pennants. . . . There is drama on the open-air stage." These lines come from an oral autobiography of a Chinese woman transcribed by a foreign missionary half a century ago (*A Daughter of Han: The Autobiography of a Chinese Working Woman.* Ida Pruitt, Stanford: Stanford University Press, 1945, 1967). Yet any Chinese person could say the same today. Lacking both the funds to attend formal entertainments and the tradition of enclosed theaters so popular in the West, Chinese are accustomed to viewing life as one great pageant. Street jugglers and musicians segue into colorful crowds, vendors, families on outings, men sleeping on the sidewalks on hot nights, to form an ever flowing river of life, all of which is joyful to look at and legitimate entertainment. Chinese mothers rarely teach their children not to stare or point at what is interesting or strange.

Westerners, alas, are unaccustomed to being part of the "drama on the open-air stage." White or black skin, blond or brown hair, blue or green eyes, hairy limbs, and foreign clothes, all make foreigners different, interesting, worth pointing at and staring at and commenting on and even holding babies up to look at. Foreigners never quite get used to this, and often wonder how Chinese people, famed for their politeness, can be so rude.

Just remember: staring and pointing at the new and different is not rude for Chinese people. It reveals Chinese lack of exposure to the outside world which is the cumulative effect of centuries of closed-door policies. In wealthier Taiwan, for example, only in remote areas do foreigners feel the zoo effect. On the mainland staring reveals poverty and lack of opportunities for education or travel. But for Chinese staring is not rude, nor is it truly racist, however much it feels like racism. You can waste your lungs yelling, and Chinese will only stare more.

Rather, try to understand being stared at in terms of China's sense of pageantry. Notice that Chinese stare just as much at other Chinese who dress, act, or talk differently, are handicapped, or are otherwise extraordinary. Most white Westerners never experience life as a racial minority, and can take their China time as a lesson in racial sensitization. Try cutting back on the staring by dressing and acting as inconspicuously as possible. Meantime, if the staring gets to be too much, withdraw.

Conflict #4: Our Great Culture: No Foreigners Allowed

Chinese call China *Zhongguo,* literally "the Middle Kingdom," the center of China's ancient world. Ever since Confucius codified the rules of human behavior over 2,500 years ago, Chinese have had a sense of knowing the correct way to live. "I have noticed," writes long-time China teacher Nancy E. Dollahite, "that every Chinese I have encountered hangs a towel on a rack the same way, wrings a wet cloth the same way, folds paper to form a parcel the same way, and chops vegetables the same way... this is within China's very bones. There is a Chinese way to do things."

Few Chinese hold foreigners to these standards of behavior, partly because some Chinese recognize legitimate differences in cultural values, but more often because they assume Westerners can't quite master all the rules of propriety. Chinese admire, feel abashed by, and envy the West's technical superiority, and argue endlessly among themselves as to which dynasty lost China's technological edge. But only the rare Chinese doubts China's cultural and moral superiority.

In practical terms, at least on the mainland, foreigners may also be excluded from much of Chinese life by segregation laws controlling housing and social centers. These rules are particularly galling for overseas Chinese, who may be welcomed to some areas off-limits to "foreigners," but excluded from others.

Segregation laws can even depend on precise racial mixes. Overseas Chinese who marry Chinese nationals can enter mainland China with a special "Visiting Your Relatives" visa, which allows limited duty-free importation and other privileges. Non-Chinese people are officially eligible for Visiting-Your-Relatives visas, and in practice may be denied, regardless of how long they've been married to a Chinese national. This is what Mark Salzman calls the Chinese bureaucratic game of "Let's make a regulation." The position of mixed-race children of such marriages is unclear. One white foreigner we know applied for a Visiting-Your-Relatives visa based on her marriage to a Chinese national, but was denied. She asked if her children would be eligible. "Is your husband pure-blooded Chinese?" the immigrations official wanted to know. Our friend assured the official he was. Then, she was told, the children would be eligible. And what about the grandchildren, if the children also married white people? After some consultation the answer came back. No, if the grandchildren were 3/4 white, they would not be eligible for a Visiting-Your-Relatives visa.

You may be angered by such rules till your face mottles purple, but rage changes nothing but your blood pressure. Someday greater education and openness will drive China's racist tendencies to the shadows. Meantime, keep explaining, encouraging your students, teachers, and colleagues to think in more open ways. Many teachers find some of their greatest satisfaction in China came from convincing a few of their students to think more logically about race, and thus, in a small way, to have left the world a better place.

Conflict #5: Black Devils

Dark-skinned people suffer out-and-out racism in China, as in much of the world. Blacks, Sri Lankans, and others are unabashedly seen as inferior to Chinese and whites. Although many regulations have been passed to improve the treatment of "African guests," the overall tenor of Chinese attitudes toward dark-skinned foreigners remains quite negative. China's intellectual community, cut off in many ways from world discourse, continues to harbor racist theories of separate evolution now debunked in the West but once credited as "scientific." The terrifying race riots of Spring 1989 in Nanjing illustrate the effects of such thinking. Fights broke out between Chinese and African students which culminated in the arrest and incommunicado incarceration of hundreds of black students, destruction of black dorms, and 3 days of marches with Chinese townspeople chanting "kill the Black Devils." Hollywood deserves a share of blame for this sad situation, for while few Chinese have ever met a black person, many have seen blacks stereotyped as hoods or maniacs in celluloid extravaganzas. Having no strong black constituency to contest these images, and few blacks around to act as contrary role models, most Chinese have swallowed these stereotypes whole. This is as true on Taiwan as in the mainland.

Conflicts with African and subcontinental exchange students have further inflated racism and xenophobia on the mainland. China invites thousands of students each year from developing nations in quid pro quo exchanges for oil and other resource rights, and in political tit-for-tats. These students, most in "developmental" disciplines such as medicine, nutrition, engineering, and sanitation, study in China for 2 to 10 years, earn a degree, and return home to contribute to national construction. While in China, their studies and housing are subsidized by China's government, which also distributes monthly per-student stipends of around 200 yuan—nearly twice the average Chinese worker's monthly wage. Most are among the elite of their own countries, and consequently have more money than their Chinese counterparts, even without stipends from the Chinese schools. Many Chinese resent special treatment for exchange students, pointing out that stipends for Chinese students hover near 15 yuan per month. Yet few Chinese understand what China gets in return for hosting these students, and the government does little to enlighten them. Further, when Chinese students or scholars go to African or subcontinental nations, they are invariably given far more special treatment than exchange students from these nations receive in China.

Economic tensions have formed the base for a vicious circle of conflicts between African/subcontinental students and Chinese students, which in turn reinforces stereotypes of dark-skinned people as violent and irrational. As a result, hundreds of small and large clashes have marred relations through the years; the 1989 Nanjing riots are just a particularly recent and vicious example.

Foreigners can ease this tragic situation by quiet insistence on more equitable discussion of race relations. If you're teaching, you could assign your students readings from Stephen Jay Gould and other debunkers of racist theories of evolution. For students, open discussions with your teachers regarding historical and economic causes of racial inequity in the U.S. are helpful. Changing people's minds doesn't happen in a week or a year or even a century, as *Western* racism itself demonstrates. But by making your small mark you help push the whole project forward.

At the same time, dark-skinned foreigners need to do some serious soul searching before heading off to China. Chinese racism toward dark-skinned people is as virulent as Western. If you can't steel yourself to maintain a measure of good humor and optimism in a land where you'll be called "Black Devil," then it's probably best not to go.

Conflict #6: Polite Refusals

"Would you like some tea?" "Oh, no." "Please, really, would you like some tea?" "No, no, of course not. I'd hate to be any trouble.""Oh, it's no trouble, really, I'd love to get you tea."Well, if it's really no trouble . . ." "No trouble at all." "Well, maybe just one cup." This exchange, almost pathological by Western standards, seems quite normal to Chinese. Proper Chinese manners require self-effacing pro forma refusals of compliments, refreshments, and gifts as part of politely accepting. Chinese would never accept refreshments from each other without 3 or 4 polite refusals first. Accepting straightaway seems proud or greedy.

All this politeness confuses foreigners, and many amusing errors have resulted when Westerners took polite refusals at face value. Many a hapless Chinese has spent a visit with a foreigner suffering from thirst after refusing a cup of tea, and never getting follow-up offers.

More Westernized Chinese understand Western directness, and may adopt Western manners when visiting foreigners. With your more sophisticated Chinese friends you'll be able to ask directly, "is that a Chinese 'no' or a Western 'no'?" But most Chinese still operate under old rules.

Westerners who omit polite refusals seem uncouth.

Compliments should also be turned aside. Polite Chinese reply to compliments with *nali, nali,* literally "where, where?" meaning "where is the trait you are complimenting, which I surely do not possess?" Chinese also never open gifts in front of the giver, and are reticent in discussing sexual matters.

If you feel comfortable, try adopting Chinese manners. Adding in a few polite refusals costs nothing and will help Chinese feel more comfortable with you. Westernized Chinese may find Sinicized foreigners quaint, but never rude. Meanwhile, meeting a foreigner who "knows a bit about manners" may just help dispel those myths about us barbarians.

Conflict #7: Truth and Consequences

Westerners value truthfulness in and of itself. We may tell "little white lies," and we may tell big lies, but we aren't proud of telling them. We put a premium on being honest with ourselves and others.

Chinese look at truth quite differently. From a philosophical standpoint, China created the Daoist and Yellow Buddhist traditions which hold that all the world is falsehood and trickery of the senses, a mirage which, if we believe in it too much, keeps us from nirvana (Buddhist) or immortality (Daoist). Imagine trying to reconcile that view with the Judeo-Christian tradition! From a practical standpoint Chinese simply feel that telling the truth for its own sake merits less emphasis than other values, such as preserving face.

Direct refusals of requests, for example, are impolite in Chinese etiquette. Chinese prefer to create reasons why doing so-and-so is impossible, rather than refuse to help. Some bus companies lack government permission to carry foreigners. Many a foreigner, asking for a seat on a bus run by such a company, has been told the seats were all full, and then fumed and fretted as the bus drove away half empty. In fact, to the Chinese, lying about the seats is far more polite than saying, "no, we cannot carry you." When Chinese lie to you, look around and see what the reasons might be. Very few Chinese lie for the sake of lying. Have you made a request which the Chinese might be unable or unwilling to carry out? If so, take the lie as a polite refusal or, at worst, as laziness. Has something perhaps gone wrong, which the Chinese might hesitate to admit to you? If so, take the lie as a polite way of avoiding discussion. You may prefer to hear all the gory details, but you can't change Chinese etiquette. Look at it this way: you never have to admit to anyone in China when you goof up, either.

"POLITICAL INDECENCY" AND OTHER INVASIONS

The Chinese customs service, both on the mainland and on Taiwan, has the legal right to open all packages sent into or out of the country to ensure that they contain no illegal material. Illegal imports for the mainland include pornography, anticommunist literature, large quantities of evangelistic religious materials, and all banned books. Illegal imports for Taiwan include pornography, communist literature, anything that advocates Taiwan independence or the overthrow of the KMT ruling party (*Kuomingtang*), and all banned books. Illegal exports from both include, among other things, national treasures (for the mainland, read: antiques that haven't been approved for export and/or on which you haven't yet paid tax).

Both post offices claim not to open letters, but many foreigners have found missing pages, steamed-open letters, and even parts of pages cut off. Phones may also be tapped, rooms may be bugged, and cameras on the street may monitor meetings. Foreigners should be very sensitive to this government scrutiny in order to avoid causing political fallout for Chinese people around them. One foreigner we know chatted with a Reuters reporter from her hotel room in Lhasa. The call was bugged and traced, and the family of the Chinese person she was traveling with were interrogated, first by the Public Security Bureau and later the National Security Bureau (China's CIA).

Political control measures are far more relaxed on Taiwan than in the mainland, and are likely to relax still further. Back in 1984, on Rebecca's first trip to Taiwan, her Chinese-English dictionary was even confiscated at customs because characters were romanized in Pinyin, the official romanization system of the mainland, and usage examples included procommunist phrases. Letters can now be sent back and forth between the "Two Sides of the Ocean Abyss," and Taiwan residents can visit the mainland fairly freely. On the mainland, however, watchfulness against political indiscretions will have to become part of your daily routine. After the 1989 democracy movements, many among the hundreds arrested were apprehended simply because they had been videotaped chatting with foreigners known to be stringers for Western news agencies.

Even though Westerners often find these political controls intolerable and may be tempted to protest, the importance of caution can never be overemphasized. Remember, before you get too caught up in a self-righteous reaction to Chinese politics, that this is not your country, and that any of your objections must be voiced with extreme tact and caution if they are to have any effect at all. However, if you learn to view problems as Chinese do, they can become a challenge. The secret is not to say anything politically controversial unless it is in person, away from ears and eyes, with someone you have good reason to trust. Some foreigners have actually made a game of thwarting their censors, writing cleverly designed letters that appear to be coded but in fact hide nothing, while others convey sensitive meanings through bland but misleading language.

ECONOMICS MAKE A BIG DIFFERENCE

Some difficulties in adjusting to China stem neither from culture nor from politics, but merely from poverty. Due to the differences in wealth, such problems appear more rarely in Taiwan. Still, even on the island these problems appear in rural areas, and to some extent in cities, where old habits die hard. The Taiwan government has instituted a 6-year, US$300 billion plan to rebuild Taiwan's infrastructure at a level commensurate with the island's newfound wealth. But for now, even in Taiwan, cities remain dirty and crowded, and the tap water undrinkable outside Taipei. On the mainland it's the same, only more so.

1. SANITATION AND HYGIENE. China's streets are often littered with filth. Open-air markets sell freshly slaughtered animals whose blood runs in the gutters. In small towns, the gutters may also act as sewers. In other words, China is a land of many smells, which can be even more overpowering than the sights.

    As is common in Third World countries, standards of hygiene also remain below First World par. Hundreds of Anti-Rat Campaigns, Anti-Spitting Campaigns, Cleanliness Campaigns, ad nauseum (one wag of our acquaintance claims what China really needs is an Anti-Campaign Campaign), have improved the situation somewhat. But most people still have no running hot water, and so must boil water for dishes, clothes washing, or baths, and therefore simply wash less often than Westerners.

    Most foreigners will contract some illness during their time in China, for the crowdedness and the still unstamped-out habit of spitting in the streets makes every common cold a city-wide event. In addition, northern and western China's dry, dusty air irritates the throat and lungs and encourages bronchitis. Finally, eating off plates washed in cold water, or maybe only dunked in a pail of suds between uses spreads many stomach ailments.

    Try to minimize your illnesses, as being sick anywhere is no fun, and being sick in unheated rooms floored with concrete is horrid. Take your vitamins, and get plenty of rest and exercise. Drink, as the Chinese do, many cups of hot liquid a day. Don't drink unboiled water. Wear surgical

masks in the winter; they protect you from the dust, the
cold, and many a floating germ. Be careful where you eat.
Street stands often have the best food but the worst sanitation; one delicious type of mutton skewer commonly sold in
the North has so often borne illness that foreigners call it
"hepatitis-on-a-stick." Many Chinese restaurants sell inexpensive disposable balsawood chopsticks. For those that
don't, carry a pair of your own. Peek into the kitchen to see
how spanking clean it is — or isn't. As a general rule, shun
any restaurant that lacks running water.

Some differences in cleanliness between China and the
West are also cultural. Chinese tend to judge cleanliness of
garments by sight, for example, while Westerners judge by
smell. We pick up a worn shirt and sniff at the armpits to
test whether or not to wear it again. Chinese peer closely for
stains. Thus the Chinese might disdain the Westerner whose
clean-smelling shirt has been smudged, while the Westerner
looks down on the Chinese whose clean-looking shirt smells
worn.

Historian Joseph Needham has also pointed out what he
calls the Chinese people's "courtyard vision of the world."
Traditional Chinese houses surround courtyards, which become the center of daily Chinese life. In traditional China,
housewives cleaned their courtyard and threw the trash just
outside it; the city bore responsibility for cleaning the
streets. Needham argues this attitude continues today, and
explains the contrast between cleanliness in private homes
and filth in the streets surrounding them. Chinese homes
may be spotless, but the yards just outside littered with old
cans, fallen leaves, disintegrating paper, and construction
debris. To the Chinese, no shame attaches to dirt outside the
courtyard of personal responsibility. The Chinese themselves say, "only shovel the snow in front of your own
door." Western selfishness centers on individuals; Chinese
selfishness centers on the family.

Remembering the cultural and economic bases of differences in cleanliness may not prevent your dismay at walking
down a street with open sewers. But it should help you
avoid regarding the locals with what old Chinese women
call "bitterness in your heart."

2. HEAT, ELECTRICITY, AND WATER. Westerners, and especially North Americans, take for granted hot showers,

cheap and reliable electricity, and heating. In China these facilities vary by the city and by the day. China abounds with leaky pipes, archaic power plants, and poorly installed wiring. In addition, drought conditions and energy emergencies occur often, during which city governments control water use not by Western-style anti-waste campaigns, but by simply shutting off supplies.

Learn to conserve. Chinese pay much more for electricity as a percentage of income than Westerners, and so are far more conscious of care with resources, and so should you be. Turn off lights when you leave rooms, turn off TVs or radios you're not listening to, avoid using electric heaters, and use electric ovens sparingly, without excessive preheating times. Most schools absorb the cost of foreigners' electric bills, but you alone using more electricity than a family of 6 down the hall will not foster good feelings. Also, stock candles, a flashlight, and/or a kerosene lamp against sudden blackouts and brownouts.

Don't waste water either, particularly in the North and West. Many Chinese recycle water, using it first to wash food, then dishes, then to scrub the floor, then finally to flush the toilets. You needn't go that far, but neither should you, in a drought-stricken country, leave the shower running while you brush your teeth. Actually, even if you have a hot shower it'll likely use a tiny self-contained water heater, giving you very little warm-shower time, so you'd be foolish to let it run anyway. And those without water heaters must shower the Chinese way: heat water on the stove, mix it with cool in a bucket, and pour it over yourself with a scoop. Always keep extra thermoses of boiled water and buckets or other containers of unboiled water available in case the water is suddenly shut off by accident or plan; shut-offs can sometimes last for days.

South of the Yangtze River no heating is permitted in schools or other public areas. This blanket (no pun intended) energy conservation measure ignores local and seasonal variation, and in cold years with snow on the ground the southern Chinese suffer. You'll suffer with them, and we advise carrying lots of thermal underwear. Even Northerners receive ungenerous heat. You may have radiators or a pot-bellied stove with a moderate supply of coal. In neither case will you swelter. Bring sweaters and long underwear.

3. TELEPHONES. Mainland Chinese cities, and rural areas on
Taiwan, still rely on ancient switching systems which
make phone calls a nightmare. International calls to China
may meet only with "this call cannot be completed in the
country you have dialed." Within China even local calls
can be blocked by a seemingly endless variety of whistles
and beeps. Long distance calls can be made direct from a
few central stations in larger cities, but generally mean
putting a call through the operator and wating several
hours, or even overnight. Once you've gotten through,
indifferent operators may take eons to connect you. If
possible, have someone who speaks Chinese well help you
place your call. If not, speak slowly and clearly, and stress
that the call is long distance and important. It may help to
identify yourself by unit rather than name; "I'm with Xi'an
University" is better than "I'm Joe Smith," and "I'm calling
from America" is best of all. Patience and good humor are
also key.

4. *GUANXI* AND *HOUMEN*: CONNECTIONS AND BACKDOOR
DEALING. The first two Chinese words many foreigners
learn, by virtue of their constant repetition, are *meiyou* and
buxing: "we have none," and "we can't." From ancient
times Chinese have suffered an economy of scarcity.
Population always outstripped resources; consumers
always outnumbered available goods and services. Desire
and ability to pay have never guaranteed possession.
     Because of this sense of struggling against limits, Chinese
have set up distribution networks for scarce goods and services unrelated to money. Most Chinese rely instead on personal relationships, which they call *guanxi:* literally "connections." Chinese call using guanxi *zou houmen:* "entering
through the back door." Westerners use guanxi and houmen
as well; the English terms "connections" and "back door"
have the same connotations as their Chinese equivalents.
We might use connections to get jobs or coveted theater
tickets. We go in the back door to buy exclusive apartments.
But China's imbalance between supply and demand forces
Chinese to use guanxi for many mundane items taken for
granted in the U.S.: train tickets, TVs, good liquor and cigarettes, and many other items can be unavailable at any price
if the buyer lacks guanxi. Notably, Taiwanese use guanxi as

well. TVs and train tickets are readily available on the island, but decent housing and good jobs are not. Guanxi is a Chinese tradition, not a communist invention. Its rampant use on the mainland is aggravated by an economy still struggling with overpopulation and profound problems of underdevelopment, to name just 2 of China's major difficulties.

Foreigners have certain advantages outside the guanxi network. Many cities offer special train-ticket windows for foreigners and high officials which sell tickets long after regular windows sell out. Friendship Stores sell many hard-to-get items, sometimes for FEC or hard currency only, and sometimes to foreigners only, regardless of currency.

But most foreigners get drawn into regular guanxi networks as well. Foreigners have much to offer in barter trade through the guanxi system; tutoring in English, foreign liquor and tobacco, tickets from the foreigner window, goods from the Friendship Store, goods from your home country, and counseling on job or school hunting in the West are all legal tender in the world of guanxi.

Beware of the manipulators most Chinese scorn as *guanxi dawang*: "guanxi masters." People who seem bent on showering you with gifts without at some point asking for something, and without any feeling of real friendship, may be setting you up for a kill ("now that we're such good friends, how about letting me use your passport to transfer some currency?"). Most Chinese prefer an even guanxi balance sheet; owing too much is bad face. Guanxi masters arrange guanxi deals professionally, taking percentages or piling up guanxi credit. Guanxi masters are China's loan sharks.

However, ordinary guanxi with ordinary people can improve your life in China and hone your understanding of the Chinese experience. Albert, for example, used guanxi with a restaurant manager to arrange lovely banquets for all our friends at restaurant cost plus a tiny margin. He created wonderful evenings and happy memories we could otherwise not have afforded.

You may tire of having your Chinese friends always asking for favors; "it's difficult," wrote one survey respondent, "to sort out who's a sincere friend and who just wants something from me." But try not to see requests as a betrayal of friendship, but rather as people sticking together in hard times. As you get a better feel for China your instinct will tell you who's a real friend using guanxi out of need, and who's a guanxi loan shark.

Do be careful, however; guanxi can be complex. Foreigners often have trouble gauging the barter worth of goods and services. It is easy for inexperienced foreigners either to get used ("I've taken you to dinner. Now will you give me English lessons once a week for a year?") or to cause Chinese to lose face by presenting gifts so valuable that the Chinese person has no way of repaying them. Also, only rarely is guanxi a direct tit-for-tat trade, such as one train ticket in return for one painting. More often a series of gifts or favors establishes a relationship, which can then be tapped.

To illustrate some of the subtleties, Rebecca was once approached by a Chinese friend's cousin, who asked her to help his wife apply to U.S. graduate schools. The friend brought several gifts—coffee, seafood, and candy. Rebecca agreed to help the wife. She at first declined the gifts, but later took them when told that accepting nothing would lose face for the husband by putting him too deeply in guanxi debt. The gifts, she was told by Chinese friends, were valuable enough to establish limited commitment on Rebecca's part.

Rebecca wrote several graduate schools for applications and helped the wife fill them out. A superior candidate, the wife was accepted with full scholarship, and began preparations to leave. The husband then appeared with more gifts: a beautiful jade necklace, and a large sum of cash. Rebecca refused these gifts. Chinese friends confirmed that accepting such large gifts would commit Rebecca to responsibility for the wife's welfare after her arrival in the States. In the end, the husband sent a lovely, but far less valuable, ink seal carved by a well-known seal artist. Helping the wife find a school was worth more than the coffee and food; the seal "paid off" the extra guanxi debt, and left everyone's "balance sheet" even.

Because guanxi can be confusing, we suggest that you avoid being drawn into guanxi trading until you have been in China long enough to develop a sense of the territory, and to make a few friendships with people whose judgment and advice you can trust.

Working:
in Spite of the School

A teacher who responded to our surveys was told one day not to work so hard preparing lessons for her conversation class. The students, explained the teacher's school official over her protests about rising test scores, were vocational pupils from the countryside. As such, they were basically stupid, and not worth the waste of time. Better to spend extra effort on the liberal arts students. This official typefies China's rigid expectations for her teachers and students, whether Chinese or foreign. Though few officials would discourage performance as openly as this one, such attitudes remain common. The college entrance exam taken in the third year of upper middle school determines much of the rest of Chinese students' lives. Based on exam results, students are not only assigned to colleges, but in many cases assigned to majors. Under economic reform this system loosened somewhat, but remains essentially intact.

Once assigned to a major, Chinese students have few or no electives. Chinese view education as a process not of learning how to think and creating an individual philosophy, but of memorizing the standard knowledge of a field. Chinese teachers and department administrators determine classes for students. Within classes, memorization and recitation are far more common pedagogical techniques than conversation or independent research. Exposure to Western teaching methods through both foreign teachers in China and Chinese teachers returned from abroad has created demand for more open education in recent years; some of these demands influenced the 1989 democracy movement. But change comes slowly and old influences remain strong.

All this affects foreign teachers and students in myriad ways. You'll have fewer choices than you're used to in classes, course content, and pedagogical techniques. Chinese students may be puzzled by Western-style teaching methods, while Chinese teachers may be offended by Western-style students. Because Chinese teachers rely largely on standardized textbooks and curriculum, even where school officials welcome new teaching methods from foreigners, few facilities exist to accommodate them. Every step in the creation of a new syllabus, from library research to photocopying to using classroom displays becomes cumbersome.

To some extent, persistent foreigners can overcome these difficulties. Your keys are patience, humor, and an understanding of the Chinese system. As our contribution to the latter, we hereby offer the following roadmap to getting things done within a Chinese educational institution.

FACILITIES, OR, "THE MAN WITH THE KEY IS ON VACATION"

From long habit Chinese institutions prefer hierarchical, clearly defined worker responsibilities. Westerners understand divisions in managerial duties, but not with material resources and facilities. In Western schools, for example, a central Audio-Visual Department controls the overhead projectors, VCRs, and other display equipment. In China each piece of equipment will likely "belong" to a "Responsible Person" (*fuze renyuan:* 负责人员); Miss Jia controls the English Department's overhead projector, and Mr. Yi controls the History Department's mimeo machine. These Responsible People bear personal responsibility for loss of or damage to equipment, and guard their "trusts" jealously. Using even the simplest facilities may require much placation of Miss Jia and Mr. Yi.

As soon as you've arrived in China and recovered from jet lag, start scouting around to find who controls all the facilities you need access to: copiers, ditto machines, thermal transfers, AV display equipment, supply rooms, library stacks, computers and printers, telephones, FAX machines (yes, many schools have them), language labs, science labs, school cars, exercise equipment, anything you might need during your stay.

Once armed with a list of names, begin your campaign of conquest. Visit each Responsible Person, introduce yourself (through an interpreter, if necessary), and express your sincere wishes for happy cooperation. Offer a token gift from home—a school pin, or postcards from your hometown, for example. Invite your "new friend" the RP to your apartment for tea (be sure to lay in a good stock of tea, soda, and snacks in case they take you up on it). Then begin feeling out how much access you'll be allowed to the facilities each RP controls. How often can you use it?

Regularly, frequently, never? Under what circumstances can you use it—can you borrow it? Use it in the RP's presence? Ask the RP to use it for you? What can you do to make life easier for the RP?

A little extra effort at the outset can reap great rewards down the road. Many resources don't exist school-wide, and departments guard their assets jealously. No amount of pleading with the Foreign Language Department Head on the benefits of students seeing *Singing in the Rain* will help if the school's only VCR lives in the Biology Department. On the other hand, a cup of tea with Clerk Bing of the Biology Department may let you not only organize an English-language videofest, but also take the machine home for a Saturday night party with expat chums.

Depending on how crucial the equipment is to your happiness in China, continued free access may merit periodic visits to the RP bearing gifts of homebaked cookies, fresh fruit, or the jet-fuel Chinese liquors known as *baijiu*. Also, keep in touch with the RP about when you'll need access. You don't want to plan your videofest for the week the RP is on vacation without arranging to borrow in advance.

Always remember that the RP bears full responsibility for all charges; no one wants to land in hot water for your misdeeds. Your visits and conduct should build up trust, and reinforce the RP's image of you as an upstanding citizen who would never cause trouble or return a busted VCR. Bear up your end of that trust. Use equipment responsibly, returning it clean and in good condition in a timely fashion. If something breaks, offer the funds to fix it. If the library RP gives you open-stack privileges, don't mess up the shelves or drop crumbs on the floor. Above all, never cause political trouble for the RP. Just because you get FAX privileges, don't use the school's FAX to submit your controversial stringer articles to UPI. You never know who is listening in on transmissions, and that's what rental FAXes in joint-venture hotels are made for.

SQUEAKY WHEELS: KEEPING YOUR NEEDS TO THE FORE

Foreign students get only slightly broader class choices than their Chinese counterparts. Large foreign-language schools use fixed curricula Smaller schools may offer more choice, but classes will still be bound by available teachers, materials, and ideology. China has no interlibrary loan system; don't ask for course reading materials from the Beijing National Archives at a school in Nanjing. Teachers tend to be specialized within institutes; don't expect classes on Suzhou embroidery at the Xi'an Railway Institute. Prevailing politics also controls class offerings. The autumn after the Tiananmen Incident and the "Beijing Spring" would be a bad time to ask for a course on the "Hundred Flowers Movement." Remember to let the school know your needs early and often; see suggestions in Chapters 4 and 5. Before arriving in China let the Chinese school know in detail the topics, books, skills, and areas you hope to study. You'll still probably have no choice between courses, but at least the courses the school arranges should be moderately relevant.

Once classes begin, continue to communicate your needs politely but firmly to your teachers. Use specifics: "Can you please show us finger methods one-on-one for the Pipa?" works much better than "I'm learning nothing in music class." Save approaching the teacher's superiors as a last resort, as it causes the teacher to lose face and may breed hard feelings.

Foreign teachers generally have even less freedom of class choice than students, as they must teach within the Chinese curriculum and only certain courses may be taught by foreigners (no, they won't assign you the Marxist Philosophy class). As with students, best provide as much information as you can as early as possible as to your background, strengths, weaknesses, and interests. If you're allergic to teaching class X, say so.

Remember, though, a limited number of courses must be shared among all the foreign teachers, and everyone likes advanced conversation, composition, and content-based classes such as History, Literature, and the ever-popular "Survey of England and America." Don't grieve if you get a class or two you're not thrilled with. But neither need you teach 6 intro grammar classes and 1 intensive remedial reading. If class distribution seems inequitable, by all means sit down with other foreign teachers and negotiate. Most waibans will agree when the foreign teachers present a united front on teaching requests.

If, on the other hand, you find yourself the new foreign teacher on the block amid crafty old pros who have conspired to give you all the intro grammar classes, consider switching schools. Early in the semester it should be easy enough to find another position, and generally just the threat will be enough to help the Bozos reconsider.

CLOSED-STACK LIBRARIES AND OTHER HURDLES

Both teachers and students should make early visits to the school library. Determine whether or not the books you need, in the languages you require, are available early enough that your friends can still ship extras from home. Don't neglect the importance of good relations with the library RPs. Most Chinese libraries are closed-stack, with card catalogs that range from the confusing to the useless. Most librarians, however, are perfectly willing to allow open-stack privileges for foreigners who appear responsible; you can even use your open-stack privileges to get books for Chinese students, colleagues, and friends, though be sure to keep a list of what you lent to whom. Teachers need to check library facilities with special care, as you can't assign your students research papers on any topic for which the library is inadequately equipped.

Academic honesty tends to blur in China, for along with the emphasis on memorization comes an assumption that the best sort of research consists of looking up the authorities on a topic and quoting them. By long tradition Chinese teachers are lax about requiring quotation marks, so be very careful about accusing Chinese students of plagiarism, even when they've copied an article word-for-word. Foreign teachers can teach about the Western emphasis on creative analysis and insist on proper documentation in their classes, but should be sensitive when students slip. Foreign students should also remember that many Chinese teachers will give higher marks to an unoriginal paper filled with quotes from known authorities than to even the best-documented and most creative paper which deviates from accepted interpretations.

Finally, many educational officials seem to care more about officialdom than education. "There are really," explains respondent David Kellogg, "two kinds of bureaucrats here: lazy, and actively obstructive." Kellogg continues with the tale of one Party secretary at his school: "This man, who has far more power than any of the actual school presidents, is a high-school drop-out himself and bears a terrible grudge against intellectuals, which pits him against the entire school." Strive for appeasement with school officials, even if good working relations appear impossible. Always praise them at banquets, and present them with gifts from your home country. They haven't nearly as much power over your life as they have over your Chinese counterparts, but they have enough to foul up your work and make your life unpleasant; a little sycophancy never hurt anyone.

Also, advises survey respondent Jon Weston, "set reasonable goals (for China) and be happy when you reach the goals. If you expect results found in Western countries, you'll go mad".

THE CHINESE TEACHER-STUDENT RELATIONSHIP: MASTER AND ACOLYTE

One winter, claims an ancient parable of Chinese propriety, the master was cold. His student, having nothing else to warm the master with, burned his shirt for firewood and subsequently perished with cold.

Now outmoded at its most exteme, this traditional respect of students for teachers continues in a host of ways. Most Chinese teachers stand erect at the front of class, reading from formal scripts. A variety of customs and events, from National Teachers Day to the detailing of students, even in university classrooms, to take turns washing the blackboard, underscore the continued respect given to teachers. In recent years, teachers' fixed salaries have fallen far behind inflation, and the profession is out of favor for young graduates. But the tradition of respect remains strong.

Students, for their part, look to teachers for advice and as role models as well as for instruction, far more explicitly than in the West. Chinese teachers routinely advise their students on dress, eating, dating, and other matters which would seem strange or improper coming from a Western teacher to Western students. The Chinese government is keenly aware of the degree to which Chinese students consciously model themselves after their teachers; after various student demonstrations, the first to be arrested have been teachers and administrators fingered as ringleaders.

Chinese expect foreigners to be different, and you shouldn't feel constrained to imitate the Chinese way. Still, enough traditional values attach to the student-teacher relationship, even with foreigners, that you should be aware of these traditions and not trammel them.

At least at first, both students and teachers should err on the side of formality in dress and action. Chinese may interpret your torn blue jeans and shabby tweeds as unprofessional or disrespectful. Carry yourself a little more formally than you might at home; don't stick your feet up on the table. Remember, not only will the Chinese expect somewhat more formal behavior, but you will also represent in their eyes Western people. Don't let the rest of us down by acting like a boor.

Your Chinese teachers will likely offer you all manner of advice. You may not have to take it, but do try to accept it graciously. Your Chinese students may turn to you with as many questions about fashion and dating as about grammar. Should you choose to answer such questions remember that you are taking on the traditional role of Master, at least in some degree, and don't answer lightly.

CRASH COURSE IN TEFL FOR THE NOVICE TEACHER

Many foreign English teachers in China are first-time teachers. As suggested in Chapter 4, if you have no teaching and/or Teaching of English as a Foreign Language (TEFL) experience or training, try to get some before leaving home. Think about your own process of learning Chinese in order to gain insight into effective language learning. Set clear goals for your classes in terms of communicative ability, and use your imagination in laying out road maps to achieve your goals. The following is a very brief overview of the 4 language areas and some ways of teaching them.

Listening

Language students learn to listen before they learn anything else. Some teaching theory so emphasizes this fact that teachers are urged not to press students to speak in the target language till they begin to voluntarily. Whether or not you agree with this, you'll need to work to fill your students' minds with English. Remember, you are probably one of very few models of native English your students will ever have.

Try to have your students listen to English in a variety of contexts: in dialogues with each other and with you; in monologues presented to the class; in pronunciation practice with minimal pairs (ship/shop); from tapes; in songs; in word games; in lectures; in conversations between several native speakers. Use your imagination and have fun!

Remember that students can usually either learn new information with old vocabulary, or new vocabulary about old information, but not both at once. Try giving listening selections on familiar topics ("How to Make Chinese Dumplings"), while introducing new vocabulary, then reinforcing the old vocabulary while listening to a new topic ("How to Make Vichyssoise").

Whenever using a lengthy listening selection, use several exercises to reinforce the students' grasp of material and vocabulary. Use pre- and post-listening comprehension questions; pre- and post-listening topic discussion; vocabulary drills; comparison with written transcripts; creative use of new vocabulary. Linguistic research suggests language learners need to hear a new word in at least 50 different contexts before the word becomes completely familiar; try to provide at least a good number in class.

And remember that students need several different types of listening skills. Listening in a general way to a casual conversation is different from listening for details from a newscast, and different again from listening for note-taking purposes in a lecture. Try to teach different skills by asking at some times for details ("how many . . . ?" "what type . . . ?"), sometimes for general comprehension ("why?" "how?"), and sometimes for main ideas ("what were the main points?").

Speaking

Chinese teachers of English tend to emphasize speaking only in rote recitation and repetition. This sort of teaching stems from traditional grammar-based curricula now generally debunked in Western teaching theory (though often, alas, still in practice in Western classrooms). Most new teaching theory emphasizes "communicative competence," the ability to effectively communicate ideas in the target language. Rather than teaching students by grammatical structure, try organizing the material in chunks of real-world communicative needs, either by topic ("at the bank," "at the doctor's office") or by "notional-functional" order ("making requests," "having an argument").

For each class, make a lesson plan. If you're an absolutely new teacher, physically write out the lesson plan; it will help you organize your thoughts. Decide which topic or notion/function you'll teach, what vocabulary and/or grammatical structures naturally attach to it, and how to get them across.

Have your students speak about the topic or notion/function in a variety of ways: repeating after you, in pair drills with each other, in small groups, in prepared skits, in unscripted situations. The more realistic you can make your students' language production, the better they'll be able to communicate. Having your students make dumplings on a hotplate in class while discussing what they're doing in English will imprint forever on their minds the words and notions/functions for foods and cooking and eating in ways no repetitious drills can touch.

And try to make your classroom a fun place, a place where students don't have to feel afraid. Never correct harshly; instead if a student uses a word or structure incorrectly, try using it in the correct context yourself, or pointing out the proper usage to the entire group without assigning blame. Have your students stand up and move around and use the entire classroom. They'll have more fun and learn more, and so will you.

Reading

We read in countless ways, from the bored skim of the cereal box to the consuming intensity with which you are doubtless devouring this book. Teach different types of reading in different ways. Teach students to scan charts, maps, menus, and phone books for specific information; to skim articles for main ideas; to read books for analytic understanding.

Chinese teachers tend to teach only intense analytic reading, from sentence patterning and breakdown of complex sentences to memorization of articles. You can help students learn analytic reading in more creative ways; teach them:

- to guess word meanings from context;
- and from common roots (anthropology, misanthropy);
- to summarize author meaning and intent rather than to memorize;
- to analyze writing critically ("we know Faulkner is supposed to be a great writer, but do you like this story, and why or why not?").

But your greatest challenge will be getting Chinese students to read English unintensively. Native readers of alphabetic languages like English relate to words on the page wholly differently from native readers of ideographic languages like Chinese. Bridging that gap is awfully difficult. Teach your students to recognize writing they don't need to read analytically and to read it quickly without looking up every new word in their dictionaries. For skimming and scanning try:

- timed reading exercises;
- bingo games and other competitions;
- reading "realia" like packages, application forms, menus, and maps.

Writing

Have students write copiously, both to reinforce vocabulary and grammar and to sharpen creative and analytic skills. For straight language skills, try sentence writing:

- have students write 5 or 10 sentences with each new vocabulary word or grammatical structure;
- or make complex sentences using connecting words (in addition, although, despite, as if);
- and use peer correcting, which reinforces reading as well as collective learning.

Teach paragraph structure as the base for longer writing:

- give students topic sentences and have them write the body of the paragraph, or vice versa;
- give lists of information to be organized into paragraphs;
- teach about language flow by giving models from great writers with straightforward language (Hemingway, et al.).

Finally, teach students to write essays and short works of fiction:

- assign writing journals, with either assigned or free topics;
- teach outlining and research;
- discuss and assign examples of different expository styles (description, comparison/contrast, classification, etc.);
- produce student-written newsletters and "books."

Straight language sentences you can mark up, or have students mark up in peer exercises, with plenty of red ink. But longer, more creative pieces you should correct in terms of structure and analysis rather than language use, as the latter discourages communication. Correct language errors by giving examples of correct use. For student newsletters and "books" assign at least 2 drafts. Finally, work together with other teachers at your school. Try coordinating assignments to reinforce vocabulary and ideas ("you have them read Poe while I teach storytelling"), or even having schoolwide projects such as a Broadway-style musical production or a weekly English paper or radio program.

All this may sound like a lot of work—and it is. Most survey respondents rated materials provided by their schools as "terrible"; you'll spend hours producing supplementary materials and arranging for dittoing. As the old saw goes, "Teaching is the easiest job in the world to do poorly and the hardest job in the world to do well." Your Chinese students, by and large, will be serious and hardworking, and deserve your best shot too.

Thriving:
Making the Most of Your Chinese Life

Your work is going smoothly and you've stopped quaking at the filthy streets; it's time to enter more deeply into Chinese life. You'll want to accomplish many things in China, from shopping to traveling to just piling up good memories. Following are some of our suggestions on how.

CULTURAL INTEGRATION

Learning to cope with cultural differences creates the foundation for a good life in China. Building on that foundation requires reaching out, joining Chinese life, and introducing Chinese people to Western life. The following suggest some activities other foreigners have used in their own process of integration.

1. ENGLISH CORNER. In most Chinese cities groups of dedicated learners meet regularly to practice English. In parks, teahouses, and school campuses, these learners enjoy talking in English, or reading English articles and discussing them. Participants range from rank beginners to the flawlessly fluent.

    Appear at English Corner and you'll learn the meaning of stardom. Ask around to find the English Corner nearest you, and try joining. You'll find there many potential friends, guides, and instructors. You may not want to commit yourself to regular English Corner attendance—too much like another class! Also, be a little wary. Some

English Corners attract English-speaking guanxi masters, who prey on easy foreigners, and they may appear at your door more often than you'd like. But occasional appearances just may remain a favorite way to meet people and relax.

2. THE ARTS OF CHINA. Many foreigners study one or more of China's traditional arts. Chinese cooking, painting, calligraphy, seal carving, embroidery, martial arts, acupuncture, and other arts continue as vibrant social traditions today. Students learn as much about Chinese life and culture as about their topic.

Mention to your students or teachers any special interests you have in anything Chinese. Rest assured they'll find someone for you to study with, either as part of a group or under private tutelage.

Traditional teachers accepted no pay. Students brought gifts of food, fuel, and other necessaries to sustain the teacher. Beyond subsistence, the joy of seeing traditions passed on was supposed to be its own reward. Today some teachers accept wages. Others still work under the old system. If you're not paying your teacher cash, be sure to bring gifts. You might tutor your teacher, or a relative, in English; bring food or liquor or cigarettes; invite your teacher to dinner regularly; or offer gifts from your home country.

3. LEARNING TO BE CHINESE. Many foreigners find their happiest days in China came when they felt themselves to be most Chinese. Every foreigner needs to escape now and then to a kvetch session with other foreigners or even to Hong Kong for the weekend. But constant separation from day-to-day Chinese life is a recipe for loneliness and disappointment. You'll have few opportunities to appreciate your Chinese friends if you spend your days saving for trips to the disco at the Beijing Great Wall Sheraton or the Taipei Lai Lai Hilton.

Instead, try joining in with daily activities at your school. Go for walks with your students or teachers. Join morning exercises. Invite Chinese friends over for dumpling-making parties. Join a sports team or a choir. Write articles for the school English newsletter. Go to school dances and parties. Even joining in the performances that schools organize for the foreigners ("I feel like a dancing

bear!" wrote one student) can be fun. In Taiwan and
Beijing these performances are occasionally televised, and
there's nothing more charming than playing the buffoon
for an audience of 1,200,000,000.

Lacking funds to hire professional entertainers, most
Chinese live quite simple lives by Western standards. Yet
China's social life provides closeness and a sense of
purpose, which you can share by joining in.

4. TEACHING THE CHINESE ABOUT US. Chinese love to learn
about the West. Set up Western activities for your students
or classmates. Teach Western cooking (we found fruit sal-
ads and deviled eggs to be perennial favorites), teach Western songs, or start a choir. Teach dances to Western rock
music. Play chess, or poker, or bridge. Start a baseball team.
Organize parties for Western holidays. Your students or
classmates will love baking Christmas cookies, learning
how to make a Seder, or coloring Easter eggs.

Your Chinese friends will love their "Western activities," and you can relieve homesickness by bringing a bit
of the West near you. Besides, togetherness promotes
international understanding, and isn't that what it's all
about?

5. BRINGING CHINA HOME WITH YOU. China changes foreigners. Your time in China will transform your ideas about
family, society, and individualism. When you return home,
you'll want to share the power of your China experience
with your family and friends. Buying souvenirs just isn't
enough.

Try keeping a journal, or writing articles for publication
at home. Write regular letters, either to individuals or the
gang. Many foreigners leave postage and copying money
with a friend or family member, and send that person
regular thick, newsy letters to be photocopied and distributed. The act of writing not only keeps your loved ones
current on the many transformative experiences you'll
have in China, but also helps you sort out feelings while
there. We found happiness in China came easier when we
had a running commentary on paper about how China was
making us tick.

You might keep a scrapbook and/or a photo album as
well. Many wonderful artifacts of Chinese life will come

your way, from old Maoist posters to bus tickets from the Qinghai/Tibet line. Keeping a collection, even while still in China, can help you make sense of your China experience.

TRAVEL IN CHINA

You can't spend a year in China and not go see the Great Wall and the Terra Cotta warriors, or the Palace Museum in Taipei, and at least a few other treasures of the world's oldest continuous culture. For students and teachers in Taiwan, travel presents little problem. The island is small and transport is good. The longest bus ride in Taiwan, from Peit'ou at the north tip to Kenting at the south, is less than 12 hours. A newly proposed train will cut the trip from Taipei, the northernmost large city, to Kaohsiung, the southernmost, to 93 minutes. Mainland-bound foreigners, however, face many problems, and need to plan their time wisely.

Your waiban should organize outings to temples, museums, and natural wonders in your area; this is one reason to live near sites you don't want to miss. More ambitious waiban also organize weekend regional trips. Larger-scale tours you'll need to organize yourself, but your waiban can help with travel arrangements; see suggestions below.

Weekend travel presents problems because China is vast and her transport slow and crowded. Some enterprising foreigners have crammed all their classes into 3 or 4 days a week in order to maximize travel time. Never press your waiban on this, however; most Chinese get only 1 day off a week, and your balking at 2 will seem babyish. Barring long weekends, weekend travel of any distance means flying; see below.

Most foreigners get 6 or 7 short vacations of 2 to 5 days each for holidays as varied as National Teacher's Day (September 10) and the Grave Sweeping Festival. Most schools allow a 4-to-6 week break between semesters at Spring Festival, and 6 to 8 weeks in the summer (summer vacation is paid only for instructors teaching consecutive years). But remember, spring break is very crowded because everyone in China travels at that time.

When traveling you'll see, if you haven't before, how the other half of foreigners in China live, the tourists ignorant of waibans and bucket-and-scoop showers who are ferried about by the China International Travel Service (CITS). You may envy them; one teacher from Jinan scrawled in despair "if I had it all to do over again, I'd see China in 3 weeks on one of those air-conditioned cruises." Just remember: those folks may not have to deal with cold-water showers, but neither will they drink mao tai in the moonlight with their students on a hillside. We all have our own goals in life.

While traveling, you can mix and match lifestyles as well. Most foreign teachers and students, especially those living within their China earnings, travel the way middle-class Chinese do, which means trains, dorms, and the public bus. Using your White Card it's possible to see China on US $6 or $7 a day. But remember you're on vacation, not an endurance contest. When you tire of Chinese-style travel you can always pay for planes, nice hotels, or air-conditioned tour vans. Bring extra cash so you can treat yourself to a private room now and again.

Some foreigners even invite along a Chinese companion when they travel, from among their students, teachers, waiban personnel, or classmates. A Chinese travel companion can negotiate for hotels and tickets; you may end up saving money even after paying the companion's travel expenses. Be careful, however; register any Chinese travel companions with your waiban, and get an official waiban letter introducing the Chinese person as your tour guide. It's also best not to share hotel rooms with a Chinese person you're not married to. In the case of opposite-sex travel companions, you can't; Chinese hotels check Chinese peoples' marriage licenses.

Tickets

Travel tickets, whether train, plane, bus, or boat, are a hassle to get in China. No computers link nationwide systems for ground transport. The only way to buy round-trip or connecting tickets is to get a package tour from CITS; they start at US$50 per day. Also, many more Chinese want to travel than Chinese transportation has seats for, especially at Spring Festival time. Consider seeing fewer cities in more depth; city-hopping without a package tour can be very stressful.

Traveling as Chinese do you'll need to buy tickets in each city to the next stop on your tour. Depending on relations and his or her prestige, your waiban may be able to arrange connecting tickets using guanxi, getting people in the cities you'll visit to wait in line for you. That way you can make detailed plans ahead. Otherwise as soon as you arrive in each city, get in line for your ongoing ticket and plan your sight-seeing only when you know how many days till you leave.

Chinese ticket classes are as follows:

Air

Domestic Chinese air travel, except between a few coastal cities, is monopolized by the Civil Aviation Association of China (CAAC). CAAC planes offer First Class and Coach seats and, aside from occasional indifferent service, compare with any international airline. Given China's distances, if you want to cover much ground quickly, you'll have to fly.

Airfares have shot up in recent years; at last check a one-way flight Beijing to Urumqi was 700 yuan RMB, even with a White Card, and climbing. The same trip via train cost 90 yuan, but took 5 days. CAAC hawks tickets at airports and at downtown ticket offices.

Trains

Slow as they are, trains are the travel mode of choice for most students and teachers, allowing countryside viewing at a stately pace. Chinese trains offer the following 5 classes of service. Because train trips can last several days, choosing a class merits serious thought.

1. SOFT SLEEPER cars hold 10 to 12 rooms, each containing 4 berths with mattresses, sheets, blankets, quilts, a small table, thermoses of hot water, and a private luggage rack. Only in Soft Sleepers can doors lock and the train announcements be shut off. Also, Soft Sleeper companions will either be other foreigners or Party cadres, frequently with incomprehensible accents. At last check a Soft Sleeper berth from Qingdao to Beijing cost 180 yuan RMB with White Card.

2. HARD SLEEPER cars hold 18 to 20 rows of padded bunks in 3 tiers, arranged perpendicularly to one wall with tables between rows, while a narrow aisle with fold-down chairs runs along the other wall. Hard Sleeper berths include sheets, blankets, and no privacy, but unless your neighbors chain smoke or yell all night, Hard Sleeper is quite pleasant. Most teachers and students try for Hard Sleeper tickets. At last check, a Hard Sleeper berth Qingdao to Beijing cost 70 yuan RMB with White Card.

3. SOFT SEAT offers rows of cushy armchairs around tables with sunny plastic flowers, and servers who pour tea. For day trips Soft Seat is very comfortable. Soft Seat Qingdao-Beijing, when offered, costs 70 yuan RMB with White Card.

4. HARD SEAT cars contain thinly padded benches surrounding large plywood tables, chickens hanging from the luggage racks, squatters stuffed in the aisles, and much misery. During the day Hard Seat is merely loud and filthy. At night it can be unbearable. Hard Seat Qingdao-Beijing costs 35 yuan RMB with White Card.

5. HARD STAND—see under Boats.

All passengers in Hard classes must carry their own mugs to fetch boiled water from a central urn. Dining cars serve meals to passengers in Soft and

Hard Sleeper and Soft Seat. Others can carry their own food, or buy from hawkers at station stops.

Buying train tickets involves advanced guanxi maneuvering. Some train stations offer foreigners-only windows; you may or may not get White Card rates there. CITS also often has ticket offices, which sell tickets only days in advance and charge service fees. Otherwise, it's the huge lines at the general windows, the scalpers outside, or boarding without a ticket. Should you brave the general windows, find out which to wait at before you step in line; some cities sell Soft and Hard classes or same-day and advance tickets at different addresses. Also be careful: theft at train stations has shot up. Should you board without a ticket, bustle past the ticket collector muttering *shang che bu piao* ("I'll buy it on the train"), and then run—don't walk—to the on-train ticket stand (usually in car #8), proffer cigarettes, and start haggling for a sleeper berth. We recommend this last method for over night trips only for the daring with solid Chinese-language abilities, or for the desperate. For day trips, bring a tiny folding bamboo stool. Sitting on one in the space between cars can be quite bearable.

Buses

Long-distance Chinese buses are rattly, smoke-choked affairs best avoided except for trips to places accessible only by bus. Most buses leave from train stations on an irregular schedule (as soon as they have enough passengers); buy tickets at a ticket window near the bus stops or from the driver.

Boats

Passenger boats ply China's rivers and seacoast offering stately travel for those not in a rush. Riverboats sell 6 classes of tickets. 1st Class is rarely sold, consisting of 1 or 2 luxury staterooms reserved for VIPs. 2d Class staterooms contain 2 curtained beds with mattresses, linens, and quilts, maid service, and thermoses of hot water. First and 2d classes contain foreigners and cadres only, for the most part. 3d Class staterooms offer 5 bunks, heat, and a private sink; 4th Class, 8 bunks, no heat, and no sink; and 5th Class, tiers of bunks massed in the boiler room and no linens. Most teachers and students try for 3d or 4th Class. 6th Class, or *sanxipiao* (散票) ("loose seating"), like Hard Stand on the trains, is a class created for people who need to travel but have no money. For token fares poor Chinese travelers can squat in unheated freight cars on the trains and in the stairwells and aisles of the boats. Chinese will not sell Hard Stand or sanxi tickets to foreigners, and believe us, you wouldn't want them anyway.

Ocean boat classes are the same as riverboats, except that 5th Class gets linens and there is no 6th Class.

Room and Board

Use your vacation travel to sample China's culinary varieties. As in most countries, hotel restaurants offer the blandest fare. Get out into the neighborhoods and eat like the locals. But remember the safety cautions in Chapter 6 under "Hygiene." Hotels in China range from 5-star joint ventures with 5-star prices to hostels. Generally only the better hotels accept foreigners. Most joint-venture hotels don't accept White Cards, but Chinese hotels do; you're entitled to pay RMB at Chinese rate. Some hotel managers will deny this; how much you care to argue depends on your personal balance between blood pressure and finance.

Most cities have at least one budget-rate hotel that accepts foreigners and offers spartan rooms and/or dorms; get a good tourist guidebook for advice (see Appendix B for suggestions). Your waiban may also be able to arrange stays in school dorms. Even without specific arrangements, try to get a general letter of introduction from your waiban when you travel; other waibans will often allow you in based on such a letter. School dorms usually offer cheap, clean rooms and access to other facilities, such as bicycles. In some relaxed cities you can also stay in any inn. The best way to find out is just to march up and ask for a room. If the innkeeper accepts you, it's fine.

SHOPPING

China offers unparalleled shopping opportunities for purchasers of knick-knacks, handicrafts, and cheap consumer goods. Shopping on Taiwan is much like shopping in the West. The basic types of mainland shopping are as follows:

Department Stores

Department stores are large, government-run stores selling consumer goods and occasionally handicrafts. They're usually the best place to start looking for things, as prices are fixed and low. Note that the "departments" are hardly as clearly separated as in the West; tea kettles may be next to tape recorders. Also, all goods are kept on shelves or behind glass counters; you have to ask service people to see things, and most speak no English. In many stores you'll buy tickets for items and may need to wait some time to pick up the goods. For large-ticket items, ask a Chinese friend for help.

Government Food Stores

State food stores are the culinary equivalent of department stores. Once again, because prices are cheap and fixed, they are the best places to start looking for things. We found staples, spices, canned goods, and, when available, fresh produce tended to be great buys at state food stores, but their meat was moldy a bit too often for our tastes.

Small Stores

Many small stores crowd China's streets, hawking everything from eggs to auto parts. Some are public, some are run by danwei cooperatives, and some are private. You can usually tell the first two because the workers will be wearing those little white caps. Prices at public stores are fixed. Private stores invite haggling. Prices at small stores tend to be higher than at the large state stores, but selections are often better, and hours more convenient.

Freemarkets

Since economic reform private peddlers have been able to set up stalls at neighborhood markets throughout China. Most cities also have at least one large central freemarket. Freemarket size is arguably the best measure of current government tolerance for liberalization. For the foreseeable future, freemarkets will continue to thrive, as even during the 1989 crackdown the leadership stressed the sanctity of economic reform.

Freemarkets are wheeling, dealing, open air markets full of pig farmers selling porkers from baskets slung on the backs of their bikes, old women hawking embroidery, and young men touting electronic gewgaws. Freemarkets have the best variety of goods in China, the freshest foods (farmers come daily to the freemarkets, and in the better ones give discounts on day-old eggs!), and the widest price range. Always check prices in state stores first to get some idea of what you should pay. Expect to pay 30–50% more in the freemarket than you would in a state store, though in some cases, freemarket prices may be at or below state levels. But don't get suckered in by what we call the "foreigner tax." Many freemarket sellers see foreigners as marks, and that 18-yuan sweater will suddenly cost 128 yuan when you ask the price. Learn to haggle, or bring a Chinese friend who is adept at bargaining.

Also, beware of freemarket antique stands. Fakes are increasingly common. Then too, by law all antiques must be inspected by the government, and only those not classed as "national treasures" may be exported. In practice, this means that virtually all goods over 120 years old, and many newer high quality goods, are illegal exports. The only legal place to buy exportable antiques is at state antique stores, where you'll pay a hefty surcharge for that red wax seal on the bottom which satisfies customs. You can try your luck smuggling out freemarket purchases, but customs has the right to confiscate anything they find which even looks old but has no seal. Some unscrupulous peddlers, in fact, work hand-inglove with customs, bribing corrupt officials for confiscated items, which they then resell to other foreigners.

Friendship Stores

Friendship Stores are large state stores selling items of particular interest to foreigners, from handicrafts to export-only goods. They are generally pricier than regular state department stores, and if you can find comparable items, better buy them at department stores. Some Friendship Stores are open to Chinese, others to foreigners only; some require purchase in FEC, and may or may not accept White Cards. Larger cities may also offer state "Arts and Crafts" stores and "Antique" stores.

MOONLIGHTING

Living in China offers many chances to further your professional goals. Don't neglect these opportunities.

Writers can publish articles in both Chinese and foreign periodicals; work as stringers for Western news agencies; update tourist guidebooks and business directories, or plug China experiences into first novels. Writing requires no special permission from your waiban; be sensitive, however. Never transmit politically sensitive material using school equipment or use the real names of any Chinese people you know in your writing, particularly in sensitive contexts.

Many Chinese companies need foreigners to check English-language technical documents or promotional literature; to help with videotapes; or to do part-time translation. Check with your waiban before doing any paid work for an outside danwei, as some schools and programs have restrictions.

Foreign companies also often need extra help with translation, writing, sales, research, and many other areas. Resident foreigners in China who appear with resume in hand can often pick up lucrative and interesting part-time jobs that the company couldn't justify relocating a full-time employee for. Some foreigners have found this sort of part-time work led later to full-time careers.

So long as your outside activities don't interfere with your schoolwork, most waibans will be very supportive. A happy foreigner means a good working relationship, for them as well as you.

Leaving:
Fruitful Farewells

"I wish my mother lived in a trailer park," survey respondent John Weston bemoaned. "Everything I could buy as a gift or receive as a gift would find a fitting home." As your time to leave China draws near, friends will load you down with pink plastic poodle tumblers, mass-produced ceramic horses, and machine-embroidered rayon wall-hangings featuring scenes from Suzhou.

Take it all as the tribute it is to international friendship and to the relationships you've developed. And remember: it's not that they have no taste, it's just that they have no money. Your students probably spent a lot of time selecting that puce-and-mauve ashtray, so accept it graciously. Years from now you may still be displaying it proudly as a war trophy.

Aside from how to thank the donor of your third machine-made tricolor horse, many factors will occupy your time and mind in your last days in China, from shipping and routes home to saying your goodbyes. Pay these last-minute activities the attention they deserve. To paraphrase the old saw, "you never get a second chance on a last impression." It's easy in the rush of things to get argumentative about promises not met or to "forget" to say goodbye to a troublesome waiban official. In the end, though, the taint on your memories won't be worth it. Take the time to do it right; you'll feel better in the long run.

And remember to leave room in your bags for the pink poodle tumblers.

1. SHIPPING. Depending on the wealth of your material goods, your best bet is probably sea shipment. China's post office

is expensive, slow, and notorious about loss and breakage. Air shipment is both pricey and restrictive. And given the difficulty of transfers in China, you'll not want to carry much with you. Instead, your waiban and/or Chinese friends can help you arrange for sea shipment. A 1–cubic-meter crate (which your waiban can probably get made for free, though you may be charged for it) costs approximately US$150 to ship to North America regardless of weight (less to New Zealand or Australia and more to Europe); many waibans will ship for free as part of the foreigner's benefits. You can pack a good-sized apartmentful of goods into a cubic meter, and it'll arrive at your home seaport about 2 months later.

Remember to pack tightly with plenty of padding; most breakage in sea shipment occurs from jostling within the crates. Close and ship off your crate as late as possible so as to have room for those last-minute gifts (surely you have a cousin living in a trailer park somewhere who'll appreciate the rayon wall-hangings). Add liberal amounts of mothballs and desiccants to the crate to protect against shipboard rats and salt spray. And if you've room left in your crate, see it as an opportunity to spend those extra unconvertible RMB. Many items you may have come to take for granted in your Chinese life would make fine additions to your home or excellent gifts, from woks and other Chinese cookware to those surprisingly effective Chinese thermoses to bicycles to handicrafts from the Friendship Store.

Customs in your home country will unlikely charge duty on gifts or items for personal use. One exception is any new luxury items, such as hand-loomed carpets or expensive jewelry. For this reason buy any luxury items early, use them in China, and import them as used goods.

Actually, even commercial importation on a small scale is remarkably easy. In the U.S. any commercial goods bought for less than $1,800 in total can be imported "informally," with a standard 10% duty rate and minimal inspection. One enterprising college student filled the space left in her crate with silk scarves and resold them in her college's dining hall for enough to pay for her next China trip.

2. TRAVEL HOME. Be as specific as you can as to your travel plans, especially if the Chinese institution will buy your ticket home. If you request early, for example, they may be able to route you with a stopover in, say, Tokyo or Singapore. But once tickets have been bought, adding stopovers ranges from the expensive to the impossible. If you plan extensive travel in Asia before going home, best fly out of Hong Kong. Arrange for a lengthy Hong Kong stopover, then buy bargain Asian airfares there, and return to Hong Kong for your flight home. If you plan to leave via one of the more exotic routes, overland through Pakistan, Nepal, or the Soviet Union, best travel very light and consult early and often with your waiban and a good travel guidebook (see Appendix B). Trans-Siberian railroad fares can be bought from other foreigners at cheap hotels in Beijing, or from CITS.

3. BUSINESS CONTACTS. Make the rounds of anyone you've done any moonlighting for, especially if you hope for more work from them in the future. Leave them with your business card, memories perhaps of a farewell banquet, and some idea of how you can continue to serve them from your home country. One foreign teacher we know set up contacts before leaving China with several export trade companies, and started a thriving import business at home.

4. GOODBYES. If you can, try to leave a week or so between your final exams or when grades are due and your flight out. Your school will likely give at least one farewell banquet for all foreign teachers and/or students, and many other friends will want to invite you out. At farewell banquets you'll probably be asked for your overall impressions of your time in China. Remember this is a pro-forma question, and not the time for you to remind the waiban that the heat was never hooked up in your room. Chinese put great store on face and smooth impressions. Whatever has gone before, try to leave on good terms.

You should also do something for your Chinese friends. Take time to go round with gifts for all your friends and for those who have done things for you (yes, even the ones you didn't get along with); by now you should understand what we mean by "leave your guanxi balance sheets even." Go and talk with anyone you may have crossed swords with and be sure all is, at least on the surface, forgiven. You might also consider putting on farewell banquets of your own, either in a restaurant (expensive), or at your home (you can always hire in a chef if your own culinary skills rank low: about 50 to 100 yuan would be a generous amount for the service).

Even if you think you'll never go to China again, your Chinese contacts can be useful, sending you handicrafts or meeting your Aunt Jane at the airport when she goes to Beijing. Then too, however you feel now, you may just start hankering for China again someday. You'll want to have folks there feel able to welcome you home.

CHINA

Autonomous Regions

List of Schools by Province

This directory lists all schools in the PRC, followed by all schools in Taiwan, that accept foreigners as teachers and/or students. The information in this directory was gathered from a variety of sources. Our starting points were 2 directories/atlases of education in China published in Chinese by the PRC government, and a directory, Higher Education in the ROC, *published in English by Taiwan's government. We translated the PRC directories and reorganized information from the Taiwan directory, then cross-checked our data with U S Department of Education Information. We then sent out surveys to each of the schools listed asking for updates and new information. Responses varied, and so accordingly does the amount of information in each listing. Wherever information in a directory listing appears in quotation marks, it is a direct quote from a survey respondent; we include these tidbits for flavor, with the proviso that they represent the views of individual respondents and not necessarily those of the authors.*

The PRC portion of the directory is arranged in alphabetical order of province, and schools within each province are grouped by type of school: University, Minorities/Politics and Law, Arts/Music, Finance/Commerce/Economics, Foreign Languages, Normal, Medical, and Technical. Please note that schools are also cross-referenced in Appendix D by lists of Key Universities. Key Universities are noted throughout the directory by an asterisk (*).

Anhui Most famous as home of Huang Shan, China's most often-painted mountain, Anhui is also a newly developed industrial region, with production at the capital Hefei having increased by a factor of more than 10,000 since 1949. The provincial museum at Hefei also features archeological and artistic treasures from throughout the region. Foreign residents in Anqing and Wuhu, along with unparalleled opportunities for climbing Huang Shan, have been able to study with local monks. Language is fairly heavily accented Mandarin, weather temperate, and food bland but rich in produce.

Universities

ANHUI UNIVERSITY*
Responsible Bureau: Provincial Education Administration
Departments: Radio Technology, Chinese, History, Philosophy, Foreign Languages, Library Science, Mathematics, Computer Science, Physics, Biology, Economics, Law
Foreign Students: 15-20
ForeignTeachers: 5-10
Teachers: can teach English, Western Culture
Students: growing program in Chinese Language/Culture

Contact: Foreign Affairs Office, Anhui University, Hezuohua Rd., Hefei, Anhui PRC Tel: 62655

BENGBU UNIFIED UNIVERSITY
Responsible Bureau: City Government
Departments: Textile Dye Arts, Inorganic Industrial Chemistry, Agricultural Construction, Secretarial Science, Management, Statistics, Packaging
Contact: Foreign Affairs Office, Bengbu Unified University, Dongfengsi St., Bengbu, Anhui PRC Tel: 4188

CHINA UNIVERSITY OF SCIENCE AND TECHNOLOGY*
Responsible Bureau: State Department of Science
Departments: High Temperature Physics Engineering, RadioTechnology, Systems Science, Computer Science, Precision Mechanics, Mathematics, Physics, Chemistry, Power Studies, Earth and Atmospheric Sciences, Biology
Foreign Teachers: 8-10
Teachers: Key University w/ good science facilities; can teach English, technical subjects
Contact: Foreign Affairs Office, China University of Science and Technology, Jinzhai Rd., Hefei, Anhui PRC Tel: 63300

HEFEI UNIFIED UNIVERSITY
Responsible Bureau: Provincial Education Administration
Departments: Management, Finance and Accounting, Taxation, Mechanical Electronics, Environmental Studies and Industrial Chemistry, Information Science, Architecture, Chinese, Foreign Languages, Economics, Experimental Technology, Applied Microbiology
Contact: Foreign Affairs Office, Hefei Unified University, Huangshan Rd., Hefei, Anhui PRC Tel: 61969

HUAINAN UNIFIED UNIVERSITY
Responsible Bureau: City Government
Departments: Radiation, Industrial Chemistry, Agricultural Construction, Secretarial Science, Management, Statistics, Packaging
Contact: Foreign Affairs Office, Huainan Unified University, Tianjiaxiang, Huainan, Anhui PRC Tel: 4914

MA'ANSHAN UNIFIED UNIVERSITY
Responsible Bureau: City Government
Departments: Mechanics, Computer Science, Agricultural Construction, Chinese, Industrial Management, Accounting
Contact: Foreign Affairs Office, Ma'anshan Unified University, Ma'anshan, Anhui PRC Tel: 4117

WUHU UNITY UNIVERSITY
Responsible Bureau: City Government
Departments: Mechanics, Management, Agricultural Construction, Farming Technology, Geology, English, Secretarial Sciences, History, Finance and Accounting
Contact: Foreign Affairs Office, Wuhu Unity University, Zhuangyuanfang, Wuhu, Anhui PRC Tel: 4722

Finance/Economics

ANHUI INSTITUTE OF FINANCE AND TRADE
Responsible Bureau: Ministry of Commerce
Departments: Commercial Economics, Statistics, Finance, Commercial Goods, Cotton Processing
Contact: Foreign Affairs Office, Anhui Institute of Finance and Trade, Hongye Village, Bengbu, Anhui PRC Tel: 7481

Foreign Languages

HEFEI FOREIGN LANGUAGE TECHNICAL INSTITUTE
Responsible Bureau: Provincial "93 Studies" Society
Departments: English, Japanese
Contact: Foreign Affairs Office, Hefei Foreign Language Technical Institute, Dongchengang, Hefei, Anhui PRC Tel: 74711

Normal Schools

ANHUI NORMAL UNIVERSITY
Responsible Bureau: State Education Commission/Provincial Government
Departments: Education, Politics, Chinese, History, Geology, Biology, Mathematics, Physics, Chemistry, Physical Education, Art, Music, Foreign Languages, Experimental Physics, Environmental Protection
Chinese Students: 5,700
Sister School: Germany—Univ of Osnabrück
Contact: Foreign Affairs Office, Anhui Normal University, Wuhu, Anhui PRC Tel: 2065

ANQING NORMAL SCHOOL
Responsible Bureau: Provincial Education Administration
Departments: Political Education, Chinese, History, Mathematics, Physics, Chemistry, English, Biological Pharmacological Production
Contact: Foreign Affairs Office, Anqing Normal School, Linghu S. Rd., Anqing, Anhui PRC Tel: 4877

FUYANG NORMAL SCHOOL
Responsible Bureau: Provincial Education Administration
Departments: Political Education, Chinese, Mathematics, Physics, Chemistry, Industrial Arts, Foreign Languages
Contact: Foreign Affairs Office, Fuyang Normal School, Xiqinghe, Fuyang,Anhui PRC Tel: 2882

HUAIBEI MINING NORMAL SCHOOL
Responsible Bureau: Ministry of Coal Mining
Departments: Political Education, Chinese, Mathematics, Physics, Chemistry, Physical Education, Arts, English
Contact: Foreign Affairs Office, Huaibei Mining Normal School, Huaibei, Anhui PRC Tel: 2559

Medical Schools

ANHUI COLLEGE OF CHINESE MEDICINE
Responsible Bureau: Provincial Administration of Sanitation and Hygiene

Departments: Chinese Medicine, Acupuncture, Chinese Pharmacology
Contact: Foreign Affairs Office, Anhui College of Chinese Medicine,
Meishan Rd., Hefei, Anhui PRC Tel: 6254

ANHUI COLLEGE OF MEDICINE
Responsible Bureau: Provincial Administration of Sanitation and Hygiene
Departments: Medicine, Oral Medicine, Sanitation and Hygiene,
Management
Contact: Foreign Affairs Office, Anhui College of Medicine, Meishan Rd.
Hefei, Anhui PRC Tel: 61810

Technical Schools

ANHUI INSTITUTE OF AGRICULTURE
Responsible Bureau: Provincial Education Administration
Departments: Veterinary Medicine, Gardening, Forestry, Agricultural
Science, Crop Protection, Silkworm and Mulberry Cultivation, Agricultural
Mechanics, Agricultural Economics
Contact: Foreign Affairs Office, Anhui Institute of Agriculture, Shushan
Rd., Hefei, Anhui PRC Tel: 73720

ANHUI INSTITUTE OF MECHANICAL ELECTRONICS
Responsible Bureau: Provincial Education Administration
Departments: Mechanics, Electrical Equipment, Nutrition, Textiles,
Industrial Arts
Contact: Foreign Affairs Office, Anhui Institute of Mechanical Electronics,
Jihe Rd., Wuhu, Anhui PRC Tel: 2763

ANHUI POLYTECHNICAL UNIVERSITY*
Responsible Bureau: Ministry of Mechanics
Departments: Mechanical Production, Power Production Mechanics,
Electrical Equipment, Management
Contact: Foreign Affairs Office, Anhui Polytechnical University, Liu'an
Rd., Hefei, Anhui PRC Tel: 75553

BENGBU MEDICAL COLLEGE
Responsible Bureau: Provincial Administration of Sanitation and Hygiene
Departments: Medicine, Medical Examination
Chinese Students: 1,300
Contact: Foreign Affairs Office, Bengbu Medical College, 108 Zhihuai Rd.,
Bengbu, Anhui PRC Tel: 4243

HEFEI INSTITUTE OF TECHNOLOGY
Responsible Bureau: Ministry of Mechanics
Departments: Geology, Electrical Equipment, Industrial Chemical Material,
Mechanics, Precision Timing Equipment, Management, Computer Science,
Architecture, Civil Engineering, Physics
Contact: Foreign Affairs Office, Hefei Institute of Technology, Tunxi Rd.,
Hefei, Anhui PRC Tel: 74711

HUAINAN INSTITUTE OF MINING
Responsible Bureau: Ministry of Coal Mining
Departments: Geology, Materials and Mining, Mechanical Electronics,

Industrial Chemistry
Contact: Foreign Affairs Office, Huainan Institute of Mining, Dongshan, Huainan, Zhejiang PRC Tel: 4797

MA'ANSHAN INSTITUTE OF STEEL
Responsible Bureau: Ministry of Industrial Metals
Departments: Industrial Metals, Industrial Chemistry, Mechanics, Industrial Automation, Economic Management
Contact: Foreign Affairs Office, Ma'anshan Institute of Steel, Hudong Rd., Ma'anshan, Anhui, PRC Tel: 3235

Beijing Capital of the PRC, second largest city, political and cultural hub of the Chinese universe, Beijing is a world unto itself. No other city in China comes close to the capital's cultural and historical treasures, or to the access the city provides to the halls of power. The Imperial Palace, the Great Wall, Tiananmen Square, the Summer Palace, the Temple of Heaven, the nation's greatest museums—the list of attractions goes on. Beijing also offers nightly cultural performances, and the opportunity to visit the Great Hall of the People (home of China's legislative branch) and other government organs. All the cuisines of China are featured in the capital restaurants, as are all traveling cultural troupes.

By one government official's estimate, nearly 50% of all resident foreigners in China live in Beijing. This means several things, of course: competition is fierce, and foreigners are nothing special in Beijing, will get precious little support for any independent projects they may conceive, and will be herded and watched precisely because they are so close to the government's power. Very discreet, clever, and motivated foreign residents have gained unparelleled access to research and governmental facilities in Beijing; one longtime British resident reportedly tutors central leaders inside the fortresslike compound at Zhongnanhai. For many, however, living in the capital means more of a headache than it's worth. "I feel like in a year here I've learned nothing of China," complained one student. "It's like trying to learn about the American Southwest from D.C., or the Scottish Highlands from London. China is somewhere else."

But Beijing remains one of the world's great cities, capital for 7 centuries of the world's most enduring nation. Weather is abominable, furnace-like and polluted in summer, harshly dry and windy in winter. Language, while standard Mandarin, bears the acrid nasal "r's" of the Beijing accent. But Beijing remains the capital, and the fact that foreigners still pour in to view her treasures is ample proof for Chinese of her continuing status as center of the central kingdom of the world.

Universities

BEIFANG TRANSPORTATION UNIVERSITY*
Responsible Bureau: Ministry of Railroads
Departments: Mechanics, Computer Science, Agricultural Construction, Shipping, Economics, Communications Control, Materials
Chinese Students: 3,600

Sister Schools: 5 in US and Germany
Contact: Foreign Affairs Office, Beifang Transportation University, Xizhimenwai, Beijing PRC Tel: 890561

BEIJING UNIFIED UNIVERSITY
Responsible Bureau: Beijing City Higher Education Bureau
Departments: Mechanical Engineering, Light Industry, Finance, Foreign Languages, Humanities, Medicine, Radio Electronics
Contact: Foreign Affairs Office, Beijing Unified University, Haidian District, Beijing PRC Tel. 277881

BEIJING UNIVERSITY*
Responsible Bureau: State Education Committee
Departments: Mathematics, Physics, Engineering, Applied Physics, Geophysics, Radiology, Computer Science, Chemistry, Geology, Sociology, Japanese, Russian, Western Languages, Psychology, Library Science, Geography, Economics, Law, International Politics, Chinese, History, Archaeology, Philosophy
Chinese Students: 12,000+
Foreign Students: 500+
Foreign Teachers: 25-30
Sister Schools: over 50 in over 20 countries
Accommodations: small, but pretty; 2-3 rms in old bldg, w/ cooking facilities, TV, tape recorder, bike (students 2/rm, no cooking facilities); strict curfew, and visitors strongly discouraged; in walled compound, isolated from Chinese students, at edge of lovely but huge campus
Teacher Salary/Benefits: 700-3,000Y/mo (Teacher/Foreign Technical Expert)
FAO: huge office with mixed quality among staff; includes cleaning staff, fleet of cars and drivers, interpreters and guides for high-level foreign experts
Teaching Conditions: 10-16 hrs/wk; excellent language lab and library, but student access limited; Beijing Univ is China's most prestigious university
Student Tuition/Expenses: variable; many students are enrolled through home-country universities
Learning Conditions: both good and bad; have some of best-trained teachers in China and excellent facilities, but very isolated from life of university; "I feel like I've learned more about European nations from my neighbors, than about China from my classes"
Contact: Foreign Affairs Office, Beijing University, Haidian District, Beijing PRC Tel: 282471

BEIJING UNIVERSITY OF TECHNOLOGY*
Responsible Bureau: City Higher Education Bureau
Departments: Mechanics, Radio Engineering, Agricultural Construction, Environmental Chemistry, Computer Science, Automation, High Temperature Engineering, Metallurgy
Chinese Students: 5,700
Contact: Foreign Affairs Office, Beijing University of Technology, PO Box 327, Eastern Suburbs, Beijing PRC Tel: 781127 (x2965 FAO, x2275 English Dept)

CHINESE PEOPLE'S UNIVERSITY (RENDA)*
   Responsible Bureau: State Education Committee
   Departments: Languages and Literatures, Journalism, History, Philosophy, File Management, International Politics, Party History, Population Studies, Scientific Socialism, Finance, Political Law, Trade, Economic Information, Planning, Statistics
   Foreign Teachers: 9 (8 on Fullbright & other formal exchanges, 1 "free agent")
   Accommodations: not bad, but free agent can't use shared kitchen facilities
   Teacher Salary/Benefits: 350-800Y/mo, 33% in FEC; o-w airfare after 1 yr + 1,000Y Spring Festival travel allowance
   FAO: "the worst in China . . . you get the runaround, last-minute notifications . . ."
   Teaching Conditions: "classes tend to be gargantuan," sometimes 90 students to a class, "which makes conversation class a logistical impossibility"; students "great . . . very motivated"; most classes language, some liberal arts, teacher training; this year's batch of freshmen "are like nothing anyone at this university has ever seen before: very outgoing and energetic . . . everyone is amazed"
   Contact. Foreign Affairs Office, Chinese People's University (Renda), Haidian District, Beijing PRC Tel: 285431

QINGHUA UNIVERSITY*
   Responsible Bureau: State Education Committee
   Departments: Agricultural Construction, Mechanical Engineering, Power Production, Radio Electronics, Computer Science, Automation, Hydrology, High Temperature Engineering, Precision Equipment Engineering, Electronics, Chemical Engineering, Physical Engineering, Power Engineering, Economic Management, Applied Mathematics, Physics, Foreign Languages, Foreign Literatures
   Chinese Students: 20,000
   Foreign Students: 50-60
   Foreign Teachers: 7
   Accommodations: not bad; 2-3 rms in foreigner compound, w/ shared kitchen and fridge but no stove; cafeteria food poor—also have separate dining hall for foreign teachers; reasonably lax visitor registration
   Teacher Salary/Benefits: 600-800Y/mo, some in FEC, + 50Y/mo raise every year; airfare home paid after 2 yrs
   FAO: "one of the best . . . very helpful and understanding of foreign expectations (which are not always reasonable)"
   Teaching Conditions: approx 12 hrs/wk, but "school then tries to lure you, later, into teaching more classes which are so interesting they're 'hard to refuse' "; school also arranges, for minimal fees, tutoring in Chinese Language, Painting, Martial Arts, etc.
   Student Tuition/Expenses: varied; many students are from developing nations on Chinese gov't scholarships
   Learning Conditions: good variety of classes
   Contact: Foreign Affairs Office, Qinghua University, Haidian District, Beijing PRC Tel: 283326

Minorities/Politics & Law

CENTRAL MINORITIES INSTITUTE
Responsible Bureau: National Committee of Minorities
Departments: Chinese, Minority Languages, History, Minority Studies, Politics, Music, Dance, Art, Mathematical Physics
Contact: Foreign Affairs Office, Central Minorities Institute, Haidian District, Beijing PRC Tel: 892889

CHINESE PEOPLE'S UNIVERSITY OF POLICE AND SECURITY
Responsible Bureau: Ministry of Public Security
Departments: Chinese, Journalism, English, Asian and European Languages, Science and Technology, Police Protection and Safety
Foreign Teachers: 3
Accommodations: excellent; 5-1/2 rms, w/ washer, TV, tape recorder, fridge, cooking facilities, use of car and driver once weekly to Beijing (campus 45 min by car from Beijing, 1-1/2 hrs by public bus); no curfew, relaxed about visitors and guests
Teacher Salary/Benefits: 1,150Y/mo, 70% FEC (for expert) plus r-t airfare and 800Y RMB travel allowance; shipping allowance, will pay excess air baggage allowance
FAO: pretty good, not very helpful, but very flexible; never organizes trips or activities
Teaching Conditions: 16 hrs/wk; great language lab; good videos; secretarial assistance, but photocopies discouraged; library: good recent foreign newspapers and magazines, but back copies sold and only limited access for students; plenty of books in stacks but due to uncooperative librarians students are usually not able to check them out—"basically the books are being held prisoner"
Contact: Foreign Affairs Office, Chinese People's University of Police and Security, Daxing County, Beijing PRC Tel: 799844

CHINESE PEOPLE'S UNIVERSITY OF PUBLIC SECURITY
Responsible Bureau: Ministry of Public Security
Departments: Public Security Management, Law, Intelligence, Security, Protection, Political Work
Contact: Foreign Affairs Office, Chinese People's University of Public Security, Fuxingmenwai, Beijing PRC Tel: 361331

CHINESE UNIVERSITY OF POLITICS AND LAW
Responsible Bureau: Ministry of Justice
Departments: Law, Economic Law, Politics
Contact: Foreign Affairs Office, Chinese University of Politics and Law, Haidian District, Beijing PRC Tel: 667931

COLLEGE OF FOREIGN AFFAIRS AND DIPLOMACY
Responsible Bureau: Ministry of Diplomacy
Departments: Diplomacy, Foreign Affairs
Chinese Students: 900
Foreign Students: 4-5
Foreign Teachers: 10-12
Accommodations: "great"; 2 rms for teachers, 1 for students, w/ washer,

TV, kitchen; central location and very relaxed about visitor registration
Teacher Salary/Benefits: 600-1,700Y/mo, r-t int'l airfare (Foreign Experts),
or o-w (Foreign Teachers)
Teaching Conditions: not bad; 12-14 hrs/wk, great language lab and "fair"
library; classes in English, Japanese, and French; school trains diplomats, so
experienced teachers are a must; school has excellent library and film-
showing facilities; curriculum director is "a real terror, very devious," but
may be in England 1991-1992
FAO: "ineffectual and mediocre"; "the worst part of the stay is the FAO"
Contact: Foreign Affairs Office, Institute of Diplomacy, Xicheng District,
Beijing PRC Tel: 894184

INSTITUTE OF INTERNATIONAL RELATIONS
Responsible Bureau: State Education Committee
Departments: Chinese, Journalism, English, Japanese, French, International
Economics
Foreign Students: 0
Foreign Teachers: 2-3
Teaching Conditions: institute trains many of China's diplomats; students
are all children of high-ranking officials. Institute screens foreign teachers
very carefully and is extremely strict, especially about contact w/ students.
Foreign teachers are barred from living on campus; live instead in Friendship
Hotel and are picked up each day for class; "no fraternizing with students is
allowed"
Contact: Foreign Affairs Office, Institute of International Relations, Haidian
District, Beijing PRC Tel: 285631

Arts/Music

BEIJING FILM ACADEMY
Responsible Bureau: Ministry of Culture
Departments: Literature, Directing, Acting, Photography, Art, Recording
Chinese Students: 300
Sister Schools: Australia—Australian Film and Television School, Ryerson
Polytechnical Inst
Contact: Foreign Affairs Office, Beijing Film Academy, Zhu Xin Zhuang,
Deshengmenwai District, Beijing PRC Tel: 275603

BEIJING INSTITUTE OF DANCE
Responsible Bureau: Ministry of Culture
Departments: Dance Composition, Dance History, Performance, Ballet
Contact: Foreign Affairs Office, Beijing Institute of Dance, Xuanwu
District, Beijing PRC Tel: 331406

CENTRAL ACADEMY OF FINE ARTS*
Responsible Bureau: Ministry of Culture
Departments: Chinese Traditional Painting, Oil Painting, Wood Block
Painting, Comic Book Painting, Calendar Painting, Sculpture, History of Art
Chinese Students: 600
Sister Schools: US—Pennsylvania State Univ, California State Univ;
Japan—Tokyo College of Art and Design, Osaka Univ of Arts, Tokyo Univ
of Arts; Norway—National School of Arts and Crafts at Oslo; Germany—

Academy of Fine Arts at Stuttgart; India—National Inst of Design
Contact: Foreign Affairs Office, Central Academy of Fine Arts, 34
Donghuan North Rd., Dongcheng District, Beijing PRC Tel: 554731

CENTRAL CONSERVATORY OF MUSIC*
Responsible Bureau: Ministry of Culture
Departments: Composition, Piano, Wind Instruments, Chinese Traditional
Instruments
Chinese Students: 650
Teachers and Students: facilities include 1.3 million vol library; music
library with 1.4 million items
Contact: Foreign Affairs Office, Central Conservatory of Music, Xinwenhua
St., Beijing PRC Tel: 667120

CENTRAL INSTITUTE OF ARTS AND HANDICRAFTS
Responsible Bureau: Ministry of Light Industry
Departments: Special Arts and Handicrafts, Decorations, Ceramics, Dyes,
Fashion Design, Industrial Planning, Interior Decorating, History of Arts and
Handicrafts
Contact: Foreign Affairs Office, Central Institute of Arts and Handicrafts,
Dong Huan Rd., Beijing PRC Tel: 594456

CHINA CONSERVATORY OF MUSIC
Responsible Bureau: Ministry of Culture
Departments: Composition, Voice, Instruments, Opera, Musicology, Music
Theory, Musical Technology
Chinese Students: 400
Foreign Students: variable
Foreign Teachers: variable
Sister Schools: Japan—Osaka School of Music; US—Chicago Conservatory
of Music; Germany—Heidelberg Univ; Hong Kong—National Minorities
School of Music
Teachers: can teach English, Western Culture and Western musical
instruments
Students: can join any degree program
Contact: Foreign Affairs Office, China Conservatory of Music, 17 Qianhai
West St., Beijing PRC Tel: 664120

CHINESE CENTRAL INSTITUTE OF DRAMA/OPERA
Responsible Bureau: Ministry of Culture
Departments: Composition, Operatic Culture, Stage Decoration, Acting,
Directing
Contact: Foreign Affairs Office, Chinese Institute of Drama/Opera, Xuanwu
District, Bejing PRC Tel: 336288

CHINESE INSTITUTE OF TRADITIONAL OPERA
Responsible Bureau: Ministry of Culture
Departments: Operatic Culture, Acting, Stage Decorating
Contact: Foreign Affairs Office, Chinese Institute of Traditional Opera,
Dongcheng District, Beijing PRC Tel: 445269

Finance/Commerce/Economics

BEIJING INSTITUTE OF COMMERCE

Responsible Bureau: Ministry of Commerce
Departments: Commercial Economics, Management, Accounting, Statistical Planning, Storage and Shipment
Chinese Students: 1,000
Teachers and Students: facilities include 300,000 vol library with 6,000 foreign language vols
Contact: Foreign Affairs Office, Beijing Institute of Commerce, 11 Fu Cheng Rd., Haidian District, Beijing PRC Tel: 891608

BEIJING INSTITUTE OF CONSUMER GOODS
Responsible Bureau: National Bureau of Consumer Goods
Departments: Consumer Goods Management, Finance and Accounting, Labor Economics
Contact: Foreign Affairs Office, Beijing Institute of Consumer Goods, Tong County, Beijing PRC Tel: 593831

BEIJING INSTITUTE OF ECONOMICS
Responsible Bureau: City Bureau of Higher Education
Departments: Industrial Economics, Statistics, Labor Economics, Foreign Trade Economics, Finance and Accounting, Economics, Management, Security, Economic Mathematics
Contact: Foreign Affairs Office, Beijing Institute of Economics, Chaoyangmenwai, Beijing PRC Tel: 593831

BEIJING INSTITUTE OF FINANCE AND TRADE
Responsible Bureau: City Bureau of Higher Education
Departments: Management, Accounting, Finance, Financial Management, Commercial Economics
Chinese Students: 400
Contact: Foreign Affairs Office, Beijing Institute of Finance and Trade, 68 Zao Ling Front Street, Xuanwu District, Beijing PRC Tel: 363103

CENTRAL INSTITUTE OF FINANCE AND ECONOMIC POLICY
Responsible Bureau: Ministry of Finance
Departments: Economic Planning, Finance, Accounting, Economic Management, Economics of Basic Construction
Contact: Foreign Affairs Office, Central Institute of Finance and Economic Policy, Xizhimenwai, Beijing PRC Tel: 891562

UNIVERSITY OF INTERNATIONAL BUSINESS AND ECONOMICS
Responsible Bureau: Ministry of Foreign Economic Relations and Trade
Departments: Foreign Trade Management, Foreign Languages, Foreign Trade, Customs Management, International Economic Cooperation, Economic Law
Chinese Students: 3,000
Foreign Students: 100 long-term, plus several hundred on short-term exchanges through sister schools
Foreign Teachers: 10
Sister Schools: 15 in US, UK, Canada, Japan, Australia
Teachers: can teach English, Western Culture, technical subjects (business, management, economics); facilities include 2 English-language journals, 1 Japanese journal

Students: small number of students in degree program, but several hundred students on short-term study program of Chinese business and management
Contact: Foreign Affairs Office, University of International Business and Economics, Andingmenwai, Beijing PRC Tel: 4212022

Broadcasting/Foreign Languages

BEIJING INSTITUTE OF BROADCASTING
Responsible Bureau: Ministry of Radio and Television
Departments: Microwave Broadcasting, Radio Technology, Television, News, Cultural Editing, Broadcasting, Foreign Languages
Foreign Students: 0
Foreign Teachers: 4 (1 specifically in Communication and Journalism)
Teacher Salary/Benefits: 1,200Y/month (Foreign Expert), some benefits
Accommodations: nice; 2 rms for singles, 3 rms married teachers, w/ shared kitchen, relaxed visitor registration; but campus is "in the sticks," 45 mins by bike or bus from town
FAO: poor; charges foreign teachers 100Y RMB for library card, "teachers are never paid on time," "encourages students to rat on teacher"; "no one stays more than one term!"
Teaching Conditions: poor; lots of reports behind teacher's back; students very bright but unmotivated "because they know they won't be able to say what they really want to say once they are in their jobs"
Contact: Foreign Affairs Office, Beijing Institute of Broadcasting, Chaoyang District, Beijing PRC Tel: 571620

BEIJING INSTITUTE OF LANGUAGES
Responsible Bureau: State Education Committee
Departments: Foreign Languages, Languages and Literatures
Foreign Students: many
Foreign Teachers: 9
Accommodations: pretty good, "but there are often little problems that take time to straighten out"
Teacher Salary/Benefits: 700Y/mo Foreign Teacher, 1400Y/mo, Foreign Expert; benefits vary
FAO: "generally helpful, but . . . tries to take advantage of the teachers through extra charges"
Teaching Conditions: "no materials are provided, no curriculum, and a lot of confusion"; can teach English, Literature, Journalism, Writing Skills, American Culture
Student Tuition/Expenses: 3 programs: 8 wks for US$650, 10 wks for $850, 1 yr for $1,500: room and board extra; scholarships available
Learning Conditions: 1st year program "rigid," but courses more flexible in second year
Contact: Foreign Affairs Office, Beijing Institute of Languages, Haidian District, Beijing PRC Tel: 277798

BEIJING NUMBER 2 INSTITUTE OF FOREIGN LANGUAGES
Responsible Bureau: National Bureau of Tourism
Departments: English, Slavic Languages, West European Languages, Asian and African Languages, Foreign Economic Cooperation
Foreign Students: few

Foreign Teachers: 12

Accommodations: excellent; "the best living conditions for teachers in China"; large 3-rm apartments w/ kitchen, oven, TV, fridge, a/c, heating, 2 balconies; but campus 45 minutes from town, difficult to get to at night

Teacher Salary/Benefits: 800Y/mo RMB (Foreign Teacher) or 1,900Y/mo RMB (Foreign Expert), + 1,400Y travel bonus, r-t int'l airfare for Experts, 1/2 month's salary in US $ as year-end bonus, 1 month's salary in US $ as 2-year bonus

FAO: very good; "goes out of their way to treat us well"; provides bus to town 3x/wk, many trips and parties; bus can also be rented from school

Teaching Conditions: 8-16 hrs/wk; situations vary; some departments "are completely hands off the teachers, some provide some supervison, some control tightly"; students very bright, but lack ambition because "their job prospects are so dismal"; class size good, 18-20 students

Student Tuition/Expenses: US$700 tuition + room and board

Learning Conditions: "everyone is very disappointed with the program, and people are always dropping out"

Contact: Foreign Affairs Office, Beijing Number 2 Institute of Foreign Languages, Chaoyang District, Beijing PRC Tel: 571272

BEIJING UNIVERSITY OF FOREIGN STUDIES

Responsible Bureau: State Education Committee

Departments: English, Russian, Japanese, French, German, Spanish, Arabic, Slavic Languages, Asian and African Languages, Chinese

Foreign Students: many

Foreign Teachers: 10-16, divided between 3 English programs; most on Fulbright and other formal exchanges

Accommodations: "Foreign Expert housing is very nice; Foreign Teacher housing is typical Chinese apartments, which are simple but adequate"

Teacher Salary/Benefits: varies

FAO: "doesn't do much; no advance planning"

Teaching Conditions: 10-14 hrs/wk; English programs divided between 1st and 2nd English programs, and Training Center; 1st English Dept trains undergrads, 2nd English Dept trains Middle School teachers; Training Center trains workers from various danwei on short-term programs—"very little communication between the departments"; class size good, 15-20 students, + some larger lectures which break down into study groups

Learning Conditions: many foreign students—US, Canada, Japan, USSR, most in formal exchange programs, but "anyone with money can arrange something"

Contact: Foreign Affairs Office, Beijing Institute of Foreign Languages, Haidian District, Beijing PRC Tel: 890351

Normal Schools

BEIJING NORMAL SCHOOL

Responsible Bureau: State Education Committee

Departments: Education, Psychology, Chinese, Economics, Philosophy, History, Library Science, Foreign Languages, Astronomy, Geology, Biology, Mathematics, Physics, Radio Technology, Chemistry, Physical Education, Art

Contact: Foreign Affairs Office, Beijing Normal School, Xinjiekouwai,

Taiping Village, Beijing PRC Tel: 660983

BEIJING TEACHERS INSTITUTE
Responsible Bureau: City Bureau of Higher Education
Departments: Political Education, Chinese, History, Geology, Biology, Mathematics, Physics, Chemistry, Music, Art, Foreign Languages
Contact: Foreign Affairs Office, Beijing Teachers Institute, Haidian District, Beijing PRC Tel: 891545

Medical Schools

BEIJING COLLEGE OF TRADITIONAL CHINESE MEDICINE INTERNATIONAL
Responsible Bureau: Ministry of Sanitation and Hygiene
Departments: Chinese Medicine, Chinese Pharmacology, Acupuncture and Acupressure, Nursing and Care
Chinese Students: 1,500
Foreign Students: 40-50
Foreign Teachers: varies
Sister Schools: in US, UK, Japan, Australia, France, Canada, Germany, Italy
Teachers: can teach English, Western Medicine
Students: have special English-language training in traditional Chinese Medicine
Contact: Foreign Affairs Office, Beijing College of Traditional Chinese Medicine International, 11 Beisanhuan E. Ave., Beijing PRC Tel: 4213458

BEIJING UNIVERSITY OF MEDICINE
Responsible Bureau: Ministry of Sanitation and Hygiene
Departments: Medicine, Sanitation and Hygiene, Oral Medicine, Pharmacology, Nursing and Care
Contact: Foreign Affairs Office, Beijing University of Medicine, Haidian District, Beijing PRC Tel: 277604

CAPITAL INSTITUTE OF MEDICINE
Responsible Bureau: City Committee of Sanitation and Hygiene
Departments: Medicine, Pediatrics, Oral Medicine
Contact: Foreign Affairs Office, Capital Institute of Medicine, You'anmenwai, Beijing PRC   Tel: 339484

CHINA XIEHE MEDICAL UNIVERSITY
Responsible Bureau: Ministry of Sanitation and Hygiene
Departments: Medical Practice, Nursing and Care
Contact: Foreign Affairs Office, China Xiehe Medical University, Dongdan, Beijing PRC Tel: 557831

Technical Schools

BEIJING AEROSPACE UNIVERSITY*
Responsible Bureau: Aerospace Ministry
Departments: Materials, Electronics, Automation and Control, Computer Science, Management, Applied Mathematics, Applied Physics, Mechanical and Electronic Equipment, Systems Engineering, Power Production
Chinese Students: 6,500
Sister Schools: 16 in US, UK, Canada, Australia, Japan, France, Belgium
Contact: Foreign Affairs Office, Beijing Aerospace University, 37 Xueyuan

Rd., Haidian District, Beijing PRC Tel: 277378

BEIJING AGRICULTURAL UNIVERSITY
Responsible Bureau: Ministry of Agriculture, Livestock, and Fisheries
Departments: Agriculture, Gardening, Crop Protection, Soil Chemistry,
Livestock, Veterinary Medicine, Agricultural Meteorology, Nutrition,
Biology, Agricultural Economics
Contact: Foreign Affairs Office, Beijing Agricultural University, Western
Suburbs, Beijing PRC Tel: 285831

BEIJING INSTITUTE OF ARCHITECTURAL ENGINEERING
Responsible Bureau: City Architectural Committee
Departments: Architecture, Urban Planning, Electronic Equipment, Civil
Engineering
Foreign Teachers: 0 at present, may accept in future
Contact: Foreign Affairs Office, Beijing Institute of Architectural Engineer-
ing, Exhibition Rd., West City District, Beijing PRC Tel: 899781

BEIJING INSTITUTE OF COMPUTER SCIENCE
Responsible Bureau: City Committee of Science
Departments: Computer Science
Foreign Teachers: 0 at present, may accept in future
Contact: Foreign Affairs Office, Beijing Institute of Computer Science,
Haidian District, Beijing PRC Tel: 896453

BEIJING INSTITUTE OF ENGINEERING
Responsible Bureau: Ministry of Weapons and Military Equipment
Departments: Mechanics, Radiation, Automation and Control, Electronics,
Computer Science, Chemistry, Power, Vehicle Studies, Management,
Foreign Languages, Mathematics, Physics, Industrial Planning
Foreign Teachers: 0 at present, may accept in future
Contact: Foreign Affairs Office, Beijing Institute of Engineering, Haidian
District, Beijing PRC Tel: 890321

BEIJING INSTITUTE OF HYDROELECTRICITY, ELECTRIC POWER, AND ECONOMIC MANAGEMENT
Responsible Bureau: Ministry of Water and Electricity
Departments: Hydroengineering, Electric Power, Economics
Contact: Foreign Affairs Office, Beijing Institute of Hydroelectricity,
Electric Power, and Economic Management, Dingfu Village, Beijing PRC
Tel: 651624

BEIJING INSTITUTE OF INDUSTRIAL AND CHEMICAL FIBERS
Responsible Bureau: Ministry of Textiles
Departments: Industrial Chemistry, Chemistry, Electronic
Equipment
Contact: Foreign Affairs Office, Beijing Institute of Industrial and Chemical
Fibers, Andingmenwai, Beijing Special Zone, PRC Tel: 466141

BEIJING INSTITUTE OF INDUSTRIAL CHEMISTRY
Responsible Bureau: Ministry of Industrial Chemistry
Departments: Chemistry, Mechanics, Automation, Radiation Physics
Contact: Foreign Affairs Office, Beijing Institute of Industrial Chemistry,
Heping St., Andingmenwai, Beijing PRC Tel: 464089

BEIJING INSTITUTE OF INFORMATION ENGINEERING
Responsible Bureau: Ministry of Electronics
Departments: Computer Science, Management Engineering
Contact: Foreign Affairs Office, Beijing Institute of Information Engineering, Deshengmenwai, Beijing PRC   Tel: 449802

BEIJING INSTITUTE OF LIGHT INDUSTRY
Responsible Bureau: Ministry of Light Industry
Departments: Mechanics, Industrial Chemistry, Automation, Management
Chinese Students: 300
Contact: Foreign Affairs Office, Beijing Institute of Light Industry, 3 Fucheng Rd., Haidian District, Beijing PRC Tel: 892197

BEIJING INSTITUTE OF METEOROLOGY
Responsible Bureau: National Bureau of Meteorology
Departments: Meteorology, Atmospheric Physics
Contact: Foreign Affairs Office, Beijing Institute of Meteorology, Haidian District, Beijing PRC Tel: 891571

BEIJING INSTITUTE OF POST AND TELECOMMUNICATIONS*
Responsible Bureau: Ministry of Post and Telecommunications
Departments: Electronic Mail, Radio Technology, Mechanics, Management, Applied Physics
Chinese Students: 3,600
Foreign Students: 40
Foreign Teachers: 3-7
Sister Schools: France—Univ Pierre and Marie Curie; Ecole Nationale Superieure des Telecommunications de Bretagne; Univ of Brest; Inst Nationale des Telecommunications d'Evry; Ecole Nationale Superieure des Telecommunications de Paris
Contact: Foreign Affairs Office, Beijing Institute of Post and Telecommunications, 42 Xueyuan Rd., Haidian District, Beijing PRC Tel: 664549

BEIJING UNIVERSITY OF AGRICULTURAL ENGINEERING
Responsible Bureau: Ministry of Agriculture, Livestock, and Fisheries
Departments: Electric Power, Hydrology and Hydroelectric Construction, Agricultural Equipment, Agricultural Mechanization, Animal Products Processing
Contact: Foreign Affairs Office, Beijing University of Agricultural Engineering, Haidian District, Beijing Special Zone, PRC Tel: 277267

CHINA UNIVERSITY OF GEOSCIENCES
Responsible Bureau: Ministry of Geology
Departments: Geology, Geography, Chemistry, Physics, Meteorology, Biology
Chinese Students: 600
Foreign Students: 0
Foreign Teachers: 3
Accommodations: reasonable; Chinese-style apartments w/ kitchen, balcony, simple furniture
Teacher Salary/Benefits: 600-850Y/mo RMB, no airfare
FAO: "fair"

Teaching Conditions: 8-14 hrs/wk, class size varies, 12-35 students; students "moderately well motivated"
Contact: Foreign Affairs Office, China University of Geosciences, Xueyuan Lu 29, Haidian District, Beijing, 10083 PRC Tel: 202-2244 (FAO x2341)

UNIVERSITY OF NORTHERN INDUSTRY
Responsible Bureau: China National Non-Ferrous Metals Company
Departments: Industry, Architectural Engineering, Economic Management, Foreign Languages, Sociology
Contact: Foreign Affairs Office, University of Northern Industry, Shijingshan District, Beijing PRC Tel: 872812

UNIVERSITY OF SCIENCE AND TECHNOLOGY/BEIJING
Responsible Bureau: Ministry of Industrial Metal Production
Departments: Mining, Industrial Metal Production, High Temperature Studies, Materials, Mechanics, Automation, Physics, Chemistry, Management, Sociology
Accommodations: "poor, 1 small rm, w/ shared bath and cooking facilities, w/ washer, TV, strict midnight curfew, visitor registration, location central to campus, 20-25 mins walk from shops and movies"
Teacher Salary/Benefits: 400Y/mo, 120Y FEC (VIA Volunteer) plus r t airfare, 30kg shipping allowance
FAO: poor, not trustworthy or helpful; never got grain coupons, despite repeated requests," "provided no transportation or other assistance to me when I needed to go to the hospital"; reneged on promises of Chinese tutors; "asked me to forge letters for other teachers who had left"
Teaching Conditions: 14 hrs/wk, plus 2 office hours; good English reading room, but closed to students; no secretaries or photocopying
Contact: Foreign Affairs Office, University of Science and Technology/ Beijing, Haidian District, Beijing PRC Tel: 277283

Fujian Closest of the mainland provinces to Taiwan, Fujian features extraordinary coastal military facilities, particularly near the commercial center at Xiamen. Fujianese is a distinct language, related more closely to native Taiwanese than to Mandarin. In all larger cities, however, fluent Mandarin speakers abound. An important center of foreign trade and ancient home to many of the world's Overseas Chinese, Fujian is wealthy by Chinese standards, particularly in Xiamen and in the capital, Fuzhou. Food is rich and varied, featuring plenty of fresh produce and seafood. Weather is mild most of the year, though broiling in summer. While air transport is convenient, it is expensive, and railways reach only to Fuzhou. Most ground transport in Fujian involves endless hours on creaking buses.

Universities

FUZHOU UNIVERSITY*
Responsible Bureau: Provincial Higher Education Administration
Departments: Geology, Materials and Mining, Mechanical Engineering,

Electrical Mechanics, Industrial Chemistry, Computer Science, Light
Industry, Radio Technology, Agricultural Construction, Mathematics,
Physics, Chemistry, Foreign Languages, Management, Economics, Statistics,
Accounting
Contact: Foreign Affairs Office, Fuzhou University, Gongye Rd., Fuzhou,
Fujian PRC Tel: 53687

OVERSEAS CHINESE UNIVERSITY
Responsible Bureau: State Council, Overseas Chinese Association
Departments: Mechanical Engineering, Electrical Engineering, Computer
Science, Industrial Chemistry, Architecture, Civil Engineering, Chinese,
Foreign Languages, Mathematics, Physics, Biology, Travel and Tourism,
Management, Law, Industrial Arts
Foreign Teachers: 3-5
Teachers: univ privately funded by overseas Chinese benefactor; new
accommodations and some flexible programs
Contact: Foreign Affairs Office, Overseas Chinese University, Chengdong,
Quanzhou, Fujian PR Tel: 4921

XIAMEN UNIVERSITY*
Responsible Bureau: State Education Committee
Departments: Chinese, Journalism, History, Anthropology, Philosophy,
Foreign Languages, Mathematics, Computer Science, Physics, Chemistry,
Timing Equipment, Aquaculture, Biology, Economics, Management,
Statistics, Accounting, Finance, Foreign Trade, Law
Chinese Students: 6,800
Foreign Students: 55-60
Foreign Teachers: 6-10
Sister Schools: relations w/ 12 schools in US, UK, Canada, Japan, Germany,
Australia, Belgium
Teachers and Students: accepts foreign teachers of Western languages/
cultures and technical subjects; has large program in Chinese Language and
Culture for foreign students; facilities include Museum of Anthropology,
Museum of Lu Xun, 1.5 million vol library; school has one of China's
premier depts of Southeast Asian Studies (part of Anthropology)
Contact: Foreign Affairs Office, Xiamen University, Siming S. Rd., Xiamen,
Fujian PRC Tel: 25102

Finance/Economics

XIAMEN INSTITUTE OF ECONOMICS
Responsible Bureau: Provincial Government
Departments: International Economic Management
Contact: Foreign Affairs Office, Xiamen Institute of Economics, Gulang
Island, Xiamen, Fujian PRC Tel: 22094

Normal Schools

FUJIAN NORMAL SCHOOL
Responsible Bureau: Provincial Higher Education Administration
Departments: Education, Political Education, Chinese, History, Library
Science, Geology, Biology, Mathematics, Physics, Chemistry, Physical
Education, Music, Art, Foreign Languages

Contact: Foreign Affairs Office, Fujian Normal School, Cangshan District, Fuzhou, Fujian PRC Tel: 42918

Medical Schools

FUJIAN COLLEGE OF CHINESE MEDICINE
   Responsible Bureau: Provincial Higher Education Administration
   Departments: Medical Practice, Acupuncture, Chinese Pharmacology
   Contact: Foreign Affairs Office, Fujian College of Chinese Medicine, Wusi N. Rd., Fuzhou, Fujian PRC   Tel: 54708

FUJIAN MEDICAL COLLEGE
   Responsible Bureau: Provincial Higher Education Administration
   Departments: Medicine, Oral Medicine, Stomatology, Sanitation and Hygiene, Medical Examination
   Chinese Students: 2,150
   Sister Schools: US—Univ of Minneapolis-St. Paul
   Accommodations: very good; 5 rms w/ kitchen, washer, frig; no curfew; 25 min walk from downtown
   Teacher Salary/Benefits: 1,400Y/mo, 1,100 In FEC (Foreign Expert), + r-t airfare (2 yrs teaching), excursions; 1 cubic meter crate + 1,700Y shipping allowance
   FAO: very good overall
   Teaching Conditions: 12 hrs/wk; good teaching materials, library; school also open to new materials; some secretarial support
   Contact: Foreign Affairs Office, Fujian Medical College, Chatingjiaotong Rd., Fuzhou, Fujian PRC   Tel: 57861

Technical Schools

JIMEI NAVIGATION INSTITUTE
   Responsible Bureau: Ministry of Transportation
   Departments: Aviation and Shipping, Boat Mechanics, Marine Engineering, Electrical Engineering, Basic Studies
   Chinese Students: 1,050
   Foreign Students: 5
   Foreign Teachers: 2-3
   Contact: Foreign Affairs Office, Jimei Navigation Institute, Jimei District, Xiamen, Fujian PRC   Tel. 28155

XIAMEN INSTITUTE OF AQUACULTURE
   Responsible Bureau: Ministry of Agriculture, Livestock, and Fisheries
   Departments: Fishery Mechanics, Aquaculture, Aquacultural Products Processing
   Contact: Foreign Affairs Office, Xiamen Institute of Aquaculture, Jimei District, Xiamen, Fujian PRC   Tel: 28201

Gansu   Dry, dusty Gansu province stretches like a narrow bow between Inner Mongolia and Qinghai, reaching to Xinjiang in the far west and

Sichuan and Shanxi in the east. Originally settled as part of the Silk Road trading route with the Near East, Gansu still displays her origins in the layout of her cities. From Tianshui in the east to Anxi and Dunhuang in the west, all line up along the ancient trade routes, most of which are now accessed by one of China's longest railways. Gansu's desert climate has preserved astonishing art and architecture, from the centuries of Buddhist grottoes at Dunhuang to the guard towers of the Great Wall's far western tip at Jiayuguan to Yellow Lamaseries and Buddhist caves near the capital at Lanzhou. Along with standard Han food, Gansu offers dishes of the Hui and Mongolian nationalities as well as many local specialties made with the honeydew and the white lily bud. Weather is high desert; language quite standard Mandarin outside minority areas.

Universities

GANSU UNIFIED UNIVERSITY
Responsible Bureau: Provincial Education Administration
Departments: Computer Science, Grains and Nutrition, Foreign Language, Finance and Accounting
Contact: Foreign Affairs Office, Gansu Unified University, Lanzhou, Gansu PRC Tel: 21939

GOLD CITY UNIFIED UNIVERSITY
Responsible Bureau: Provincial Education Administration
Departments: Agricultural Construction, Industrial Chemistry, Computer Science, Library Science, English, Accounting, Planning and Statistics
Contact: Foreign Affairs Office, Gold City Unified University, Dongfanghong Square, Lanzhou, Gansu PRC Tel: 27491

LANZHOU UNIVERSITY*
Responsible Bureau: State Education Committee
Departments: Chinese, History, Philosophy, Politics, Library Science, Mathematics, Physics, Chemistry, Power Studies, Earth Studies, Biology, Economics, Law, Foreign Languages
Contact: Foreign Affairs Office, Lanzhou University, Tianshui Rd., Lanzhou, Gansu PRC Tel: 22991

Minorities/Politics and Law

GANSU INSTITUTE OF POLITICS AND LAW
Responsible Bureau: Provincial Justice Administration
Departments: Law
Contact: Foreign Affairs Office, Gansu Institute of Politics and Law, Anning W. Rd., Lanzhou, Gansu PRC Tel: 66843

NORTHWEST MINORITIES INSTITUTE
Responsible Bureau: National Minorities Committee
Departments: Livestock and Veterinary Medicine, Medical Practice, Languages and Literatures, History, Politics, Mathematical and Theoretical Chemistry, Industrial Arts, Trade
Foreign Teachers: 5-7
Contact: Foreign Affairs Office, Northwest Minorities Institute, Xibeixin Village, Lanzhou, Gansu PRC Tel: 24011

Commerce

LANZHOU INSTITUTE OF COMMERCE
Responsible Bureau: Ministry of Commerce
Departments: Commercial Economics, Financial Statistics, Finance
Contact: Foreign Affairs Office, Lanzhou Institute of Commerce,
Duanjiawan, Lanzhou, Gansu PRC Tel: 27901

Normal School

NORTHWEST NORMAL SCHOOL
Responsible Bureau: Provincial Education Administration
Departments: Education, Politics, Telephone Education, Chinese, History,
Geology, Biology, Mathematics, Physics, Computer Science, Physical
Education, Chemistry, Music, Art, Foreign Languages
Contact: Foreign Affairs Office, Northwest Normal School, Shilidian,
Lanzhou, Gansu PRC Tel: 66151

Medical Schools

LANZHOU MEDICAL COLLEGE
Responsible Bureau: Provincial Administration of Sanitation and Hygiene
Departments: Medicine, Pharmacology, Sanitation and Hygiene, Oral
Medicine
Contact: Foreign Affairs Office, Lanzhou Medical College, Donggang W.
Rd., Lanzhou, Gansu PRC Tel: 24311

GANSU COLLEGE OF CHINESE MEDICINE
Responsible Bureau: Provincial Administration of Sanitation and Hygiene
Departments: Acupuncture, Chinese Medicine, Chinese Pharmacology
Contact: Foreign Affairs Office, Gansu College of Chinese Medicine,
Dingxi E. Rd., Lanzhou, Gansu PRC Tel: 27121

Technical Schools

GANSU UNIVERSITY OF TECHNOLOGY
Responsible Bureau: Ministry of Mechanics
Departments: Mechanics, Automation and Control, Natural Products
Architecture, Industrial Management
Chinese Students: 2,500
Contact: Foreign Affairs Office, Gansu University of Technology,
Langongping, Lanzhou, Gansu PRC Tel: 35951

LANZHOU INSTITUTE OF RAILWAYS
Responsible Bureau: Ministry of Railways
Departments: Mechanics, Environmental Engineering, Natural Products
Architecture, Railway Shipping, Automation and Control
Contact: Foreign Affairs Office, Lanzhou Institute of Railways, Anning W.
Rd., Lanzhou, Gansu PRC Tel: 66224

Guangxi   Officially named the Guangxi Zhuang Autonomous Region, Guangxi is home to the Zhuang people, China's largest minority group, numbering just over 12 million. Lush and fertile, the province holds some of China's most fabulous natural wonders, from the stark karst mountains of Guilin to the echoing caverns of the Li River. Resident foreigners tend to congregate in the tourist capital at Guilin, but should not neglect the verdant beauty of Yangshuo or the palm-tree–lined beaches of the capital, Nanning.

Universities

GUANGXI UNIVERSITY*

Responsible Bureau: Regional Education Administration
Departments: Industrial Metals Mining, Industrial Metals Refinement, Electric Power, Mechanical Engineering, Industrial Chemistry, Light Industry, Civil Engineering, Law, Mathematics, Physics, Chemistry, Chinese, Philosophy, Foreign Languages, Economics
Contact: Foreign Affairs Office, Guangxi University, Xixiangtang Rd., Nanning, Guangxi PRC Tel: 23876

YONGJIANG UNIVERSITY

Responsible Bureau: Regional Education Administration
Departments: English, Industrial Management, Applied Microcomputers, Livestock Feed Industry
Foreign Students: 0
Foreign Teachers: 2-4
Accommodations: poor; 3 rms w/ kitchen, washer, TV, tape recorder, no curfew; but no heat or hot water. Campus is in Pu Miao, a tiny village about 45 mins from Nanning; univ provides foreign teacher w/ "weekend" rm in Nanning as well as 3 rms at Pu Miao campus
Teacher Salary/Benefits: 700Y/mo RMB + 400Y vacation bonus
FAO: no FAO; everything arranged through English Dept who were "helpful and solicitous"
Teaching Conditions: 14 hrs/wk, facilities mediocre but "they try their best"; no secretaries or photocopying
Contact: English Dept, Yongjiang University, Pumiao, Nanning, Guangxi PRC

Minorities/Politics & Law

GUANGXI INSTITUTE FOR NATIONALITIES

Responsible Bureau: Regional Minorities Committee
Departments: Politics, History, Chinese, Mathematics, Physics, Chemistry, Foreign Languages, Minority Languages
Chinese Students: 3,000
Foreign Students: 15
Foreign Teachers: 2
Teachers: teach English, Western Culture; opportunities for independent research on minorities
Students: have programs in Chinese, Chinese Culture, "China's Minorities"
Contact: Foreign Affairs Office, Guangxi Institute for Nationalities, Xixiangtang, 530006 Nanning, Guangxi PRC Tel: 34141

Arts/Music

GUANGXI INSTITUTE OF ARTS

Responsible Bureau: Regional Education Administration
Departments: Teaching, Art, Music
Contact: Foreign Affairs Office, Guangxi Institute of Arts, Jiaoyu Rd., Nanning, Guangxi PRC Tel: 24473

Normal Schools

GUANGXI NORMAL INSTITUTE
Responsible Bureau: Regional Education Administration
Departments: Chinese, Political Education, English, Mathematics, Physics, Chemistry, Geology
Contact: Foreign Affairs Office, Guangxi Normal Institute, Mingxiu Rd., Nanning, Guangxi PRC Tel: 20131

GUANGXI NORMAL SCHOOL
Responsible Bureau: Regional Education Administration
Departments: Chinese, Politics, History, Foreign Languages, Education, Mathematics, Physics, Chemistry, Biology, Physical Education
Contact: Foreign Affairs Office, Guangxi Normal School, Wangcheng, Guilin, Guangxi PRC Tel: 2915

Medical Schools

GUANGXI COLLEGE OF CHINESE MEDICINE
Responsible Bureau: Regional Education Administration
Departments: Chinese Medicine, Chinese Pharmacology, Acupuncture
Contact: Foreign Affairs Office, Guangxi College of Chinese Medicine, Mingxiu, Nanning, Guangxi PRC Tel: 27725

GUANGXI MEDICAL COLLEGE
Responsible Bureau: Regional Education Administration
Departments: Medicine, Oral Medicine, Sanitation and Hygiene
Contact: Foreign Affairs Office, Guangxi Medical College, Taoyuan Rd., Nanning, Guangxi PRC Tel: 24512

YOU RIVER INSTITUTE OF MINORITY MEDICINE
Responsible Bureau: Regional Education Administration
Departments: Medicine
Contact: Foreign Affairs Office, You River Institute of Minority Medicine, Baise, Guangxi PRC Tel: 2551

Technical Schools

GUANGXI AGRICULTURAL COLLEGE
Responsible Bureau: Regional Education Administration
Departments: Agricultural Science, Gardening, Crop Protection, Agricultural Mechanics, Agricultural Economics, Livestock and Veterinary Medicine, Fresh Water Aquaculture
Chinese Students: 2,300
Contact: Foreign Affairs Office, Guangxi Agricultural College, Xuzhou Rd., Nanning, Guangxi PRC Tel: 21223

GUANGXI INSTITUTE OF INDUSTRY
Responsible Bureau: Regional Education Administration
Departments: Mechanical Engineering, Civil Engineering, Economics, Chinese, Industrial Worker's Construction, Economic Management

Contact: Foreign Affairs Office, Guangxi Institute of Industry, Liuzhou, Guangxi PRC Tel: 25430

GUILIN INSTITUTE OF ELECTRONIC INDUSTRY
Responsible Bureau: Ministry of Electronics
Departments: Mechanical Production, Equipment Design, Communications Engineering, Surveying Technology, Applied Computer Science, Automation and Control, Production, Finance and Accounting
Contact: Foreign Affairs Office, Guilin Institute of Electronic Industry, Liuhe Rd., Guilin, Guangxi PRC Tel: 3343

GUILIN INSTITUTE OF GEOLOGY
Responsible Bureau: China National Non-Ferrous Metals Company
Departments: Geology, Materials Exploration, Chemical Exploration, Hydroengineering, Surveying, Economic Management
Chinese Students: 1,750
Contact: Foreign Affairs Office, Guilin Institute of Geology, Pingfengshan, Guilin, Guangxi PRC Tel: 2796

Guangdong   Guangdong ranks as China's wealthiest province as well as her most Westernized. Deeply influenced by neighboring Hong Kong, particularly in the border town of Shenzhen, Guangdong displays a bustle and vivacity of capitalist enterprise which, while tame compared with Hong Kong, nevertheless far outstrips China's interior. Foreigners unable to give up Western import goods and dance halls that rock till dawn would do well to stay in Guangdong. "Teachers mean nothing here," writes one respondent. "The businessman is king." Foreigners are less of a rarity in Guangdong than in many other areas, and receive less deference and attention.

Guangzhou (Canton), the capital, hosts the majority of China's foreign trade, and offers many opportunities for moonlighting in business. Shenzhen is a world unto itself (Chinese nationals need special border passes to enter the city), dedicated largely to facilitating trade with Hong Kong. Smaller cities such as Shaoguan and Shantou offer more of a view into traditional Chinese life, but remain wealthier than more northern cities. Some of China's best cooking comes from Guangdong, for with her fertile land and relative wealth, the province produces epicureans alien to the poorer, more barren interior. Guangdong weather is steamy, and her language is Cantonese, not comprehensible to students of Mandarin.

Universities

GUANGZHOU UNIVERSITY
Responsible Bureau: City Committee of Higher Education
Departments: Industrial Workers Construction, Electronics, Computer Science, English, Secretarial Science, Industrial Management, Accounting, Law, Highway Bridge Building, Speakers and Recording
Contact: Foreign Affairs Office, Guangzhou University, Xiaobeixiatang, Guangzhou, Guangdong PRC Tel: 331781

JIAYING UNIVERSITY
   Responsible Bureau: Provincial Bureau of Higher Education
   Departments: Accounting, Economic Management, English, Applied
   Computer Science
   Contact: Foreign Affairs Office, Jiaying University, Mazigang, Mei County,
   Guangdong PRC Tel: 23115

JINAN UNIVERSITY
   Responsible Bureau: State Department, Overseas Chinese Association
   Departments: Medicine, Literature, Theoretical Engineering, Economics,
   Liberal Arts, Journalism, History, Chemistry, Physics, Biology, Computer
   Science, Mathematics
   Chinese Students: 3,540
   Sister Schools: US—California State Univ, Texas Tech Univ, Miami Univ;
   UK—Simon Fraser Univ, Liverpool School of Tropical Medicine
   Teachers and Students: school has strong focus on involving overseas
   Chinese in the PRC educational system; has various programs with sister
   schools
   Contact: Foreign Affairs Office, Jinan University, Shipai, Guangzhou,
   Guangdong PRC Tel: 774511

SHANTOU UNIVERSITY
   Responsible Bureau: Provincial Bureau of Higher Education
   Departments: Economics, Information, Architecture, Computer Science,
   Medical Practice, Chinese, Foreign Languages, History, Law, Mathematics,
   Physics, Chemistry, Biology
   Chinese Students: 1500+
   Foreign Students: 6
   Foreign Teachers: 10
   Accommodations: excellent; 5 rms, w/ kitchen, A/C, TV, washer, fridge, no
   curfew, very central location
   Teacher Salary/Benefits: 300-1,200Y/mo (high-school grad to Foreign
   Expert) plus r-t airfare
   FAO: not very good; trustworthy about written contracts, otherwise
   unhelpful; also, friction between FAO and Foreign Language Dept
   Teaching Conditions: 14 hrs/wk; excellent library, but not open to students;
   campus is beautiful
   Students: all studying Chinese
   Contact: Foreign Affairs Office, Shantou University, Shantou, Guangdong
   PRC Tel. 75541

SHENZHEN UNIVERSITY*
   Responsible Bureau: Provincial Bureau of Higher Education
   Departments: Mechanics, Electronics, Architecture, Chinese, English,
   Mathematics, Physics, Industrial Management, Finance and Accounting,
   Finance, Law, Computer Science
   Chinese Students: 4,000
   Foreign Students: 65
   Foreign Teachers: 10-12
   Teachers: not bad; 1 or 2 rms, w/ shared kitchen and common rm, washer,
   TV, tape recorder, fridge, A/C, phone, plenty of hot water and no need for
   heat; use of car and driver for fee; foreigner compound somewhat isolated

and campus 20-30 mins from downtown by bus, but visitor registration lax
Teacher Salary/Benefits: 1,000-2,000Y/mo RMB, 50% convertible to US$
(FEC not used in Shenzhen) + approx 700Y utilities subsidy, some domestic
travel, 400-700Y travel bonus
Teaching Conditions: fairly good: 8-14 hrs/wk, excellent language lab,
photocoping, and AV facilities (no secretarial help for teachers, but PCs
available for use) "the library is one of the best I have seen," although may
be closed stack for students
FAO: so-so, "the people you love to hate"
Student Tuition/Expenses: 700Y/mo tuition and room; food approx 10Y/
day; foreigners can apply directly to FAO
Learning Conditions: not bad; "learned a lot, wonderful cultural experi-
ence"
Contact: Foreign Affairs Office, Shenzhen University, Nantou District,
Shenzhen, Guangdong PRC Tel: 23356

WUYI UNIVERSITY
Responsible Bureau: Provincial Bureau of Higher Education
Departments: Chinese, English, Radio Technology, Computer Science,
Trade, Industrial Workers Construction
Contact: Foreign Affairs Office, Wuyi University, Jiangmen, Guangdong
PRC Tel: 34312

ZHONGSHAN UNIVERSITY*
Responsible Bureau: Ministry of Education
Departments: Mathematics, Power Studies, Computer Science, Physics,
Electronics, Chemistry, Biology, Geology, Geography, Meteorology,
Chinese, History, Anthropology, Philosophy, Foreign Languages, Library
Science, Economics, Management, Law
Chinese Students: 9,800
Foreign Students: 65-70
Foreign Teachers: 10-15
Sister Schools: many
Teachers: high-powered campus, many "children of elite"; campus has
Museum of Anthropology, several English-language journals
Students: many good programs: Mandarin, Cantonese, business/economics;
some "isolation from everyday life"
Contact: Foreign Affairs Office, Zhongshan University, Xingang Rd.,
Guangzhou, Guangdong PRC Tel: 446300

Minorities/Politics & Law

GUANGDONG INSTITUTE OF MINORITIES
Responsible Bureau: Provincial Bureau of Higher Education
Departments: Politics, Chinese, Mathematics, Economic Mathematics,
Finance
Contact: Foreign Affairs Office, Guangdong Institute of Minorities, Shipai,
Guangzhou, Guangdong PRC Tel: 775150

Arts/Music

Guangzhou Academy of Fine Arts
Responsible Bureau: Provincial Bureau of Higher Education
Departments: Traditional Chinese Painting, Oil Painting, Printmaking,

Industrial Arts, Sculpture, Design, Fine Arts Education
Chinese Students: 360
Foreign Students: 10-30
Students: study Chinese art/music; plan summer program as well as program for degree students
Contact: Foreign Affairs Office, Guangzhou Academy of Fine Arts, 257 Changgangdong Rd., Guangzhou, Guangdong PRC Tel: 449883

SEA STAR MUSIC INSTITUTE
Responsible Bureau: Provincial Bureau of Higher Education
Departments: Voice, Minority Music, Wind and String Instruments, Piano, Composition Theory, Teaching
Contact: Foreign Affairs Office, Sea Star Music Institute, Xianliedongheng Rd., Guangzhou, Guangdong PRC Tel: 775808

Commerce/Finance/Economics

GUANGDONG COMMERCIAL COLLEGE
Responsible Bureau: Provincial Bureau of Higher Education
Departments: Commercial and Industrial Management, Finance and Accounting
Chinese Students: 2,000
Foreign Students: 20-25
Foreign Teachers: 4
Teachers: teach English, business/management
Students: 20-25 long-term foreign students in degree programs in Chinese Business/Management; also short-term spring programs in Chinese Business/ Management approx 50 students: summer program in Chinese Language/ Culture/Business, approx 200 students
Contact: Foreign Affairs Office, Guangdong Commercial College, Chisha, Haizhu District, Guangzhou, Guangdong PRC   Tel: 452110/451301

GUANGZHOU INSTITUTE OF FOREIGN TRADE
Responsible Bureau: Ministry of Foreign Trade
Departments: Foreign Trade Economics, Import and Export, Foreign Industrial Finance and Economics
Contact: Foreign Affairs Office, Guangzhou Institute of Foreign Trade, Northern Suburbs, Guangzhou, Guangdong PRC

Foreign Languages

GUANGZHOU INSTITUTE OF FOREIGN LANGUAGES
Responsible Bureau: State Education Committee
Departments: English, French, German, Spanish, Russian, Japanese, Thai, Indonesian, Vietnamese
Chinese Students: 3,000
Foreign Students: 400+
Foreign Teachers: 5-8
Sister Schools: UK—Murdoch Univ; Australia—Univ of Perth; Germany— Univ of Paderborn
Teachers: teach English, Western Culture
Students: huge complex for foreign students learning Chinese, especially for Chinese gov't scholarship students prior to entering Chinese-language degree programs; students in foreigners-only dorm

Contact: Foreign Affairs Office, Guangzhou Institute of Foreign Languages, Huangpodong, Northern Suburbs, Guangzhou, Guangdong PRC Tel: 662303

Normal Schools

GUANGZHOU TEACHERS COLLEGE
Responsible Bureau: City Education Committee
Departments: Chinese, History, Politics, English, Mathematics, Physics, Chemistry, Biology, Geology
Chinese Students: 2,000
Foreign Students: 0
Foreign Teachers: 4-5
Accommodations: very good; 2 rms, w/ washer, dryer, TV, tape recorder, space heater, fans; cafeteria food cheap and great; very central location; strict visitor registration
FAO: "not bad"
Teaching Conditions: 12-14 hrs/wk; materials and library very good
Contact: Foreign Affairs Office, Guangzhou Teachers College, Guihuagang, Guangzhou, Guangdong PRC Tel: 663805

SOUTH CHINA NORMAL SCHOOL
Responsible Bureau: Provincial Bureau of Higher Education
Departments: Chinese, Foreign Languages, Politics, History, Education, Mathematics, Physics, Chemistry, Distance Education, Biology, Geology, Physical Education, Library Science
Contact: Foreign Affairs Office, South China Normal School, Shipai, Guangzhou, Guangdong PRC   Tel: 777103

Medical Schools

GUANGDONG COLLEGE OF MEDICINE AND PHARMACOLOGY
Responsible Bureau: Provincial Bureau of Higher Education
Departments: Medicine, Sanitation and Hygiene, Pharmacology, Nursing and Care
Chinese Students: 2,000
Foreign Students: 0
Foreign Teachers: 1
Teacher: rather isolated; "not a good place for young people just out of college—it's a rather lonely gig"
Accommodations: very good; 4 rms w/ kitchen, TV, tape recorder, washer, fridge; no curfew
Teacher Salary/Benefits: 750Y/mo RMB
FAO: deal directly with personnel dept and "as no one there speaks English they will neither interfere with nor aid you in any way"
Teaching Conditions: 18 hrs/wk; good students; library short on foreign-language materials
Contact: Foreign Affairs Office, Guangdong College of Medicine and Pharmacology, Baogang St., Guangzhou, Guangdong PRC   Tel: 49735

GUANGZHOU COLLEGE OF MEDICINE
Responsible Bureau: City Education Committee
Departments: Medicine
Contact: Foreign Affairs Office, Guangzhou College of Medicine, Dongfengxi Rd., Guangzhou, Guangdong PRC Tel: 332550

GUANGZHOU COLLEGE OF TRADITIONAL CHINESE MEDICINE
Responsible Bureau: Ministry of Sanitation and Hygiene
Departments: Medical Practice, Acupuncture, Chinese Pharmacology
Chinese Students: 1,700
Foreign Students: 17
Foreign Teachers: 3-5
Sister Schools: US—Univ of Illinois Medical Center at Chicago
Teachers and Students: accepts foreign teachers of English, technical subjects; has program in Chinese Medicine for foreign students
Contact: Foreign Affairs Office, Guangzhou College of Traditional Chinese Medicine, Guoji Rd., Guangzhou, Guangdong PRC   Tel: 661233

ZHANJIANG MEDICAL COLLEGE
Responsible Bureau: Provincial Bureau of Higher Education
Departments: Medicine
Chinese Students: 300
Contact: Foreign Affairs Office, Zhanjiang Medical College, Wenming Rd., Zhanjiang, Guangdong PRC   Tel: 23544

ZHONGSHAN MEDICAL COLLEGE
Responsible Bureau: Ministry of Sanitation and Hygiene
Departments: Medicine, Oral Medicine, Sanitation and Hygiene, Stomatology, Radiation Therapy, Nursing and Care, Nutrition
Chinese Students: 2,500+
Foreign Students: 200+
Foreign Teachers: 8-10
Accommodations: small but nice: kitchens, + excellent cafeteria (students 2/rm in dorms)
Teacher Salary/Benefits: 800Y/mo + o-w airfare
FAO: conservative but pleasant
Teaching Conditions: 14 hrs/wk; school very open to new materials; huge campus—"easy to get lost"
Students: large number of Chinese gov't scholarship medical students; some self-paying acupuncture students
Contact: Foreign Affairs Office, Zhongshan Medical College, Zhongshan #2 Rd., Guangzhou, Guangdong PRC Tel: 778223

Technical Schools

GUANGDONG INSTITUTE OF MECHANICAL ENGINEERING
Responsible Bureau: Provincial Mechanics Administration
Departments: Mechanics, Automation, Computer Science, Management, Foreign Trade
Chinese Students: 1,700
Contact: Foreign Affairs Office, Guangdong Institute of Mechanical Engineering, Wushan St., Guangzhou, Guangdong PRC Tel: 775075

GUANGDONG INSTITUTE OF TECHNOLOGY*
Responsible Bureau: Provincial Bureau of Higher Education
Departments: Mechanics, Materials, Automation, Electrical Equipment, Computer Science, Geology, Environmental Studies, Industrial Chemistry, Agricultural Construction, Management, Foreign Languages
Chinese Students: 2,300

Contact: Foreign Affairs Office, Guangdong Institute of Technology, Dongfengwu Rd., Guangzhou, Guangdong PRC Tel: 776597

SOUTH CHINA AGRICULTURAL UNIVERSITY*
Responsible Bureau: Ministry of Agriculture, Livestock, and Fisheries
Departments: Agricultural Science, Crop Protection, Gardening, Silkworm and Mulberry Cultivation, Livestock and Veterinary Medicine, Agricultural Mechanics, Biology, Agricultural Education, Forestry, Agricultural Economics, Soil Chemistry
Chinese Students: 1,100
Foreign Students: 36
Foreign Teachers: 5-7
Sister Schools: US—Univ of Pennsylvania, UC-Davis, Silsoe College, Riverina-Murray Inst; Japan—Kyushu Univ; Australia—Univ of Sydney, Massey Univ; Germany—Univ of Kasetsart; Philippines—Univ of Philippines
Contact: Foreign Affairs Office, South China Agricultural University, Shipai, Guangzhou, Guangdong PRC Tel: 778136

SOUTH CHINA INSTITUTE OF TECHNOLOGY*
Responsible Bureau: Ministry of Education
Departments: Mechanical Engineering, Architectural Engineering, Ships and Boating, Radio and Telecommunications Technology, Electric Power, Automation, Computer Science, Inorganic Materials, Chemistry, Papermaking, Nutrition, Mathematics, Power Studies, Physics, Engineering Management
Chinese Students: 2,800
Sister Schools: US—Texas Tech Univ, Univ of Pittsburgh, Edinboro Univ of PA, Georgia Inst of Tech, Southern Methodist Univ; UK—City Univ of London; Hong Kong—HK Polytechnique; Germany—Univ of Braunschweig
Teachers and Students: have various exchange programs with sister schools; also accept outside foreign teachers and students; Inst has large library (approx 1 million vols), and in-school publishing house (SCIT Press)
Contact: Foreign Affairs Office, South China Institute of Technology, Shipai, Guangzhou, Guangdong PRC Tel: 777461

Guizhou   Deep in China's steamy south, Guizhou is far off the beaten tourist track. Known best for China's highest waterfall at Huangguoshu near Anshun, the province is also home to a bewildering variety of minorities, from the Miao and Buyi to the Hmong. While not so famous as neighboring Guangxi, Guizhou also offers some fabulous karst mountains and gorgeous jungle scenery. While all schools in Guizhou that accept foreigners are located in the capital at Guiyang or the industrial center at Zunyi, foreign residents have also gained permission to visit rarely accessible minority areas. Weather is warm to hot year-round, food spicy, and language in Han areas strongly influenced by Hunanese.

Universities

GUIZHOU PEOPLE'S UNIVERSITY
Responsible Bureau: Provincial Government
Departments: Secretarial Science, Law, English, Industrial Management
Contact: Foreign Affairs Office, Guizhou People's University, Xiangshi Rd.,
Guiyang, Guizhou PRC Tel: 42234

GUIZHOU UNIVERSITY*
Responsible Bureau: Provincial Education Committee
Departments: Chinese, History, Philosophy, Foreign Languages, Mathematics, Computer Science, Physics
Teachers and Students: accepts foreign teachers of Western languages/
cultures and technical subjects; has large program in Chinese Language/
Culture for foreign students
Contact: Foreign Affairs Office, Guizhou University, Huaxi District,
Guiyang, Guizhou PRC Tel: 2219

Minorities/Law

GUIZHOU MINORITIES INSTITUTE
Responsible Bureau: Provincial Education Committee
Departments: Politics, Mathematics, History, Physics, Chinese, Industrial
Arts
Contact: Foreign Affairs Office, Guizhou Minorities Institute, Huaxi
District, Guiyang, Guizhou PRC Tel: 2498

Normal Schools

GUIYANG NORMAL SCHOOL
Responsible Bureau: Provincial Education Committee
Departments: Chinese, Political Education, History, Foreign Languages,
Education, Mathematics, Physics, Chemistry, Biology, Physical Education,
Arts, Geology
Contact: Foreign Affairs Office, Guiyang Normal School, Waihuan E. Rd.,
Guiyang, Guizhou PRC Tel: 25912

Medical Schools

GUIYANG COLLEGE OF CHINESE MEDICINE
Responsible Bureau: Provincial Education Committee
Departments: Chinese Medicine, Chinese Pharmacology
Contact: Foreign Affairs Office, Guiyang College of Chinese Medicine,
Dong Rd., Guiyang, Guizhou PRC Tel: 22633

GUIYANG COLLEGE OF MEDICINE
Responsible Bureau: Provincial Committee of Higher Education
Departments: Medicine, Pharmacology, Sanitation and Hygiene
Contact: Foreign Affairs Office, Guiyang College of Medicine, Beijing Rd.,
Guiyang, Guizhou PRC Tel: 23948

ZUNYI COLLEGE OF MEDICINE
Responsible Bureau: Provincial Education Committee
Departments: Medicine, Oral Medicine
Contact: Foreign Affairs Office, Zunyi College of Medicine, Waihuan Rd.,

Zunyi, Guizhou PRC Tel: 3191

Technical Schools

GUIZHOU INSTITUTE OF TECHNOLOGY
Responsible Bureau: Provincial Education Committee
Departments: Geology, Mining, Industrial Metals, Mechanics, Electrical
Mechanics, Industrial Chemistry, Natural Products Architecture
Chinese Students: 3,200
Contact: Foreign Affairs Office, Guizhou Institute of Technology,
Caijiaguan, Guiyang, Guizhou PRC Tel: 42486

Hainan Island   Only recently separated as a province from Guangdong,
Hainan remains far poorer than her northern neighbor. Her miles of beaches,
fertile landmass, rich mineral deposits, wealth of minority peoples, and
strategic importance, however, all promise a stellar future. Haikou, China's
southernmost city and the gateway to the South China Sea, is the island's
economic and industrial center. Weather is tropical and language a variant
of Cantonese.

HAINAN UNIVERSITY
Responsible Bureau: Provincial Bureau of Higher Education
Departments: Electronics, Agricultural Construction, Law, Finance and
Accounting, Chinese, Mathematics, Chemistry, Agricultural Science,
Physical Education, Political History, English, Physics, Biology, Medicine,
Veterinary Medicine
Contact: Foreign Affairs Office, Hainan University, Haikou, Hainan, PRC
Tel: 23926

Hebei   Breadbasket of China, Hebei produces some of the finest wheat
and corn in the country. The capital at Shijiazhuang houses several important
agricultural research stations as well as a number of major schools and
industries. Zhangjiakou on the Great Wall is home of some of the earliest
archaeological finds in China, including the site of "Peking Man." Chengde
(Jehol) in northern Hebei was the summer hunting lodge of the Qing
Emperors, who had replicas of the most famous temples and towers of all
China built in the Chengde hills for their amusement. Beidaihe on the coast
is the summer resort of today's leaders, and many Chinese tourists to
Beidaihe's beaches amuse themselves guessing which villa houses Deng
Xiao-ping. Weather is hot in summer, cold in winter, and dry. Food is hearty,
grain-based fare, featuring plenty of *man-tou* (steamed bread) and noodles.
Language is remarkably standard Mandarin.

Universities

HANDAN UNIVERSITY
Responsible Bureau: City Government
Departments: Secretarial Science, Management, Art, Mechanics, Computer Science, Agricultural Construction
Contact: Foreign Affairs Office, Handan University, Zhuhe Rd., Handan, Hebei PRC Tel: 22892

HEIBEI UNIVERSITY
Responsible Bureau: Provincial Education Committee
Departments: Education, Chinese, History, Library Science, Philosophy, Foreign Languages, Mathematics, Physics, Chemistry, Biology, Economics, Law
Chinese Students: 8,300
Foreign Students: 10-15
Foreign Teachers: 7-10
Sister Schools: US—CAEE
Teachers: can teach English, Western Culture, technical subjects
Students: have special program in Chinese Language and Culture
Contact: Foreign Affairs Office, Hebei University, Hezuo Rd., Baoding, Hebei PRC Tel: 2928

SHIJIAZHUANG UNIVERSITY
Responsible Bureau: Provincial Education Committee
Departments: Computer Science, Agricultural Construction, Mechanics
Contact: Foreign Affairs Office, Shijiazhuang University, Xinhuaxi Rd., Shijiazhuang, Hebei PRC Tel: 31869

TANGSHAN UNIVERSITY
Responsible Bureau: City Government
Departments: Mechanics, Chemical Engineering, Agricultural Construction, Chinese, Economic Policy, Physics, Foreign Languages
Contact: Foreign Affairs Office, Tangshan University, Jianshe Rd., Tangshan, Hebei PRC Tel: 26209

ZHANGJIAKOU UNIVERSITY
Responsible Bureau: City Government
Departments: Agricultural Science, English, Economic Policy
Contact: Foreign Affairs Office, Zhangjiakou University, Xihuozi St., Zhangjiakou, Hebei PRC Tel: 3940

Finance/Economics

HEBEI INSTITUTE OF FINANCE AND ECONOMICS
Responsible Bureau: Provincial Education Committee
Departments: Economic Policy, Finance, Planning, Statistics, Management
Foreign Teachers: 2
Accommodations: pretty good; 2 rms + bath, w/ TV, washer, fridge, A/C, no kitchen, no curfew; centrally located for campus, 20 min bike to downtown; special cook for foreign teachers
Teacher Salary/Benefits: 800Y/mo, 70% in FEC + o-w airfare, excursions, reimbursement for health expenses; some domestic travel
FAO: not very helpful, moderately trustworthy—"often needed reminding,

never took initiative"
Teaching Conditions: 14 hrs/wk; good ditto machine but no secretaries or
photocopies; library poor, not open to students and only unpredictably to
teachers
Contact: Foreign Affairs Office, Hebei Institute of Finance and Economics,
Hongqi Ave., Shijiazhuang, Hebei PRC Tel: 32618

Normal Schools

HEBEI NORMAL INSTITUTE
Responsible Bureau: Provincial Education Committee
Departments: Political Education, Chinese, History, Mathematics, Physics,
Chemistry, Arts and Industries, Foreign Languages
Contact: Foreign Affairs Office, Hebei Normal Institute, Hongqi Ave.,
Shijiazhuang, Hebei PRC Tel: 34262

HEBEI TEACHERS UNIVERSITY
Responsible Bureau: Provincial Education Commission
Departments: Political Education, Chinese Language and Literature,
Geology, Education, Physics, Chemistry, Biology, Physical Education,
Mathematics, Music, Art, Foreign Languages, Literature, History, Population
Research, A-V Teaching Skills
Chinese Students: 5,200
Foreign Students: 20
Foreign Teachers: 3-4
Sister Schools: US—Univ of Northern Iowa, College of Staten Island (NY),
City Univ of NY, Drake Univ (Iowa); Simpson College (Iowa); UK—York
Univ; Australia—Univ of New South Wales
Teachers: teach English, Literature
Students: study in Chinese Language and Culture program (classes in
Chinese Language/Literature, Landscape Painting, Folk Music, Martial Arts)
Contact: Foreign Affairs Office, Hebei Teachers University, Yuhuazhong
Rd., Shijiazhuang, Hebei PRC Tel: 49941

Medical Schools

CHENGDE INSTITUTE OF MEDICINE
Responsible Bureau: Provincial Education Committee
Departments: Medicine, Chinese Medicine, Nursing and Care
Contact: Foreign Affairs Office, Chengde Institute of Medicine, Cuiqiao
Rd., Chengde, Hebei PRC Tel: 5269

HEBEI INSTITUTE OF CHINESE MEDICINE
Responsible Bureau: Provincial Administration of Sanitation and Hygiene
Departments: Chinese Medicine
Contact: Foreign Affairs Office, Hebei Institute of Chinese Medicine,
Xinshinan Rd. Shijiazhuang, Hebei PRC Tel: 31500

HEBEI INSTITUTE OF MEDICINE
Responsible Bureau: Provincial Education Committee
Departments: Medicine, Sanitation and Hygiene, Oral Medicine,
Pharmacology
Contact: Foreign Affairs Office, Hebei Institute of Medicine, Chang'an Rd.,
Shijiazhuang, Hebei PRC Tel: 48744

ZHANGJIAKOU INSTITUTE OF MEDICINE
Responsible Bureau: Provincial Education Committee
Departments: Medicine, Chinese Medicine, Medical Testing and Examination
Contact: Foreign Affairs Office, Zhangjiakou Institute of Medicine, Changqing Rd., Zhangjiakou, Hebei PRC Tel: 3571

Technical Schools

HEBEI INSTITUTE OF ARCHITECTURAL ENGINEERING
Responsible Bureau: Provincial Education Committee
Departments: Architectural Engineering
Contact: Foreign Affairs Office, Hebei Institute of Architectural Engineering, Jianguo Rd., Zhangjiakou, Hebei PRC Tel: 2953

HEBEI INSTITUTE OF CHEMICAL ENGINEERING
Responsible Bureau: Provincial Education Committee
Departments: Chemical Engineering, Environmental Studies, Mechanics, Textiles, Light Industry
Contact: Foreign Affairs Office, Hebei Institute of Chemical Engineering, Yuhua Rd,, Shijiazhuang, Hebei PRC Tel. 47916

HEBEI INSTITUTE OF COAL MINING ARCHITECTURE AND ENGINEERING
Responsible Bureau: Ministry of Coal Mining
Departments: Geology, Mining, Mechanics, Electrical Equipment, Natural Products Architecture and Engineering
Contact: Foreign Affairs Office, Hebei Institute of Coal Mining Architecture and Engineering, Guangming Rd., Handan, Hebei PRC Tel: 25034

HEBEI INSTITUTE OF ENGINEERING
Responsible Bureau: Provincial Education Committee
Departments: Automation, Mechanics, Chemistry, Agricultural Construction, Industrial Management, Computer Science
Contact: Foreign Affairs Office, Hebei Institute of Engineering, Hongqiao District, Tianjin, Hebei PRC Tel: 67211

HEBEI INSTITUTE OF GEOLOGY
Responsible Bureau: Ministry of Geology and Mining
Departments: Geology, Water Engineering, Materials and Resources, Economic Management
Contact: Foreign Affairs Office, Hebei Institute of Geology, Yihua District, Zhangjiakou, Hebei PRC Tel: 2649

HEBEI INSTITUTE OF MECHANICAL AND ELECTRICAL ENGINEERING
Responsible Bureau: Provincial Education Committee
Departments: Mechanics, Automation, Management
Contact: Foreign Affairs Office, Hebei Institute of Mechanical and Electrical Engineering, Xinhuaxi Rd., Shijiazhuang, Hebei PRC Tel: 23853

NORTH CHINA INSTITUTE OF HYDROLOGY AND HYDROELECTRICITY
Responsible Bureau: Ministry of Hydroelectricity
Departments: Hydrology, Geology, Power Production, Mechanical Engineering
Chinese Students: 1,950

Sister School: UK—Univ of Warwick
Contact: Foreign Affairs Office, North China Institute of Hydrology and Hydroelectricity, Zhonghua Rd., Handan, Hebei PRC Tel: 4860

NORTH CHINA INSTITUTE OF ELECTRONICS
Responsible Bureau: Ministry of Water and Electricity
Departments: Power Production, Electric Power, Electronics, Mechanics
Contact: Foreign Affairs Office, North China Institute of Electronics, Qingnian Rd., Baoding, Hebei PRC Tel: 4951

SHIJIAZHUANG RAILROAD INSTITUTE
Responsible Bureau: Ministry of Railways
Departments: Railway Construction, Mechanical Engineering, Railroad Technology, Architecture
Contact: Foreign Affairs Office, Shijiazhuang Railroad Institute, Beihuandong Rd., Shijiazhuang, Hebei PRC Tel: 47223

TANGSHAN INSTITUTE OF ENGINEERING TECHNOLOGY
Responsible Bureau: Provincial Education Committee
Departments: Mining and Materials, Industrial Metals Production, Mechanics, Automation, Industrial Chemistry, Agricultural Construction, Industrial Management
Contact: Foreign Affairs Office, Tangshan Institute of Engineering Technology, Xinhuadong District, Tangshan, Hebei PRC Tel: 23841

Heilongjiang   China's northernmost province and home to the annual Ice Festival, Heilongjiang borders with Inner Mongolia, Siberia, and Jilin. Heavily influenced in architecture and culture by the Soviet Union, the province has a more European feel than most of China, with solid, granite-faced cities nestled in deep, virgin forests. Weather is a serious consideration; the province receives plentiful coal, so central heating is generous. But outdoors winter temperatures regularly drop to -50°F without the windchill factor. Summers are mild, and spring and fall cool. Heilongjiang cuisine is very hearty by Chinese standards, featuring large portions of meat and many potato dishes, as well as exotica of the northern forests, from bear's paw to pheasant. The capital, Harbin, is a major industrial and transportation center, and also the most important center for Soviet Studies in the PRC. Daqing houses China's premier oil fields, while Qiqiha'er and Mudanjiang offer important border region and minority studies. The border with Siberia is heavily patrolled, but foreign residents have gained access for camping and hiking to backcountry trails normally sealed off to foreigners. Language is fairly standard Mandarin.

Universities

HARBIN UNIVERSITY OF SCIENCE AND TECHNOLOGY*
Responsible Bureau: Ministry of Mechanics
Departments: Mechanics, Electronics, Technical Physics, Management, Japanese

Contact: Foreign Affairs Office, Harbin University of Science and
Technology, Xuefu Rd., Harbin, Heilongjiang PRC Tel: 61168

HARBIN UNIVERSITY OF TECHNOLOGY
   Responsible Bureau: Aerospace Ministry
   Departments: Precision Equipment Engineering, Power Production,
   Computer Science, Control, Industrial Workers Construction, Radio
   Technology, Electrical Equipment, Chemistry, Mechanics, Metallurgy,
   Management, Physics, Mathematics, Power Engineering
   Contact: Foreign Affairs Office, Harbin University of Technology, Xidazhi
   St., Harbin, Heilongjiang PRC Tel: 33051

HEILONGJIANG UNIVERSITY
   Responsible Bureau: Provincial Education Committee
   Departments: Chinese, History, Philosophy, Foreign Languages,
   Mathematics, Physics, Chemistry, Computer Science, Library Investigation,
   Economics, Law
   Chinese Students: 4,300
   Foreign Students: 20-25
   Foreign Teachers: 5-8
   Accommodations: pretty good; 1-1/2 rms w/ kitchen, TV, tape recorder,
   fridge, plenty of heat, bus 2x/wk to downtown (else 1 hr on public bus)
   Teacher Salary/Benefits: benefits include r-t airfare, several excursions
   FAO: "horrible," get things in writing; most personnel speak only Japanese
   Teaching Conditions: 14 hrs/wk; excellent language lab, great library but
   students have no access; also tendency to "isolate" foreign teachers from
   meetings and "the life of the department"—"it pays to fight for things around
   here"
   Students: have program in Chinese Language/Culture
   Contact: Foreign Affairs Office, Heilongjiang University, 24 Xuefu Rd.,
   Harbin, Heilongjiang PRC Tel: 64259

JIAMUSI UNIVERSITY
   Responsible Bureau: City Government
   Departments: Mechanical Arts, Chinese, Secretarial Arts, Russian
   Chinese Students: 2,150
   Foreign Students: 0
   Foreign Teachers: 1-2
   Sister School: US—Florida College
   Teachers: can teach English, technical subjects
   Contact: Foreign Affairs Office, Jiamusi University, Sifeng Rd., Jiamusi,
   Heilongjiang PRC Tel: 24024

JIXI UNIVERSITY
   Responsible Bureau: City Government
   Departments: Mechanical Electronics, Chinese, Computer Science,
   Industrial Management
   Contact: Foreign Affairs Office, Jixi University, Jiguan District, Jixi,
   Heilongjiang PRC

MUDANJIANG UNIVERSITY
   Responsible Bureau: City Government

Departments: Secretarial Science, Industrial Management, Commercial Management, Industrial Chemistry, Dyes, Industrial Workers Construction
Contact: Foreign Affairs Office, Mudanjiang University, Beishan, Mudanjiang, Heilongjiang PRC Tel: 2170

UNIVERSITY OF HARBIN
Responsible Bureau: City Government
Departments: Industrial Worker's Construction, Nutrition, Industrial Management, Chinese, Law, Packaging, Fashion
Contact: Foreign Affairs Office, University of Harbin, Daowai District, Harbin, Heilongjiang PRC Tel: 87132

Finance/Commerce/Economics

HEILONGJIANG INSTITUTE OF COMMERCE
Responsible Bureau: Ministry of Commerce
Departments: Oil Storage, Electronics, Mechanics, Nutrition, Commercial Goods Management, Chinese Pharmacological Production, Commercial Economics
Contact: Foreign Affairs Office, Heilongjiang Institute of Commerce, Tongda St., Harbin, Heilongjiang PRC Tel: 45571

Normal Schools

HARBIN NORMAL SCHOOL
Responsible Bureau: Provincial Education Committee
Departments: Education, Politics, Chinese, History, Geology, Biology, Mathematics, Physics, Chemistry, Physical Education, Music, Art, Foreign Languages
Contact: Foreign Affairs Office, Harbin Normal School, Hexing Rd., Harbin, Heilongjiang PRC Tel: 63737

MUDANJIANG NORMAL SCHOOL
Responsible Bureau: Provincial Education Committee
Departments: Politics, Chinese, Biology, Mathematics, Physics, Physical Education, English
Contact: Foreign Affairs Office, Mudanjiang Normal School, Dongjingchengzhen, Ning'an County, Heilongjiang PRC

QIQIHA'ER NORMAL SCHOOL
Responsible Bureau: Provincial Education Committee
Departments: Pre-education Training, Political Education, Chinese, History, Geology, Biology, Mathematics, Physics, Chemistry, Physical Education, Music, Foreign Languages
Contact: Foreign Affairs Office, Qiqiha'er Normal School, Xihongqiao, Qiqiha'er, Heilongjiang PR Tel: 25286

Medical Schools

HARBIN MEDICAL COLLEGE
Responsible Bureau: Provincial Education Committee
Departments: Medicine, Oral Medicine, Sanitation and Hygiene
Contact: Foreign Affairs Office, Harbin Medical College, Nangang District, Harbin, Heilongjiang PRC Tel: 62911

HEILONGJIANG COLLEGE OF TRADITIONAL CHINESE MEDICINE

Responsible Bureau: Provincial Education Committee
Departments: Acupuncture, Chinese Medicine, Chinese Pharmacology
Contact: Foreign Affairs Office, Heilongjiang College of Traditional
Chinese Medicine, Huhe Rd., Harbin, Heilongjiang PRC Tel: 55665

JIAMUSI COLLEGE OF MEDICINE
Responsible Bureau: Provincial Education Committee
Departments: Medicine, Oral Medicine, Pharmacology
Contact: Foreign Affairs Office, Jiamusi College of Medicine, Dexiang St.,
Jiamusi, Heilongjiang PRC Tel: 21821

Technical Schools

DAQING PETROLEUM INSTITUTE*
Responsible Bureau: Ministry of Petroleum
Departments: Oil Exploration, Oil Development, Oil Refinement, Oil
Mechanics, Computers and Control, Industrial Management
Contact: Foreign Affairs Office, Daqing Petroleum Institute, Anda,
Heilongjiang PRC Tel: 31133

HARBIN INSTITUTE OF ARCHITECTURAL ENGINEERING
Responsible Bureau: City Ministry of Architecture and Environmental
Protection
Departments: Architecture, Urban Planning, Architectural Materials,
Mechanical and Electrical Management Engineering
Contact: Foreign Affairs Office, Harbin Institute of Architectural Engineer-
ing, Xidazhi St., Harbin, Heilongjiang PRC Tel: 34942

HARBIN INSTITUTE OF ELECTRICAL ENGINEERING
Responsible Bureau: Ministry of Mechanics
Departments: Electrical Mechanics, Control, Electrical Engineering
Materials, Mechanics, Management, Political Education
Chinese Students: 1,500
Sister School: Japan—Chiba Univ
Contact: Foreign Affairs Office, Harbin Institute of Electrical Engineering,
Daqing St., Harbin, Heilongjiang PRC Tel: 54913

HARBIN INSTITUTE OF SHIP AND BOAT ENGINEERING*
Responsible Bureau: China General Ship and Boat Company
Departments: Ships and Boats, Ship Engineering, Power Production,
Automation and Control, Sonar, Mechanics, Electronics, Management,
Political Education
Chinese Students: 2,700
Sister Schools: US—Southern Louisiana Univ; Japan—Nagasaki Inst of
Applied Sciences; Germany—Hamburg Univ
Contact: Foreign Affairs Office, Harbin Institute of Ship and Boat
Engineering, Wenmiao St., 11/F, Nangang District, Harbin, Heilongjiang
PRC Tel: 34615

HEILONGJIANG INSTITUTE OF MINING
Responsible Bureau: Ministry of Coal Mining
Departments: Materials and Mining Engineering, Electrical Equipment and
Resource Choice, Mechanical Engineering, Architectural Engineering

Chinese Students: 2,000
Foreign Students: 0 long term; many on short-term programs through the Foreign Trade Department
Foreign Teachers: 7-8
Accommodations: not bad; 2 rms w/ bath, kitchen, TV, tape recorder, phone, plenty of hot water, occasional use of car and driver; dorm central to campus, 30 min walk from downtown
Teacher Salary/Benefits: 500-800Y/mo, 50% convertible to FEC, + r-t int'l airfare
FAO: respondents provided no comments
Teaching Conditions: good; close cooperation between Chinese, foreign staff; school invites Russian teachers from Komsomolsk-on-Amur Polytechnical Institute in USSR as well as English teachers, which provides interesting opportunities for cultural exchange; no photocopying or secretarial assistance; library poor
Contact: Foreign Affairs Office, Heilongjiang Institute of Mining, Jiguan District, Jixi, Heilongjiang PRC Tel: 2875

JIAMUSI INSTITUTE OF INDUSTRY

Responsible Bureau: Provincial Economic Committee
Departments: Mechanics, Power Production Mechanics, Agricultural Mechanics, Computer Science, Industrial Management, Mechanical Electronics
Contact: Foreign Affairs Office, Jiamusi Institute of Industry, Xinangang, Jiamusi, Heilongjiang PRC Tel: 21751

NORTHEAST INSTITUTE OF AGRICULTURE

Responsible Bureau: Provincial Administration of Agriculture, Livestock, and Fisheries
Departments: Agricultural Science, Gardening, Agricultural Industry, Livestock and Veterinary Medicine, Agricultural Economics
Contact: Foreign Affairs Office, Northeast Institute of Agriculture, Gongbin Rd., Harbin, Heilongjiang, PRC Tel: 51115

NORTHEAST INSTITUTE OF HEAVY MECHANICS

Responsible Bureau: Ministry of Mechanics
Departments: Industrial Metals Mechanics, Mechanical Engineering, Automation and Control, Management, Political Education
Contact: Foreign Affairs Office, Northeast Institute of Heavy Mechanics, Fula'erji, Qiqiha'er, Heilongjiang PRC Tel: 83984

QIQIHA'ER INSTITUTE OF LIGHT INDUSTRY

Responsible Bureau: Provincial Economic Committee
Departments: Light Industry, Chemistry, Automation, Mechanics, Management Engineering
Contact: Foreign Affairs Office, Qiqiha'er Institute of Light Industry, Wenhua St., Qiqiha'er, Heilongjiang PRC Tel: 72316

Henan   An important center of ancient Chinese culture, dry, dusty Henan houses some of China's most important archaelogical treasures, from the Buddhist grottoes at Longmen near Luoyang to Shang Dynasty ruins in the capital at Zhengzhou. China's early Jewish community was also centered in Henan, particularly in Kaifeng, whose people no longer adhere to Judaism but eschew pork because "it is our tradition." Language is fairly standard Mandarin and food is heavy by Chinese standards, and includes many wheat products. Henan weather features four distinct seasons, but, away from the Yellow River valley and the rich agricultural lands near Zhengzhou, is dusty and windy year-round.

Universities

HENAN UNIVERSITY*
Responsible Bureau: Provincial Higher Education Committee
Departments: Chinese, Political Education, History, Education, Mathematics, Physics, Chemistry, Geology, Physical Education, Art, Computer Science, Law, Foreign Languages
Chinese Students: 8,000
Foreign Students: 19
Foreign Teachers: 3
Sister School: US exchange program with Lee College, Cleveland, TN
Comment: we received a letter which contained facts asked for in our survey but which read as though it had been copied by a non-native speaker. Therefore, we have not included some of the more dubious information.
Accommodations: 2 rms, hot water in the morning only, kitchen
Contact: Foreign Affairs Office, Henan University, Minglun St., Kaifeng, Henan PRC Tel: 22461

KAIFENG UNIVERSITY
Responsible Bureau: City Government
Departments: Politics, Industrial Management, Finance and Accounting, Chinese, Geology, Secretarial Science, Mechanics, Computer Software
Contact: Foreign Affairs Office, Kaifeng University, Xiangyang Rd., Kaifeng, Henan PRC Tel: 32905

LUOYANG UNIVERSITY
Responsible Bureau: City Government
Departments: Mechanics, Computer Science, Management, Industrial Workers Construction, Finance and Accounting, Foreign Languages, Chinese, Archaeology
Contact: Foreign Affairs Office, Luoyang University, Tanggong W. Rd., Luoyang, Henan PRC Tel: 36339

PINGYUAN UNIVERSITY
Responsible Bureau: City Government
Departments: Applied Micromechanics, Secretarial Science, Economics, Industrial Management, Physical Education, Statistics, Cotton Textiles
Contact: Foreign Affairs Office, Pingyuan University, Luotuowan, Xinxiang, Henan PRC Tel: 53321

ZHENGZHOU UNIVERSITY*
Responsible Bureau: Provincial Education Committee

Departments: Mathematics, Computer Science, Physics, Chemistry, Electronics, Chinese, Journalism, Foreign Languages, Philosophy, Politics, Law, Economics, History, Library Science
Contact: Foreign Affairs Office, Zhengzhou University, Daxue Rd., Zhengzhou, Henan PRC Tel: 46455

Finance/Economics

HENAN INSTITUTE OF ECONOMICS AND FINANCE
Responsible Bureau: Provincial Education Committee
Departments: Economics, Statistics, Trade, Economic Policy and Finance, Secretarial Science
Contact: Foreign Affairs Office, Henan Institute of Economics and Finance, Nongye Rd., Zhengzhou, Henan PRC Tel: 31968

Normal Schools

HENAN NORMAL SCHOOL
Responsible Bureau: Provincial Higher Education Committee
Departments: Mathematics, Physics, Chemistry, Biology, Political Education, Physical Education, Chinese, Education, Foreign Languages
Contact: Foreign Affairs Office, Henan Normal School, Muye Village, Xinxiang, Henan PRC Tel: 54813

Medical Schools

HENAN COLLEGE OF CHINESE MEDICINE
Responsible Bureau: Provincial Higher Education Committee
Departments: Chinese Medicine, Chinese Pharmacology, Acupuncture
Contact: Foreign Affairs Office, Henan College of Chinese Medicine, Jinshui Rd., Zhengzhou, Henan PRC Tel: 25090

HENAN COLLEGE OF MEDICINE
Responsible Bureau: Provincial Education Committee
Departments: Medicine, Sanitation and Hygiene, Oral Medicine, Pediatrics
Contact: Foreign Affairs Office, Henan College of Medicine, Daxue Rd., Zhengzhou, Henan PRC Tel: 26473

Technical Schools

LUOYANG INSTITUTE OF INDUSTRY
Responsible Bureau: Ministry of Mechanics
Departments: Mechanics, Agricultural Equipment, Electrical Equipment Automation, Management, Sociology
Contact: Foreign Affairs Office, Luoyang Institute of Industry, Xiyuan Rd., Luoyang, Henan PRC Tel: 22957

ZHENGZHOU INSTITUTE OF AVIATION INDUSTRY AND MANAGEMENT
Responsible Bureau: Ministry of Aviation
Departments: Financial Management, Planning Management, Consumer Goods Management, Personal File Management
Contact: Foreign Affairs Office, Zhengzhou Institute of Aviation Industry and Management, Hanghai Rd., Zhengzhou, Henan PRC Tel: 25862

ZHENGZHOU INSTITUTE OF LIGHT INDUSTRY
Responsible Bureau: Ministry of Light Industry
Departments: Control Engineering, Nutritional Engineering, Industrial

Chemistry, Mechanics, Finance and Accounting, Industrial Management
Chinese Students: 2,300
Sister Schools: US—Univ of Kansas, Univ of Pittsburgh
Contact: Foreign Affairs Office, Zhengzhou Institute of Light Industry, Wenhua Rd., Zhengzhou, Henan PRC Tel: 32551

ZHENGZHOU INSTITUTE OF TECHNOLOGY
Responsible Bureau: Ministry of Industrial Chemistry
Departments: Mechanical Engineering, Industrial Chemistry, Natural Products Engineering, Mechanical Electronics Engineering, Hydrology, Economic Management
Chinese Students: 2,850
Sister Schools: US—Univ of Oakland, Univ of Delaware; UK—Worcester Polytechnic; Japan—Northeast Univ
Contact: Foreign Affairs Office, Zhengzhou Institute of Technology, 52 Wenhua Rd., Zhengzhou, Henan PRC Tel: 32654

Hubei   China's industrial heartland, Hubei province produces much of the nation's steel and houses most of her heavy industry. The capital, Wuhan, is actually three closely interlinked cities—Wuchang, Hanyang, and Hankou. A key transportation center, Wuhan hosts excellent flight, water, and rail connections to most of China's major cities. As one respondent wrote, "it's hot as hell here in summer, and freezing in winter, but at least it's easy to escape." Where the Chang Jiang (Yangtze) flows through Hubei it has cut the spectacular "Three Gorges," beloved of Chinese poets and painters, and many river valley towns, such as tiny Yichang, back onto cliffs so sheer the towns are accessible only by water. Hubei food is hearty, her weather extreme (and no heating allowed in Wuhan and other south-of-the-Chiang-Jiang towns), and her language heavily accented Mandarin.

Universities

HUBEI UNIVERSITY
Responsible Bureau: Provincial Education Committee
Departments: Political Education, Education Management, Chinese, History, Geology, Physics, Biology, Mathematics, Chemistry, Physical Education, English, Economic Management
Contact: Foreign Affairs Office, Hubei University, Wuchang, Baoji'an, Wuhan, Hubei PRC Tel: 74753

JIANGHAN UNIVERSITY
Responsible Bureau: City Education Committee
Departments: Economic Management, Political Law, Accounting and Statistics, Chinese and Secretarial Science, Foreign Languages, Mechanical Electronics, Urban Planning and Environmental Protection, Mathematical Statistics, Physical Education, Industrial Arts, Agricultural Science
Contact: Foreign Affairs Office, Jianghan University, Hankou, Zhaojiatiao,

Wuhan, Hubei PRC Tel: 21142

WUHAN UNIVERSITY*
Responsible Bureau: Ministry of Education
Departments: Chinese, Journalism, History, Philosophy, Politics, Economics, Economic Management, Law, Library Science, Intelligence Gathering, Foreign Languages, Mathematics, Computer Science, Physics, Chemistry, Environmental Science, Biology, Water Resource Exploration, Atmospheric Physics, Epidemiology
Foreign Students: approx 250
Sister Schools: many
Accommodations: excellent; 4 students each in 2br suites w/ central living space, own bathroom, no cooking facilities but hotplates OK, also cafeteria; "the food and service are both great if you treat the staff well, but bad if you are rude"; also good private restaurants on campus; dorms central to campus, 20 min bus ride from downtown
FAO: "very helpful, no obstructive *'ni shi shui'* attitude"
Learning Conditions: excellent Chinese classes, w/ int'l student population (many Chinese gov't scholarship students and European students); classes in Law, Economics, etc. open to foreigners who speak Chinese
Contact: Foreign Affairs Office, Wuhan University, Wuchang, Luojiashan, Wuhan, Hubei PRC Tel: 812712

Minorities/Politics & Law

SOUTH CENTRAL INSTITUTE OF MINORITIES
Responsible Bureau: National Minorities Committee
Departments: Politics, Chinese, Mathematics, Physics, Chemistry, Foreign Languages, Economic Management
Contact: Foreign Affairs Office, South Central Institute of Minorities, Wuchang, Minyuan Rd., Wuhan, Hubei PRC Tel: 70426

SOUTH CENTRAL INSTITUTE OF POLITICS AND LAW
Responsible Bureau: Ministry of Justice
Departments: Law, Economic Law
Chinese Students: 3,500
Foreign Students: 0
Foreign Teachers: 2
Sister Schools: Australia—relations with Sydney University
Teachers: teach English, Western Politics, Law
Students: no foreign students at present; hoping to establish exchange programs
Contact: Foreign Affairs Office, South Central Institute of Politics and Law, Wuchang District, Wuhan, Hubei PRC Tel: 77586

Arts/Music

HUBEI ACADEMY OF FINE ARTS
Responsible Bureau: Provincial Education Committee
Departments: Arts, Industrial Arts, Teaching
Contact: Foreign Affairs Office, Hubei Academy of Fine Arts, Wuchang, Huzhong Village, Wuhan, Hubei PRC Tel: 77201

WUHAN MUSIC ACADEMY
Responsible Bureau: Provincial Education Committee
Departments: Composition, Voice, Minority Music, Piano, Wind and String Instruments, Music
Contact: Foreign Affairs Office, Wuhan Music Academy, Wuchang, Jiefang Rd., Wuhan, Hubei PRC Tel: 72026

Finance/Commerce/Economics

SOUTH CENTRAL UNIVERSITY OF ECONOMICS AND FINANCE
Responsible Bureau: Ministry of Finance
Departments: Economics, Politics, Accounting, Finance, Statistics, Economic Information, Architecture
Contact: Foreign Affairs Office, South Central University of Economics and Finance, Wuchang, Wuluo Rd., Wuhan, Hubei PRC   Tel: 75901

Normal Schools

HUBEI COLLEGE OF EDUCATION
Responsible Bureau: Provincial Education Committee
Departments: Politics, Chinese, English, Mathematics, Physics, Chemistry, History
Chinese Students: 250
Contact: Foreign Affairs Office, Hubei College of Education, 23 Wuluo Rd., Wuchang, Hubei PRC Tel: 4545

HUAZHONG NORMAL SCHOOL
Responsible Bureau: State Education Committee
Departments: Education, Politics, Telephone Education, Languages and Literatures, History, Library Science, Intelligence Gathering, Geology, Physics, Biology, Mathematics, Chemistry, Physical Education, Foreign Languages
Contact: Foreign Affairs Office, Huazhong Normal School, Wuchang, Guizishan, Wuhan, Hubei PRC Tel: 75601

Medical Schools

HUBEI INSTITUTE OF CHINESE MEDICINE
Responsible Bureau: Provincial Education Committee
Departments: Acupuncture, Chinese Medicine, Chinese Pharmacology
Contact: Foreign Affairs Office, Hubei Institute of Chinese Medicine, Wuchang, Yunjiaqiao, Wuhan, Hubei PRC Tel: 75694

HUBEI INSTITUTE OF MEDICINE
Responsible Bureau: Provincial Higher Education Administration
Departments: Medicine, Pediatrics, Oral Medicine, Population Planning, Management
Contact: Foreign Affairs Office, Hubei Institute of Medicine, Wuchang, Gaojiawan, Wuhan, Hubei PRC Tel: 811495

TONGJI COLLEGE OF MEDICINE
Responsible Bureau: Ministry of Sanitation and Hygiene
Departments: Medicine, Pediatrics, Sanitation and Hygiene, Environmental

Health, Obstetrics and Gynecology, Stomatology, Pharmacology,
Management
Contact: Foreign Affairs Office, Tongji College of Medicine, Hankou,
Hangkong Rd., Wuhan, Hubei PRC Tel: 56811

Technical Schools

CHINA UNIVERSITY OF GEOLOGICAL SCIENCE*
Responsible Bureau: Ministry of Geography
Departments: Geology, Mining Production, Water Resource Management,
Exploration, Exploration Engineering, Economic Management, Earth
Chemistry, Computer Science
Sister Schools: Germany—Univ of Hanover, Univ of Clausthal
Contact: Foreign Affairs Office, China University of Geological Science,
Wuchang, Yujiashan, Wuhan, Hubei PRC Tel: 70481

GEZHOUBA INSTITUTE OF HYDROELECTRICAL ENGINEERING
Responsible Bureau: Ministry of Hydroelectric Power
Departments: Hydrology and Hydroelectric Power, Shipping Mechanics,
Electrical Equipment Automation
Chinese Students: 2,000
Foreign Students: 0
Foreign Teachers: 1-2
Teachers: "it's a pretty lonely job, but everyone's very nice"
Contact: Foreign Affairs Office, Gezhouba Institute of Hydroelectrical
Engineering, Wangzhougang, Yichang, Hubei PRC Tel: 22011

HUAZHONG INSTITUTE OF TECHNOLOGY
Responsible Bureau: State Education Committee
Departments: Mathematics, Chemistry, Physics, Power Studies, Biology,
Radiation, Architecture, Mechanics, Electronics, Power Production, Solid
State Electronics, Electric Power, Automation and Control, Computer
Science, Ships and Boating, Management, Foreign Languages, Chinese,
Information Science
Contact: Foreign Affairs Office, Huazhong Institute of Technology,
Wuchang, Guanshankou, Wuhan, Hubei PRC Tel: 70152

HUBEI INSTITUTE OF TECHNOLOGY
Responsible Bureau: Provincial Education Committee
Departments: Mechanical Engineering, Electrical Equipment, Papermaking,
Plastics, Yeasts and Leavening, Arts, Industrial Workers Construction,
Industrial Management
Contact: Foreign Affairs Office, Hubei Institute of Technology, Wuchang,
Nanhu, Wuhan, Hubei PRC Tel: 73865

WUHAN CITY INSTITUTE OF CONSTRUCTION
Responsible Bureau: City Bureau of Construction and Environmental
Protection
Departments: Urban Planning, Urban Construction, Environmental
Engineering, Landscape Gardening
Contact: Foreign Affairs Office, Wuhan City Institute of Construction,
Wuchang, Xujiashan, Wuhan, Hubei PRC Tel: 70150

WUHAN INDUSTRIAL UNIVERSITY
   Responsible Bureau: National Bureau of Architectural Materials
   Departments: Silicon Processing, Automation, Mechanics, Non-metallic
   Mining, Construction, Management, English
   Contact: Foreign Affairs Office, Wuhan Industrial University, Wuchang,
   Mafangshan, Wuhan, Hubei PRC Tel: 73048

WUHAN INSTITUTE OF CHEMICAL TECHNOLOGY
   Responsible Bureau: Ministry of Industrial Chemistry
   Departments: Mining, Industrial Chemistry, Mechanics, Automation,
   Economic Management
   Chinese Students: 1,900
   Contact: Foreign Affairs Office, Wuhan Institute of Chemical Technology,
   Wuchang, Lujiaxiang, Wuhan, Hubei PRC Tel: 70369

WUHAN INSTITUTE OF HYDROELECTRICAL ENGINEERING
   Responsible Bureau: Ministry of Hydroelectric Power
   Departments: Chemistry, Environmental Engineering, Automation, Applied
   Computer Science, Hydrology, Mechanical Electronics, River Protection and
   Control, Industrial Workers Construction, Shipping, High Temperature Areas
   Theory, Mechanics
   Contact: Foreign Affairs Office, Wuhan Institute of Hydroelectrical
   Engineering, Wuhan, Luojiashan, Wuhan, Hubei PRC Tel: 812212

WUHAN INSTITUTE OF MARINE SHIPPING
   Responsible Bureau: Ministry of Transportation
   Departments: Ships and Boating, Power Production, Mechanics,
   Management
   Contact: Foreign Affairs Office, Wuhan Institute of Marine Shipping,
   Wuchang, Yujiatou, Wuhan, Hubei, PRC Tel: 66191

WUHAN INSTITUTE OF STEEL
   Responsible Bureau: Ministry of Industrial Metals
   Departments: Mine Site Choice, Industrial Metals, Industrial Chemistry,
   Materials, Mechanics, Automation, Management, Electrical
   Equipmentization
   Contact: Foreign Affairs Office, Wuhan Institute of Steel Wuchang, Renjia
   Rd., Wuhan, Hubei PRC Tel: 663212

WUHAN INSTITUTE OF TECHNOLOGY
   Responsible Bureau: China National Vehicle Company
   Departments: Mechanics, Cars and Tractors, Electrical Engineering,
   Management Engineering
   Contact: Foreign Affairs Office, Wuhan Institute of Technology, Wuchang,
   Mafangshan, Wuhan, Hubei PRC Tel: 74807

WUHAN INSTITUTE OF TEXTILES
   Responsible Bureau: Ministry of Textiles
   Departments: Textiles, Mechanical Electronics, Textile Chemistry
   Engineering
   Contact: Foreign Affairs Office, Wuhan Institute of Textiles, Wuchang,
   Guanshan, Wuhan, Hubei PRC Tel: 70185

Hunan   Hunan, birthplace of Mao Ze-dong, remains a center of traditional agriculture. The province's rich alluvial flatlands host a farming life
whose rhythms remain essentially what they were when the young Mao
wrote his influential "Report on the Peasant's Movement of Hunan." The
capital, Changsha, is an important center for education and medical research,
while Mao's birthplace at Shaoshan hosts key study centers of Communist
history. Hunan food is hearty and spicy, and her language is Mandarin, but
with a thick accent. Weather can be extreme and heating is not allowed, so
pack accordingly.

Universities

CHANGSHA UNIVERSITY
Responsible Bureau: City Government
Departments: Mechanical Control, Textiles, Industrial Workers Construc-
tion, Computer Science, Journalism, Secretarial Science, English, Industrial
Management, Commercial Accounting, Political Propaganda, Law, Finance
and Accounting
Contact: Foreign Affairs Office, Changsha University, Xining St.,
Changsha, Hunan PRC   Tel: 28780

HUNAN UNIVERSITY*
Responsible Bureau: Ministry of Mechanics
Departments: Natural Products Engineering, Mechanics, Electrical
Equipment, Industrial Chemistry, Architecture, Environmental Design,
Computer Science, Economic Management, Basic Science
Contact: Foreign Affairs Office, Hunan University, Yuelushan, Changsha,
Hunan PRC   Tel: 83171

HUNAN UNIVERSITY OF SCIENCE AND TECHNOLOGY*
Responsible Bureau: Provincial Committee of Science
Departments: Life Science, Linguistics, Management Science, Information
Science, Physics, Resource Science, Architecture, Nutrition, Travel and
Tourism
Contact: Foreign Affairs Office, Hunan University of Science and
Technology, Jinwanzi, Changsha, Hunan PRC Tel: 34908

XIANGTAN UNIVERSITY
Responsible Bureau: Provincial Education Committee
Departments: Mechanics, Industrial Chemistry, History, Foreign Lan-
guages, Philosophy, Economics, Law, Computer Science, Mathematics,
Physics, Chemistry
Foreign Students: 0
Foreign Teachers: 2-4
Accommodations: very good; 2 or 3 rms, w/ TV, tape recorder, fridge, fan;
no kitchen but can use hotplate; no curfew, relaxed visitor registration,
central location
Teacher Salary/Benefits: 590-690Y/mo (up to 1,000 for Foreign Experts)
FAO: so-so, extremely inflexible about vacations
Teaching Conditions: 14 hrs/wk; teachers also do thesis advising for fourth-
year students; very good teaching materials; foreign teachers have set up
student reading room

Contact: Foreign Affairs Office, Xiangtan University, Western Suburbs, Xiangtan, Hunan PRC   Tel: 24812

Finance/Commerce/Economics

HUNAN INSTITUTE OF FINANCE AND ECONOMICS
Responsible Bureau: Chinese People's Bank
Departments: Finance, Economic Policy, Economics, Statistics, Information
Contact: Foreign Affairs Office, Hunan Institute of Finance and Economics, Shijiachong, Changsha, Hunan PRC   Tel: 83101

HUNAN TECHNICAL SCHOOL OF INTERNATIONAL ECONOMIC MANAGEMENT
Responsible Bureau: Provincial Committee of Foreign Economic Relations
Departments: International Economics, International Trade
Contact: Foreign Affairs Office, Hunan Technical School of International Economic Management, Yuhua Rd., Changsha, Hunan PRC Tel: 32066

Normal Schools

HUNAN NORMAL UNIVERSITY
Responsible Bureau: Provincial Education Committee
Departments: Chinese, Politics, History, Education, Foreign Languages, Industrial Arts, Mathematics, Physics, Chemistry, Biology, Geology, Physical Education
Foreign Students: 15-20
Foreign Teachers: 5-6
Accommodations: OK; 2 rms w/ shared bath, kitchen, washer, TV, tape recorder, fridge, oven, bike, VCR, A/C, fan; location central to campus but 30 min walk from downtown; strict 11 p.m. curfew, and Chinese students discouraged from visiting
Teacher Salary/Benefits: 340Y/mo, + r-t airfare, excursions, shipping allowance
FAO: "sweet and sour"—flexible on travel/vacations, but untrustworthy and "ruthless"
Teaching Conditions: 6-10 hrs/wk; terrible materials, but good library and photocopy facilities
Learning Conditions: great teachers and materials
Contact: Foreign Affairs Office, Hunan Normal University, Hexi, Changsha, Hunan PRC   Tel: 83131

Medical Schools

HUNAN COLLEGE OF TRADITIONAL CHINESE MEDICINE
Responsible Bureau: Provincial Education Committee
Departments: Acupuncture, Chinese Medicine, Chinese Pharmacology
Chinese Students: 2,500
Foreign Students: 20-30
Foreign Teachers: 2
Sister Schools: no programs presently, but attempting to establish
Teaching Conditions: 14 hrs/wk; poor materials but open to new; library short on English materials
Accommodations: OK; 4 rms w/ kitchen, TV, washer, fridge, bike, A/C; heat and hot water broke frequently; no curfew, "lax" visitor registration,

location central to campus and free market, 20 min. walk from downtown
Student Tuition/Expenses: 2,500Y FEC/semester + rm and board
FAO: very good; "I came here because I knew they were good, and they've
lived up to their reputation"
Learning Conditions: "great" courses in Acupuncture/Accupressure,
Traditional Chinese Medicine; but "don't bother with the library"
Contact: Foreign Affairs Office, Hunan College of Traditional Chinese
Medicine, 107 Shaoshan Rd., 410007 Changsha, Hunan PRC   Tel: 33123

HUNAN MEDICAL COLLEGE
Responsible Bureau: Ministry of Sanitation and Hygiene
Departments: Medicine (Oncology, Pharmacology, Dentistry), Sanitation
and Hygiene
Chinese Students: 2,100
Foreign Students: varies
Foreign Teachers: 15-20
Sister Schools: US—Yale Univ, Univ of Colorado, Harvard Univ, Iowa
Univ, Univ of Nebraska, San Francisco State Univ, Univ of Washington;
Hong Kong—Hong Kong Univ
Teachers and Students: very old college, w/ several long-standing exchange
programs, including Yale-China (oldest continuing US-China exchange); has
various programs w/ sister schools and also accepts outside foreign teachers
Contact: Foreign Affairs Office, Hunan Medical College, North District,
Changsha, Hunan PRC   Tel: 24411

Technical Schools

CHANGSHA INSTITUTE OF HYDROLOGY AND HYDROELECTRIC POWER
Responsible Bureau: Ministry of Water and Electricity
Departments: Electric Power, Chinese, Mathematics, Physics, Chemistry,
Foreign Languages, Finance and Economics
Contact: Foreign Affairs Office, Changsha Institute of Hydrology and
Hydroelectric Power, Yaojin Rd., Changsha, Hunan PRC   Tel: 34808

CHANGSHA INSTITUTE OF TRANSPORTATION
Responsible Bureau: Ministry of Transportation
Departments: Architectural Engineering, Civil Engineering, Mechanical
Engineering, Management
Chinese Students: 300
Contact: Foreign Affairs Office, Changsha Institute of Transportation,
Southern Suburbs, Changsha, Hunan PRC   Tel: 35622

CHANGSHA RAILWAY INSTITUTE
Responsible Bureau: Ministry of Railways
Departments: Mechanics, Vehicles, Electronics, Agricultural Construction,
Shipping, Foreign Languages
Contact: Foreign Affairs Office, Changsha Railway Institute, Shaoshan Rd.,
Changsha, Hunan PRC   Tel: 35211

HUNAN INSTITUTE OF AGRICULTURE
Responsible Bureau: Provincial Education Committee
Departments: Agricultural Science, Gardening, Livestock and Veterinary
Medicine, Agricultural Equipment, Agricultural Economics, Examination

Contact: Foreign Affairs Office, Hunan Institute of Agriculture, Eastern Suburbs, Changsha, Hunan PRC   Tel: 24871

SOUTH CENTRAL UNIVERSITY OF TECHNOLOGY
Responsible Bureau: China National Non-Ferrous Metals Company
Departments: Geology, Materials and Mining, Industrial Metals, Mining Engineering, Materials, Metallurgy, Mechanics, Automation and Control, Computer Science, Chemistry, Management, Mathematical Theory, Politics, Foreign Languages
Chinese Students: 1,000
Foreign Students: 0
Foreign Teachers: 5
Teachers: teach English and/or technical subjects
Contact: Foreign Affairs Office, South Central University of Technology, Yuelushan, Changsha, Hunan PRC   Tel: 83111

XIANGTAN INSTITUTE OF MINING
Responsible Bureau: Ministry of Coal Mining
Departments: Materials and Mining, Geology, Mechanics, Automation
Contact: Foreign Affairs Office, Xiangtan Institute of Mining, Xiangtan, Hunan PRC   Tel: 24625

Inner Mongolia   Arching across China's northern border with the Mongolian People's Republic, Inner Mongolia was divided off as a Chinese province in 1947. The vast, windswept grasslands of the Mongolian steppes and the colorful Mongolian people, many of whom still follow traditional nomadic ways of life, make Inner Mongolia one of the PRC's most exotic destinations. Most foreign residents are concentrated in the capital at Hohot (Huhehaote), economic center of the region as well as home to Mongolia's Yellow Lamaist hierarchy.The industrial center at Baotou, however, and the grasslands town of Tongliao, offer isolated but fascinating destinations for those who want to get truly off the beaten track. Weather is chill and windy most of the year, food hearty but unvarying, consisting primarily of mutton, flatbreads, and powdered goat-cheese tea. Language is Mongolian, though in the cities Mandarin speakers are common.

Universities

FENGZHOU UNITY UNIVERSITY
Responsible Bureau: Regional Education Administration
Departments: Commercial Economic Management, Applied Computer Science
Contact: Foreign Affairs Office, Fengzhou Unity University, Haila'er Elementary School, Hohot, Inner Mongolia PRC   Tel: 22683

GREEN MOUNTAIN UNIVERSITY
Responsible Bureau: Regional Education Committee

Departments: Industrial Workers Construction, Chinese Language and Literature, English, Industrial Management, Electrical Power Plants and Electrical Systems
Contact: Foreign Affairs Office, Green Mountain University, Bali Village, Hohot, Inner Mongolia PRC   Tel: 33410

UNIVERSITY OF INNER MONGOLIA*
Responsible Bureau: Regional Education Administration
Departments: Mongolian Language and Literature, Chinese Language and Literature, History, Philosophy, Economics, Law, Foreign Languages, Physics, Chemistry, Biology, Electronics
Students: have student program in Mongolian language and culture
Contact: Foreign Affairs Office, University of Inner Mongolia, Xincheng District, Hohot, Inner Mongolia PRC   Tel: 43141

Finance/Economics

INNER MONGOLIA INSTITUTE OF ECONOMIC POLICY
Responsible Bureau: Regional Education Administration
Departments: Finance, Economic Policy, Industrial Economics, Commercial Economics, Planning and Statistics, Industrial Management, Sales Finance
Contact: Foreign Affairs Office, Inner Mongolia Institute of Economic Policy, Haila'er Rd., Hohot, Inner Mongolia PRC Tel: 23380

Normal Schools

INNER MONGOLIA MINORITIES NORMAL SCHOOL
Responsible Bureau: Regional Education Administration
Departments: History, Politics, Mathematics, Chinese Language and Literature, Mongolian Language and Literature, Physics, Chemistry, English, Geology
Contact: Foreign Affairs Office, Inner Mongolia Minorities Normal School, Tongliao, Inner Mongolia, PRC

INNER MONGOLIA NORMAL SCHOOL
Responsible Bureau: Regional Education Administration
Departments: Education and Schools, Mongolian Language and Literature, Chinese Language and Literature, Foreign Languages, Political Education, History, Music, Art, Mathematics, Physics, Chemistry
Contact: Foreign Affairs Office, Inner Mongolia Normal School, Xincheng District, Hohot, Inner Mongolia PRC   Tel: 41291

Medical Schools

BAOTOU INSTITUTE OF MEDICINE
Responsible Bureau: Regional Education Administration
Departments: Medicine, Sanitation and Hygiene
Contact: Foreign Affairs Office, Baotou Institute of Medicine, Gangtie Ave., Baotou, Inner Mongolia PRC   Tel: 26122

INNER MONGOLIA INSTITUTE OF MEDICINE
Responsible Bureau: Regional Education Administration

Departments: Medicine, Pharmacology, Chinese Medicine, Mongolian Medicine, Medical Practice
Contact: Foreign Affairs Office, Inner Mongolia Institute of Medicine, Xinhua St., Hohot, Inner Mongolia PRC Tel: 34910

INNER MONGOLIA INSTITUTE OF MINORITY MEDICINE
Responsible Bureau: Regional Education Administration
Departments: Medicine, Mongolian Medicine
Contact: Foreign Affairs Office, Inner Mongolia Institute of Minority Medicine, Tongliao, Inner Mongolia PRC Tel: 3560

Technical Schools

BAOTOU INSTITUTE OF STEEL
Responsible Bureau: Ministry of Industrial Metals
Departments: Materials and Mining Engineering, Industrial Metals, Mechanical and Electrical Engineering, Architecture
Chinese Students: 2,500
Contact: Foreign Affairs Office, Baotou Institute of Steel, Kundulun District, Baotou, Inner Mongolia PRC Tel: 25845

INNER MONGOLIA INSTITUTE OF AGRICULTURE AND LIVESTOCK
Responsible Bureau: Regional Education Administration
Departments: Livestock, Grasslands, Veterinary Medicine, Agricultural Science, Crop Protection, Agricultural Economics, Vegetables
Contact: Foreign Affairs Office, Inner Mongolia Institute of Agriculture and Livestock, Hohot, Inner Mongolia PRC Tel: 44746

INNER MONGOLIA INSTITUTE OF INDUSTRY
Responsible Bureau: Regional Education Administration
Departments: Material Arts, Chemistry, Power Production, Architecture, Electrical Equipment, Management, Industrial Workers Construction
Contact: Foreign Affairs Office, Inner Mongolia Institute of Industry, Aimin Rd., Hohot, Inner Mongolia PRC Tel: 41707

Jiangsu Home of scenic Suzhou, Wuxi, Yangzhou, and Yixing as well as of bustling Nanjing, Jiangsu houses, according to one Chinese official, nearly a fifth of all foreign teachers and students in China. A major center of industry, transportation, and research, Nanjing also houses several of China's largest universities as well as beautiful temples and museums. Breathtaking Suzhou, replete with Ming and Qing gardens; Wuxi, home of Lake Tai; ancient Yangzhou, where Marco Polo once was mayor; and Yixing, cradle of Purple-Sand ceramics, offer some of the most gorgeous scenery in China. Jiangsu food is varied and delicious, featuring dozens of different dumplings and buns. Weather is mostly mild, though pollution in Nanjing is atrocious. Language is thickly accented Mandarin.

Universities

JIANGNAN UNIVERSITY
Responsible Bureau: City Government
Departments: Mechanics, Automation, Radio Technology, Computer Science, Chemistry, Textiles, Agricultural Construction, Management, Chinese, Foreign Languages, Medical Practice
Contact: Foreign Affairs Office, Jiangnan University, Yanxi Rd., Wuxi, Jiangsu PRC   Tel: 11056

NANJING UNIVERSITY*
Responsible Bureau: State Education Committee
Departments: Chinese, History, Philosophy, Library Science, Foreign Languages, Economics, Law, Computer Science, Mathematics, Physics, Chemistry, Environmental Studies, Geology, Geography, Atmosperic Studies, Astronomy, Biology
Chinese Students: 10,300
Foreign Students: 200
Foreign Teachers: 5-10
Sister Schools: US—CIEE, other schools
Accommodations: reasonable; 1 lg rm, w/ TV, fridge, no kitchen, cafeteria food "inedible"; 10 min walk from downtown
Teacher Salary/Benefits: 1,100Y/mo, 900 in FEC (Foreign Expert), + r-t airfare, excursions
FAO: very poor—tend to renege even on written contracts
Teaching Conditions: 12 hrs/wk; materials terrible, no language lab, library OK but no secretarial support
Students: very large programs in Chinese Language, Culture, some short term, organized through Sister Schools; others long term. Some foreign students able to share dorm rooms with Chinese students
Contact: Foreign Affairs Office, Nanjing University, 22 Hankou Rd., Nanjing, Jiangsu PRC   Tel: 33307

PENGCHENG UNIVERSITY
Responsible Bureau: City Government
Departments: Agricultural Construction, Mechanical Electronics, Industrial Management, Literature
Contact: Foreign Affairs Office, Pengcheng University, Southern Suburbs, Xuzhou, Jiangsu PRC   Tel: 88930

SUZHOU UNIVERSITY
Responsible Bureau: Provincial Bureau of Higher Education
Departments: Chinese, Politics, History, Foreign Languages, Physical Education, Mathematics, Physics, Chemistry, Economic Policy, Law
Contact: Foreign Affairs Office, Suzhou University, Shizi St., Suzhou, Jiangsu PRC   Tel: 23614

UNIVERSITY OF RIVERS AND OCEANS
Responsible Bureau: Ministry of Water and Electricity
Departments: Hydroelectric Power, Marine Shipping and Aquaculture, Field Irrigation, Surveying, Power Studies, Automation, Agricultural Construction, Management

Foreign Students: many
Foreign Teachers: 10-15
Teachers: can teach English, Western Culture, technical subjects
Students: school formerly had 100+ Chinese gov't scholarship students; was site of 1989 anti-African student riots; number of foreign students currently in flux
Contact: Foreign Affairs Office, University of Rivers and Oceans, Xikang Rd., Nanjing, Jiangsu PRC   Tel: 32106

Finance/Commerce/Economics

NANJING INSTITUTE OF FINANCE AND TRADE
Responsible Bureau: City Government
Departments: Industrial Management, Foreign Trade, Accounting, Finance, Taxation
Contact: Foreign Affairs Office, Nanjing Institute of Finance and Trade, Fenhuang W. St., Nanjing, Jiangsu PRC Tel: 48647

Arts/Music

NANJING ACADEMY OF ARTS
Responsible Bureau: Provincial Bureau of Higher Education
Departments: Arts, Music
Contact: Foreign Affairs Office, Nanjing Academy of Arts, Huju N. Rd., Nanjing, Jiangsu PRC   Tel: 34259

Normal Schools

NANJING NORMAL SCHOOL
Responsible Bureau: Provincial Bureau of Higher Education
Departments: Politics, Education, Chinese, Foreign Languages, Mathematics, Physics, Chemistry, Biology, Geology, Music, Art, Physical Education, History
Contact: Foreign Affairs Office, Nanjing Normal School, Ninghai Rd., Nanjing, Jiangsu PRC   Tel: 31636

XUZHOU RAILWAY NORMAL SCHOOL
Responsible Bureau: Ministry of Railways
Departments: Chinese, Mathematics, Biology, History, Chemistry, English
Contact: Foreign Affairs Office, Xuzhou Railway Normal School, Renmin Rd., Xuzhou, Jiangsu PRC   Tel: 6183

XUZHOU TEACHERS COLLEGE
Responsible Bureau: Provincial Education Commission
Departments: Chinese, History, Foreign Languages, Political Education, Mathematics, Physics, Chemistry, Physical Education, Geology, Biology
Chinese Students: 4,500
Foreign Students: 0 long term; several short-term programs
Foreign Teachers: 2-3
Sister School: Australia—University of Melbourne
Accommodations: great; 4 rms w/ kitchen (in cookhouse across courtyard) bath, washer, TV, tape recorder, plenty of hot water, A/C, vacuum cleaner, bike, use of car and driver when needed, no curfew; cook provided if wish;

dorm central to campus and 15 min walk from downtown
Teacher Salary/Benefits: 600-1,000Y/mo, 50% in FEC, + o-w int'l airfare,
400Y travel allowance
FAO: excellent; "they have always tried their best to help us—they even
gave us a garden"; FAO also very responsive to cooperation from foreigners:
1 respondent's salary was raised 400Y/mo after respondent began volunteering to tutor evening classes
Teaching Conditions: workload heavy; 16-24 hrs/wk but students excellent;
no photocopying, but secretarial assistance available, + foreign teachers get
own office; excellent library, w/ subscriptions to many foreign magazines,
including *Time, Newsweek, Life, Harpers, Atlantic Monthly,* etc.
Contact: Foreign Affairs Office, Xuzhou Teachers College, Heping Rd.,
Xuzhou, Jiangsu PRC   Tel: 35520

YANGZHOU NORMAL SCHOOL
Responsible Bureau: Provincial Bureau of Higher Education
Departments: Chinese, History, Politics, English, Mathematics, Physics,
Chemistry, Physical Education, Commercial Economics
Contact: Foreign Affairs Office, Yangzhou Normal School, Western
Suburbs, Yangzhou, Jiangsu PRC   Tel: 43011

Medical Schools

JIANGSU COLLEGE OF MEDICINE
Responsible Bureau: Ministry of Atomic Industry
Departments: Medicine, Radiation Therapy, Politics
Contact: Foreign Affairs Office, Jiangsu College of Medicine, Renmin Rd.,
Suzhou, Jiangsu PRC   Tel: 22662

NANJING COLLEGE OF CHINESE MEDICINE
Responsible Bureau: Provincial Bureau of Higher Education
Departments: Chinese Medicine, Chinese Pharmacology, Acupuncture,
Acupressure
Contact: Foreign Affairs Office, Nanjing College of Chinese Medicine,
Hanzhong Rd., Nanjing, Jiangsu PRC   Tel: 41462

NANJING COLLEGE OF MEDICINE
Responsible Bureau: Provincial Bureau of Higher Education
Departments: Medicine, Pediatrics, Oral Medicine, Sanitation and Hygiene,
Nursing and Care
Contact: Foreign Affairs Office, Nanjing College of Medicine, Hanzhong
Rd., Nanjing, Jiangsu PRC   Tel: 49282

NANJING COLLEGE OF PHARMACOLOGY
Responsible Bureau: National Medical and Pharmacological Bureau
Departments: Pharmacology, Chinese Pharmacology; Pharmacological
Production, Chemistry
Chinese Students: 500
Sister Schools: Japan—Gifu College of Pharmacology, US—Univ of
Pittsburgh
Contact: Foreign Affairs Office, Nanjing College of Pharmacology,
Tongjiagang, Nanjing, Jiangsu PRC   Tel: 31611

NANJING RAILWAY COLLEGE OF MEDICINE
Responsible Bureau: Ministry of Railways
Departments: Medicine, Sanitation and Hygiene
Contact: Foreign Affairs Office, Nanjing Railway College of Medicine, Dingjiaqiao Rd., Nanjing, Jiangsu PRC   Tel: 31508

NANTONG COLLEGE OF MEDICINE
Responsible Bureau: Ministry of Transportation
Departments: Medicine, Aviation and Shipping Medicine
Contact: Foreign Affairs Office, Nantong College of Medicine, Qixiu Rd., Nantong, Jiangsu PRC   Tel: 7191

XUZHOU COLLEGE OF MEDICINE
Responsible Bureau: Provincial Bureau of Higher Education
Departments: Medicine
Chinese Students: 1,120
Contact: Foreign Affairs Office, Xuzhou College of Medicine, Huaihai W. Rd., Xuzhou, Jiangsu PRC   Tel: 24932

YANGZHOU COLLEGE OF MEDICINE
Responsible Bureau: Provincial Bureau of Higher Education
Departments: Medicine, Chinese Medicine, Obstetrics and Gynecology
Contact: Foreign Affairs Office, Yangzhou College of Medicine, Huaihai Rd., Yangzhou, Jiangsu PRC   Tel: 42331

ZHENJIANG COLLEGE OF MEDICINE
Responsible Bureau: Provincial Bureau of Higher Education
Departments: Examination, Medicine
Contact: Foreign Affairs Office, Zhenjiang College of Medicine, Jiefang Rd., Zhenjiang, Jiangsu PRC   Tel: 21733

Technical Schools

CHANGZHOU INSTITUTE OF INDUSTRIAL ARTS
Responsible Bureau: City Government
Departments: Mechanics, Computer Science, Industrial Automation, Industrial Management, Foreign Languages, Secretarial Sciences, Agricultural Construction
Contact: Foreign Affairs Office, Changzhou Institute of Industrial Arts, Zhoujiaxiang, Changzhou, Jiangsu PRC   Tel: 33521

CHINESE INSTITUTE OF MINING
Responsible Bureau: Ministry of Coal Mining
Departments: Coal Field Geology, Resource Exploration and Surveying, Materials and Mining, Coal Mining Construction and Techniques, Mechanics, Unified Coal Theory and Use, Automation, Coal Industry Management
Contact: Foreign Affairs Office, Chinese Institute of Mining, Xuzhou, Jiangsu PRC   Tel: 88653

EAST CHINA INSTITUTE OF INDUSTRY
Responsible Bureau: Ministry of Weapons and Military Equipment
Departments: Mechanics, Industrial Chemistry, Electronics, Mechanical Control Arts, Computer Science, Radiation Electronics Technology, High

Temperature Physics Engineering, Aviation Power Studies, Automation and
Control, Management, Basic Sciences
Contact: Foreign Affairs Office, East China Institute of Industry,
Xiaolingwei, Nanjing, Jiangsu PRC   Tel: 47612

JIANGSU INSTITUTE OF AGRICULTURE
Responsible Bureau: Provincial Bureau of Higher Education
Departments: Agricultural Science, Gardening, Livestock, Veterinary
Medicine, Mechanical Electronics, Field Irrigation, Animal Products
Processing, Livestock Feed and Nutrition, Nutrition and Hygiene, Village
Construction
Contact: Foreign Affairs Office, Jiangsu Institute of Agriculture, Western
Suburbs, Yangzhou, Jiangsu PRC   Tel: 42521

JIANGSU INSTITUTE OF INDUSTRIAL CHEMISTRY
Responsible Bureau: Provincial Administration of Industrial Chemistry
Departments: Non-organic Industrial Chemistry, Industrial Chemistry
Mechanics, Management Engineering
Contact: Foreign Affairs Office, Jiangsu Institute of Industrial Chemistry,
Jichang Rd., Changzhou, Jiangsu PRC   Tel: 33311

JIANGSU INSTITUTE OF TECHNOLOGY
Responsible Bureau: Ministry of Mechanics
Departments: Electrical Equipment, Power Production, Mechanics,
Information, Management, Agricultural Mechanics, Agricultural
Mechanization
Contact: Foreign Affairs Office, Jiangsu Institute of Technology, East
Suburbs, Zhenjiang, Jiangsu PRC   Tel: 24071

NANJING AERONAUTICAL INSTITUTE
Responsible Bureau: Ministry of Aviation
Departments: Airplanes, Generators, Automation and Control, Electronics,
Mechanics, Management, Wind Power Production, Computer Science
Chinese Students: 5,200
Sister Schools: US—Univ of New Mexico, Univ of Tennessee, Georgia Inst
of Technology; UK—Univ of Glasgow, Univ of Nottingham, Oxford Univ,
Manchester Univ; Japan—Kyushu Univ; Sweden—Univ of Stockholm
Contact: Foreign Affairs Office, Nanjing Aeronautical Institute, 29 Yudao
St., Nanjing, Jiangsu PRC   Tel: 41191

NANJING AGRICULTURAL UNIVERSITY
Responsible Bureau: Ministry of Agriculture, Livestock, and Fisheries
Departments: Agricultural Sciences, Crop Protection, Soil Chemistry,
Gardening, Livestock, Veterinary Medicine, Agricultural Economics,
Agricultural Mechanization, Nutrition, Animal Products Processing
Contact: Foreign Affairs Office, Nanjing Agricultural University,
Zhongshanmenwai, Nanjing, Jiangsu PRC   Tel: 41420

NANJING COLLEGE OF FOOD ECONOMICS
Responsible Bureau: Ministry of Commerce
Departments: Planning and Statistics, Finance and Accounting, Economics,
Grain and Oils Storage

Chinese Students: 1,200
Contact: Foreign Affairs Office, Nanjing College of Food Economics,
Fujian Rd., Nanjing, Jiangsu PRC   Tel: 85178

NANJING INSTITUTE OF ARCHITECTURE AND ENGINEERING
Responsible Bureau: City Ministry of Construction and Environmental
Protection
Departments: Agricultural Construction, Mechanics, Geology of Rivers and
Lakes, Water Surveying, Architectural Economic Management
Contact: Foreign Affairs Office, Nanjing Institute of Architecture and
Engineering, Zhongshan N. Rd., Nanjing, Jiangsu PRC   Tel: 32976

NANJING INSTITUTE OF INDUSTRIAL CHEMISTRY
Responsible Bureau: Ministry of Industrial Chemistry
Departments: Industrial Chemistry, Mechanics, Applied Chemistry
Contact: Foreign Affairs Office, Nanjing Institute of Industrial Chemistry,
Xinmofan Blvd., Nanjing, Jiangsu PRC   Tel: 335592

NANJING INSTITUTE OF INDUSTRY
Responsible Bureau: State Education Committee
Departments: Architectural Engineering, Mechanical Engineering, Power
Production, Radio Technology, Civil Engineering, Environmental Studies,
Electronics, Mathematical Power Studies, Automation and Control,
Computer Science, Physical Chemistry, Biological Medicine, Materials,
Sociology, Management
Contact: Foreign Affairs Office, Nanjing Institute of Industry, Sipai
Building, Nanjing, Jiangsu PRC   Tel: 35503

NANJING INSTITUTE OF METEOROLOGY*
Responsible Bureau: National Bureau of Meteorology
Departments: Weather-Driven Power Production, Weather, Meteorology,
Atmospheric Exploration, Atmospheric Physics, Agricultural Meteorology
Chinese Students: 1,300
Sister School: UK—Univ of Edinburgh
Contact: Foreign Affairs Office, Nanjing Institute of Meteorology, Pukou
District, Nanjing, Jiangsu PRC   Tel: 51336

NANJING INSTITUTE OF POST AND TELECOMMUNICATIONS
Responsible Bureau: Ministry of Post and Telecommunications
Departments: Electronic Mail, Radio Technology, Computer Science, Mail
Routes
Contact: Foreign Affairs Office, Nanjing Institute of Post and Telecommuni-
cations, Guangdong Rd., Nanjing, Jiangsu PRC   Tel: 33862

NANJING INSTITUTE OF RESOURCE ENGINEERING
Responsible Bureau: Provincial Science Committee
Departments: High Temperature Studies, Electrical Equipment, Industrial
Water Conservation, Nuclear Power Plants, Village Resources, Scientific
Personal File Management
Contact: Foreign Affairs Office, Nanjing Institute of Resource Engineering,
Jiangwangmiao, Nanjing, Jiangsu PRC   Tel: 46331

NANJING UNIVERSITY OF FORESTRY
Responsible Bureau: Ministry of Forestry
Departments: Forestry, Forest Disease Prevention and Control, Park Forests, Forestry Management, Forest Products Chemistry, Lumber Processing, Lumber Water Shipment, Forestry Mechanics, Lumber Trade
Chinese Students: 2,400
Contact: Foreign Affairs Office, Nanjing University of Forestry, Shaoshan Rd., Nanjing, Jiangsu PRC   Tel: 43771

NANTONG TEXTILES INSTITUTE
Responsible Bureau: Provincial Bureau of Higher Education
Departments: Mechanical Electronics, Textiles, Economic Management
Contact: Foreign Affairs Office, Nantong Textiles Institute, Yijiaqiaodong, Nantong, Jiangsu PRC   Tel: 2084

SUZHOU CITY INSTITUTE OF CONSTRUCTION AND ENVIRONMENTAL PROTECTION
Responsible Bureau: City Construction and Environmental Protection Ministry
Departments: Architecture, Urban Planning, Environmental Engineering, Environmental Planning and Management
Contact: Foreign Affairs Office, Suzhou City Institute of Construction and Environmental Protection, Fengqiao, Suzhou, Jiangsu PRC   Tel: 31417

SUZHOU SILK AND BROCADE INSTITUTE
Responsible Bureau: China National Silks and Brocades Company
Departments: Silks and Brocades, Dye and Fiber Chemistry, Mechanics and Electrical Equipment, Industrial Management, Industrial Arts
Chinese Students: 1,900
Contact: Foreign Affairs Office, Suzhou Silk and Brocade Institute, Xiangmenwai, Suzhou, Jiangsu PRC Tel: 25614

WUXI INSTITUTE OF LIGHT INDUSTRY
Responsible Bureau: Ministry of Light Industry
Departments: Nutritional Science, Yeasts and Leavening, Grains and Oils, Mechanics, Automation, Industrial Chemistry, Textiles, Industrial Design
Chinese Students: 2,500
Sister Schools: US—Rutgers, UC-Davis, Kansas Univ; Japan—Kyushu Univ, Gifu Univ
Contact: Foreign Affairs Office, Wuxi Institute of Light Industry, Qingshanwan, Wuxi, Jiangsu PRC   Tel: 21243

ZHENJIANG INSTITUTE OF SHIPS AND BOATS
Responsible Bureau: China General Ships and Boating Company
Departments: Ships and Boats, Mechanics, Automation and Control, Management
Foreign Students: 0
Foreign Teachers: 3
Sister School: USSR—Nikclayev Shipbuilding Inst
Teaching Conditions: small school with outstanding waiban
Contact: Foreign Affairs Office, Zhenjiang Institute of Ships and Boats, Huancheng Rd., Zhenjiang, Jiangsu PRC   Tel: 22291

Jiangxi   Center since ancient times of China's porcelain industry, Jiangxi remains today the world's premier porcelain-producing region, from the ancient kilns at Jingdezhen to the "kaolin" trading centers in the capital at Nanchang. The province was also important in Republican-era and revolutionary history, and towns such as Nanchang and Ganzhou house large historical collections. Weather is mild spring and fall, steamy in summer and cool in winter. Language is a mixture of thickly accented Mandarin and Fujianese, food richly varied with many dishes related to Guangdong cooking.

Universities

JIANGXI UNIVERSITY*
Responsible Bureau: Ministry of Education
Departments: Chinese, Journalism, History, Philosophy, Library Science, Foreign Language, Mathematics, Information, Computer Science, Physics, Radio Technology, Chemistry, Nutrition, Biology, Microbiology, Fresh Water Aquaculture, Political Economics, Management, Law
Chinese Students: 4,000
Contact: Foreign Affairs Office, Jiangxi University, Disi Jiaotong Rd., Nanchang, Jiangxi PRC Tel: 67800

Finance/Economics

JIANGXI INSTITUTE OF ECONOMICS AND FINANCE
Responsible Bureau: Ministry of Finance
Departments: Statistics, Finance and Accounting, Finance, Basic Construction Economics, Economics, Industrial Economics, Agricultural Economics, Commercial Economics
Contact: Foreign Affairs Office, Jiangxi Institute of Economics and Finance, Xialuo, Nanchang, Jiangxi PRC Tel: 67858

Normal Schools

GANNAN NORMAL SCHOOL
Responsible Bureau: Provincial Higher Education Administration
Departments: Chinese, Political Education, Foreign Languages, Mathematics, Physics, Chemistry, Physical Education, Music, Art
Contact: Foreign Affairs Office, Gannan Normal School, Hongqi Blvd., Ganzhou, Jiangxi PRC Tel: 3687

JIANGXI NORMAL UNIVERSITY
Responsible Bureau: Provincial Education Administration
Departments: Chinese, History, Foreign Languages, Political Education, Education, Music, Art, Mathematics, Physics, Chemistry, Geology, Computer Science, Physical Education
Chinese Students: 5,000
Sister Schools: US—Oklahoma State Univ, Eastern Michigan Univ; Canada—Univ of Western Ontario
Contact: Foreign Affairs Office, Jiangxi Normal University, Disi Jiaotong Rd., Nanchang, Jiangxi PRC Tel: 67801

Medical Schools

JIANGXI INSTITUTE OF CHINESE MEDICINE
Responsible Bureau: Provincial Administration of Sanitation and Hygiene
Departments: Chinese Medicine, Pharmacology
Contact: Foreign Affairs Office, Jiangxi Institute of Chinese Medicine, Bayi Blvd., Nanchang, Jiangxi PRC Tel: 63936

NANCHANG COLLEGE OF MEDICINE
Responsible Bureau: Provincial Administration of Sanitation and Hygiene
Departments: Medicine, Pediatrics, Oral Medicine, Sanitation and Hygiene
Contact: Foreign Affairs Office, Nanchang College of Medicine, Bayi Blvd., Nanchang, Jiangxi PRC Tel: 64936

Technical Schools

EAST CHINA GEOLOGICAL INSTITUTE
Responsible Bureau: Ministry of Atomic Industry
Departments: Geology, Materials Exploration, Experimentation, Water Exploration, Water Resource Management
Foreign Students: 0
Foreign Teachers: 2-5
Sister School: US—Univ of Texas, El Paso
Teachers: can teach English, Geology, Hydrogeology
Students: Geology Dept can accept foreign students, but none attending at present
Contact: Foreign Affairs Office, East China Geological Institute, Fuzhou, Jiangxi PRC Tel: 3831

EAST CHINA UNIVERSITY OF TRANSPORTATION
Responsible Bureau: Ministry of Railways
Departments: Architecture, Mechanics, Electrical Equipment, Economic Management
Contact: Foreign Affairs Office, East China University of Transportation, Shuanggang, Nanchang, Jiangxi PRC Tel: 67815

JIANGXI INDUSTRIAL UNIVERSITY
Responsible Bureau: Provincial Education Administration
Departments: Mechanics, Electrical Mechanics, Industrial Chemistry, Agricultural Construction, Nutrition
Contact: Foreign Affairs Office, Jiangxi Industrial University, Disi Jiaotong Rd., Nanchang, Jiangxi PRC Tel: 67926

JIANGXI INSTITUTE OF INDUSTRIAL METALS
Responsible Bureau: China National Non-Ferrous Metals Company
Departments: Mining, Mechanical Engineering, Industrial Metals, Automation, Management
Contact: Foreign Affairs Office, Jiangxi Institute of Industrial Metals, Ganzhou, Jiangxi PRC Tel: 4775

JINGDEZHEN INSTITUTE OF PORCELAIN
Responsible Bureau: Ministry of Light Industry
Departments: Engineering, Mechanics, Industrial Management

Contact: Foreign Affairs Office, Jingdezhen Institute of Porcelain, Eastern Suburbs, Jingdezhen, Jiangxi PRC Tel: 3845

NANCHANG INSTITUTE OF AVIATION INDUSTRY
Responsible Bureau: Ministry of Aviation
Departments: Materials, Industrial Chemistry, Mechanics, Electronics
Contact: Foreign Affairs Office, Nanchang Institute of Aviation Industry, Shanghai Rd., Nanchang, Jiangxi PRC Tel: 64846

Jilin The center of Qing Dynasty Manchuria (colonial-era Manchukuo), Jilin today retains a split personality. At Changchun, the capital, the province seems a major center of science and technology, home to China's auto industry, one of her most famous film studios, and some of her top medical research. In border towns like Tonghua and Yanji, the province seems a small Korea, fortified against military crossings, but the site of much quiet small-scale trade (Tonghua is one of the few towns in the world where U.S. citizens can sample freshly made North Korean *kim chee*). To the west lie the Changbaishan Mountains, dotted with ski resorts, hiking trails, winter-olympics training centers, and farmers searching for the almost unimaginably valuable wild Changbaishan Ginseng. Weather is far northern, food bland but hearty, and language fairly standard Mandarin.

Universities

JILIN CITY UNITY UNIVERSITY
Responsible Bureau: City Government
Departments: English, Law, Biology, High Temperature Engineering, Industrial Worker's Construction, Computer Science
Contact: Foreign Affairs Office, Jilin City Unity University, Jilin Ave., Jilin City, Jilin PRC Tel: 22501

JILIN INDUSTRIAL UNIVERSITY
Responsible Bureau: Ministry of Mechanics
Departments: Agricultural Engineering, Vehicles, High Temperature Energy Production, Mechanics, Electronics, Computer Science, Materials, Mathematical Theory, Management Theory, Intelligence Gathering
Contact: Foreign Affairs Office, Jilin Industrial University, Stalin Ave., Changchun, Jilin PRC Tel: 23397

JILIN UNIVERSITY*
Responsible Bureau: Ministry of Education
Departments: Chinese, History, Politics, Library Science, Philosophy, Foreign Languages, Mathematics, Physics, Chemistry, Electronics, Computer Science, Biology, Law, Economics
Chinese Students: 6,500
Contact: Foreign Affairs Office, Jilin University, 77 Jiefang Ave., Changchun, Jilin PRC Tel: 23189

JILIN UNIVERSITY OF SCIENCE AND TECHNOLOGY*
Responsible Bureau: Provincial Education Administration
Departments: Nursing, Political History, Mathematics, Japanese, Biology,
Industrial Management, English, Library Science, Intelligence Gathering,
Applied Computer Science, Law
Contact: Foreign Affairs Office, Jilin University of Science and Technology, Weixing Rd., Changchun, Jilin PRC Tel: 54081

YANBIAN UNIVERSITY
Responsible Bureau: Provincial Education Committee
Departments: Mathematics, Chemistry, Physics, Geology, English, Politics,
History, Foreign Languages, Industrial Arts, Physical Education
Contact: Foreign Affairs Office, Yanbian University, Yanji, Jilin PRC
Tel: 5921

Arts/Music

JILIN ACADEMY OF ARTS
Responsible Bureau: Provincial Cultural Administration
Departments: Music, Opera, Art
Contact: Foreign Affairs Office, Jilin Academy of Arts, Ziyou Blvd.,
Changchun, Jilin PRC Tel: 55646

Finance/Commerce

JILIN INSTITUTE OF FINANCE AND TRADE
Responsible Bureau: Provincial Education Committee
Departments: Accounting and Statistics, Economic Policy and Finance,
Trade Economics, Foreign Trade, Grains
Contact: Foreign Affairs Office, Jilin Institute of Finance and Trade, Stalin
Ave., Changchun, Jilin PRC Tel: 22050

Foreign Languages

CHANGCHUN FOREIGN LANGUAGES TECHNICAL COLLEGE
Responsible Bureau: Provincial Education Committee
Departments: English, Russian, Japanese
Contact: Foreign Affairs Office, Changchun Foreign Languages Technical
College, Hongqi St., Changchun, Jilin PRC Tel: 53105

Normal Schools

CHANGCHUN NORMAL SCHOOL
Responsible Bureau: China National Non-Ferrous Metals Company
Departments: Chinese, Foreign Languages, Mathematics, Physical
Education, Political History, Chemistry, Physics, Music
Contact: Foreign Affairs Office, Changchun Normal School, Changjiu
Highway, Changchun, Jilin PRC Tel: 42393

JILIN NORMAL SCHOOL
Responsible Bureau: Provincial Education Committee
Departments: Chinese, Mathematics, Politics, History, Physics, Chemistry,
Foreign Languages

Contact: Foreign Affairs Office, Jilin Normal School, Jiangnan St., Jilin City, Jilin PRC Tel: 26321

NORTHEAST NORMAL UNIVERSITY
Responsible Bureau: State Education Committee
Departments: Education, Political Education, History, Chinese, Foreign Languages, Music, Art, Mathematics, Physics, Chemistry, Biology, Geology, Physical Education, Library Science, Telephone Education
Chinese Students: 6,400
Foreign Students: 105
Foreign Teachers: 5-10
Sister Schools: US—Univ of Wisconsin, Univ of Mississippi, Univ of California, Univ of Michigan, S. Illinois Univ, Stanford; Japan—Univ of Miyagi, Univ of Okayawa, Obirin College; Canada—Univ of Saskatchewan
Teachers and Students: facilities include 2.3 million vol library, Museum of Biology, Museum of Ancient Chinese History
Contact: Foreign Affairs Office, Northeast Normal University, Stalin Ave., Changchun, Jilin PRC Tel: 22009

SIPING NORMAL SCHOOL
Responsible Bureau: Provincial Education Administration
Departments: Chinese, Politics, History, Foreign Languages, Mathematics, Physics, Chemistry, Biology, Geology, Physical Education
Contact: Foreign Affairs Office, Siping Normal School, Tiexi District, Siping, Jilin PRC Tel: 3009

TONGHUA NORMAL SCHOOL
Responsible Bureau: Provincial Education Committee
Departments: Politics, History, Chinese, Mathematics, Education, Physics, Chemistry, English, Biology, Physical Education
Contact: Foreign Affairs Office, Tonghua Normal School, Laozhan St., Tonghua, Jilin PRC Tel: 6022

Medical Schools

BETHUNE INSTITUTE OF MEDICINE
Responsible Bureau: Ministry of Sanitation and Hygiene
Departments: Medicine, Pediatrics, Oral Medicine, Environmental Medicine, Nutritional Examination
Chinese Students: 2,600
Sister Schools: Canada—Univ of Saskatchewan; Japan—Kyushu Univ, Tohoku Univ
Contact: Foreign Affairs Office, Bethune Institute of Medicine, 6 Xinmin Ave., Changchun, Jilin PRC Tel: 54678

CHANGCHUN INSTITUTE OF CHINESE MEDICINE
Responsible Bureau: Provincial Sanitation and Hygiene Administration
Departments: Chinese Medicine, Chinese Pharmacology
Contact: Foreign Affairs Office, Changchun Institute of Chinese Medicine, Gongneng Blvd., Changchun, Jilin PRC Tel: 52265

JILIN INSTITUTE OF MEDICINE
Responsible Bureau: Provincial Sanitation and Hygiene Administration

Departments: Medicine, Examination
Contact: Foreign Affairs Office, Jilin Institute of Medicine, Beijing Rd.,
Jilin City, Jilin PRC Tel: 23181

YANBIAN MEDICAL COLLEGE
Responsible Bureau: Provincial Sanitation and Hygiene Administration
Departments: Medical Practice, Pharmacology
Chinese Students: 1,000+
Foreign Students: 0
Foreign Teachers: 2-3
Accommodations: poor; 5 rms for 2 people, w/ kitchen, washer, TV, tape
recorder, fridge, plenty of heat but no hot water; also special cook for foreign
teachers approx 50Y/mo; no curfew and lax visitor registration
Teacher Salary/Benefits: 350Y/mo RMB, + 1,000Y/yr travel bonus,
shipping allowance
FAO: reasonable, but "a certain amount of deliberate obfuscation"; also, "no
one in the waiban speaks English"
Teaching Conditions: 12 hrs/wk; materials and library poor; secretarial help
available, but no photocopying
Contact: Foreign Affairs Office, Yanbian Medical College, Yanji, Jilin PRC
Tel: 2147

Technical Schools

CHANGCHUN INSTITUTE OF GEOLOGY
Responsible Bureau: Ministry of Geology and Mineral Resources
Departments: Geology, Hydroengineering, Materials Exploration, Timing
Equipment, Mining Exploration, Equipment Management, Political
Education
Contact: Foreign Affairs Office, Changchun Institute of Geology, Geology
Palace, Changchun, Jilin PRC Tel: 24087

CHANGCHUN INSTITUTE OF POST AND TELECOMMUNICATIONS
Responsible Bureau: Ministry of Post and Telecommunications
Departments: Electronic Mail, Radio Technology, Computer Science,
Management
Contact: Foreign Affairs Office, Changchun Institute of Post and Telecom-
munications, Nanhu Blvd., Changchun, Jilin PRC Tel: 54223

CHANGCHUN INSTITUTE OF PRECISION RADIATION MECHANICS
Responsible Bureau: Ministry of Weapons and Military Equipment
Departments: Radiation, Physics, Electronics, Materials, Mechanics,
Management, Basic Science, Statistics
Contact: Foreign Affairs Office, Changchun Institute of Precision Radiation
Mechanics, Weixing Rd., Chanchun, Jilin PRC Tel: 54644

JILIN INSTITUTE OF ARCHITECTURAL ENGINEERING
Responsible Bureau: Provincial and City Administrations of Environmental
Protection
Departments: Architecture, Construction Management, Labor Salaries
Contact: Foreign Affairs Office, Jilin Institute of Architectural Engineering,
Hongqi St., Changchun, Jilin PRC Tel: 52230

JILIN INSTITUTE OF INDUSTRIAL CHEMISTRY
Responsible Bureau: Provincial Oil and Chemistry Administration
Departments: Industrial Chemistry, Chemical Mechanics
Contact: Foreign Affairs Office, Jilin Institute of Industrial Chemistry,
Longtan District, Jilin City, Jilin PRC Tel: 38181

JILIN INSTITUTE OF INDUSTRY
Responsible Bureau: Provincial Education Committee
Departments: Mechanics, Materials, Electronics, Management, Light
Industrial Chemistry
Contact: Foreign Affairs Office, Jilin Institute of Industry, Yan'an Rd.,
Changchun, Jilin PRC Tel: 55521

NORTHEAST INSTITUTE OF ELECTRIC POWER ENGINEERING
Responsible Bureau: Ministry of Water and Electricity
Departments: Power Production, Electric Power, Architecture, Applied
Chemistry
Chinese Students: 1,800
Accommodations: pretty good; 2 rms, w/ TV, tape recorder, fridge,
"inadequate" hot water and kitchen, "inadequate heat until I complained;"
some use of car and driver, central to campus and markets, but 30 mins by
bus to downtown
Teacher Salary/Benefits: 1,500Y/mo, 70% FEC
FAO: "administration is ambivalent towards foreign teachers," at times
generous, at other times stingy about petty matters
Contact: Foreign Affairs Office, Northeast Institute of Electric Power
Engineering, Chanchun Rd., Jilin City, Jilin PRC Tel: 24186

Liaoning Strategically crucial Liaoning province has changed owner-
ship more often in the last 2 centuries than any other Chinese province, as the
Russians battled for a warm-water port, the Japanese struggled for a foothold
in Manchuria, the Europeans coveted rail lines, and the U.S. searched for
influence after Yalta. This importance is reflected still today. The capital,
Shenyang, is the only mid-sized Chinese city with sizeable numbers of
foreign consulates and the port city of Dalian (Dairen) is the northernmost
of China's Special Economic Zones and a major center of foreign trade.
Weather is harsh in the province's northern end, more mild on the coast.
Liaoning cuisine is rich in seafood but not overly varied in produce.
Language is fairly standard Mandarin.

Universities

ANSHAN UNIVERSITY
Responsible Bureau: City Government
Departments: Chinese, Finance, Mechanical Electronics, Medical Practice,
Architecture
Contact: Foreign Affairs Office, Anshan University, Shijiao, Anshan,
Liaoning PRC

BENXI UNIVERSITY
Responsible Bureau: City Government
Departments: Mechanical Control, Electrification, Industrial Management,
Industrial Worker's Construction, Financial Accounting, Statistics, Medical
Practice
Contact: Foreign Affairs Office, Benxi University, Pingshan District, Benxi,
Liaoning PRC Tel: 85777

DALIAN UNIVERSITY
Responsible Bureau: City Government
Departments: 3 colleges: *Medicine* (Medicine, Nursing, Acupuncture,
Stomatology and Medical Inspection); *Teaching* (General Liberal Arts);
Engineering (Electrical Equipment, High Temperature Studies,
Micromechanics, Agricultural Construction, Scientific Intelligence
Gathering, Consumer Goods Management, Accounting, Packaging, Industrial
Management, Mechanical Control, Statistics, Organical Chemical Engineer-
ing, Industrial Design)
Chinese Students: 4,165
Foreign Students: 58-60
Foreign Teachers: 4
Teachers: can teach English, Western Culture, technical subjects
Students: training center in Chinese Language and Culture, including classes
in Calligraphy, Tai Chi Chuan, Chinese Cooking, and excursions
Student Tuition/Expenses: tuition US$750/semester; dorms: $4/day for
double room; $2/day for 4 in a room; Meals: $2/day
Contact: Foreign Affairs Office, Dalian University, 142 Sanyuan St. Xigang
District, Dalian, Liaoning PRC Tel: 336461

DANDONG UNIVERSITY
Responsible Bureau: City Government
Departments: Industrial Economics, Architectural Engineering, Textiles,
Management Engineering, Finance and Accounting
Contact: Foreign Affairs Office, Dandong University, Zhenan District,
Dandong, Liaoning PRC Tel: 264243

FUSHUN UNIVERSITY
Responsible Bureau: City Government
Departments: Industrial Chemistry, Textiles, Silicate Industry, Mechanical
Weaving, Industrial Workers Construction, Environmental Engineering,
Medical Practice, Industrial Management
Contact: Foreign Affairs Office, Fushun University, Xinfu District, Fushun,
Liaoning PRC Tel: 73378

JINZHOU UNIVERSITY
Responsible Bureau: City Bureau of Education
Departments: Agricultural Economics, Secretarial Science, Industrial
Chemistry, Industrial Management, Orchard Production, Livestock and
Veterinary Medicine
Contact: Foreign Affairs Office, Jinzhou University, Shizhuan School,
Jinzhou, Liaoning PRC Tel: 8200

LIAONING UNIVERSITY*
Responsible Bureau: Provincial Bureau of Higher Education
Departments: Chinese, Journalism, History, Personal File Management, Philosophy, Law, Political Economics, Finance, Statistics, Foreign Languages, Mathematics, Physics, Chemistry, Biology, Accounting, Insurance
Chinese Students: 6,300
Foreign Students: 65-70
Foreign Teachers: 5
Sister Schools: US—Southern Illinois Univ, Univ of Denver; Japan—Kansai Univ, Toyama Univ
Teachers and Students: facilities include 1.2 million vol library, in-school publishing house (LU Press); has large program in Chinese Language and Culture
Contact: Foreign Affairs Office, Liaoning University, Chongshan W. Rd., Shenyang, Liaoning PRC Tel: 62541

SHENYANG UNIVERSITY*
Responsible Bureau: Provincial Bureau of Higher Education
Departments: Industrial Automation, Mechanical Production, Environmental Protection, Industrial Workers Construction, Finance, Statistics, Industrial Economics
Foreign Teachers: 8-10
Accommodations: pretty good, spacious, plenty of heat, flowering plum trees outside of windows
Contact: Foreign Affairs Office, Shenyang University, Dadong District, Shenyang, Liaoning PRC Tel: 442070

Arts/Music

LU XUN ACADEMY OF FINE ARTS
Responsible Bureau: Provincial Bureau of Higher Education
Departments: Handicrafts and Arts, Teaching, Fashion, Photography, Arts Design
Chinese Students: 700
Contact: Foreign Affairs Office, Lu Xun Academy of Fine Arts, 1 Sanhao St., Shenyang, Liaoning PRC Tel: 482635

Finance/Commerce/Economics

NORTHEAST INSTITUTE OF FINANCE AND ECONOMICS
Responsible Bureau: Ministry of Finance
Departments: Economics, Planning and Statistics, Accounting, Foreign Trade, Finance, Industrial Management
Accommodations: OK; 3 rms, some w/ kitchen, fridge, TV; strict 11 p.m. curfew, "obnoxious" doorman w/ gate locked on inside—"dangerous; if there were a fire we'd be foreign toast"; cafeteria poor
Teacher Salary/Benefits: 600Y/mo RMB, + r-t airfare
FAO: not bad
Teaching Conditions: 12-14 hrs/wk; good language lab, reasonable materials, no secretarial support or photocopying

Contact: Foreign Affairs Office, Northeast Institute of Finance and Economics, Heishijiao, Dalian, Liaoning PRC Tel: 91101

SHENYANG INSTITUTE OF ECONOMICS AND FINANCE
Responsible Bureau: City Government
Departments: Labor Economics, Industrial Management, Accounting, Statistics, Commercial Management, Economic Policy, Foreign Trade Economic Management, Information Management
Contact: Foreign Affairs Office, Shenyang Institute of Economics and Finance, Beiling Ave., Shenyang, Liaoning PRC Tel: 65826

Foreign Languages

DALIAN FOREIGN LANGUAGES INSTITUTE
Responsible Bureau: Provincial Higher Education Committee
Departments: English, Russian, Japanese, French
Contact: Foreign Affairs Office, Dalian Foreign Languages Institute, Zhongshan District, Dalian, Liaoning PRC Tel: 28741

Normal Schools

JINZHOU NORMAL INSTITUTE
Responsible Bureau: Provincial Bureau of Higher Education
Departments: Chinese, Political History, Mathematics, Physics, Chemistry, Foreign Languages
Contact: Foreign Affairs Office, Jinzhou Normal Institute, Anhe St., Jinzhou, Liaoning PRC Tel: 2723

LIAONING FOREIGN LANGUAGE NORMAL INSTITUTE
Responsible Bureau: Provincial Bureau of Higher Education
Departments: English, Russian, Japanese
Contact: Foreign Affairs Office, Liaoning Foreign Language Normal Institute, Qingnian St., Liaoyang, Liaoning PRC Tel: 25309

LIAONING NORMAL SCHOOL
Responsible Bureau: Provincial Bureau of Higher Education
Departments: Education and Schools, Political Education, Japanese, History, Library Science, Geology, Biology, Mathematics, Computer Science, Mathematics, Physics, Chemistry, Physical Education, Foreign Languages
Contact: Foreign Affairs Office, Liaoning Normal School, Shahekou District, Dalian, Liaoning PRC Tel: 41181

SHENYANG NORMAL INSTITUTE
Responsible Bureau: Provincial Bureau of Higher Education
Departments: Political Education, Education Management, Chinese, Foreign Languages, Biology, Mathematics, Physics, History of the Chinese Communist Party
Contact: Foreign Affairs Office, Shenyang Normal Institute, Huanghe Ave., Shenyang, Liaoning PRC Tel: 66049

Medical Schools

CHINESE UNIVERSITY OF MEDICAL SCIENCE
Responsible Bureau: Ministry of Sanitation and Hygiene
Departments: Medicine, Pediatrics, Oral Medicine, Sanitation and Hygiene,
Stomatology, Registered Nursing
Contact: Foreign Affairs Office, Chinese University of Medical Science,
Nanjing St., Shenyang, Liaoning PRC Tel: 32578

DALIAN INSTITUTE OF MEDICINE
Responsible Bureau: Provincial Administration of Sanitation and Hygiene
Departments: Medicine, Oral Medicine, Sanitation and Hygiene
Management
Chinese Students: 1,500
Sister Schools: US—Boston Univ School of Medicine; Japan—Tokyo
Medical Univ
Contact: Foreign Affairs Office, Dalian Institute of Medicine, 220 Xinghai
#3 Station, Dalian, Liaoning PRC Tel: 91242

JINZHOU INSTITUTE OF MEDICINE
Responsible Bureau: Provincial Administration of Sanitation and Hygiene
Departments: Medicine and Pharmacology
Contact: Foreign Affairs Office, Jinzhou Institute of Medicine, Le'an St.,
Jinzhou, Liaoning PRC Tel: 5369

LIAONING INSTITUTE OF CHINESE MEDICINE
Responsible Bureau: Provincial Adminstration of Sanitation and Hygiene
Departments: Acupuncture, Chinese Bone Treatment, Chinese
Pharmacology
Contact: Foreign Affairs Office, Liaoning Institute of Chinese Medicine,
Beiling Ave., Shenyang, Liaoning PRC Tel: 62567

SHENYANG INSTITUTE OF MEDICINE
Responsible Bureau: Provincial Bureau of Higher Education
Departments: Composition, Direction, Voice, Music, Instruments, Musical
Education
Contact: Foreign Affairs Office, Shenyang Institute of Medicine, Sanhao St.,
Shenyang, Liaoning PRC Tel: 482223

SHENYANG INSTITUTE OF PHARMACOLOGY
Responsible Bureau: National Medical and Pharmacological Bureau
Departments: Pharmacology, Japanese, Chinese Pharmacology, Chemical
Pharmacological Production, Microproduction, Pharmacological
Management
Contact: Foreign Affairs Office, Shenyang Institute of Pharmacology,
Wenhua Rd., Shenyang, Liaoning PRC Tel: 482706

Technical Schools

ANSHAN INSTITUTE OF STEEL
Responsible Bureau: Ministry of Industrial Metals

Departments: Materials and Metals, Industrial Metals, Mechanics, Automation and Control, Industrial Chemistry
Contact: Foreign Affairs Office, Anshan Institute of Steel, Zhonghua Rd., Anshan, Liaoning PRC Tel: 25951

CHINESE INSTITUTE OF XINGSHI POLICE
Responsible Bureau: Ministry of Public Security
Departments: Xingshi Intelligence, Clue Investigation, Document Investigation, Chemical Investigation, Photography, Police Medicine
Contact: Foreign Affairs Office, Chinese Institute of Xingshi Police, Houtawan St., Shenyang, Liaoning PRC Tel: 61829

DALIAN INSTITUTE OF AQUACULTURE
Responsible Bureau: Ministry of Agriculture, Livestock, and Fisheries
Departments: Fishery Mechanics, Fishing Port Architecture, Aquaculture, Economic Management, Aquatic Breeding
Contact: Foreign Affairs Office, Dalian Institute of Aquaculture, Heishijiao Village, Dalian, Liaoning PRC Tel: 91025

DALIAN INSTITUTE OF INDUSTRY
Responsible Bureau: State Education Committee
Departments: Mechanics, Materials, Shipbuilding, Electronics, Computer Science, Architecture, Hydrology, Industrial Chemistry, Management, Sociology, Mathematics, Physics, Power Science, Foreign Languages
Contact: Foreign Affairs Office, Dalian Institute of Industry, Luanjin Village, Dalian, Liaoning PR Tel: 91511

DALIAN INSTITUTE OF LIGHT INDUSTRY
Responsible Bureau: Ministry of Light Industry
Departments: Chemistry, Mechanical Electronics, Nutrition, Textiles, Fashion
Contact: Foreign Affairs Office, Dalian Institute of Light Industry, Ganjingzi District, Dalian, Liaoning PRC Tel: 52952

DALIAN INSTITUTE OF MARINE SHIPPING
Responsible Bureau: Ministry of Transportation
Departments: Sailing, Steamer Mechanics, Computer Science, Electronics, Marine Shipping Management
Contact: Foreign Affairs Office, Dalian Institute of Marine Shipping, Lingshuiqiao, Dalian, Liaoning PRC Tel: 91395

DALIAN RAILWAY INSTITUTE
Responsible Bureau: Ministry of Railways
Departments: Mechanical Cars and Vehicles, Materials, Mechanics, Electrical Equipment Engineering
Contact: Foreign Affairs Office, Dalian Railway Institute, Shahekou District, Dalian, Liaoning PRC Tel: 44323

FUSHUN INSTITUTE OF PETROLEUM
Responsible Bureau: China National Petroleum and Chemicals General Company
Departments: Mechanics, Automation, Oil Chemistry, Management
Contact: Foreign Affairs Office, Fushun Institute of Petroleum, Wanghua

NINGXIA INSTITUTE OF INDUSTRY
Responsible Bureau: Regional Economic Committee
Departments: Industrial Workers Construction, Mechanical Control, Industrial Management
Contact: Foreign Affairs Office, Ningxia Institute of Industry, Xinshi District, Yinchuan, Ningxia PRC Tel: 7401

NINGXIA UNIVERSITY*
Responsible Bureau: Regional Education Administration
Departments: Politics, History, Chinese, Journalism, Mathematics, Physics, Chemistry, Biology
Contact: Foreign Affairs Office, Ningxia University, Wencui N. Rd., Yinchuan, Ningxia PRC Tel: 7800

Qinghai   Once largely part of Tibet, Qinghai retains much of the varied culture of that region. The capital at Xining offers study of dozens of minority cultures, from tiny Bayi villages to the Tibetan Yellow Lamaists at the Ta'ersi Lamasery. Qinghai Lake, China's largest salt lake, offers fabulous bird-watching, while the region's immensely varied topography provides constant photo opportunities. The soft, temperate green hills of Xining give way to frozen crags in the south at Geladaintong, the headwaters of the Yellow, Yangtze, and Mekong rivers, and to harsh salt flats in the west. Ge'ermu (Golmud) in the west is the overland gateway to Tibet as well as the supply station for most of the labor camps in China's vast gulag system. Language is fairly standard Mandarin among Han residents, varied among minorities. Food is varied among minority regions, with lots to chose from in Xining. Weather in Xining offers four distinct seasons, none especially harsh, but gets fiercer in higher-altitude regions.

QINGHAI COLLEGE OF MEDICINE
Responsible Bureau: Provincial Education Administration
Departments: Medicine, Chinese Medicine, Rodent Control
Chinese Students: 730
Contact: Foreign Affairs Office, Qinghai College of Medicine, 84 Kunlun Rd., Xining, Qinghai PRC Tel: 23168

QINGHAI COLLEGE OF NATIONALITIES
Responsible Bureau: Provincial Minorities Committee
Departments: Political Education, Languages and Literatures, Law, Mathematics, Theoretical Chemistry
Chinese Students: 2,000
Foreign Students: 10-15
Foreign Teachers: 5
Teachers and Students: excellent ethnology programs; many opportunities for field study of minority groups; FAO has high marks; reasonable library (approx .5 million vols)
Contact: Foreign Affairs Office, Qinghai College of Nationalities, 25 Bayi

Rd., Xining, Qinghai PRC   Tel: 75310

QINGHAI INSTITUTE OF ENGINEERING AND AGRICULTURE
Responsible Bureau: Provincial Education Administration
Departments: Mechanics, Industrial Chemistry, Natural Products Architecture, Hydroelectricity, Agricultural Science, Plant Protection
Teachers and Students: library 240,000 vols; school emphasizes science and technology teaching
Contact: Foreign Affairs Office, Qinghai Institute of Engineering and Agriculture, North Suburbs, Xining, Qinghai PRC Tel: 24230

QINGHAI NORMAL SCHOOL
Responsible Bureau: Provincial Education Administration
Departments: Political Education, Chinese, History, Geology, Biology, Mathematics, Physics, Education, Chemistry, Foreign Languages, Physical Education, Industrial Arts
Chinese Students: 1,200
Contact: Foreign Affairs Office, Qinghai Normal School, Wusi Ave., Xining, Qinghai, PRC Tel: 55451

Shaanxi Shaanxi, and particularly the capital at Xi'an, is one of China's most popular tourist destinations. Xi'an houses some of China's most famed cultural and historical treasures, from the terra-cotta warriors of Qinshihuangdi to the Ming Dynasty Drum Tower and City Walls, and is one of the mainland's most international cities. Yan'an in the north was the endpoint of Mao's Long March and remains a mecca for historians of Chinese communism. Shaanxi summers are hot and dry, and winters cold and windy, particularly in the Western Hills at Baoji. Food is hearty, greasy, and mildly spiced, featuring many thick noodle soups and buns. Language is heavily accented Mandarin. While many of the region's archaeological treasures have yet to be excavated, and others remain under wraps for lack of funds for adequate display, resident foreigners have gained superb access to documents and artifacts for study and research.

Universities

BAOJI UNIVERSITY
Responsible Bureau: City Bureau of Education
Departments: Mechanical Production, Computer Science, Industrial Automation, Management
Contact: Foreign Affairs Office, Baoji University, Gongyuan Rd., Baoji, Shaanxi PRC   Tel: 3587

NORTHWEST UNIVERSITY*
Responsible Bureau: Provincial Bureau of Higher Education
Departments: Chinese, History, Philosophy, Foreign Languages, Mathematics, Computer Science, Physics, Chemistry, Industrial Chemistry, Geography, Geology, Biology, Economics

Chinese Students: 8,000
Teachers and Students: accepts foreign teachers of both English and technical subjects; has large program in Chinese Culture
Contact: Foreign Affairs Office, Northwest University, Xiaonanmenwai, Xi'an, Shaanxi PRC Tel: 25036

XI'AN TRANSPORTATION UNIVERSITY*
Responsible Bureau: State Education Committee
Departments: Mechanics, Materials, Power Production, Chemical Engineering, Electrical Equipment, Electronics, Computer Science, Information and Control, Agricultural Construction, Mathematics, Power Studies, Physics, Foreign Languages, Library Science, Intelligence Gathering
Chinese Students: 10,300
Foreign Students: 100+
Foreign Teachers: 10-15
Sister Schools: relations with 21 schools in Canada, France, Germany, Italy, UK and US
Teacher Accommodations: not bad: 3 rms, w/ TV, fridge, cooking facilities; cafeteria unpleasant; "cafeteria doesn't want us there, they are too busy overcharging wedding parties"; strict 11 p.m. curfew; location central to campus, 45 min walk from downtown
Salary and Benefits: 600Y/mo plus r-t airfare, domestic travel and excursions
FAO: "the worst waiban in China," drove out many foreign teachers
Teaching Conditions: 14 hrs/wk; students great, but no cooperation from dept; no secretarial help or photocopying
Students: have large programs in Chinese Language and Culture, students housed in dorms
Contact: Foreign Affairs Office, Xi'an Transportation University, 26 Xianning Rd., Xi'an, Shaanxi PRC Tel: 31011

YAN'AN UNIVERSITY
Responsible Bureau: Provincial Bureau of Higher Education
Departments: Political Education, Chinese, Mathematics, Physics, Chemistry, English
Chinese Students: 3,000+
Foreign Students: 40 (potential)
Foreign Teachers: 6
Teachers: school very eager to have foreign teachers; will be very generous
Teacher Accommodations: very good; 4 rms, w/ kitchen, tv, tape recorder, fridge, use of car and driver; no curfew, liberal on student visits
Salary and Benefits: 1,050-1,200 Y/mo RMB + 150Y/mo food allowance, r-t airfare for Foreign Experts
FAO: terrific and helpful, but not trustworthy about oral promises (or even always written)
Teaching Conditions: 8-9 hrs/wk; poor materials, but school open to new ideas, staff extremely helpful; both photocopying and secretaries available
Students: no foreign students now; school is working to set up program in Chinese Language/Culture; "willing to give very generous terms"
Contact: Foreign Affairs Office, Yan'an University, Yangjialing, Yan'an, Shaanxi PRC Tel: 3011

Arts/Music

XI'AN ACADEMY OF ART
Responsible Bureau: Provincial Bureau of Higher Education
Departments: Chinese Traditional Painting, Oil Painting, Woodblock Painting
Contact: Foreign Affairs Office, Xi'an Academy of Art, Southern Suburbs, Xi'an, Shaanxi PRC Tel: 52517

XI'AN MUSIC ACADEMY
Responsible Bureau: Provincial Bureau of Higher Education
Departments: Composition, Voice, Instrumental Music, Wind and String Instruments, Piano, Accordion
Contact: Foreign Affairs Office, Xi'an Music Academy, Chang'an Central Rd., Xi'an, Shaanxi PRC Tel: 51694

Minorities/Politics and Law

NORTHWEST INSTITUTE OF POLITICS AND LAW
Responsible Bureau: Ministry of Justice
Departments: Philosophy, Political Economics, Law, Economic Law, Labor Reform Management
Contact: Foreign Affairs Office, Northwest Institute of Politics and Law, Chang'an S. Rd., Xi'an, Shaanxi PRC Tel: 52056

TIBETAN MINORITY INSTITUTE
Responsible Bureau: District Education Administration
Departments: Politics, Languages and Literatures, History, Physical Education, Medicine, Economics
Contact: Foreign Affairs Office, Tibetan Minority Institute, Chengyang, Shaanxi PRC Tel: 3078

Finance/Economics/Commerce

SHAANXI INSTITUTE OF FINANCE AND ECONOMICS
Responsible Bureau: People's Bank, Central Branch
Departments: Industrial Economics, Trade Economics, Consumer Goods, Statistics, Accounting, Finance
Chinese Students: 2,600
Contact: Foreign Affairs Office, Shaanxi Institute of Finance and Economics, Cuihua Rd., Xi'an, Shaanxi PRC Tel: 52221

Foreign Languages

SHAANXI PROVINCE TECHNICAL NORMAL INSTITUTE OF FOREIGN LANGUAGES
Responsible Bureau: Provincial Education Administration
Departments: English, Russian
Contact: Foreign Affairs Office, Shaanxi Province Technical Normal Institute of Foreign Languages, Zhenhua N. Rd., Xi'an, Shaanxi PRC Tel: 61067

XI'AN FOREIGN LANGUAGES INSTITUTE
Responsible Bureau: Provincial Bureau of Higher Education

Departments: English, Russian, Japanese, German, French, Spanish, Travel and Tourism
Teachers: teach English and other Western languages, Western Culture, some teacher-training
Students: large program in Chinese Language and Culture
Contact: Foreign Affairs Office, Xi'an Foreign Languages Institute, Southern Suburbs, Xi'an, Shaanxi PRC Tel: 52956

Normal Schools

BAOJI NORMAL SCHOOL
Responsible Bureau: Provincial Bureau of Higher Education
Departments: Political Education, Chinese, Mathematics, Physics, Chemistry, English, History
Contact: Foreign Affairs Office, Baoji Normal School, Shibahe, Baoji, Shaanxi PRC Tel: 4323

SHAANXI NORMAL SCHOOL
Responsible Bureau: State Education Committee
Departments: Education, Political Education, Chinese, History, Biology, Geology, Mathematics, Physics, Chemistry, Physical Education, Foreign Languages, Distance Education
Accommodations: good; 4 rms w/ kitchen, bath, TV, fridge, A/C; fairly strict 10:30 p.m. curfew; location on edge of campus, 1 hr. walk to downtown
Teacher Salary/Benefits: 1,400Y/mo, 50% in FEC, + r-t int'l airfare (Foreign Expert)
FAO: very good
Teaching Conditions: 8-10 hrs/wk; photocopying available, students good, but library poor and access difficult
Contact: Foreign Affairs Office, Shaanxi Normal School, Chang'an S. Rd., Xi'an, Shaanxi PRC Tel: 52946

Medical Schools

XI'AN MEDICAL COLLEGE
Responsible Bureau: Ministry of Sanitation and Hygiene
Departments: Medicine, Oral Medicine, Sanitation and Hygiene, Stomatology, Pharmacology
Chinese Students: 2,500
Teachers and Students: accepts foreign students in all degree programs; accepts foreign teachers of English, technical subjects. Foreigners have also helped edit school's foreign-language publications; *Acta Academiae Medicinae Xian* (Quarterly): *Medical Education Study;* and *Medical Geography Abroad*
Contact: Foreign Affairs Office, Xi'an Medical College, Southern Suburbs, Xi'an, Shaanxi PRC Tel: 52921

YAN'AN MEDICAL COLLEGE
Responsible Bureau: Provincial Bureau of Higher Education
Departments: Medicine

Contact: Foreign Affairs Office, Yan'an Medical College, Dufuquan, Yan'an, Shaanxi PRC Tel: 3293

Technical Schools

NORTHWEST INSTITUTE OF ARCHITECTURAL ENGINEERING
Responsible Bureau: City Ministry of Architecture and Environmental Protection
Departments: Natural Products Architecture, Mechanical Electronics Engineering
Contact: Foreign Affairs Office, Northwest Institute of Architectural Engineering, Xiaozhai, Xi'an, Shaanxi PRC Tel: 51407

NORTHWEST INSTITUTE OF TELECOMMUNICATIONS ENGINEERING
Responsible Bureau: Ministry of Electronics
Departments: Information, Electronics, Computer Science, Physics, Management Engineering, Mathematics, Foreign Languages
Sister Schools: US—Univ of Wisconsin
Teachers: accepts foreign teachers of both English and technical subjects
Contact: Foreign Affairs Office, Northwest Institute of Telecommunications Engineering, Taibai Rd., Xi'an, Shaanxi PRC Tel: 51321

NORTHWEST INSTITUTE OF TEXTILE SCIENCE AND TECHNOLOGY
Responsible Bureau: Ministry of Textiles
Departments: Textiles, Mechanical Electronics, Fashion, Textile Chemistry, Industrial Management
Chinese Students: 1,000
Contact: Foreign Affairs Office, Northwest Institute of Textile Science and Technology, Jinhua S. Rd., Xi'an, Shaanxi PR Tel: 31963

SHAANXI INSTITUTE OF MECHANICAL ENGINEERING
Responsible Bureau: Ministry of Mechanics
Departments: Materials Engineering, Mechanical Engineering, Precision Engineering, Printing Technology, Automation and Control, Hydrology and Hydaulic Engineering, Industrial Management and Economic Engineering
Chinese Students: 4,200
Sister Schools: US—Rochester Inst of Technology, Northern Illinois Univ; Japan—Kyoto Univ, Fukui Univ; Italy—Univ of Rome
Teachers: accepts foreign teachers in both English and technical subjects; library 460,000 vols
Contact: Foreign Affairs Office, Shaanxi Institute of Mechanical Engineering, Jinhua S. Rd., Xi'an, Shaanxi PRC Tel: 31236

XI'AN INSTITUTE OF GEOLOGY
Responsible Bureau: Ministry of Geography and Mining Products
Departments: Geological Exploration, Surveying
Contact: Foreign Affairs Office, Xi'an Institute of Geology, Yanta Rd., Xi'an, Shaanxi PRC Tel: 52196

XI'AN INSTITUTE OF METALLURGY AND CONSTRUCTION ENGINEERING
Responsible Bureau: Ministry of Industrial Metals
Departments: Architecture, Environmental Studies, Industrial Metals, Materials and Mining, Mechanical Electronics, Management

Chinese Students: 5,900
Sister Schools: Australia—Univ of Wollongong; Japan—Kyushu Univ;
US—Old Dominion Univ
Teachers and Students: accepts teachers of both English and technical
subjects
Contact: Foreign Affairs Office, Xi'an Institute of Metallurgy and
Construction Engineering, Hepingmenwai, Xi'an, Shaanxi PRC
Tel: 52871

XI'AN INSTITUTE OF MINING
Responsible Bureau: Ministry of Coal Mining
Departments: Materials and Mining, Mechanical Electronics, Geology
Contact: Foreign Affairs Office, Xi'an Institute of Mining, Yanta Rd., Xi'an,
Shaanxi PRC Tel: 52931

XI'AN INSTITUTE OF PETROLEUM
Responsible Bureau: Ministry of Petroleum
Departments: Mechanical Engineering, Timing Equipment and Automation,
Industrial Economics, Petroleum Development, Computer Science
Contact: Foreign Affairs Office, Xi'an Institute of Petroleum, Lingyuan Rd.,
S. Section, Xi'an, Shaanxi PRC Tel: 53380

XI'AN INSTITUTE OF TECHNOLOGY
Responsible Bureau: Ministry of Engineering and Electronics Industry
Departments: Computer Science, Finance, Economics, Radiation, Precision
Mechanics, Electronics
Chinese Students: 2,500
Foreign Students: 0
Foreign Teachers: 2-4
Teachers: opportunities for English teachers and tech experts
Students: working to set up program for foreign students
Contact: Foreign Affairs Office, Xi'an Institute of Technology, 7 Jinhua N.
Rd., Eastern Suburbs, Xi'an, Shaanxi PRC Tel: 721921

XI'AN UNIVERSITY OF INDUSTRY
Responsible Bureau: Ministry of Aviation
Departments: Mathematical Theory and Power Studies, Mechanics,
Materials, Shipping, Electronics, Military Engineering, Automation and
Control, Computer Science, Management, Natural Products Architecture,
Sociology
Contact: Foreign Affairs Office, Xi'an University of Industry, Youyi W.
Rd., Xi'an, Shaanxi PRC Tel: 53355

Shandong
Birthplace of Confucius and center of Yellow River culture, Shandong is rich with historical and architectural treasures, from the ancient tombs at Zibo to the Buddhist temples and caverns at Lingyansi near Jinan. For more recent history the port city of Qingdao, built largely during the German occupation and resembling a "little Bavaria," offers many insights into Republican-era struggles, while industry in the capital at Jinan has been

important to the economic development of "New China." Language is
heavily accented Mandarin, and food richly varied during most of the year,
featuring much seafood and reduced to white-cabbage blandness only in the
depths of winter. Weather in the interior is broiling in summer, freezing in
winter; along the coast mild most of the year but with harsh winter blasts.

Universities

QINGDAO UNIVERSITY
Responsible Bureau: Provincial Higher Education Administration
Departments: Mathematics, Industrial Management, Foreign Languages,
Physics, Chemistry, Environmental Protection, Electrical Equipment,
Chinese, History
Chinese Students: 1,000+
Foreign Students: 5-10
Foreign Teachers: 5-6
Sister School: US—Connecticut College
Accommodations: not bad; 2-4 rms, w/ kitchen, TV, fridge, shared washer,
bikes; little heat and hot water; central to campus and freemarket, but 45 min.
bus ride from downtown
Teacher Salary/Benefits: 550-900Y/mo RMB, + o-w or r-t airfare,
excursions
FAO: "proceed with caution"
Teaching Conditions: 10-16 hrs/wk; class size good, excellent language lab,
good library but tight on student access; foreign teachers have set up "student
library;" "Qingdao U. is a new school still very much under construction;
lots of flexibility, but many things still 'to be worked out'"
Student Tuition/Expenses: varied, starting at approx US$800/semester
Learning Conditions: all student programs individualized; work closely w/
FAO before and after arrival to see your needs are met
Contact: Foreign Affairs Office, Qingdao University, Shinan District,
Qingdao, Shandong PRC Tel: 84186

SHANDONG UNIVERSITY*
Responsible Bureau: State Education Committee
Departments: Chinese, History, Philosophy, Law, Foreign Languages,
Library Science, Mathematics, Computer Science, Physics, Radio Technol-
ogy, Radiation, Chemistry, Biology, Microbiology, Scientific Socialism
Chinese Students: 2,400
Foreign Students: 110
Foreign Teachers: 6-10
Sister Schools: US—Harvard Univ, Indiana Univ, City College of NY;
Japan—Yamaguchi Univ; UK—Univ of Regina; Australia—Univ of
Adelaide
Accommodations: smallish; 2-3 rms, but pleasant, w/ kitchen, washer, tape
recorder, TV, shared bikes; in walled compound on leafy campus
Teacher Salary/Benefits: 600-1,000Y/mo RMB; most o-w airfare, 1/2 cubic
meter shipping allowance, excursions
FAO: some difficulties; "get it in writing"
Teaching Conditions: 12-18 hrs/wk, great students—Key Univ w/ good
facilities (library 1.7 million vol, in-school publishing house [SU Press])
Student Tuition/Expenses: vary by program

Learning Conditions: many programs (esp Chinese Language/Culture) set curricula, fairly inflexible; if want to design own curricula, be in touch early and often w/ waiban
Contact: Foreign Affairs Office, Shandong University, Jinan, Shandong, PRC Tel: 43861

SHANDONG UNIVERSITY OF OCEANOGRAPHY

Responsible Bureau: State Education Committee
Departments: Physics, Aquaculture, Chemistry, Oceanology, Geology, Aquatic Products, Aquatic Breeding, Mathematics, Marine Engineering, Foreign Languages
Chinese Students: 2,000+
Foreign Students: 0
Foreign Teachers: 2-3
Accommodations: very good in some ways, but small; nice old bldg w/ wood paneling in the interior; plentiful heat, cooking facilities, TV, bike
Teacher Salary/Benefits: 900Y/mo RMB, + 1 cubic meter shipping allowance and US$100 bonus for M.A. in TESOL
FAO: "quite nice, but will readily take advantage of you if allowed; get everything in writing and review your contract before signing"
Teaching Conditions: 14 hrs/wk; "at first I was required to correct 100 writing essays per week, but when I complained about this the English Dept was quite flexible about dropping this requirement"
Students: no foreign students now, school trying to set up exchange program
Contact: Foreign Affairs Office, Shandong University of Oceonography, Yushan Rd., Qingdao, Shandong PRC Tel: 83593

YANTAI UNIVERSITY

Responsible Bureau: Provincial Education Administration
Departments: Architecture, Mechanics, Chemistry, Foreign Languages, Mathematics, Physics, Law, Industrial Workers Construction
Chinese Students: 900+
Foreign Students: 0
Foreign Teachers: 3-6
Accommodations: very good; 6 rms w/ balconies, kitchen, view of sea, shared washer, TV, fridge, bike; cafeteria "cheap but sloppy;" dorm central to campus, 20 min from downtown by bus; strict visitor registration
Teacher Salary/Benefits: 700Y/mo RMB, + vacation bonus, excursions, 250Y RMB shipping allowance
FAO: reasonably helpful, somewhat inflexible about vacations
Teaching Conditions: 12 hrs/wk; good language lab and library; secretarial support
Contact: Foreign Affairs Office, Yantai University, Qingquanzhai, Yantai, Shandong PR Tel: 24657

Arts/Music

SHANDONG ACADEMY OF FINE ARTS

Responsible Bureau: Provincial Cultural Administration
Departments: Music, Arts, Opera, Applied Arts, Arts Education
Contact: Foreign Affairs Office, Shandong Academy of Fine Arts, Wenhua E. Rd., Jinan, Shandong PRC Tel: 42814

Finance/Economics

SHANDONG INSTITUTE OF ECONOMICS
Responsible Bureau: Provincial Economic Committee
Departments: Accounting, Statistics, Economic Policy, Finance,
Economics, Foreign Trade, Teaching
Chinese Students: 1,700
Contact: Foreign Affairs Office, Shandong Institute of Economics,
Yanzishan E. Alley, Jinan, Shandong PRC Tel: 44162

Normal Schools

QUFU TEACHERS UNIVERSITY
Responsible Bureau: Provincial Higher Education Administration
Departments: Chinese, Politics, History, Foreign Languages, Education,
Mathematics, Physics, Industrial Arts, Physical Education, Chemistry,
Biology, Geology
Chinese Students: 4,000
Foreign Students: 0 now; plans for 200
Foreign Teachers: 5
Sister Schools: US—Skidmore College; Canada—McGill Univ
Accommodations: pretty good; 2-4 rms w/ kitchen,TV, tape recorder,
washer, bike; no curfew, fairly lax visitor registration; location central to
campus, easy bike ride from downtown
Teacher Salary/Benefits: 600-1,200Y (Foreign Teacher–Foreign Expert),
+ r-t airfare
FAO: mostly pleasant
Teaching Conditions: 10-16 hrs/wk, dedicated students, poor materials but
reasonable library, school "very helpful" (e.g., aided 1 foreign teacher to
make nationwide contact with Chinese Shakespeare scholars)
Students: no foreign students now, but school planning new program in
Chinese Language and Culture; expenses will be US$250 for 4-wk course, +
US$8/day room and board
Contact: Foreign Affairs Office, Qufu Teachers University, Xiguan, Qufu,
Shandong PRC

SHANDONG NORMAL SCHOOL
Responsible Bureau: Provincial Education Administration
Departments: Education, Politics, History, Chinese, Foreign Languages,
Mathematics, Computer Science, Physics, Chemistry, Biology, Moral
Education, Geology, Industrial Arts, Physical Education
Contact: Foreign Affairs Office, Shandong Normal School, Wenhua E. Rd.,
Jinan, Shandong PRC Tel: 43711

VICTORY OIL FIELD NORMAL SCHOOL
Responsible Bureau: Ministry of Petroleum
Departments: Chinese, Mathematics, Physics, Chemistry, Foreign
Languages, Political History, Industrial Arts, Physical Education
Foreign Students: 0
Foreign Teachers: 2-5
Teachers: teach English; "pretty lonely, but the terms are very generous"
Contact: Foreign Affairs Office, Victory Oil Field Normal School,

Dongying, Shandong PRC Tel: 25167

YANTAI TEACHERS COLLEGE
Responsible Bureau: Provincial Higher Education Administration
Departments: Chinese, Politics, English, Mathematics, Physics, Chemistry,
Physical Education, Biology
Chinese Students: 2,700
Contact: Foreign Affairs Office, Yantai Teachers College, Southern
Suburbs, Yantai, Shandong PRC Tel: 23567

Medical Schools

CHANGWEI MEDICAL COLLEGE
Responsible Bureau: Provincial Administration of Sanitation and Hygiene
Departments: Medicine, Sanitation and Hygiene Management
Contact: Foreign Affairs Office, Changwei Medical College, Shengli Ave.,
Weifang, Shandong PRC Tel: 4931

QINGDAO MEDICAL COLLEGE
Responsible Bureau: Provincial Administration of Sanitation and Hygiene
Departments: Medical Practice, Pediatrics, Medical Examination, Radiation,
Sanitation and Hygiene Management
Chinese Students: 800+
Foreign Students: 0
Foreign Teachers: 4
Teachers: teach English, Western Culture; nice accommodations and
pleasant students; campus in downtown Qingdao
Contact: Foreign Affairs Office, Qingdao Medical College, Huangtai Rd.,
Qingdao, Shandong PRC Tel: 24523

SHANDONG COLLEGE OF CHINESE MEDICINE
Responsible Bureau: Provincial Administration of Sanitation and Hygiene
Departments: Medicine, Chinese Pharmacology
Contact: Foreign Affairs Office, Shandong College of Chinese Medicine,
Jingshi Rd., Jinan, Shandong, PRC Tel: 46911

SHANDONG COLLEGE OF MEDICINE
Responsible Bureau: Ministry of Sanitation and Hygiene
Departments: Medicine, Oral Medicine, Sanitation and Hygiene,
Pharmacology
Contact: Foreign Affairs Office, Shandong College of Medicine, Wenhua
W. Rd., Jinan, Shandong PRC Tel: 21682

TAI'AN COLLEGE OF MEDICINE
Responsible Bureau: Provincial Administration of Sanitation and Hygiene
Departments: Medicine, Radiation Therapy, Nursing and Care
Contact: Foreign Affairs Office, Tai'an College of Medicine, Taishan W.
Rd., Tai'an, Shandong PRC Tel: 2734

Technical Schools

QINGDAO INSTITUTE OF ARCHITECTURAL ENGINEERING
Responsible Bureau: Ministry of Industrial Metals

Departments: Architectural Engineering, Environmental Studies,
Mechanics, Mining, Industrial Management
Chinese Students: 1,000
Foreign Students: 0
Foreign Teachers: 4-5
Accommodations: good; 2-3 rms in nice old bldg, w/ kitchen, shared bath,
TV, tape recorder, bike; central location and reasonable doorman
Teacher Salary/Benefits: 450-1,000Y/mo RMB, + o-w airfare
FAO: "not bad"
Teaching Conditions: 14-16 hrs/wk; students good
Contact: Foreign Affairs Office, Qingdao Institute of Architectural
Engineering, Fushun Rd., Qingdao, Shandong PRC Tel: 33532

SHANDONG AGRICULTURAL UNIVERSITY
Responsible Bureau: Provincial Agricultural Administration
Departments: Agricultural Science, Crop Protection, Soil Chemistry,
Forestry, Gardening, Livestock and Veterinary Medicine, Agricultural
Equipment, Agricultural Economics
Contact: Foreign Affairs Office, Shandong Agricultural University, Tai'an,
Shandong PRC Tel: 3451

SHANDONG INSTITUTE OF ARCHITECTURAL ENGINEERING AND MATERIALS
Responsible Bureau: National Bureau of Architectural Materials
Departments: Material Science, Applied Chemistry, Automation,
Non-metallic Mining
Contact: Foreign Affairs Office, Shandong Institute of Architectural
Engineering and Materials, Baihushan Rd., Zhibo, Shandong PRC Tel: 168

SHANDONG INSTITUTE OF ARCHITECTURAL ENGINEERING
Responsible Bureau: Provincial, City, and County Construction Committees
Departments: Architecture, Mechanical Electronics, Urban Planning,
Architectural Engineering
Contact: Foreign Affairs Office, Shandong Institute of Architectural
Engineering, Heping Rd., Jinan, Shandong PRC Tel: 42404

SHANDONG INSTITUTE OF LIGHT INDUSTRY
Responsible Bureau: Provincial Number One Light Industrial
Administration
Departments: Mechanical Electronics, Light Industrial Chemistry, Silicate
Industry, Art Design
Contact: Foreign Affairs Office, Shandong Institute of Light Industry,
Huangtai N. Rd., Jinan, Shandong PRC Tel: 44221

SHANDONG INSTITUTE OF MINING
Responsible Bureau: Ministry of Coal Mining
Departments: Geology, Coal Mine Architecture and Construction, Coal
Exploration, Electrical Equipment, Coal Mine Mechanics, Computer Center
Contact: Foreign Affairs Office, Shandong Institute of Mining, Tai'an,
Shandong PRC Tel: 3310

SHANDONG PETROLEUM INSTITUTE
Responsible Bureau: Ministry of Petroleum
Departments: Basic Science, Exploration, Resource Development, Oil

Refinement, Mechanics, Automation, Management, Computer Science
Chinese Students: 3,400
Teachers: considering setting up exchange programs w/ several US and
Canadian univs
Contact: Foreign Affairs Office, Shandong Petroleum Institute, Dongying,
Shandong PRC Tel: 24901

SHANDONG POLYTECHNICAL UNIVERSITY
Responsible Bureau: Provincial Bureau of Higher Education
Departments: Mechanical Engineering, Electrical Engineering, Power
Production, Electric Power, Electric Equipment, Electronics, Computer
Science, Chemistry, Hydrology, Management Engineering, Basic Studies
Chinese Students: 4,600
Sister School: Coventry Polytechnic
Contact: Foreign Affairs Office, Shandong Polytechnical University, Jingshi
Rd., Jinan, Shandong PRC Tel: 25081

SHANDONG TEXTILE ENGINEERING COLLEGE
Responsible Bureau: Provincial Textile Administration
Departments: Textile Engineering, Mechanical Electronic Engineering,
Textile Chemistry, Management Engineering, Applied Arts
Chinese Students: 700+
Foreign Students: 0
Foreign Teachers: 3
Accommodations: pretty good; 2-3 rms, w/ kitchen, TV, tape recorder, bike;
central location; major curfew and visitor registration problems ("doorkeeper
was nasty ogre")
Teacher Salary/Benefits: 600Y/mo RMB + RMB reimbursement for o-w
airfare, 1/2 cubic meter crate shipping allowance
FAO: very good; "in general when I have a complaint about something they
have been reasonable and willing to compromise"
Teaching Conditions: 14 hrs/wk; good students but poor materials
Contact: Foreign Affairs Office, Shandong Textile Engineering College,
Fushun Rd., Qingdao, Shandong PRC Tel: 33272

Shanghai   The largest city in China and the second largest in the world,
the Shanghai Special Zone houses nearly 20 million people. This vibrant,
bustling city is one of the most modern and international in China, with
tremendous cultural and economic opportunities. The Bund, built during the
colonial era, and the city's other commercial centers offer unparalleled
shopping. Transport is convenient, and foreign residents have many opportunities to moonlight in business and journalism. Foreigners are no rarity in
Shanghai, and will rarely receive special attention, for better or worse. Many
foreign residents compare Shanghai with New York—"the people have a
hard edge," wrote one respondent. "It can be abrasive, but it's very exciting."
Shanghai cuisine is one of the finest in China, though sweeter and more oily
than many foreign palates prefer. Weather is chilly and damp in winter, mild

spring and fall, and suffocating in summer. The Shanghainese language is not comprehensible to Mandarin speakers, but nearly everyone in the city speaks Mandarin if pushed.

Universities

FUDAN UNIVERSITY*
Responsible Bureau: State Education Committee
Departments: Languages and Literatures, Journalism, History, Economics, Philosophy, International Politics, World Economics, Law, Mathematics, Physics, Atomic Science, Electronics, Chemistry, Biology, Management, Power Studies, Materials, Radiation Physics, Statistics, Mathematical Operational Research, Foreign Languages
Chinese Students: 10,000
Foreign Students: 300-400
Foreign Teachers: 12
Sister Schools: US—State Univ of New York at Albany, St. Mary's College, MD, Univ of Southern Maine, UC Fullerton, many others
Accommodations: all foreigners in walled compound; teachers 2-3 rms w/ kitchen, TV, tape recorder; students 2 per rm; rather cut off from campus life
Teacher Salary/Benefits: 700-1,100Y/mo RMB, + r-t airfare, shipping allowance, excursions
FAO: "waiban very helpful, with a lot of power"
Teaching Conditions: 12-16 hrs/wk; great facilities, but students "discouraged from too much contact." Fudan is one of China's top schools—many students children of elite
Student Tuition/Expenses: variable; many students enroll through univs in home country
Learning Conditions: few opportunities to practice Chinese within compound: "English, French, and Japanese prevail"; libraries "excellent," but card catalogs all in Chinese
Contact: Foreign Affairs Office, Fudan University, Handan Rd., Shanghai PRC Tel: 484906

SHANGHAI POLYTECHNICAL UNIVERSITY*
Responsible Bureau: City Bureau of Higher Education
Departments: Mechanics, Electrical Mechanics, Industrial Automation, Industrial Metallurgy, Computer Science, Industrial Chemistry, Management
Contact: Foreign Affairs Office, Shanghai Polytechnical University, Yanchang Rd., Shanghai PRC Tel: 650744

SHANGHAI TRANSPORTATION UNIVERSITY*
Responsible Bureau: State Education Committee
Departments: Shipping and Marine Aquaculture, Power Production Mechanics, Electric Power, Automation and Control, Computer Science, Electronic Communication, Materials, Mechanical Mathematics, Precision Engineering, Applied Physics, Power Studies, Applied Chemistry, Management, Foreign Trade, Scientific Foreign Languages, Sociology
Chinese Students: 4,000
Foreign Students: 50-60
Foreign Teachers: 10-15
Teachers: teach English, Western Culture, variety of technical subjects;

"Jiaoda" is a Key Univ, one of China's most famous
Students: various programs in Chinese Language/Culture, as well as degree
programs
Contact: Foreign Affairs Office, Shanghai Transportation University,
Huashan Rd., Shanghai PRC Tel: 378517

SHANGHAI UNIVERSITY
Responsible Bureau: City Bureau of Higher Education
Departments: Chinese, History, Law, Library Science, Sociology,
Mechanics, Electronics, Microelectronics and Automation, Radio
Technology, Foreign Languages, Art Design, Oil Painting, Chinese Painting,
Sculpture, Politics
Chinese Students: 7,200
Foreign Students: 30-35
Contact: Foreign Affairs Office, Shanghai University, Haixuan Rd.,
Shanghai PRC Tel: 524433

TONGJI UNIVERSITY*
Responsible Bureau: State Education Committee
Departments: Architecture, Agricultural Construction Design, Highways
and Transportation, Minerology, Surveying, Materials, Environmental
Studies, Mechanics, Electronics, Management, Economic Information,
Marine Aquaculture and Geology, Foreign Languages, Mathematics, Power
Studies, Physics, Chemistry
Teachers and Students: one of China's premier institutions with very large
programs for foreign teachers and students
Contact: Foreign Affairs Office, Tongji University, Siping Rd., Shanghai
PRC Tel: 462121

Arts/Music

SHANGHAI CONSERVATORY OF MUSIC
Responsible Bureau: Ministry of Culture
Departments: Composition, Direction, Voice, Wind and String Instruments,
Minority Instruments, Piano, Musicology
Chinese Students: 800+
Foreign Students: 20-25
Foreign Teachers: 5-8
Teachers: can teach English, Western Culture
Students: can study Chinese Language, Culture, traditional musical
instruments; school "very flexible"
Contact: Foreign Affairs Office, Shanghai Conservatory of Music, 20
Fenyang Rd., Shanghai PRC Tel: 370137

SHANGHAI DRAMA/OPERA INSTITUTE
Responsible Bureau: Ministry of Culture
Departments: Acting, Stage Decoration, Operatic Culture, Directing
Contact: Foreign Affairs Office, Shanghai Drama/Opera Institute, Jing'an
District, Shanghai PRC   Tel: 521909

Politics and Law

EAST CHINA INSTITUTE OF POLITICS AND LAW
Responsible Bureau: Ministry of Justice
Departments: Law
Chinese Students: 2,500
Foreign Students: 30+
Foreign Teachers: 6-8
Accommodations: 2-4 rms in quiet area of campus, w/ TV, tape recorder, shared bike, kitchen; campus 2 min walk from Zhongshan Park, 20 min bus ride from Bund
Teacher Salary/Benefits: 800-1,200Y/mo RMB; other benefits vary
FAO: "not bad, but get things in writing"
Teaching Conditions: 12-14 hrs/wk; students very sharp
Learning Conditions: "lots of good teachers, but the program is pretty unstructured, so you have to be self-motivated"
Contact: Foreign Affairs Office, East China Institute of Politics and Law, Wanhangdu Rd., Shanghai PRC Tel: 520611

Finance/Commerce/Economics

SHANGHAI COLLEGE OF ECONOMICS AND FINANCE
Responsible Bureau: Ministry of Finance
Departments: Economics, Industrial Economics, Trade Economics, Economic Information, Statistics, Accounting, Finance, World Economics
Contact: Foreign Affairs Office, Shanghai College of Economics and Finance, Hongkou District, Shanghai PRC Tel: 664690

SHANGHAI INSTITUTE OF FOREIGN TRADE*
Responsible Bureau: Ministry of Foreign Trade
Departments: Foreign Trade Economics, Foreign Trade Foreign Languages, International Economic Law, Industrial Management
Chinese Students: 1,080
Foreign Students: 40
Foreign Teachers: varies
Sister Schools: US—Univ of San Francisco, Univ of Lincoln, Eastern Washington Univ, Columbia Univ; Ausrtalia—Univ of Sydney; Japan—Univ of Tokyo, Southwestern College
Accommodations: great; bedrm, shared kitchen and bath, Western toilet and "10 sq. meter bathtub," washer, dryer, TV, tape recorder, fridge; heat and A/C "great when they turn it on"
Teacher Salary/Benefits: 700-900Y/mo, 30% convertible to FEC + o-w int'l airfare, 300Y travel bonus, great health care
FAO: "I think we can't complain"; overall helpful, but only moderately trustworthy on oral promises; most personnel tops but "one guy is a pill—we call him 'Fat Happy'; he smiles a lot, is fat, and doesn't do anything!"
Teaching Conditions: 10-12 hrs/wk; students great, "love 'em to death!" little photocopying, but secretarial assistance available; library "fairly well equipped," including subscriptions to *Time, Newsweek,* etc., but closed to undergrads
Contact: Foreign Affairs Office, Shanghai Institute of Foreign Trade, 620 Gubei Rd., Shanghai PRC Tel: 598181

Foreign Languages

SHANGHAI FOREIGN LANGUAGES INSTITUTE*
Responsible Bureau: State Education Committee
Departments: English, German, Foreign Trade, French, Arabic, Russian, Japanese, Spanish, Chinese
Chinese Students: 2,000+
Foreign Students: 350+
Foreign Teachers: 10-15
Teachers: can teach Western Culture, languages
Students: study Chinese Language, Culture; many Chinese government scholarship students learning Chinese prior to entering Chinese-language degree programs; large foreigner compound, "it can be hard to practice Chinese"
Contact: Foreign Affairs Office, Shanghai Foreign Languages Institute, 119 Tiyuhui Rd., Shanghai PRC Tel: 664900

Normal Schools

EAST CHINA NORMAL UNIVERSITY*
Responsible Bureau: State Education Committee
Departments: Education, Political Education, Chinese, History, Geology, Mathematics, Physics, Chemistry, Biology, Library Sciences, Foreign Languages, Electronic Education, Industrial Arts, Physical Education, Psychology, Computer Science, Mathematical Theory, Statistics, Electronic Science and Technology, Economics
Chinese Students: 8,300
Foreign Students: 120
Foreign Teachers: varies
Contact: Foreign Affairs Office, East China Normal University, 3663 Zhongshan N. Rd., Shanghai PRC Tel: 549498

SHANGHAI NORMAL SCHOOL
Responsible Bureau: City Bureau of Higher Education
Departments: Political Education, Chinese, History, Mathematics, Physics, Chemistry, Foreign Languages, Industrial Arts, Physical Education, Geology, Computer Science
Contact: Foreign Affairs Office, Shanghai Normal School, Xuhui District, Shanghai PRC Tel: 384301

SHANGHAI TEACHERS COLLEGE OF TECHNOLOGY
Responsible Bureau: City Bureau of Higher Education
Departments: Chinese, English, Political Education, Mathematics, Physics, Chemistry, Biology, Mechanics, Architecture
Chinese Students: 1,800
Foreign Students: 0
Foreign Teachers: 1-2
Sister School: US—Glendale Community College
Contact: Foreign Affairs Office, Shanghai Teachers College of Technology, Fengxian County, 201418 Shanghai PRC Tel: 747540/747541

Medical Schools

SHANGHAI COLLEGE OF TRADITIONAL CHINESE MEDICINE
Responsible Bureau: City Bureau of Higher Education
Departments: Chinese Medicine, Chinese Pharmacology, Acupuncture and Acupressure
Chinese Students: 1,400
Foreign Students: 25
Foreign Teachers: varies
Sister Schools: US—Harvard Medical School, Univ of San Francisco; Japan—Kawasaki Medical School, Showa Univ; Germany—Univ of Groningen
Students: has program in Traditional Chinese Medicine for foreign students
Contact: Foreign Affairs Office, Shanghai College of Traditional Chinese Medicine, 539 Lingling Rd., Xuhui District, Shanghai PRC Tel: 388400

SHANGHAI NUMBER ONE COLLEGE OF MEDICINE*
Responsible Bureau: Ministry of Sanitation and Hygiene
Departments: Medicine, Sanitation and Hygiene, Pharmacology
Contact: Foreign Affairs Office, Shanghai Number One College of Medicine, Yixueyuan Rd., Shanghai PRC Tel: 311900

SHANGHAI NUMBER TWO COLLEGE OF MEDICINE
Responsible Bureau: City Bureau of Higher Education
Departments: Medicine, Pediatrics, Oral Medicine, Medical Examination, Biological Medicine
Chinese Students: 3,750
Foreign Students: 60
Foreign Teachers: varies
Sister Schools: US—Univ of Missouri (Kansas City), UC San Francisco; Japan—Osaka Univ; France—Univ of Rene Descartes, Univ d'Aix-Marseilles; Belgium—Univ of Antwerp
Contact: Foreign Affairs Office, Shanghai Number Two College of Medicine, 280 Chongqing S. Rd., Luwan District, Shanghai PRC
Tel: 260760

SHANGHAI RAILWAY SCHOOL OF MEDICINE
Responsible Bureau: Ministry of Railroads
Departments: Medicine, Oral Medicine
Contact: Foreign Affairs Office, Shanghai Railway School of Medicine, Zhabei District, Shanghai PRC Tel: 661774

Technical Schools

CHINESE UNIVERSITY OF TEXTILES
Responsible Bureau: Ministry of Textiles
Departments: Textiles, Mechanics, Automation, Textile Chemistry, Management, Fashion, Chemical Fibers
Contact: Foreign Affairs Office, Chinese University of Textiles, Yan'an W. Rd., Shanghai PRC Tel: 522430

EAST CHINA INSTITUTE OF TECHNOLOGY
Responsible Bureau: State Education Committee

Departments: Chemistry, Industrial Chemistry, Biological Chemistry, High Radiation Materials, Organic Materials, Automation and Control, Mechanics, Environmental Studies, Mathematics, Physics, Management, Foreign Languages, Sociology, Computer Science

Accommodations: good; 2 rms, w/ washer, TV, tape recorder, fridge, shortwave radio, no kitchen but cafeteria cheap and good; no curfew, lax visitor registration; central to campus (east side by Sun Yat-sen tomb—pretty countryside, 45 min by bus to Bund)

Teacher Salary/Benefits: 450Y/mo RMB, + r-t airfare, excursions

FAO: "East China Inst has the best FAO I've seen in China (out of 6 schools where I have taught)"

Teaching Conditions: 15 hrs/wk, + 8 office hrs; classes include International Trade; language lab excellent; library and materials so-so

Contact: Foreign Affairs Office, East China Institute of Technology, Meilung Rd., Shanghai PRC Tel: 380811

SHANGHAI CITY INSTITUTE OF CONSTRUCTION

Responsible Bureau: City Construction Committee

Departments: Architecture, Management, Urban Planning, Heating and Air Conditioning, Architectural and Construction Mechanics

Contact: Foreign Affairs Office, Shanghai City Institute of Construction, Yangpu District, Shanghai PRC Tel: 461580

SHANGHAI FISHERIES UNIVERSITY

Responsible Bureau: Ministry of Agriculture, Livestock, and Fisheries

Departments: Aquaculture, Marine Products Processing, Aquatic Breeding, Aquaculture Economics and Management

Chinese Students: 2,000

Contact: Foreign Affairs Office, Shanghai Fisheries University, 334 Jungong Rd., Shanghai PRC Tel: 431090

SHANGHAI INSTITUTE OF AGRICULTURE

Responsible Bureau: City Agricultural Committee

Departments: Agricultural Science, Crop Protection, Livestock and Veterinary Medicine, Gardening, Agricultural Economics

Chinese Students: 1,100

Sister School: Japan—Univ of Osaka

Contact: Foreign Affairs Office, Shanghai Institute of Agriculture, Shanghai County, Qibao Hamlet, Shanghai PRC   Tel: 389081

SHANGHAI INSTITUTE OF ARCHITECTURAL ENGINEERING AND MATERIALS

Responsible Bureau: National Bureau of Architectural Materials

Departments: Materials, Mechanical Electronics, Industrial Management

Contact: Foreign Affairs Office, Shanghai Institute of Architectural Engineering and Materials, Jiangwanwu E. Rd., Shanghai PRC   Tel: 485136

SHANGHAI INSTITUTE OF ELECTRIC POWER

Responsible Bureau: Ministry of Water and Electricity

Departments: Power Production, Electric Power, Management

Contact: Foreign Affairs Office, Shanghai Institute of Electric Power, Pingliang Rd., Shanghai PRC   Tel: 430410

SHANGHAI INSTITUTE OF MECHANICAL ENGINEERING
Responsible Bureau: Ministry of Mechanics
Departments: Timing Mechanisms and Devices, Power Production Mechanics, Systems Engineering and Automation, Computer Science, Scientific and Technological Foreign Languages
Chinese Students: 3,500
Sister Schools: US—MIT, Indiana Univ; Hong Kong—Hong Kong Polytechnic; Japan—Univ of Tokyo; Switzerland—Federal Inst of Technology; Germany—Univ of Stuttgart
Contact: Foreign Affairs Office, Shanghai Institute of Mechanical Engineering, 516 Jungong Rd., Shanghai PRC Tel: 433040

SHANGHAI INSTITUTE OF RAILWAYS
Responsible Bureau: Ministry of Railways
Departments: Railway Shipping, Mechanics, Electrical Equipment, Natural Materials Engineering, Electronic Mail and Computer Science
Chinese Students: 3,000
Contact: Foreign Affairs Office, Shanghai Institute of Railways, 1 Zhennan Rd., Shanghai PRC Tel: 506344

SHANGHAI MARITIME UNIVERSITY
Responsible Bureau: Ministry of Transportation
Departments: Maritime Boats, Ship Mechanics, Mechanics, Computer Science, Water Transport Management, International Marine Shipping, Foreign Languages
Chinese Students: 3,000
Foreign Students: 0
Foreign Teachers: 2
Accommodations: very good; 5 rms, w/ kitchen, TV, fridge, tape recorder, bike; 11:30p.m. curfew, but flexible; visitors must register; SMU is in Pudang, an isolated area by Shanghai standards
Teacher Salary/Benefits: very good salary, + r-t airfare every 2 yrs, shipping allowance
FAO: "lazy but well-meaning"; quite flexible about vacations
Teaching Conditions: 16-18 hrs/wk; school materials poor, but open to new; library good and open to students
Contact: Foreign Affairs Office, Shanghai Maritime University, 1550 Pudong Rd., Shanghai PRC Tel: 840911

SHANGHAI SCIENCE AND TECHNOLOGY CADRES INSTITUTE
Responsible Bureau: City Bureau of Higher Education
Departments: Materials, Physics, Radio Electronics, Mathematics, Micromechanics, Computer Science, Chemistry, Biology
Foreign Students: 0
Foreign Teachers: 1-3
Accommodations: good; 3 rms, w/ kitchen, TV; 10 p.m. curfew; bold new location is fairly isolated, too far from Shanghai for a day trip, but cooler and cleaner than the city
Teacher Salary/Benefits: 650Y/mo RMB, + r-t airfare
FAO: no official waiban, but 1 "pleasant" man acts as liaison
Teaching Conditions: 15 hrs/wk, students great (older cadres); no language lab

Contact: Foreign Affairs Office, Shanghai Science and Technology Cadres Institute, Jiading County, Shanghai Special Zone, PRC Tel: 950433

SHANGHAI UNIVERSITY OF ENGINEERING TECHNOLOGY
  Responsible Bureau: City Economic Committee
  Departments: Mechanics, Electronics and Electrical Equipment, Management, Industrial Chemistry, Materials, Vehicle Studies, Textiles, Mechanical Electronics, Textile Chemistry
  Contact: Foreign Affairs Office, Shanghai University of Engineering Technology, Xianxia Rd., Shanghai PRC Tel: 597051

Shanxi Heavily hit by cutbacks in government subsidies to mining, Shanxi is one of China's poorest regions. The capital at Taiyuan offers dozens of lovely temples and several fine museums, and the Buddhist grottoes at Datong rank among China's finest. Mt. Wutai, one of China's holiest Buddhist mountains, offers centuries of temples and shrines, including the oldest extant Buddhist temple in China. However, due to the region's poverty, the local government tends to be leery of outside eyes. Even Mt. Wutai is officially a closed area, and while travel permits are routinely granted, foreigners are closely tracked. Foreign residents have much better access to the region than travelers, and one Datong teacher reported studying ancient sutras found at Lianyungang with some local scholars. Still, this is not a region for those who want free access to nightclubs. Food is bland but hearty, with many noodle dishes; weather dry, dusty, and harsh in winter; and language thickly accented Mandarin.

Universities

SHANXI UNIVERSITY
  Responsible Bureau: Provincial Education Administration
  Departments: Chinese, Law, Library Science, History, Education, Philosophy, Politics, Foreign Languages, Mathematics, Computer Science, Physics, Chemistry, Biology, Environmental Protection, Economics, Law, Physical Education, Art/Music
  Chinese Students: 6,300
  Foreign Students: 45-50
  Foreign Teachers: 10-15
  Sister Schools UK—Sussex Univ; US—Univ of South Carolina, Connecticut College
  Teachers: teach English language and/or technical subjects
  Students: have large program in Chinese Language/Culture
  Contact: Foreign Affairs Office, Shanxi University, Wucheng Rd., 030006 Taiyuan, Shanxi PRC   Tel: 773441

TAIYUAN UNIVERSITY
  Responsible Bureau: City Government
  Departments: Mechanics, Steel and Iron Patternmaking, Computer

Software, Industrial Chemistry, Industrial Workers Construction, Crop
Protection, Nursing and Care, Chinese, Politics, History, Planning and
Statistics, Finance
Contact: Foreign Affairs Office, Taiyuan University, Jingangli, Taiyuan,
Shanxi PRC Tel: 20059

YUNZHONG UNIVERSITY
Responsible Bureau: City Government
Departments: Coal and Industrial Chemistry, Sanitation and Hygiene,
Industrial Management, Education Management
Contact: Foreign Affairs Office, Yunzhong University, Xinjian S. Rd.,
Datong, Shanxi PRC Tel: 32347

Finance/Commerce/Economics

SHANXI INSTITUTE OF ECONOMIC POLICY
Responsible Bureau: Ministry of Commerce
Departments: Commercial Economics, Statistics, Accounting, Finance
Contact: Foreign Affairs Office, Shanxi Institute of Economic Policy,
Nanneihuan St., Taiyuan, Shanxi PRC Tel: 22156

Normal Schools

SHANXI NORMAL SCHOOL
Responsible Bureau: Provincial Education Administration
Departments: Chinese, Political Education, History, Geology, Biology,
Mathematics, Chemistry, Physical Education, Foreign Languages
Contact: Foreign Affairs Office, Shanxi Normal School, Linfen, Shanxi
PRC Tel: 3932

Medical Schools

SHANXI INSTITUTE OF MEDICINE
Responsible Bureau: Provincial Education Administration
Departments: Medicine, Sanitation and Hygiene
Contact: Foreign Affairs Office, Shanxi Institute of Medicine, Xinjian S.
Rd., Taiyuan, Shanxi PRC Tel: 21511

Technical Schools

SHANXI AGRICULTURAL UNIVERSITY*
Responsible Bureau: Provincial Education Administration
Departments: Agricultural Science, Crop Protection, Soil Chemistry,
Gardening, Forestry, Livestock, Veterinary Medicine, Agricultural
Mechanics, Agricultural Economics, Nutrition
Contact: Foreign Affairs Office, Shanxi Agricultural University, Taigu
County, Taiyuan, Shanxi PRC

SHANXI INSTITUTE OF MINING
Responsible Bureau: Ministry of Coal Mining
Departments: Materials and Mining, Geology, Mining Construction and
Techniques, Mechanics, Electrical Equipment
Contact: Foreign Affairs Office, Shanxi Institute of Mining, Yingzexi Ave.,
Taiyuan, Shanxi PRC Tel: 66402

TAIYUAN INSTITUTE OF HEAVY MECHANICS
Responsible Bureau: Ministry of Mechanics
Departments: Mechanics, Library Science
Contact: Foreign Affairs Office, Taiyuan Institute of Heavy Mechanics,
Taiyuan, Shanxi PRC Tel: 65447

TAIYUAN INSTITUTE OF MECHANICS
Responsible Bureau: Ministry of Weapons and Military Equipment
Departments: Mechanics, Automative Control, Industrial Chemistry
Contact: Foreign Affairs Office, Taiyuan Institute of Mechanics, Shanglan
Village, Taiyuan, Shanxi PRC Tel: 59411

TAIYUAN UNIVERSITY OF TECHNOLOGY*
Responsible Bureau: Provincial Education Commission
Departments: Mechanics, Electrical Machinery, High Temperature Studies,
Information Control and Engineering, Computer Science, Agricultural
Construction, Industrial Chemistry, Applied Chemistry, Hydrology,
Mathematics, Power Science
Chinese Students: 6,000
Foreign Students: 0
Foreign Teachers: 10-12
Sister Schools: UK—Univ of Liverpool, Polytechnic of Newcastle-upon-
Tyne; US—Univ of South Carolina, Oberlin College
Teachers: can teach English, Western Culture, technical subjects
Contact: Foreign Affairs Office, Taiyuan University of Technology, 11
Yingzexi Ave., Taiyuan, Shanxi PRC Tel: 66517

Sichuan   Lush and steamy Sichuan, irrigated by the Chang Jiang
(Yangtze), Yalong, and Jialing Rivers, is China's most populous province
and one of her most fertile areas. Ranging from the subtropics at Dukou to
dry, temperate weather at Se'erxu, Sichuan never offers freezing conditions
(except on her mountaintops), and her farmers harvest some of China's finest
produce year-round. Sichuan cuisine is spicy, her people almost exclusively
Han in the East and North, mixing with Shani in the South and Tibetan and
Chang in the West. Two of China's most famous mountains (holy Buddhist
Mt. Emei and the Giant Buddha Mountain at Leshan) tempt climbers, and the
province offers unparalleled wildlife viewing activities, including the only
preserve in the world offering a fair shot at seeing giant pandas in the wild.
Millennia of Buddhist and secular art and architecture grace Sichuan,
particularly in the temples of the capital at Chengdu, of Qingchengshan, and
of Emei Shan, and in the caves at Dazu. Near Qingchengshan ancient
Dujiangyan, the world's oldest man-made irrigation project, still stands in
tribute to China's ancient technology. The mighty Chang Jiang (Yangtze) is
the province's main transportation artery, and the lifeblood of Chongqing,
the province's largest city and key commercial center. Language is thickly
accented Mandarin.

Universities

CHENGDU UNIVERSITY OF SCIENCE AND TECHNOLOGY*
Responsible Bureau: Ministry of Education/Provincial Government
Departments: Mechanical Engineering, Electrical Engineering, Chemistry, Hydrology, Metallurgy, High Energy Radiation Materials, Computer Science, Power Studies, Mathematics, Physics, Management, Politics
Chinese Students: 6,500
Teachers and Students: accepts foreign teachers of English, scientific English, and technical subjects; accepts foreign students in Chinese Language and degree programs; excellent waiban, good financial packages, large libraries and good facilities
Contact: Foreign Affairs Office, Chengdu University of Science and Technology, Xinnanmen, Chengdu, Sichuan PRC Tel: 52967

CHENGDU UNIVERSITY
Responsible Bureau: City Government
Departments: Industrial Management, Mechanics, Electrical Equipment Engineering and Chemistry, Mathematical Theory, Chinese, Foreign Languages
Contact: Foreign Affairs Office, Chengdu University, Renmin N. Rd., Chengdu, Sichuan PRC Tel: 31183

CHONGQING UNIVERSITY*
Responsible Bureau: State Education Committee
Departments: Mechanical Engineering, Radiation, Precision Equipment Engineering, High Temperature Studies, Radio and Telecommunications Technology, Computer Science, Management, Mathematics, Applied Physics, Applied Chemistry
Chinese Students: 6,500
Sister Schools: US—Univ of California, Western Washington State Univ, Univ of San Diego, Univ of Virginia
Accommodations: pretty good; 1-2 rms w/ kitchen, A/C, washer, TV, no curfew, central location
Teacher Salary/Benefits: 1,400Y/mo, 50% FEC plus r-t airfare (Foreign Expert contract negotiated through British Council)
FAO: quite good, "very fortunate with FAO personnel"
Teaching Conditions: 14 hrs/wk, terrible materials; library well equipped but a "state secret" and tough to get into
Contact: Foreign Affairs Office, Chongqing University, Shazheng St., Chongqing, Sichuan PRC Tel: 661789

HANZHIHUA UNIVERSITY
Responsible Bureau: City Government
Departments: Industrial Worker's Construction, Computer Science, Mechanical Control, Chinese, Political Management, Teaching, Secretarial Science
Contact: Foreign Affairs Office, Hanzhihua University, Bingcaogang, Dukou, Sichuan PRC Tel:

SICHUAN UNIVERSITY*
Responsible Bureau: State Education Committee

Departments: Chinese, Journalism, History, Personal Files, Philosophy, Foreign Languages and Literatures, Library Science, Mathematics, Physics, Radio Technology, Chemistry, Biology, Computer Science, Economics, Management, Commerce, Trade, Law
Accommodations: excellent; 3-5 rms w/ kitchen, TV, tape recorder, bike, A/C; but in walled compound and very strict about Chinese visitors
Teacher Salary/Benefits: varied; many Fulbright Experts—individuals generally get poor contracts here
FAO: notoriously unpleasant and inflexible waiban official (e.g. waiban charged 1 foreign teacher 30Y per night "guest fee" when his wife visited)
Teaching Conditions: Key University with top-notch students, good facilities—but staff tends toward inflexibility
Learning Conditions: students in foreign compound; "I felt I had to go off campus to practice my Chinese"
Contact: Foreign Affairs Office, Sichuan University, Wangjianglou, Chengdu, Sichuan PRC Tel: 54111

YUZHOU UNIVERSITY
Responsible Bureau: City Bureau of Education
Departments: Mechanics, Electronics, Economic Management, Chemistry, Biology, Chinese, Mathematics, Physics, Foreign Languages, Physical Education, Statistics
Contact: Foreign Affairs Office, Yuzhou University, Xianfeng St., Chongqing, Sichuan PRC Tel: 663746

Minorities/Politics and Law

SOUTHWEST INSTITUTE OF POLITICS AND LAW*
Responsible Bureau: Ministry of Justice
Departments: Law, Economic Law, Criminal Investigation, Administrative Management, Labor Reform Management
Contact: Foreign Affairs Office, Southwest Institute of Politics and Law, Shapingba District, Chongqing, Sichuan PRC Tel: 661223

SOUTHWEST MINORITIES INSTITUTE
Responsible Bureau: National Bureau of Minorities
Departments: Livestock and Veterinary Medicine, Politics, History, Chinese, Minority Languages, Mathematics, Theoretical Chemistry
Teacher Accommodations: so-so; 2 rms, w/ kitchen, TV, tape recorder, bike; strict curfew and registration of visitors
Teacher Salary/Benefits: 500Y/mo, 30% FEC plus 400Y/semester domestic travel
FAO: extremely flexible and quite helpful
Teaching Conditions: 14 hrs/wk; students great; materials provided bad, but library good
Student Tuition and Expenses: US$600/term plus 350Y/term housing, 10Y/day food
Learning Conditions: fairly good; library resources limited and teaching methods and materials traditional
Contact: Foreign Affairs Office, Southwest Minorities Institute, Qinglong Village, Chengdu, Sichuan PRC Tel: 52403

Arts/Music

SICHUAN ACADEMY OF ARTS
Responsible Bureau: Provincial Bureau of Higher Education
Departments: Industrial Arts, Painting, Plastics, Decoration Design
Contact: Foreign Affairs Office, Sichuan Academy of Arts, Jiulongbo District, Chongqing, Sichuan PRC Tel: 23423

SICHUAN CONSERVATORY OF MUSIC
Responsible Bureau: Provincial Bureau of Higher Education
Departments: Voice, Musical Instruments, Wind and String Instruments, Composition, Minority Music
Contact: Foreign Affairs Office, Sichuan Conservatory of Music, Xinnanmenwai, Chengdu, Sichuan PRC Tel: 22181

Finance/Commerce/Economics

SOUTHWEST INSTITUTE OF FINANCE AND ECONOMICS
Responsible Bureau: Chinese People's Bank
Departments: Finance, Political Economics, Agricultural Economics, Accounting, Statistics, Economic Policy, Economic Management
Contact: Foreign Affairs Office, Southwest Institute of Finance and Economics, Xiguanghua Village, Chengdu, Sichuan PRC Tel: 23116

Foreign Languages

SICHUAN FOREIGN LANGUAGE INSTITUTE
Responsible Bureau: Bureau of Higher Education
Departments: English, Russian, Japanese, French, German
Teachers and Students: accepts foreign teachers of Western languages/ cultures; has large Chinese Language program for foreign students
Contact: Foreign Affairs Office, Sichuan Foreign Language Institute, Lieshi Rd., Chongqing, Sichuan PRC Tel: 661737

Normal Schools

CHONGQING NORMAL SCHOOL
Responsible Bureau: Provincial Bureau of Higher Education
Departments: Chinese, History, Foreign Languages, Mathematics, Physics, Chemistry, Biology, Geology, Chinese
Contact: Foreign Affairs Office, Chongqing Normal School, Tianchen Rd., Chongqing, Sichuan PRC Tel: 661275

NANCHONG NORMAL SCHOOL
Responsible Bureau: Provincial Bureau of Higher Education
Departments: Chinese, Foreign Languages, Politics, History, Mathematics, Physics, Chemistry, Biology
Contact: Foreign Affairs Office, Nanchong Normal School, Renmin N. Rd., Nanchong, Sichuan PRC Tel: 2244

SICHUAN NORMAL SCHOOL
Responsible Bureau: Provincial Bureau of Higher Education
Departments: Chinese, Political Education, Foreign Languages, History,

Education, Mathematics, Physics, Chemistry, Biology, Geology
Contact: Foreign Affairs Office, Sichuan Normal School, Dongcheng
District, Chengdu, Sichuan PRC Tel: 42612

SOUTHWEST NORMAL SCHOOL
Responsible Bureau: State Education Committee
Departments: History, Music, Art, Mathematics, Physics, Chemistry,
Biology, Geology, Physical Education, Telephone Technology, Pre-
education Training, Politics, Chinese, Library Management, Foreign
Languages, Political Education
Contact: Foreign Affairs Office, Southwest Normal School, Beipei,
Chongqing, Sichuan PRC

Medical Schools

CHENGDU COLLEGE OF CHINESE MEDICINE
Responsible Bureau: Provincial Bureau of Higher Education
Departments: Chinese Medicine, Acupuncture, Chinese Pharmacology,
Western Medicine
Contact: Foreign Affairs Office, Chengdu College of Chinese Medicine,
Xiluo Rd., Chengdu, Sichuan PRC Tel: 27241

CHONGQING COLLEGE OF MEDICINE
Responsible Bureau: Provincial Bureau of Higher Education
Departments: Medicine, Pediatrics, Medical Examination, Population
Planning
Contact: Foreign Affairs Office, Chongqing College of Medicine, Shapingba
District, Chongqing, Sichuan PRC Tel: 23695

SICHUAN MEDICAL COLLEGE
Responsible Bureau: Ministry of Sanitation and Hygiene
Departments: Medicine, Stomatology, Oral Medicine, Sanitation and
Hygiene Inspection, Pharmacology, Pharmacological Chemistry, Nutrition
Chinese Students: 3,700
Sister Schools: US—Univ of Washington; Canada—Univ of British
Columbia, Univ of Toronto
Teachers and Students: accepts foreign teachers of English, technical
subjects; has program for foreign students in Chinese Medicine
Contact: Foreign Affairs Office, Sichuan Medical College, Chengdu,
Sichuan PRC Tel: 54411

Technical Schools

CHENGDU COLLEGE OF GEOLOGY
Responsible Bureau: Ministry of Geology
Departments: Geology, Mining Production and Exploration and Research,
Applied Chemistry, Water Resource Geology, Global Physics, Nuclear
Materials, Mining Exploration, Applied Mathematics, Sociology
Chinese Students: 3,800
Sister Schools: Australia—Univ of Adelaide; France: Univ of Lower Saxony
Contact: Foreign Affairs Office, Chengdu College of Geology, Northeast
Suburbs, Chengdu, Sichuan PRC Tel: 34712

CHENGDU INSTITUTE OF METEOROLOGY
Responsible Bureau: National Bureau of Meteorology
Departments: Meteorology, Exploration and Surveying, Electronics,
Finance and Economics
Contact: Foreign Affairs Office, Chengdu Institute of Meteorology, Renmin
S. Rd., Chengdu, Sichuan PRC Tel: 52580

CHENGDU INSTITUTE OF RADIO ENGINEERING
Responsible Bureau: Ministry of Electronic Industry
Departments: Radio and Telecommunications Technology, Electromagnetic
Fields, Electronics, Applied Chemistry, Mechanics, Computer Science,
Social Science, Mathematics, Physics
Chinese Students: 4,920
Sister Schools: Japan—Keio Univ; Germany—Fachhochschule Aachen
Contact: Foreign Affairs Office, Chengdu Institute of Radio Engineering,
Eastern Suburbs, Chengdu, Sichuan PRC Tel: 33312

CHONGQING INSTITUTE OF ARCHITECTURAL ENGINEERING*
Responsible Bureau: City Ministry of Construction and Environmental
Protection
Departments: Agricultural Construction, Electronics, Automation,
Mechanics, Management, Secretarial Sciences, Politics
Chinese Students: 5,400
Sister Schools: US—Univ of Minnesota, Univ of Washington, Univ of
Tennessee, Univ of Michigan; Canada—Univ of Manitoba; Japan—Univ of
Waseda
Contact: Foreign Affairs Office, Chongqing Institute of Architectural
Engineering, Shapingba District, Chongqing, Sichuan PRC Tel: 661989

CHONGQING INSTITUTE OF POST AND TELECOMMUNICATIONS
Responsible Bureau: Ministry of Post and Telecommunications
Departments: Electronic Mail, Radio Technology, Management
Accommodations: not very good, 4 rms, cooking facilities, appliances
didn't always work
Teacher Salary/Benefits: 900Y, 33% FEC, o-w airfare
FAO: conservative and semieducated, not very helpful, not very flexible, but
trustworthy
Teaching Conditions: 15 hrs/wk; teaching materials terrible, but school
open to new materials
Contact: Foreign Affairs Office, Chongqing Institute of Post and Telecom-
munications, Nan'an District, Chongqing, Sichuan PRC Tel: 481726

CHONGQING INSTITUTE OF TRANSPORTATION
Responsible Bureau: Ministry of Transportation
Departments: Highways and Bridges, Management, Mechanics, Marine
Shipping Ports
Contact: Foreign Affairs Office, Chongqing Institute of Transportation,
Dahuang Rd., Chongqing, Sichuan PRC Tel: 482653

SOUTHWEST INSTITUTE OF PETROLEUM
Responsible Bureau: Ministry of Petroleum
Departments: Resource Exploration, Mechanics, Applied Chemistry,

Management, Petroleum Geology
Contact: Foreign Affairs Office, Southwest Institute of Petroleum, Shiyou E.
Rd., Nanchong, Sichuan PRC Tel: 22771

SOUTHWEST UNIVERSITY OF AGRICULTURE
Responsible Bureau: Ministry of Agriculture, Livestock, and Fisheries
Departments: Agricultural Science, Gardening, Crop Protection, Soil
Chemistry, Nutrition, Silkworm and Mulberry Cultivation, Agricultural
Mechanics, Agricultural Economics, Aquatic Products, Agricultural
Education, Livestock and Veterinary Medicine, Finance and Accounting,
Statistics
Accommodations: very good, 6 rms for 2 people, w/ kitchen, TV, tape
recorder, bike, shared washer; cafeteria food inedible
Teacher Salary/Benefits: 650-750Y/mo, 30% FEC, + o-w airfare
FAO: so-so; tight about money
Teaching Conditions: 12-15 hrs/wk; shortage of materials
Contact: Foreign Affairs Office, Southwest University of Agriculture,
Beipei, Chongqing, Sichuan PRC Tel: 3965

SICHUAN INSTITUTE OF TECHNOLOGY
Responsible Bureau: Provincial Bureau of Higher Education
Departments: Mechanical Engineering, Vehicles, Power Production,
Nutrition, Architectural Engineering, Materials
Chinese Students: 650
Contact: Foreign Affairs Office, Sichuan Institute of Technology, Bi
County, Chengdu, Sichuan PRC Tel: 21271

SOUTHWEST UNIVERSITY OF TRANSPORTATION*
Responsible Bureau: Ministry of Railways
Departments: Agricultural Construction, Mechanics, Mechanical Cars and
Vehicles, Electrical Equipment, Computer Science, Shipping, Materials,
Mathematics, Management, Power Studies, Finance and Accounting,
Sociology, Foreign Languages
Contact: Foreign Affairs Office, Southwest University of
Transportation, Emei County, Sichuan PRC Tel: 5151

Tianjin   China's third largest city, Tianjin (the Tianjin Special Zone)
connects Bejing with the Bohai Gulf, forming a crucial economic corridor.
One of China's most important centers of foreign trade, the zone offers
resident foreigners excellent moonlighting opportunities in business, finance,
and trade. The zone also has spectacular shopping opportunities in the new
Fashion District, Food District, and indoor freemarkets downtown as well as
a wealth of cultural activities. Too far from Beijing for a convenient day trip,
the city is very accessible to the capital for weekend visits. Several important
museums grace Tianjin, as do a number of important historic districts,
particularly those reflecting the city's treaty port years and those important
in the life of Zhou En-lai. Weather is temperate, though windy in winter.
Food is excellent and quite varied. Language is standard Mandarin.

Universities

NANKAI UNIVERSITY*
Responsible Bureau: State Education Committee
Departments: Chinese, History, Philosophy, Library Science, Sociology, Economics, International Economics, Law, Foreign Languages, Finance, Mathematics, Physics, Biology, Chemistry
Chinese Students: 5,000
Foreign Students: 200 short term and 150 long term
Foreign Teachers: 30
Sister Schools: US—Temple Univ, Univ of Minnesota, Kansas Univ, State Univ of NY, Indiana Univ; Japan—Ritsumeikan Univ; Australia—Univ of Melbourne, Australian National Univ, Laval Univ; Canada—McGill Univ, McMasters Univ
Teachers: Nankai is one of China's premier univs; accepts foreign teachers and experts in various fields; facilities include 1.9 million vol library, 2 English-language quarterly journals, 2 in-school publishing houses (NU Press, NU Publishing House)
Students: has special programs in Chinese Canguage/Culture, as well as students in degree programs; students in walled compound
Contact: Foreign Affairs Office, Nankai University, Nankai District, Tianjin PRC Tel: 331640

TIANJIN UNIVERSITY*
Responsible Bureau: State Education Committee
Departments: Mechanics, Microengineering, High Temperature Physical Engineering, Electrical Engineering, Water Power, Ships and Boats, Management, Chemical Engineering, Applied Chemistry, Architecture, Computer Science, Physics
Chinese Students: 10,500
Sister Schools: Canada, Japan, France, Germany, US
Teachers and Students: facilities 1.1 million vol library
Contact: Foreign Affairs Office, Tianjin University, 92 Wei Jin Rd., Nankai District, Tianjin PRC Tel: 333704

Arts/Music

TIANJIN INSTITUTE OF ART
Responsible Bureau: City Bureau of Higher Education
Departments: Teaching, Painting, Handicraft Arts, Pattern Design, Fashion, Dyes
Contact: Foreign Affairs Office, Tianjin Institute of Art, Tianwei District, Tianjin PRC Tel: 62186

TIANJIN INSTITUTE OF MUSIC
Responsible Bureau: City Bureau of Higher Education
Departments: Composition Theory, Voice, Minority Instruments, Wind and String Instruments, Teaching
Contact: Foreign Affairs Office, Tianjin Institute of Music, Hedong District, Tianjin PRC Tel: 40061

Finance/Commerce/Economics

TIANJIN INSTITUTE OF COMMERCE
Responsible Bureau: Ministry of Commerce
Departments: Packaging Engineering, Nutrition Engineering, Management
Engineering, Frozen Goods Engineering, Industrial Management
Contact: Foreign Affairs Office, Tianjin Institute of Commerce, Northern
Suburbs, Tianjin PRC Tel: 64345

TIANJIN INSTITUTE OF FINANCE AND ECONOMICS
Responsible Bureau: City Bureau of Higher Education
Departments: Foreign Trade, Finance, Economic Policy and Accounting,
Industrial Management, Commercial Economics
Contact: Foreign Affairs Office, Tianjin Institute of Finance and Economics,
Hexi District, Tianjin PRC Tel: 82657

TIANJIN INSTITUTE OF FOREIGN TRADE
Responsible Bureau: Ministry of Foreign Trade and Economics
Departments: Foreign Trade and Economics, Foreign Trade English
Contact: Foreign Affairs Office, Tianjin Institute of Foreign Trade, Hebei
District, Tianjin PRC Tel: 65610

Foreign Languages

TIANJIN FOREIGN LANGUAGES INSTITUTE
Responsible Bureau: City Bureau of Higher Education
Departments: English, Japanese, Western Languages
Contact: Foreign Affairs Office, Tianjin Foreign Languages Institute, Hexi
District, Tianjin PRC Tel: 397101

Normal/Medical Schools

TIANJIN COLLEGE OF CHINESE MEDICINE
Responsible Bureau: City Bureau of Higher Education
Departments: Chinese Medicine, Acupuncture, Chinese Pharmacology,
Chinese Bone Treatment, Chinese External Medicine
Contact: Foreign Affairs Office, Tianjin College of Chinese Medicine,
Nankai District, Tianjin Special Zone PRC Tel: 23427

TIANJIN INSTITUTE OF MEDICINE
Responsible Bureau: City Bureau of Higher Education
Departments: Medicine, Oral Medicine, Sanitation and Hygiene, Nursing
and Care, Precision Medical Timing Equipment
Chinese Students: 2,000
Contact: Foreign Affairs Office, Tianjin Institute of Medicine, 62 Qi Xiang
Tai Rd., Heping District, Tianjin PRC Tel: 334390

TIANJIN NORMAL SCHOOL
Responsible Bureau: City Bureau of Higher Education
Departments: Political Education, Chinese, History, Education,
Mathematics, Physics, Chemistry, Biology, Geology, Foreign Languages
Contact: Foreign Affairs Office, Tianjin Normal School, Hexi District,
Tianjin PRC Tel: 333665

Technical Schools

CIVIL AVIATION INSTITUTE OF CHINA
Responsible Bureau: National Bureau of Civil Aviation
Departments: Aviation Management, Aviation Mechanics, Aviation Timing Control Electronics, Aviation Radio
Chinese Students: 1,600
Foreign Students: 0
Foreign Teachers: 2
Accommodations: excellent; 4 rms w/ kitchen, washer, TV, phone, fan, A/C, plenty of heat/hot water, use of car and driver Saturday a.m.; location central to campus and markets but 2 hrs from downtown by public bus; 30 min by school shuttle—last shuttle leaves downtown 5:40 p.m.—to have evening downtown must take taxi, approx 40Y
Teacher Salary/Benefits: 800Y/mo, 50% in FEC, + r-t airfare, excursions
FAO: "totally incapable"
Teaching Conditions: 8 hrs/wk; good students, excellent library; staff very sophisticated; CAIC is specialized training school for civil aviation, run by CAAC; students mix of trainees and professionals; in addition to 2 long-term foreign English teachers, have frequent short-term foreign technical experts
Contact: Foreign Affairs Office, Civil Aviation Institute of China, Zhanggui Village, East Suburbs, Tianjin PRC Tel: 47602

TIANJIN INSTITUTE OF LIGHT INDUSTRY
Responsible Bureau: Ministry of Light Industry
Departments: Mechanical Engineering, Nutritional Engineering, Chemical Engineering, Electrical Equipment Technology and Automation, Organic Chemistry, Heavy Transport and Mechanics
Chinese Students: 600
Contact: Foreign Affairs Office, Tianjin Institute of Light Industry, 1486 Da Gu S. Rd., Hexi District, Tianjin PRC Tel: 82965

TIANJIN INSTITUTE OF TECHNOLOGY
Responsible Bureau: City Bureau of Higher Education
Departments: Radio Technology, Automation, Mechanics, Microengineering, Chemical Engineering, Computer Science, Mathematics, Physics, Foreign Languages, Management Engineering
Contact: Foreign Affairs Office, Tianjin Institute of Technology, Hexi District, Tianjin PRC

TIANJIN TEXTILES INSTITUTE
Responsible Bureau: Ministry of Textiles
Departments: Textile Engineering, Fashion, Mechanics, Automation, Industrial Management
Contact: Foreign Affairs Office, Tianjin Textiles Institute, Hedong District, Tianjin PRC Tel: 43251

Tibet   Surely one of the most exotic of study/teaching abroad destinations, Tibet University offers some excellent programs in Tibetan language and culture and invites up to 10 foreign teachers a year. The program is often suspended due to political difficulties, however, and even at the best of times, foreigners admit to many difficulties, from coping with altitude sickness to nightly curfews and house-to-house searches. Not for the faint of heart!

TIBET UNIVERSITY*
Responsible Bureau: District Educational Administration
Departments: Mathematical Theory, Politics, Languages and Literatures, Music and Art, Tibetan Language and Literature, History, Chemistry, Biology, Geology
Teachers: accepts foreigners as English/Western-culture teachers; "fascinating, but lots of strict curfews, and they keep pretty close tabs on us"
Students: had program in Tibetan Language/Culture; program suspended temporarily 10/89; write for current status
Contact: Foreign Affairs Office, Tibet University, Lhasa, Tibet PRC
Tel: 23213

Xinjiang   China's northwesternmost province, Xinjiang is a land of extremes from the lowest desert basin in the world to the massive peaks of the Altan mountains, from the howling Gobi and Taklamakan deserts "of no return" to the gracious, shaded oases of Turpan and Kashgar. Most famous for the architectural and sculptural wonders remaining from her Silk Road history, Xinjiang is also rich with minority cultures, particularly that of the Uighurs, a central Asian people closer in language and custom to the Arab nations than to the Han Chinese. Major cities are Urumqi, the bustling capital; Kashgar, on the border of Pakistan (from which enterprising tourists can apply to enter Soviet Central Asia or to travel the Karakoram highway); and Turpan, where resident foreigners can watch Uighur dancers under grape trellises in the shadow of Suleiman's Minaret. Food is Central Asian— mutton, beef, flatbreads, noodles, and lots of raisins, melons, and dried peaches and plums. Weather throughout Xinjiang is high desert: broiling in the day, freezing at night, wind-swept year-round, and searingly dry. Language is fairly   standard Mandarin in Han areas, variable among minorities.

KASHGAR NORMAL SCHOOL
Responsible Bureau: Regional Education Administration
Departments: Political Education, Languages and Literatures, Mathematics, Physical Chemistry, Physical Education
Contact: Foreign Affairs Office, Kashgar Normal School, Kashgar, Xinjiang PRC Tel: 2302

XINJIANG COLLEGE OF CHINESE MEDICINE
Responsible Bureau: Regional Administration of Sanitation and Hygiene
Departments: Chinese Medicine, Acupuncture

Accommodations: spacious, tree-lined campus; rare in Urumqi
Contact: Foreign Affairs Office, Xinjiang College of Chinese Medicine, Beijing Rd., Urumqi, Xinjiang PRC Tel: 41554

XINJIANG INSTITUTE OF ECONOMICS AND FINANCE
Responsible Bureau: Regional Economics Commission
Departments: Finance and Economics, Planning and Statistics, Finance and Accounting, Finance
Contact: Foreign Affairs Office, Xinjiang Institute of Economics and Finance, Ergong, Urumqi, Xinjiang PRC Tel: 38754

XINJIANG INSTITUTE OF INDUSTRY
Responsible Bureau: Regional Education Administration
Departments: Mechanics, Electrical Mechanics and Electrical Equipment Timing Devices, Industrial Chemistry, Light Industry, Civil and Architectural Engineering
Contact: Foreign Affairs Office, Xinjiang Institute of Industry, Youhao Rd., Urumqi, Xinjiang PRC Tel: 41911

XINJIANG INSTITUTE OF PETROLEUM
Responsible Bureau: Regional Petroleum Bureau
Departments: Geology, Mechanics, Management Engineering
Contact: Foreign Affairs Office, Xinjiang Institute of Petroleum, Mingyuan, Urumqi, Xinjiang PRC Tel: 42892

XINJIANG MEDICAL COLLEGE
Responsible Bureau: Regional Education Administration
Departments: Medical Practice, Pharmacology, Public Sanitation and Hygiene, Rodent Control
Contact: Foreign Affairs Office, Xinjiang Medical College, Xinyi Rd., Urumqi, Xinjiang PRC Tel: 41601

XINJIANG NORMAL SCHOOL
Responsible Bureau: Regional Education Administration
Departments: Political Education, Languages and Literatures, Foreign Languages, Education, Mathematics, Physics, Chemistry
Contact: Foreign Affairs Office, Xinjiang Normal School, Kunlun Rd., Urumqi, Xinjiang PRC Tel: 42513

XINJIANG UNIVERSITY
Responsible Bureau: Regional Education Administration
Departments: Chinese, History, Politics, Foreign Languages, Mathematics, Physics, Chemistry, Biology, Geology, Law
Contact: Foreign Affairs Office, Xinjiang University, Nanliang, Urumqi Xinjiang PRC Tel: 22483

YILI NORMAL SCHOOL
Responsible Bureau: Regional Education Administration
Departments: Languages and Literatures, Mathematics, Physics, Chemistry, Foreign Languages, Physical Education
Contact: Foreign Affairs Office, Yili Normal School, Jiefang Rd., Yining, Xinjiang PRC Tel: 3710

Yunnan   Bordered by Burma, Vietnam, and Laos as well as by Sichuan, Guizhou, and Guangxi, Yunnan is peopled with a greater variety of minorities than any other Chinese province. Deep in the southern jungles of Xishuangbanna foreigners can eat fried bumblebees while howler monkeys shriek from the banyan trees. In the capital at Kunming, the "City of Eternal Spring," traders from the border regions meet on gracious, tree-lined avenues near Dianchi, the "Inland Sea." Ancient ocean floors cracked into a fairy tale "Stone Forest" in Lunan County's "Valley of the Gods." Dali in the lush green Erhai Valley, nestled against the blue Cangshan mountains, surely ranks among the world's remaining paradises. Climate throughout the province is mild (tending toward steamy in Xishuangbanna), and the area traditionally relaxed about foreigners. Food is rich and varied, including many tropical fruit dishes. Language is fairly standard Mandarin in Han areas, variable among minorities.

Universities

KUNMING UNIVERSITY
Responsible Bureau: City Government
Departments: Mechanical Production, Electrical Mechanics and Electrical Equipment, Industrial Worker's Construction, Rubber Arts, Chinese Language and Literature, Industrial Finance and Accounting, Industrial Management
Contact: Foreign Affairs Office, Kunming University, Cuihu N. Rd., Kunming, Yunnan PRC Tel: 82465

YUNNAN UNIVERSITY*
Responsible Bureau: Provincial Education Administration
Departments: Chinese Language and Literature, Journalism, History, Personal File Studies, Philosophy, Foreign Languages, Mathematics, Computer Science, Physics, Radio Technology, Chemistry, Meteorology, Biology, Economics
Teacher Salary/Benefits: 800Y/mo, + benefits
Teaching Conditions: 10-12 hrs/wk; school "very open to new ideas"
Learning Conditions: fairly progressive teachers; small, but very pretty; campus, overall quite beautiful
Contact: Foreign Affairs Office, Yunnan University, Cuihu N. Rd., Kunming, Yunnan PRC Tel: 23901

Minorities/Politics and Law

YUNNAN INSTITUTE OF NATIONALITIES
Responsible Bureau: Provincial Minority Committee
Departments: Politics, Chinese Language and Literature, Minority Languages and Literatures, History, Foreign Languages
Chinese Students: 2,750
Contact: Foreign Affairs Office, Yunnan Institute of Nationalities, Lianhuachi, Kunming, Yunnan PRC Tel: 28587

Arts/Music

YUNNAN ACADEMY OF ART
Responsible Bureau: Provincial Education Administration

Departments: Art, Industrial Arts, Composition, Minority Music, Voice, Wind Instruments, Opera
Contact: Foreign Affairs Office, Yunnan Academy of Art, Mayuan, Kunming, Yunnan PRC Tel: 82173

Finance/Commerce

YUNNAN INSTITUTE OF FINANCE AND TRADE
Responsible Bureau: Provincial Economic Committee
Departments: Finance, Commercial Economics, Economic Policy, Basic Construction Finance and Credit, Planning and Statistics
Accommodations: good; 1 rm + bath, no kitchen; has TV, washer, fairly stiff 11:30 p.m. curfew; location central to campus, 30 min from downtown by bike; cafeteria cheap and good
Teacher Salary/Benefits: 600Y/mo RMB, + some domestic travel, 500Y travel bonus
FAO: excellent
Teaching Conditions: 16 hrs/wk, excellent language lab, no photocopying or secretaries; library easily accessible, lots of economy books, "few readable novels or short-story collections"
Contact: Foreign Affairs Office, Yunnan Institute of Finance and Trade, Shangma Village, Kunming, Yunnan PRC Tel: 26262

Normal Schools

YUNNAN NORMAL SCHOOL
Responsible Bureau: Provincial Education Administration
Departments: School Education, Chinese, History, English, Physical Education, Physics, Chemistry, Biology
Contact: Foreign Affairs Office, Yunnan Normal School, Xizhan, Kunming, Yunnan PRC Tel: 26051

Medical Schools

DALI COLLEGE OF MEDICINE
Responsible Bureau: Provincial Education Administration
Departments: Medical Practice
Chinese Students: 830
Foreign Students: 2
Foreign Teachers: 2
Sister Schools: US—China Institute of Chinese Medicine
Teacher Accommodations: excellent; 1 large rm, w/ washer, dryer, TV, tape recorder; no kitchen, but cafeteria cheap and good; no guest rooms
Teacher Salary/Benefits: 500-800Y/mo, 40% FEC
FAO: very good except with small practical matters
Teaching Conditions: 12-14 hrs/wk; staff pleasant, although sometimes "slowness of bureaucracy made it difficult to get things done"
Contact: Foreign Affairs Office, Dali College of Medicine, Xiaguan, Dali, Yunnan PRC Tel: 5757

KUNMING COLLEGE OF MEDICINE
Responsible Bureau: Provincial Education Administration
Departments: Clinical Medicine, Preventive Medicine, Stomatology, Forensic Medicine

Chinese Students: 2,600
Foreign Students: 10
Foreign Teachers: 4-5
Sister Schools: France—Ecole Parisien; Australia: Univ of Sydney Medical School; US—Washington Univ
Teacher Accommodations: poor, but to be improved when new dorm completed, 1992; now 1 rm/teacher w/ shared bath, TV, tape recorder, fridge, bike, space heater, typewriter; no kitchen, cafeteria poor; dorm central to campus, 30 min walk from downtown
Teacher Salary/Benefits: 750Y/month RMB, + 600Y RMB vacation bonus
FAO: very good; but not wholly trustworthy on oral promises
Teaching Conditions: 14 hrs/wk, good variety of courses, excellent students; no secretarial help or photocopies; library good for medical materials, poor for general reading
Students: some short courses in Chinese Medicine available
Contact: Foreign Affairs Office, Kunming College of Medicine, Renminxi Rd., 650031 Kunming, Yunnan PRC Tel: 81933

YUNNAN COLLEGE OF TRADITIONAL CHINESE MEDICINE
Responsible Bureau: Provincial Education Administration
Departments: Chinese Medicine, Acupuncture and Acupressure, Chinese Pharmacology
Contact: Foreign Affairs Office, Yunnan College of Traditional Chinese Medicine, Baita Rd., Kunming, Yunnan PRC   Tel: 24972

Technical Schools

KUNMING INSTITUTE OF TECHNOLOGY
Responsible Bureau: China National Non-Ferrous Metals Company
Departments: Geology, Materials and Mining, Metallurgy, Metallurgical Materials and High Temperature Control, Mechanical Engineering, Automation and Control, Environmental Engineering, Foreign Languages, Architectural Engineering and Power Studies
Sister Schools: US—South Dakota School of Mines and Technology, Lehigh Univ, Colorado State Univ; France—Inst Nationale de Science Appliques de Lyon; Germany—Univ of Karlsruhe
Teachers and Students: accepts foreign teachers in both English and technical subjects; has large library (approx 650,000 vols) and Museum of Geology
Contact: Foreign Affairs Office, Kunming Institute of Technology, Lianhuachi, Kunming, Yunnan PRC Tel: 29028

YUNNAN INSTITUTE OF TECHNOLOGY
Responsible Bureau: Provincial Education Administration
Departments: Mechanical Engineering, Vehicle Engineering, Electrical Equipment Engineering, Architectural Engineering, Glue and Paper Manufacturing, Chemical Engineering, Nutrition Engineering
Chinese Students: 730
Contact: Foreign Affairs Office, Yunnan Institute of Technology, Huancheng Donglu, Xizi, Kunming, Yunnan PRC   Tel: 28205

Zhejiang   "Heaven," claims the old Chinese saying, "has paradise. The earth has Suzhou and Hangzhou." Home of West Lake with its dozens of spectacular temples, mountains, and groves, Hangzhou, the capital of Zhejiang, ranks among China's most beloved tourist destinations. The ancient port city of Wenzhou, now a bustling mercantile center; the charming temples and lively intellectual life of Ningbo; Shaoxing, home of one of China's finest traditional liquors; and proximity to Shanghai and to Jiangsu Province (home of Suzhou) complete the region's charms. Resident foreigners have been able to explore every crag around West Lake and gain access to Putuoshan, the only of China's major Buddhist mountains not regularly open to foreigners. Zhejiang weather is mild, and food is rich and varied with much seafood and produce. Language is a variant of Fujianese, but Mandarin speakers abound.

Universities

HANGZHOU UNIVERSITY
Responsible Bureau: Provincial Bureau of Education
Departments: Philosophy, Economics, Law, Chinese, History, Education, Foreign Languages, Psychology, Geology, Mathematics, Statistical Mechanics, Physics, Chemistry, Biology, Physical Education
Chinese Students: 6,600
Foreign Students: 15-20
Foreign Teachers: 6-8
Sister Schools: relations w/ 17 schools in US, Canada, Australia, Germany, Belgium, Japan
Teachers and Students: has various exchange programs w/ sister schools
Contact: Foreign Affairs Office, Hangzhou University, Tianmushan Rd., Hangzhou, Zhejiang PRC Tel: 81224

NINGBO UNIVERSITY
Responsible Bureau: City Government
Departments: Art, Computer Science, History, Foreign Languages, Chemistry, Physics
Foreign Students: 0
Foreign Teachers: 3-5
Teachers: can teach English, Western Culture; Ningbo is still under construction; lots of carpentering going on, but setting lovely
Contact: Foreign Affairs Office, Ningbo University, Ningbo, Zhejiang PRC

WENZHOU UNIVERSITY
Responsible Bureau: City Government
Departments: Industrial Management, Secretarial Science, Foreign Trade Economics, Electronics, Nutrition, Agricultural Construction
Contact: Foreign Affairs Office, Wenzhou University, Jiaoxiangxiang, Wenzhou, Zhejiang PRC Tel: 5682

ZHEJIANG UNIVERSITY*
Responsible Bureau: State Education Committee
Departments: Mathematics, Physics, Chemistry, Power Studies, Geology, Electrical Equipment, Industrial Chemistry, Agricultural Construction, Mechanics, Radio Electronics, Radiation Timing Equipment, Materials, High Temperature Physics, Scientific Experimentation Timing Equipment, Computer Science, Management, Languages, Sociology

Chinese Students: 11,000
Foreign Students: 10-15
Foreign Teachers: 5-7
Sister Schools: US—Univ of Utah, Univ of Massachussetts, Rochester Inst
of Technology, Rutgers, Georgia Inst of Technology, Univ of Maryland,
California State Univ, Northridge Univ; Germany—Berlin Tech Univ, Univ
of Wurzburg; Belgium—Univ of Ghent, Univ of Lund
Teachers and Students: has various short-term study and other programs w/
sister schools, also small program in Chinese Language and Culture for long-
term foreign students; facilities include 1.1 million vol library
Contact: Foreign Affairs Office, Zhejiang University, Yuquan, Hangzhou,
Zhejiang PRC Tel: 21701

Arts/Music

ZHEJIANG ACADEMY OF FINE ARTS
Responsible Bureau: Ministry of Culture
Departments: Chinese Traditional Painting, Oil Painting, Woodblock
Painting, Plastics, Industrial Arts
Chinese Students: 500
Contact: Foreign Affairs Office, Zhejiang Academy of Fine Arts, Nanshan
Rd., Hangzhou, Zhejiang PRC Tel: 22634

Finance/Commerce/Economics

HANGZHOU INSTITUTE OF COMMERCE
Responsible Bureau: Ministry of Commerce
Departments: Management, Planning and Statistical Financial Accounting,
Nutrition, Electronics, Information
Chinese Students: 2,400
Sister Schools: US—Univ of South Florida
Contact: Foreign Affairs Office, Hangzhou Institute of Commerce, Jiaogong
Rd., Hangzhou, Zhejiang PRC Tel: 81024

Normal Schools

HANGZHOU NORMAL SCHOOL
Responsible Bureau: City Committee of Humanities Education
Departments: Chinese, Political History, Foreign Languages, Mathematics,
Physics, Chemistry, Biology, Music, Physical Education
Contact: Foreign Affairs Office, Hangzhou Normal School, Wenyi Rd.,
Hangzhou, Zhejiang PRC Tel: 88124

NINGBO NORMAL SCHOOL
Responsible Bureau: City Bureau of Higher Education
Departments: Chinese, Mathematics, Physics, Chemistry, Political History,
English, Physical Education, Geology
Contact: Foreign Affairs Office, Ningbo Normal School, Sanguantang,
Ningbo, Zhejiang PRC Tel: 56188

ZHEJIANG NORMAL UNIVERSITY
Responsible Bureau: Provincial Education Committee
Departments: Chinese, Politics, History, Foreign Languages, Geology,
Mathematics, Physics, Chemistry, Biology, Physical Education, Music

Chinese Students: 4,200
Contact: Foreign Affairs Office, Zhejiang Normal University, Gao Village, Jinhua, Zhejiang PRC Tel: 3800

Medical Schools

WENZHOU COLLEGE OF MEDICINE
  Responsible Bureau: Provincial Administration of Sanitation and Hygiene
  Departments: Medicine, Pediatrics
  Contact: Foreign Affairs Office, Wenzhou College of Medicine, Wenzhou, Zhejiang PRC Tel: 4941

ZHEJIANG COLLEGE OF TRADITIONAL CHINESE MEDICINE
  Responsible Bureau: Provincial Administration of Sanitation and Hygiene
  Departments: Chinese Medicine, Acupuncture
  Chinese Students: 500
  Contact: Foreign Affairs Office, Zhejiang College of Traditional Chinese Medicine, Qingchun St., Hangzhou, Zhejiang PRC Tel: 71911

ZHEJIANG UNIVERSITY OF MEDICINE
  Responsible Bureau: Provincial Government
  Departments: Medicine, Pharmacology, Stomatology, Biomedical Engineering, Infectious Diseases, Cardiology, Demography
  Chinese Students: 3,000
  Sister Schools: US—Stanford Univ, Missouri Univ; Japan—Gifu Univ, Yamagata Univ; Germany—Univ of Mons, Univ of Lubeck
  Contact: Foreign Affairs Office, Zhejiang University of Medicine, Hanzhou, Zhejiang PRC Tel: 22501

Technical Schools

CHINA INSTITUTE OF MEASUREMENT AND SURVEYING
  Responsible Bureau: National Bureau of Measurement and Surveying
  Departments: Surveying, Power Measurement and Surveying, High Temperature Measurement, Electromagnetic Measurement, Radio Measurement
  Contact: Foreign Affairs Office, China Institute of Measurement and Surveying, Jiaogongsan Rd., Hangzhou, Zhejiang PRC Tel: 85024

HANGZHOU INSTITUTE OF ELECTRONICS AND INDUSTRY
  Responsible Bureau: Ministry of Electronics
  Departments: Mechanics, Industrial Economics, Management, Electronics
  Contact: Foreign Affairs Office, Hangzhou Institute of Electronics and Industry, Wenyi Rd., Hangzhou, Zhejiang PRC   Tel: 83214

ZHEJIANG FORESTRY INSTITUTE
  Responsible Bureau: Provincial Forestry Administration
  Departments: Forestry, Economic Forestry
  Contact: Foreign Affairs Office, Zhejiang Forestry Institute, Lin'an County, Zhejiang PRC Tel: 231

ZHEJIANG INSTITUTE OF AQUACULTURE
  Responsible Bureau: Provincial Aquaculture Administration
  Departments: Mechanics, Aquaculture, Aquatic Breeding, Marine Products,

Nutrition
Contact: Foreign Affairs Office, Zhejiang Institute of Aquaculture,
Pingyangpu, Putuo County, Zhejiang PRC Tel: 3851

ZHEJIANG INSTITUTE OF SILK AND BROCADE INDUSTRY
Responsible Bureau: China National Silk and Brocade Company
Departments: Silks and Brocades, Fashion, Mechanical Electronics, Dyes
Chinese Students: 1,200
Accommodations: good; 3 rms w/ kitchen, bath, TV, fridge, no curfew,
occasional use of car and driver; location central to campus, 90 min walk
from downtown
Teacher Salary/Benefits: 800Y/mo FEC + 400Y/mo RMB (Amity
contract), + r-t int'l airfare, 1,500Y shipping allowance
FAO: moderate
Teaching Conditions: moderate course load, good students but terrible
language lab, library; some photocopying, secretaries provided
Contact: Foreign Affairs Office, Zhejiang Institute of Silk and Brocade
Industry, Wenyi Rd., Hangzhou, Zhejiang PRC Tel: 86137

ZHEJIANG INSTITUTE OF TECHNOLOGY
Responsible Bureau: Provincial Education Committee
Departments: Industrial Chemistry, Mechanical Engineering, Electrical
Engineering, Management, Civil Engineering, Light Industry
Chinese Students: 3,700
Sister Schools: Japan—Ashikaga Inst of Engineering
Contact: Foreign Affairs Office, Zhejiang Institute of Technology,
Mishixiang, Hangzhou, Zhejiang PRC Tel: 88514

ZHEJIANG UNIVERSITY OF AGRICULTURE*
Responsible Bureau: Ministry of Agriculture, Livestock, and Fisheries/
Provincial Government
Departments: Agricultural Science, Gardening, Crop Protection, Soil
Chemistry, Mulberry and Silkworm Cultivation, Livestock and Veterinary
Medicine, Tea Cultivation, Agricultural Economics, Agricultural Mechanics,
Environmental Protection, Agricultural Education, Nutrition
Chinese Students: 1,000
Foreign Students: 10-12
Foreign Teachers: 3-5
Sister Schools: US—Univ of Maryland, Oregon State Univ, Virginia
Polytechnic Inst, State Univ of Virginia; Japan—Tokyo Univ, Shimane Univ;
UK—Univ of Newcastle-upon-Tyne; Germany—Univ of Berlin
Contact: Foreign Affairs Office, Zhejiang University of Agriculture,
Huajiachi, Hangzhou, Zhejiang PRC Tel: 42605

Taiwan   Also called "Formosa," (from a Portugese phrase meaning
"Beautiful Island"), Taiwan is a semi-tropical jewel in the South China Sea,
some 100 miles off the coast of Fujian Province. Ruled since 1949 by the

Nationalist Party (Kuomintang, or KMT), the island suffered for nearly 40 years under martial law as KMT leaders insisted the island would one day "take back" the mainland. Though Taiwan's government lifted martial law in 1987, and declared peace with the mainland in 1991, relations between the two areas remain tense.

Taiwan has a modern, international economy, and her shops, at least in the cities, carry everything you might desire. In rural areas you can also see something of traditional culture. Most of the island's cultural and economic resources are centered in the capital at Taipei, though Kaohsiung in the south is a major center of heavy industry. Excellent scenery abounds throughout the island, particularly at the Sun-Moon Lake resort and the Hualien Gorge in the island's center, and at Kenting National Park in the South. Weather is broiling and humid in the summer, mild spring and fall, and damp and occasionally chill in the winter. Food is international, featuring cuisines from throughout China as well as many international restaurants. Indigenous Taiwanese cuisine is very light, focusing on seafood and heavily influenced by Japanese style. For more on these topics, see Chapter 2.

CHANG GUNG INSTITUTE OF NURSING
Departments: full nursing program
Chinese Students: 1,100
Teachers and Students: school has excellent internship and training programs in cooperation w/ Linkou Chang Gung Memorial Hospital; no special programs for foreigners
Contact: Personnel Office, Chang Gung Institute of Nursing, 261 Wen-hwa #1 Rd., Kwei-shan, Tauyuan, Taiwan   Tel: (03) 328-1200

CHANG GUNG MEDICAL COLLEGE
Departments: Medicine, Medical Technology, Nursing, Pathology
Chinese Students: 350
Teachers and Students: school offers graduate programs in medicine only, in association w/ Chang Gung Memorial Hospital; no special programs for foreigners
Contact: Personnel Office, Chang Gung Medical College, 259 Wen-hwa #1 Rd., Kwei-shan, Taoyuan, Taiwan   Tel: (03) 328-3016

CHEN-HSIU JUNIOR COLLEGE OF TECHNOLOGY
Departments: Chemical Engineering, Electrical Engineering, Civil Engineering, Electronic Engineering, Industrial Engineering and Management, Mechanical Engineering, Architectural Engineering
Chinese Students: 6,600
Teachers and Students: private college training technicians for industry; has some programs for Overseas Chinese
Contact: Personnel Office, Chen-Hsiu Junior College of Technology, 840 Cheng-Ching Rd., 83305 Niaau-sung Village, Kaohsiung County, Taiwan Tel: (07) 731-0606 (Office of Foreign Student Affairs: x8)

CHIH-LEE COLLEGE OF BUSINESS
Departments: International Trade, Business Administration, Accounting and Statistics, Secretarial Science, Banking and Insurance
Chinese Students: 5,000
Teachers and Students: private, comprehensive business school; no special

programs for foreigners
Contact: Personnel Office, Chih-Lee College of Business, 313 Wen-hwa Rd., Section 1, Panchiao City, Taiwan

CHINA JUNIOR COLLEGE OF TECHNOLOGY
Departments: Mechanical Engineering, Electrical Engineering, Electronic Engineering
Chinese Students: 4,000
Teachers and Students: school has excellent technical facilities; no special programs for foreigners, but does provide adviser to help foreigners with cultural/other difficulties; can arrange language tutoring
Contact: Personnel Office, China Junior College of Technology, 245 Yanchiuyuan Rd., Section 3, Nankang District, Taipei, Taiwan
Tel: (02) 782-1683 (Foreign Student Adviser)

CHINA JUNIOR COLLEGE OF MARINE TECHNOLOGY
Departments: Navigation, Marine Engineering, Fisheries, Marine Products Processing, Shipping and Management, Electronic Communications
Chinese Students: 3,800
Teachers and Students: school focuses on providing trained technical personnel for the marine and aquaculture industries; no special programs for foreigners
Contact: Personnel Office, China Junior College of Marine Technology, 212 Yen-ping N. Rd., Section 9, Shih-lin District, Taipei, Taiwan

CHINA MEDICAL COLLEGE
Departments: 9 depts including Chinese Traditional Medicine, Chinese Pharmaceutical Science
Chinese Students: 4,300
Teachers and Students: accepts foreign teachers in Western Medicine depts, and foreign students, especially in Chinese Medicine
Contact: Personnel Office, China Medical College, 91 Hsueh-shih Rd., Taichung, Taiwan   Tel: (04) 231-7153 (Foreign Student adviser)

CHINESE CULTURE UNIVERSITY
Departments: 52 depts in 9 colleges: Liberal Arts, including Chinese Literature (classic and modern), History, Philosophy; Foreign Languages, including Oriental Languages, Western Languages; Law, including Political Science, Sino-American Relations, Dr. Sun Yat-Sen's Thought; Journalism and Communication; Arts, including Music (Western and Chinese), Fine Arts, Drama (Chinese Opera and Film); Science; Engineering; Agriculture; Business, including Int'l Trade, Tourism
Chinese Students: 14,500
Teachers and Students: has several programs for foreign students in various depts. Accepts teachers in several depts; campus on beautiful mountainside, close to Taipei and bordering the National Palace Museum
Contact: Personnel Office, Chinese Culture University, Hwa Kang, Yang Ming Shan, Taipei, Taiwan   Tel: (02) 861-0511 x449 (Office of Overseas Chinese and Foreign Student Affairs)

CHIN-YI INSTITUTE OF TECHNOLOGY
Departments: Mechanical Engineering, Electrical Engineering, Electronic

Engineering, Chemical Engineering, Industrial Engineering and Management, Business Management
Teachers and Students: school trains technical personnel; no special programs for foreigners
Contact: Personnel Office, Chin-Yi Institute of Technology, 35 Lane 215, Chung Shan Rd., Section 1, 41111 Taipin, Taichung, Taiwan
Tel: (04) 270-4505 (International Student Affairs Center)

CHUNG HWA JUNIOR COLLEGE OF MEDICAL TECHNOLOGY
Departments: Nursing, Midwifery, Food and Nutrition, Medical Technology, Hospital Administration
Chinese Students: 2,800
Teachers and Students: school prepares students for technical medical positions; no special programs for foreigners
Contact: Personnel Office, Chung Hwa Junior College of Medical Technology, 31 Lane 373, Chung Sheng Rd., Jen Te Village, Tainan County, Taiwan   Tel: (06) 267-1214

CHUNG SHAN MEDICAL AND DENTAL COLLEGE
Departments: Dental Medicine, Medicine, Medical Technology, Nursing, Nutrition, Rehabilitation
Chinese Students: 2,900
Teachers and Students: no special programs for foreigners
Contact: Personnel Office, Chung Shan Medical and Dental College, 113 Tachin St., Section 2, Taichung, Taiwan

CHUNG YUAN CHRISTIAN UNIVERSITY
Departments: 19 departments in 3 colleges: Engineering, Science, Business (including International Trade, Business Administration)
Chinese Students: 10,400
Contact: Personnel Office, Chung Yuan Christian University, 32023 Chung Li, Taiwan

CHUNG-YU COLLEGE OF BUSINESS ADMINISTRATION
Departments: Business Administration, Accounting and Statistics, Banking and Insurance, International Trade, Secretarial Science
Chinese Students: 4,700
Teachers and Students: comprehensive business school; no special programs for foreigners
Contact: Personnel Office, Chung-Yu College of Business Administration, 40 Yi Rd. 7, Keelung, Taiwan

DEH YU NURSING JUNIOR COLLEGE
Departments: Midwifery and Nursing, Food Health
Chinese Students: 1,800
Teachers and Students: no special programs for foreigners
Contact: Personnel Office, Deh Yu Nursing Junior College, 336 Fu Hsing Rd., Keelung, Taiwan

FAR EAST ENGINEERING COLLEGE
Departments: Chemical Engineering, Electrical Engineering, Mechanical Engineering, Electronic Engineering, Industrial Engineering

Chinese Students: 3,000
Teachers and Students: school grants associate's degrees only; no special programs for foreigners
Contact: Personnel Office, Far East Engineering College, 49 Chung-hwa Rd., Hsi-chih Town, Tainan, Taiwan   Tel: (06) 598-9143

FENG CHIA UNIVERSITY
Departments: 27 depts in 4 colleges: Engineering; Business (including Int'l Trade); Science; Management; also program in Chinese Literature
Chinese Students: 18,100
Sister Schools: has exchanges with 12 institutions in US, Belgium, Philippines, Thailand, Korea, Japan
Teachers and Students: cooperative programs w/ sister schools include exchanges of faculty, students, and publications. Also has Chinese Language Teaching Center
Contact: Personnel Office, Feng Chia University, 100 Wenhwa Rd., Seatwen District, Taichung, Taiwan   Tel: (04) 252-2250 (Int'l Affairs Committee)

FOO YIN JUNIOR COLLEGE OF NURSING AND MEDICAL TECHNOLOGY
Departments: Basic Nursing, Maternity Nursing, Pediatric Nursing, Surgical Nursing, Public Health Nursing, Psychiatric Nursing
Chinese Students: 2,950
Teachers and Students: comprehensive nursing program with good labs and other facilities; no special programs for foreigners
Contact: Personnel Office, Foo Yin Junior College of Nursing and Medical Technology, 151 Chin-hsueh Rd., 83101 Ta-liao Village, Kaohsiung County, Taiwan   Tel: (07) 781-1151

FU JEN CATHOLIC UNIVERSITY
Departments: 35 depts in 6 colleges: Liberal Arts (Chinese Literature, History, Philosophy); Art; Foreign Languages (English, German, French, Spanish, Japanese, Translation and Interpretation, Linguistics); Science and Engineering; Law; Management (Int'l Trade, Business Administration)
Chinese Students: 16,000
Sister Schools: in several countries
Teachers and Students: has Chinese Language Program for foreign students and accepts many foreign teachers in several depts
Contact: Personnel Office, Fu Jen Catholic University, 510 Chung Tsung Rd., Taipei, Hsinchuang District, Taiwan

HSING WU COLLEGE OF COMMERCE
Departments: Accounting, Business Administration, International Trade, Tourism, Banking and Insurance
Chinese Students: 5,100
Teachers and Students: comprehensive business program; no special programs for foreigners
Contact: Personnel Office, Hsing Wu College of Commerce, Shieh Yang, Kang Linkou, Taipei County, Taiwan   Tel: (02) 601-1411

HUNG-KUANG JUNIOR COLLEGE OF NURSING
Departments: Nursing and Midwifery, Food Science and Nutrition, Nursing,

Industrial Safety and Health
Chinese Students: 3,800
Teachers and Students: school has excellent lab facilities, many extracurricular clubs, some sister relationships with foreign schools; no special programs for foreigners
Contact: Personnel Office, Hung-Kuang Junior College of Nursing, 34 Chung-chie Rd. 43309 Sha-lu, Taichung County, Taiwan   Tel: (046) 318-652

HWA HSIA COLLEGE OF TECHNOLOGY
Departments: 5 depts, all Engineering related
Chinese Students: 3,700
Contact: Personnel Office, Hwa Hsia College of Technology, 111 Hun-Hsin St., 23557 Chung-Ho City, Taipei County, Taiwan   Tel: (02) 944-1724 (Foreign Student Advisor)

KAOHSIUNG MEDICAL COLLEGE
Departments: 10 depts, all related to Medicine or Nursing
Contact: Personnel Office, Kaohsiung Medical College, 100 Shih-chuan First Rd., Kaohsiung, Taiwan   Tel: (07) 312-1101 x106 (Information for Foreign Students)

KOUCHI JUNIOR COLLEGE OF COMMERCE
Departments: Accounting and Statistics, Banking and Insurance, Business Administration, International Trade, Finance and Taxation, Tourism
Chinese Students: 3,000
Teachers and Students: comprehensive business school; no special programs for foreigners
Contact: Personnel Office, Kouchi Junior College of Commerce, 84 Sang Do 2 Rd., 80223 Kaohsiung, Taiwan   Tel: (07) 761-5171

KUANG SHAN INSTITUTE OF TECHNOLOGY
Departments: Chemical Engineering, Textile Engineering, Mechanical Engineering, Electrical Engineering, Electronic Engineering, Industrial Engineering and Management, Environmental Engineering
Chinese Students: 4,800
Teachers and Students: school trains technicians and professional engineers; no special programs for foreigners
Contact: Personnel Office, Kuang Shan Institute of Technology, 94 Da Wan Rd., Yung Kang Village, Tainan County, Taiwan   Tel: (06) 237-5175

KUANG WU JUNIOR COLLEGE OF TECHNOLOGY
Departments: Mechanical Engineering, Electrical Engineering, Electronic Engineering, Chemical Engineering
Chinese Students: 5,300
Teachers and Students: no special programs for foreigners
Contact: Personnel Office, Kuang Wu Junior College of Technology, 151 I-Te St., 11271 Peito, Taipei County, Taiwan

LIENHO JUNIOR COLLEGE OF TECHNOLOGY
Departments: Electrical Engineering, Electronic Engineering, Chemical Engineering, Architectural Engineering, Industrial Engineering , Management, Ceramic Engineering, Industrial Design, Optical Engineering,

Environmental Engineering
Chinese Students: 3,700
Teachers and Students: school is technical college preparing skilled
personnel for industry; dept of industrial design is particularly well known
for designing footwear; no special programs for foreigners
Contact: Personnel Office, Lienho Junior College of Technology, Miao Li,
Taiwan   Tel: (037) 320-610

LING TUNG COLLEGE
Departments: 13 depts including Int'l Trade and Business Administration
Chinese Students: 5,200
Contact: Personnel Office, Ling Tung College, 1 Ling Tung Rd., Nantun
Taichung, Taiwan   Tel: (04) 389-5624

LUNG-HWA JUNIOR COLLEGE OF TECHNOLOGY AND COMMERCE
Departments: Mechanical Engineering, Electrical Engineering, Electronic
Engineering, Chemical Engineering, Industrial Management
Chinese Students: 3,700
Teachers and Students: school is on south face of Long-Shou mountain;
grants associate's degrees only, prepares skilled technicians for industry; no
special programs for foreigners
Contact: Personnel Office, Lung-hwa Junior College of Technology and
Commerce, Tao yuan, Taiwan

MEI-HO JUNIOR COLLEGE OF NURSING
Departments: full Nursing program
Teachers and Students: school provides 5-year program for middle-school
graduates, equivalent to high school + 2-year nursing degree; no special
programs for foreigners
Contact: Personnel Office, Mei-Ho Junior College of Nursing, 23 Ping-kung
Rd., Mei-Ho District, Nei-pu Village, Pingtung, Taiwan
Tel: (08) 779-9821

MING CHUAN COLLEGE
Departments: 9 depts, all business related, including Int'l Trade and Tourism
Chinese Students: 10,500
Teachers and Students: accepts foreign teachers, particularly in dept of
Tourism, as teachers of English, Japanese, Spanish
Contact: Personnel Office, Ming Chuan College, 250 Chung Shan N. Rd.,
Section 5, Taipei, Taiwan   Tel: (02) 882-7123 (Foreign Student Information)

NAN-TAI JUNIOR COLLEGE OF TECHNOLOGY
Departments: Electronic Engineering, Electrical Engineering, Mechanical
Engineering, Chemical Engineering, Industrial Engineering and Manage-
ment, Automobile Engineering, Int'l Trade, Business Administration
Chinese Students: 6,000
Teachers and Students: no special programs for foreigners
Contact: Personnel Office, Nan-Tai Junior College of Technology,
1 Nan-tai St., Yung Kung Village, Tainan County, Taiwan

NANJEON JUNIOR COLLEGE OF TECHNOLOGY
Departments: 7 depts, all Engineering related
Chinese Students: 2,800

Contact: Personnel Office, Nanjeon Junior College of Technology, 178
Chiao Chin Rd., 73701 Yenshui Chen, Tainan County, Taiwan
Tel: (06) 6523112-4 (Office of Foreign Students)

NATIONAL CENTRAL UNIVERSITY
Departments: 14 depts in 4 colleges: Liberal Arts, including Chinese
Literature, Philosophy; Science; Engineering; Management, including
Business Administration, Financial Management
Chinese Students: 3,323
Teachers and Students: school accepts foreign teachers of English,
technical subjects, and foreign students in all depts; no special programs for
foreigners; campus dominates lovely hill in small town, called "Garden of
Chungli City"
Contact: Personnel Office, National Central University, 32054 Chungli City,
Taiwan

NATIONAL CHANGHUA UNIVERSITY OF EDUCATION
Departments: 9 depts including English and Business
Chinese Students: 2,440
Teachers and Students: accepts foreign teachers in English and Business
depts and foreign students; campus located on mountainside
Contact: Personnel Office, National Changhua University of Education,
50058 Changhua City, Taiwan   Tel: (04) 723-2105-212 (Foreign Student
Affairs)

NATIONAL CHENGCHI UNIVERSITY
Departments: 27 depts in 5 colleges, Liberal Arts and Sciences, including
Chinese Literature, Education, History; Foreign Languages, including
Oriental Languages and Cultures, Western Languages and Literature, Arabic
Language and Literature; Communication; Law, including East Asian
Studies and China Border Area Study; Commerce
Teachers and Students: Chengchi accepts more foreign students in degree
programs than any other Taiwan univ, as well as 20-25 foreign teachers in
Western Languages and Culture; Chengchi is in mountainous picturesque
suburb of Taipei and is one of the most prestigious univs in Taiwan
Contact: Personnel Office, National Chengchi University, 64 Chih-nan Rd.,
Section 2, 11623 Wenshan, Taiwan   Tel: (02) 939-8335/(02) 939-3091 (for
foreign students, x 301)

NATIONAL CHENG KUNG UNIVERSITY
Departments: 30 depts in 5 colleges, Liberal Arts, including Chinese
Literature, Foreign Languages and Literature, History; Science; Engineering;
Management Science; Medicine
Chinese Students: 11,400
Teachers and Students: NCKU is most famous for its medical research, but
accepts foreigners as teachers in the Foreign Languages and Literature Dept,
and as students
Contact: Personnel Office, National Cheng Kung University, 1 Ta-hsueh
Rd., 70101 Tainan, Taiwan   Tel: (06)236-1111 x205

NATIONAL CHIAO TUNG UNIVERSITY
Departments: 12 depts in 3 colleges: Engineering; Science; Management

Chinese Students: 4,890
Teachers and Students: NCTU is a science-focused univ which cooperates with the Hsinchu Science Industrial Park; no special programs for foreigners
Contact: Personnel Office, National Chiao Tung University, Hsinchu, Taiwan Tel: (035) 712-1212-211

NATIONAL CHIAYI INSTITUTE OF AGRICULTURE
Departments: 13 depts all Agricultural Science related, including aquaculture
Chinese Students: 4,000
Teachers and Students: one of Taiwan's major agricultural schools, with cooperative extension program and active student clubs; no special programs for foreigners
Contact: Personnel Office, National Chiayi Institute of Agriculture, 84 Horng Mau Bei, Luh Lau Li 60083, Chiayi, Taiwan   Tel: (15) 276-6141-202

NATIONAL CHUNG CHENG UNIVERSITY
Departments: 10 depts in 5 Colleges (Liberal Arts, including Chinese Literature and Foreign Language; Sciences; Social Sciences; Engineering; Management)
Chinese Students: 170
Teachers and Students: no special programs for foreign students
Contact: Personnel Office, National Chung Cheng University, Ming-hsiung, 62117 Chiayi, Taiwan   Tel: (05) 226-3410-17

NATIONAL CHUNG HSING UNIVERSITY
Departments: 48 depts in 7 colleges: Agriculture; Science; Engineering; Liberal Arts, including Chinese Literature, History, Foreign Languages and Literature; Evening School, including all Liberal Arts depts plus Business and Accounting; plus 2 schools of law and commerce at Taipei campus; *see following listing*
Chinese Students: 13,460
Teachers and Students: accepts foreign teachers in Western Languages and Culture and foreign students (majority at Taipei campus)
Contact: Personnel Office, National Chung Hsing University, Kuo-Kuong Rd., Taichung, Taiwan

NATIONAL CHUNG HSING UNIVERSITY, COLLEGE OF LAW AND COMMERCE
Departments: 10 depts in both day and evening schools including Law, Business Administration, Cooperative Economics, Land Economics and Administration
Chinese Students: 7,000
Teachers and Students: accepts foreigners as both teachers and students in various depts
Contact: Personnel Office, National Chung Hsing University, College of Law and Commerce, 69 Chien Kuo North Rd., Section 2, Taipei, Taiwan Tel: (01) 502-1520 x286 (Foreign Students office)

NATIONAL I-IAN INSTITUTE OF AGRICULTURE AND TECHNOLOGY
Departments: 10 depts in 2 colleges: Agriculture, including aquaculture; Technology

Chinese Students: 3,100
Teachers and Students: accepts foreigners
Contact: Personnel Office, National I-Ian Institute of Agriculture and Technology, 1 Shang Nung Rd., I-Ian City, Taiwan   Tel: (039) 323-783 (Foreign Students Office)

NATIONAL INSTITUTE OF THE ARTS
Departments: 4 depts including Music, Fine Arts, Theater, Dance; also has research center in traditional and folk arts and traditional theater and music
Chinese Students: 600
Teachers and Students: campus in wooded area at edge of Taipei
Contact: Personnel Office, National Institute of the Arts, 172 Chung Cheng Rd., 24702 Lu Chou, Taipei County, Taiwan

NATIONAL KAOHSIUNG INSTITUTE OF MARINE TECHNOLOGY
Departments: 16 depts including Fisheries, Aquaculture, Seafood Technology, and other marine-related sciences
Chinese Students: 2,500
Teachers and Students: no special programs for foreigners
Contact: Personnel Office, National Kaohsiung Institute of Marine Technology, 142 Hai-chuan Rd., Nan-tzu District, 81105 Kaohsiung, Taiwan

NATIONAL KAOHSIUNG INSTITUTE OF TECHNOLOGY
Departments: 7 depts, all in Engineering
Chinese Students: 7,500
Teachers and Students: sister-school relations with: US— Univ of Akron, Tri-County Technology, Texas State Technical Inst; Korea—Daelim Inst of Technology; important industrial-related scientific inst
Contact: Personnel Office, National Kaohsiung Institute of Technology, 415 Chieh-kung Rd., 80782 Kaohsiung, Taiwan   Tel: (07) 381-4526

NATIONAL KAOHSIUNG NORMAL UNIVERSITY
Departments: 7 depts including Chinese, English, Education
Chinese Students: 3,500
Teachers and Students: accepts several foreign teachers, especially in graduate inst of English Education; has program in Chinese for foreign students at graduate inst of Chinese Language and Literature
Contact: Personnel Office, National Kaohsiung Normal University, 116 Ho-ping First Rd., Kaohsiung, Taiwan   Tel: (07) 751-7161 x 214 (Office of Foreign Affairs)

NATIONAL OPEN UNIVERSITY
Departments: Business, Humanities, Social Sciences
Chinese Students: 37,000
Foreign Students: 0
Foreign Teachers: varies
Teachers: open univ offers televised continuing-education courses; foreigners have occasionally taught English through Open Univ
Contact: Personnel Office, National Open University, 172 Chung Cheng Rd., 24702 Lu Chow, Taipei, Taiwan

NATIONAL PINGTUNG INSTITUTE OF AGRICULTURE
Departments: 14 depts, all focused on Agriculture and Aquaculture
Chinese Students: 2,900
Foreign Students: approx 200
Teachers and Students: lovely rural setting, w/ largest campus in Taiwan, including model livestock and crop farms, aquaculture ponds, gardens; offers 1-1/2 yr training programs for foreign students, mostly from Southeast Asia
Contact: Personnel Office, National Pingtung Institute of Agriculture, 1 Hsueh-fu Rd., 91207 Nei-pu Village, Ping Tung County, Taiwan
Tel: (08) 770-3715 (Office of Registrar)

NATIONAL SUN YAT-SEN UNIVERSITY
Departments: 14 depts in 5 colleges, Liberal Arts, including Chinese Literature, Foreign Language and Literature, Music; Science; Engineering; Management; Marine Science
Chinese Students: 2,700
Teachers and Students: accepts foreign teachers in Western Languages and Culture, and foreign students
Contact: Personnel Office, National Sun Yat Sen University, Hsi-Tzu Beach, Kaohsiung, Taiwan   Tel: (07) 531-617 x2501 (Overseas and Foreign Students Office)

NATIONAL TAIPEI COLLEGE OF BUSINESS
Departments: Accounting, Statistics, Banking, Insurance, Business Administration, Finance and Taxation, Computer Science, Secretarial Science, International Trade
Chinese Students: approx 5,200 in regular short and long term programs, and approx 6,000 enrolled in televised "distance learning" classes
Teachers and Students: NTCB is one of the island's premier business schools; often accepts foreign teachers for Language, International Trade classes; no special programs for foreign students
Contact: Personnel Office, National Taipei College of Business, 321 Chi-nan Rd., Section 1, Taipei, Taiwan   Tel: (02) 341-9534 (Information Center for Prospective Foreign Students, x227)

NATIONAL TAIPEI COLLEGE OF NURSING
Departments: full Nursing program
Chinese Students: 1,000
Teachers and Students: NTCN is a fully accredited nursing school, including large program in midwifery; no special programs for foreigners
Contact: Personnel Office, National Taipei College of Nursing, 365 Ming-te Rd., Peitou, Taiwan

NATIONAL TAIPEI INSTITUTE OF TECHNOLOGY
Departments: Mechanical Engineering, Electrical Engineering, Chemical Engineering, Materials and Minerals Resources Engineering, Civil Engineering, Electronic Engineering, Textiles, Industrial Design
Chinese Students: 7,500 in regular programs; 2,400 in distance-learning programs
Teachers and Students: accepts foreign teachers of technical subjects; student courses include internships in factories and other workplaces; no special programs for foreigners

Contact: Personnel Office, National Taipei Institute of Technology, 1 Chung-hsiao East Rd., Section 3, 10643 Taipei, Taiwan
Tel: (02) 771-4800 (Dean of Academic Affairs)

NATIONAL TAIWAN ACADEMY OF ARTS
Departments: 10 depts including Chinese Music, Traditional Chinese Dance
Chinese Students: 2,400
Teachers and Students: accepts foreign students in all depts
Contact: Personnel Office, National Taiwan Academy of Arts, 59 Tah Kuan Rd., Section 1, Pan Chiao, Taipei, Taiwan   Tel: (02) 967-6414

NATIONAL TAIWAN INSTITUTE OF TECHNOLOGY
Departments: Industrial Management, Electronic Engineering, Mechanical Engineering, Textile Engineering, Construction Engineering, Electrical Engineering, Chemical Engineering, Business Administration, Information Management
Chinese Students: 4,100
Teachers and Students: NTIT has excellent computer and other technical facilities; no special programs for foreigners
Contact: Personnel Office, National Taiwan Institute of Technology, 43 Keelung St., Section 4, Taipei, Taiwan

NATIONAL TAIWAN NORMAL UNIVERSITY
Departments: 22 depts in 4 colleges: Education; Liberal Arts, including Chinese, English, History; Science; Fine and Applied Arts; also has large Mandarin Training Center
Chinese Students: 12,300
Foreign Students: 1,000+ (most at Mandarin Training Center)
Teachers: accepts teachers of Western Languages/Literature/Culture and of technical subjects
Students: accepts foreigners in all depts, and at MTC; MTC offers no dorms, but assists with finding local housing; tuition is by class, ranging from NT$1,440 for calligraphy classes (30 students) to NT$24,000 for quarter-long individual language tutorials; class load is normally 2 hrs/day for regular or 4 hrs/day for intensive enrollment, and focuses on straight language instruction; MTC can assist, however, in finding tutors for martial arts, Chinese Music, etc.
Contact: Personnel Office, National Taiwan Normal University, 162 Ho-ping E. Rd., Section 1, 10610 Taipei, Taiwan   Tel: (02) 362-5621 (Office of Foreign Student Affairs)

NATIONAL TAIWAN OCEAN UNIVERSITY
Departments: 15 depts in 3 colleges: Maritime Science; Fisheries Science; Science and Engineering
Chinese Students: 3,300
Teachers and Students: school on Taiwan's north coast, w/ excellent technical and aquaculture research facilities; close to several fisheries and shipbuilding firms, w/ which able to arrange internships; no special programs for foreigners
Contact: Personnel Office, National Taiwan Ocean University, 2 Pei-ning Rd., Keelung, Taiwan   Tel: (032) 622-192

NATIONAL TAIWAN UNIVERSITY
Departments: 47 depts in 7 colleges: Liberal Arts, including Chinese Literature, Foreign Languages and Literature, History, Philosophy; Sciences; Law, including Political Science and 3 Principals of the People Studies; Medicine; Engineering; Agriculture; Management
Chinese Students: 18,000
Contact: Personnel Office, National Taiwan University, Main Campus: Section 4, Roosevelt Rd., (College of Law, College of Management: Hsu Chow Rd.), (College of Medicine: Jen Ai Rd.), Taipei, Taiwan

NATIONAL TSING HUA UNIVERSITY
Departments: 12 depts in 4 colleges: Science; Engineering; Nuclear Science; Humanities and Social Sciences, including Foreign Languages, Chinese Literature and Linguistics, Economics, History, Linguistics, Sociology and Anthropology, Literature
Chinese Students: 4,300
Teachers and Students: school emphasizes basic and applied sciences, works closely with Hsinchu Science and Industrial Park; often accepts foreign teachers for Humanities classes; no special programs for foreign students
Contact: Personnel Office, National Tsing Hua University, 101 Kuang Fu Rd., Section 2, Hsinchu City, Taiwan

NATIONAL UNIVERSITY PREPARATORY SCHOOL FOR OVERSEAS CHINESE STUDENTS
Departments: 28 classes in 4 "groups": Science and Engineering; Liberal Arts; Medicine and Agriculture; Law and Commerce
Teachers and Students: school established by government to prepare "returning overseas Chinese students" for enrolling in Taiwan univs; includes intensive Mandarin training, basic skills, "Living Guidance," many extra-curricular activities and clubs; rarely accepts foreign teachers
Contact: Personnel Office, National University Preparatory School for Overseas Chinese Students, 46 Hsin Liau Rd., Lin Kou, Taipei County, Taiwan

NATIONAL YANG MING MEDICAL COLLEGE
Departments: Medicine, Dentistry, Medical Technology, Neuroscience, Microbiology and Immunology, Biochemistry, Medical Engineering, Physiology, Pharmacology, Public Health, Nursing, Clinical Medicine, Rehabilitation Medicine, Anatomical Sciences, Genetics, Hospital Administration
Chinese Students: 1,700
Teachers and Students: comprehensive medical school; no special programs for foreigners
Contact: Personnel Office, National Yang Ming Medical College, 155 Li-nung Rd., Section 2, Shih-pai District, Taipei, Taiwan

NATIONAL YUNLIN INSTITUTE OF TECHNOLOGY
Departments: Mechanical Engineering, Manufacturing, Mechanical Design, Electrical Engineering, Optical Engineering, Automation
Chinese Students: 2,900
Teachers and Students: small school w/ strong industrial focus, including large program in automobile design; no special programs for foreigners

Contact: Personnel Office, National Yunlin Institute of Technology, 64 Wun Hua Rd., 63208 Huwei, Yunlin, Taiwan   Tel: (056) 329-642

OVERSEAS CHINESE COLLEGE OF COMMERCE
Departments: 5 depts including Int'l Trade and Business Administration
Chinese Students: 4,800
Teachers and Students: private college that stresses Foreign Language Education, especially English
Contact: Personnel Office, Overseas Chinese College of Commerce, 100 Chiao Kwang Rd., 40721 Taichung, Taiwan

PRIVATE CHUNG CHOU JUNIOR COLLEGE OF TECHNOLOGY
Departments: Mechanical Engineering, Electrical Engineering, Electronic Engineering
Chinese Students: 2,600
Teachers and Students: school trains professional engineers; no special programs for foreigners
Contact: Personnel Office, Private Chung Chou Junior College of Technology, 6 Lane 2, Shan Chiao Rd., Section 3, Yuanlin, Changhua, Taiwan Tel: (04) 834-1098

PROVIDENCE UNIVERSITY
Departments: 18 depts divided between day and evening, undergrad and grad schools, including Western Languages and Literature, Chinese Literature, Tourism, Business
Chinese Students: 5,300
Contact: Personnel Office, Providence University, 200 Chungchi Rd., 43309 Shalu, Taichung County, Taiwan

SHIH CHIEN COLLEGE
Departments: 12 depts including Int'l Trade, Business Administration, Communication Design
Chinese Students: 6,300
Contact: Personnel Office, Shih Chien College, 3 Alley 62, Ta-chi St., Taipei, Taiwan   Tel: (02) 503-8151-5

SHU-TEN JUNIOR COLLEGE OF TECHNOLOGY
Departments: Mechanical Engineering, Electrical Engineering, Chemical Engineering, Industrial Engineering and Management
Chinese Students: 3,500
Teachers and Students: no special programs for foreigners
Contact: Personnel Office, Shu-Ten Junior College of Technology, 11 Taching St., Section 2, 40202 Taichung, Taiwan   Tel: (04) 261-6640

SOOCHOW UNIVERSITY
Departments: 22 depts in 3 colleges: Arts (Chinese Literature, History, Philosophy); Foreign Languages and Literatures (English, Japanese, German); Science; Law; Business (Int'l Trade, Business Administration)
Chinese Students: 13,700
Sister Schools: US— UCLA; St. Olaf's College (MN), Univ of Wisconsin at Stevens Point; Japan—Takushoku Univ

Teachers and Students: has various exchange programs w/ sister schools; also has large Chinese Studies Program for foreign students; accepts foreign teachers in various depts, especially as language teachers
Contact: Personnel Office, Soochow University, Main Campus: 70 Lin-hsi Rd., Wai-shuang-hsi, Shihlin, 11102, (Downtown Campus: 56 Kueiyang St., Sec. 1, 10001) Taipei, Taiwan Tel: (02) 881-9471 x332 (Chinese Studies for Foreign Students)

TAHAN JUNIOR COLLEGE OF ENGINEERING AND BUSINESS
Departments: Mechanical Engineering, Civil Engineering, Mining and Metallurgical Engineering, International Trade, Taxation and Finance, Accounting and Statistics
Chinese Students: 2,100
Teachers and Students: school prepares skilled technicians and workers for business and industry; no special programs for foreigners
Contact: Personnel Office, Tahan Junior College of Engineering and Business, 1 Sujen St., Peipu, Hualien, Taiwan

TA HWA JUNIOR COLLEGE OF TECHNOLOGY
Departments: Chemical Engineering, Electrical Engineering, Industrial Engineering and Management, Mechanical Engineering, Electronic Engineering and Computer Science
Chinese Students: 4,000
Teachers and Students: school has sister relationships w/ several schools in Korea and the US, and occasionally sets up programs w/ these schools; excellent facilities in peaceful rural setting, w/ opportunities for cooperation w/ Hsinchu Science and Industrial Park
Contact: Personnel Office, Ta Hwa Junior College of Technology, 1 Ta-hwa Rd., Chunglin, Hsinchu, Taiwan Tel: (035) 921-247; Taipei Office: (02) 754-2180

TAINAN JUNIOR COLLEGE OF HOME ECONOMICS
Departments: Home Economics, Accounting and Statistics, Fashion Design, Arts and Crafts, Music, Interior Design
Chinese Students: 7,000
Teachers and Students: students primarily women; school prepares students for technical business positions and for "family education"; no special programs for foreigners
Contact: Personnel Office, Tainan Junior College of Home Economics, 529 Chung Cheng Rd., Yung Kang, Tainan, Taiwan Tel: (06) 253-2106

TAIPEI MEDICAL COLLEGE
Departments: Medicine, Pharmacy, Dentistry, Medical Technology, Nursing, Nutrition and Health, Graduate Institute of Pharmaceutical Sciences
Teachers and Students: comprehensive medical school; no special programs for foreigners
Contact: Personnel Office, Taipei Medical College, 250 Wu-hsing St., Taipei, Taiwan Tel: (02) 736-1661

TAIPEI MUNICIPAL TEACHERS COLLEGE
Departments: 8 depts including Languages and Literature Education and

Music Education
Chinese Students: 1,000
Contact: Personnel Office, Taipei Municipal Teachers College, 1 Ai-Kuo W.
Rd., Taipei, Taiwan   Tel: (02) 311-3040

TAIPEI PHYSICAL EDUCATION COLLEGE
Departments: 21 professional athletic programs, including Judo, Karate,
Taekwon Do, and "Chinese Fencing"
Chinese Students: 720
Teachers and Students: school trains physical educators and professional
athletes; no special programs for foreigners
Contact: Personnel Office, Taipei Physical Education College, 5 Tun Hwa
N. Rd., 10590 Taipei, Taiwan   Tel: (02) 711-4621

TAIWAN PROVINCIAL CHIAYI TEACHERS COLLEGE
Departments: 4 depts including Languages Education
Chinese Students: 900
Contact: Personnel Office, Taiwan Provincial Chiayi Teachers College, 151
Lin-sen E. Rd, 60059 Chiayi City, Taiwan   Tel: (06) 277-0442

TAIWAN PROVINCIAL HSIN-CHU TEACHERS COLLEGE
Departments: Elementary Education, Languages and Literature Education,
Social Studies Education, Mathematics and Science Education, Fine Arts
Education
Chinese Students: 1,000
Teachers and Students: school trains elementary school teachers; no special
programs for foreigners
Contact: Personnel Office, Taiwan Provincial Hsin-chu Teachers College,
521 Nan Dah Rd., Hsin-chu, Taiwan   Tel: (035) 213-1328

TAIWAN PROVINCIAL HUALIEN NORMAL COLLEGE
Departments: Elementary Education, Language Education, Science and
Mathematics Education, Social Studies Education
Teachers and Students: school trains elementary and secondary school
teachers; no special programs for foreigners
Contact: Personnel Office, Taiwan Provincial Hualien Normal College,
Hualien, Taiwan

TAIWAN PROVINCIAL PINGTUNG TEACHERS COLLEGE
Departments: Elementary Education, Chinese Language and Literature
Education, Social Studies Education, Mathematics and Science Education,
Early Childhood Development
Chinese Students: 1,200
Teachers and Students: strong teacher-training programs and good facilities
(including ERIC research files on CD-ROM); accepts many foreign teachers
in Languages and Literature, has some short-term Chinese Language and
Culture programs for foreign students; campus on outskirts of the lovely
Kenting National Park (tropical rainforest/wildlife preserve)
Contact: Personnel Office, Taiwan Provincial Pingtung Teachers College,
1 Lin Sen Rd., Pingtung, Taiwan   Tel: (08) 722-6141 (Foreign Student
Adviser: x22)

TAIWAN PROVINCIAL TAICHUNG TEACHERS COLLEGE
Departments: 4 depts including Linguistics and Literary Education
Chinese Students: 1,150
Contact: Personnel Office, Taiwan Provincial Taichung Teachers College, 140 Min-sheng Rd., Taichung City West, Taiwan   Tel: (04) 226-3181-4

TAIWAN PROVINCIAL TAINAN TEACHERS COLLEGE
Departments: 5 depts including Languages and Literature Education
Chinese Students: 3,200
Contact: Personnel Office, Taiwan Provincial Tainan Teachers College, 33 Su Lin St., Section 2, Tainan, Taiwan

TAIWAN PROVINCIAL TAIPEI TEACHERS COLLEGE
Departments: 5 depts including Languages and Literature Education and Music Education
Chinese Students: 3,400
Contact: Personnel Office, Taiwan Provincial Taipei Teachers College, 134 Ho-ping East Rd., Section 2, Taipei, Taiwan   Tel: (02) 735-5764

TAIWAN PROVINCIAL TAITUNG TEACHERS COLLEGE
Departments: 5 depts including Chinese Language Education
Chinese Students: 750
Teachers and Students: has program in Chinese Language for foreign students; local student population includes members of several aboriginal tribes
Contact: Personnel Office, Taiwan Provincial Taitung Teachers College, 684 Chunghua, Section 1, 95004 Taitung, Taiwan Tel: (089) 318-855 (Foreign Student Adviser)

TAJEN PHARMACEUTICAL COLLEGE
Departments: 5 depts including Pharmacy, Industrial Safety and Health, Food Sanitation, Pollution Control
Chinese Students: 3,000
Contact: Personnel Office, Tajen Pharmaceutical College, 20 Wei-hsin Rd., 90703 Hsin-erh Village, Yen-pu Hsiang, Pingtung County, Taiwan Tel: (08) 762-4002-5 (Foreign Student Adviser)

TAMKANG UNIVERSITY
Departments: 31 depts in 5 colleges: Liberal Arts (Chinese, English, Spanish, German, French, Japanese, History, European Studies, American Studies, Latin American Studies, Western Languages and Literature); Science; Engineering; Business (Int'l Trade, Economics); Management (Int'l Affairs and Strategic Studies, Information Management)
Chinese Students: 20,475
Teachers and Students: several exchange programs w/ sister schools; also large Chinese Language and Culture program for foreign students; accepts foreign teachers in many depts, especially languages and Western Area Studies
Contact: Personnel Office, Tamkang University, Main Campus: 151 Ying-chuan Rd., Tamsui, 25137, (City Campus: 18 Li-shui St., 10620) Taipei, Taiwan

TAMSUI OXFORD COLLEGE
Departments: 9 depts including Tourism, Int'l Trade, Business Management
Chinese Students: 6,500
Contact: Personnel Office, Tamsui Oxford College, 32 Chen Li St., Tamsui,
Taipei County, Taiwan   Tel: (02) 621-3200

TATUNG INSTITUTE OF TECHNOLOGY
Departments: Mechanical Engineering, Electrical Engineering, Chemical
Engineering, Business Management, Industrial Design, Information
Engineering, Materials Engineering, Biological Engineering, Applied
Mathematics
Chinese Students: 1,700
Teachers and Students: private college, founded and run by the Tatung
Corporation; school conducts extensive research for corporation, provides
excellent hand-on experience for students; no special programs for foreigners
Contact: Personnel Office, Tatung Institute of Technology, 40 Chung Shan
N. Rd., Section 3, Taipei, Taiwan

TUNG FANG JUNIOR COLLEGE OF TECHNOLOGY
Departments: Food Engineering, Chemical Engineering, Industrial
Engineering and Management, Industrial Arts, Electrical Engineering,
Electronic Engineering
Chinese Students: 3,100
Teachers and Students: sister college relations w/: Japan—Bunri College;
US—Pacific Union College; has various student exchanges w/ sister schools
Contact: Personnel Office, Tung Fang Junior College of Technology, 61
Lane 301, Chung Shan Rd., Section 1, 82901 Hu-nei Village, Kaohsiung
County, Taiwan   Tel: (07) 693-2011

TUNGHAI UNIVERSITY
Departments: 29 depts in 7 colleges: Liberal Arts (Chinese Literature,
Foreign Languages and Literature, History, Music, Philosophy); Science;
Engineering; Management (International Trade); Law (Social Work, Public
Administration); Agriculture; Evening School (Liberal Arts and Accounting)
Chinese Students: 11,700
Sister Schools: relations with sister schools in the US, Canada, England,
Ireland, Finland, Germany, Japan, Korea
Teachers and Students: has many exchange programs with sister schools
and also accepts independent foreign teachers; over 1/5 of Tunghai faculty
are foreign appointees; Tunghai also has large program in Chinese Language
and Culture for foreign students
Contact: Personnel Office, Tunghai University, Taichung, Taiwan

TUNG NAN JUNIOR COLLEGE OF TECHNOLOGY
Departments: 6 depts, all Engineering related
Chinese Students: 4,250
Contact: Personnel Office, Tung Nan Junior College of Technology, 92 Wan
Shun Hamlet, Shen Kun Village, Taipei County, Taiwan
Tel: (02) 662-3722 (Foreign Student Adviser Office)

VAN NUNG INSTITUTE OF TECHNOLOGY
Departments: 9 depts, most Engineering related including Int'l Trade and

Business Administration
Chinese Students: 4,150
Contact: Personnel Office, Van Nung Institute of Technology, 63-1 Shui-wei Li, Chungli, Taoyuan, Taiwan   Tel: (03) 453-2636 (Foreign Student Adviser Office)

WEN TZAO URSULINE JUNIOR COLLEGE OF MODERN LANGUAGES
Departments: English, French, German, Spanish
Chinese Students: 2,000
Teachers and Students: accepts foreign language teachers
Contact: Personnel Office, Wen Tzao Ursuline Junior College of Modern Languages, 900 Mintsu 1 Rd., 80760 Kaohsiung, Taiwan

WORLD COLLEGE OF JOURNALISM, THE
Departments: Newspaper Administration, News Editing and Reporting, Broadcasting and Television, Public Relations, Library Science, Motion Picture Production, Printing and Photography, Tourism Promotion
Chinese Students: 5,900
Teachers and Students: one of Taiwan's premier schools of Journalism; runs 2 college dailies and produces many films and promotional videos; school frequently accepts foreign teachers in Language, Communication, Journalism, and Broadcasting
Contact: Personnel Office, The World College of Journalism, 1 Lane 17, Mushan Rd., Section 1, 11603 Taipei, Taiwan

WU FENG INDUSTRIAL JUNIOR COLLEGE
Departments: Electrical Engineering, Electronic Engineering, Mechanical Engineering, Chemical Engineering
Chinese Students: 3,100
Teachers and Students: school trains technicians and professional engineers for industry; has arrangements w/ many businesses for internships; no special programs for foreigners
Contact: Personnel Office, Wu Feng Industrial Junior College, 117 Chien Kuo Rd., Section 2, Min Hsiung, Chia Yi, Taiwan   Tel: (05) 226-2454

YAN YA JUNIOR COLLEGE OF TECHNOLOGY
Departments: Chemical Engineering, Textile Engineering, Civil Engineering, Mechanical Engineering, Architectural Engineering
Chinese Students: 3,500
Teachers and Students: school prepares skilled technicians for industry; no special programs for foreigners
Contact: Personnel Office, Yan Ya Junior College of Technology, 414 Chung Shan East Rd., Section 3, 32034 Chungli, Taiwan

YUANPEI JUNIOR COLLEGE OF MEDICAL TECHNOLOGY
Departments: Medical Administration, Medical Technology, Radiological Technology
Chinese Students: 1,900
Teachers and Students: school trains medical technicians; no special programs for foreigners
Contact: Personnel Office, Yuanpei Junior College of Medical Technology, 306 Yuanpei St., Hsin-chu, Taiwan

YUNG TA JUNIOR COLLEGE OF TECHNOLOGY
Departments: Chemical Engineering, Electronic Engineering, Mechanical Engineering, Electrical Engineering, Industrial Engineering and Management
Chinese Students: 3,200
Teachers and Students: school trains skilled workers for industry; provides in-service training in many businesses; no special programs for foreigners
Contact: Personnel Office, Yung Ta Junior College of Technology, 316 Chung Shan Rd., Lin Lo District, 90902 Ping Tung, Taiwan

Teacher Sending Organizations

This directory lists organizations which recruit, send, or place foreign teachers for posts in the PRC or Taiwan (we have also included a few listings for posts in Hong Kong. All listings are alphabetical by name of program. Please note that each listing represents a separate program, and that therefore some of the largest sending organizations have more than one listing. The authors would like to acknowledge the Institute of International Education's Teaching Abroad Directory, which provided the basic format for this directory, as well as some of our data. The IIE directory is international, updated yearly, and available from IIE (see listing in Appendix C).

PLEASE NOTE: A number of large organizations have specifically requested NOT to be listed in our directory. These are primarily religious organizations with a strong missionary focus. Should you wish to participate in such an organization, inquire about it carefully. Should you encounter members of such organizations in China, be aware of their agenda.

AMERICAN SCHOOL OF GUANGZHOU

ASG is a private co-ed primary school, founded in 1981; current enrollment 42; 90% of faculty US nationals

Positions Available: general: 4 full and part-time positions; ESL: none; administrators: 1 full-time

Requirements for Teachers: B.A. in elementary education required; 2 yrs teaching experience and int'l experience preferred.

Requirements for Administrators/ Others: M.A. in educational administration and administrative experience required; int'l experience preferred

Duration: 1-2 yrs; renewable

Salary: teachers: US$16,000-27,000/acad yr; administrators: negotiated, based on experience, but usually approx $42,000/acad yr

Benefits: r-t airfare from US and paid home leave for overseas hires only

Academic Calendar: Sep-Jun

Training and Support Services: 1 wk on-site orientation

Application Deadline: Apr 1

Other: most of staff hired locally; school does not recruit teachers from overseas

Contact: Principal, American School of Guangzhou, AMCONGEN, Box 100, FPO, San Francisco, CA 96655-0002

AMITY FOUNDATION

Amity is a joint Chinese-foreign institution originally founded by Quakers

Positions Available: places ESL and Western culture teachers in institutions throughout China

Requirements for Teachers: B.A. any field; positive recommendation from overseas sponsoring agency (primarily church-related organizations); contact Amity for additional info

Duration: 1 yr; renewable

Salary: 1,700Y/mo; 1,300 FEC; 400 RMB

Benefits: provided by sponsoring agencies

Academic Calendar: Sep-Jul

Training and Support Services: orien-

tation; some teaching materials; mid-yr conference; visit by Chinese/foreign staff
Any Special Focus/Affiliation: some religious orientation, primarily academic
Contact: Director, Amity Foundation, 17 Da Jian Yin Xiang, Nanjing, PRC Tel (86) 649-701 FAX 741053 Telex 34136 GL YNJCN *or* Amity Foundation, Overseas Coordinator, 4 Jordan Road, Kowloon, Hong Kong (3) 71233692

BRITISH COUNCIL
The Council offers one of the most attractive financial packages we have seen for non-technical teachers/foreign experts working in a Chinese institution
Positions Available: places 40+ teacher trainers in TEFL and up to 6 lecturers in various institutions in China as part of Britain's aid program in China
Requirements for Teachers: UK citizen; teacher trainers in TEFL; TEFL qualification: master's degree in Applied Linguistics or TEFL, relevant experience; lecturers: relevant master's degree, relevant experience
Duration: 1 yr; renewable
Salary: subsidy: 10,000-12,000 pounds sterling/yr from British Council;
Benefits: r-t airfare from England for appointee and up to 2 dependents (no children over 12); accommodations; domestic travel if placed outside Beijing; baggage allowance; superannuation contribution and private medical insurance
Academic Calendar: Sep-Jul
Training and Support Services: project materials provided; resource center in Beijing; visits from English Language Officers; regular conference
Application Deadline: as stated in advertisements in press
Any Special Focus/Affiliation: administered on behalf of UK government's Overseas Development Administration
Contact: Director, British Council, 65 Davies Street, London, W1Y 2AA Tel (01) 930-8466 FAX (01) 493-5035 Telex 8952201 BRICON 6

CANADIAN BAPTIST INTERNATIONAL MINISTRIES

Positions Available: general: places ESL and Western culture teachers at various institutions in China
Requirements for Teachers: must be affiliated with a Canadian Baptist Federation church and be accredited in the teaching profession; the candidate will have proven ability in teaching ESL
Requirements for Administrators/Others: same as above
Duration: 1 yr; renewable
Salary: 350Y RMB/mo, paid for by Chinese institution
Benefits: r-t airfare from Canada for appointee; housing; 1,000Y RMB domestic travel bonus/acad yr; health insurance; up to CAN$300 excess baggage allowance
Academic Calendar: Sep-Jul
Training and Support Services: C.B.I.M. facilitates placement of candidate overseas; "provided moral and spiritual support only—we needed material support too"
Any Special Focus/Affiliation: Baptist association
Contact: Director, Canadian Baptist International Ministries, 7185 Millcreek Dr., Mississaugua, Ont L5N 5R4 Tel (416) 826-3441

CAPS
Positions Available: general: places ESL and Western culture teachers at various institutions in China
Duration: 1 yr; renewable
Academic Calendar: Sep-Jul
Contact: Director CAPS, P.O. Box 831, Shatin, Central, Hong Kong

CHINA EDUCATIONAL EXCHANGE
Contact: China Educational Exchange, Winnipeg, Manitoba

CHINA TEACHING SPECIALIST PROGRAM
CTP focuses on training program in US; functions only as placement agency for teaching posts in China; CTP also offers placement-only option for $450
Positions Available: general: places teachers and foreign experts at schools throughout China; offers optional training programs
Requirements for Teachers: foreign teacher: B.A. required; foreign expert:

M.A. required
Duration: 1 yr; renewable
Salary: foreign teacher: 600-700Y/mo, 30% FEC; foreign expert: 1,000 -1,200Y/mo, 50-70% FEC
Benefits: housing, health insurance, domestic travel and excursions; foreign experts also receive int'l airfare
Academic Calendar: training: spring session, early Apr-late May; summer session, late Jun to mid-Aug; fall session, early Oct-early Dec; teaching Sep-Jul
Training and Support Services: CTP provides training program in TESOL, Chinese Language and Culture, Geography and History, cultural adaptation and preparation for life in China; training program tuition (which includes placement) $700 WA residents, $750 non-residents
Application Deadline: spring session: Mar 8; summer session: May 31; fall session: Sep 6
Any Special Focus/Affiliation: academic
Contact: Erica Littlewood Work, Director, China Teaching Specialist Program, Western Washington State University, Old Main 530A, Bellingham, WA 98225 Tel (206) 676-3753

CHINESE AMERICAN EDUCATIONAL EXCHANGE
CAEE is a non-profit educational organization founded in 1980; recruits teachers for Chinese universities and designs and administers study programs for academic institutions, professional organizations and individuals.
Positions Available: university level teaching in PRC; academic fields include, American and British Literature, Linguistics, ESL, Accounting and Business, Economics, Medicine, Public Health; 15-20 positions available on an on-going basis each yr
Requirements for Teachers: university teaching: master's degree or equivalent required, Ph.D. preferred; ESL instructors: master's degree preferred, teaching experience preferred; undergraduate and graduate courses taught in English; occasional university-wide lectures; teaching

internships also available for college graduates with BA
Duration: 3 mos-1 yr; renewable
Salary: determined on the basis of applicants academic background and teaching experience
Benefits: r-t transportation provided for experts; housing for appointee and dependents; health insurance, education for children and other benefits provided; EEO/AA employer
Academic Calendar: last wk in Aug-mid-July; half year appointments available
Training and Support Services: orientation in US
Application Deadline: open, on-going programs; application forms sent on request
Contact: Dr. Judith Stelboum or Dr. Teresa O'Connor, Director/Chinese American Educational Exchange, College of Staten Island, Room A-324, 715 Ocean Terrace, Staten Island, NY 10301 Tel (718) 390-7654

EDUCATION DEPARTMENT
The department has launched a 2-yr pilot program hiring native English speakers to strengthen English teaching in Hong Kong
Positions Available: teaching positions in pre-K, primary, and secondary schools for English-speaking children in Hong Kong; for a list of English-speaking schools write to the address listed below and request "Information Sheet: Education Facilities for English-Speaking Children."
Contact: Julie Chen, Education Officer, Education Department, Lee Gardens, 33-37 Hysan Avenue, Causeway Bay, Hong Kong Tel (852-5) 839-2233

EDUCATIONAL SERVICES EXCHANGE WITH CHINA
ESEC provides English and Business teachers; training for disabled Chinese; economic development programs for China's poorest regions; works directly w/ Foreign Experts Bureau in Beijing
Positions Available: ESL teachers at several Chinese universities
Duration: 1 yr; renewable
Salary: 650Y/mo, 30% FEC
Benefits: r-t airfare for appointee; hous-

ing; domestic travel and excursions; health insurance

Academic Calendar: Sep-Jul; training and support services: 8 wks of summer training (cultural, curricular) in the US; teaching materials; mid-yr conference; short-term experts visit

Any Special Focus/Affiliation: Christian association

Contact: Director, Educational Services Exchange with China, 1641 West Main Street, Suite 401, Alhambra, CA 91801 Tel (818) 284-7955

ELS International

ELS is a placement agency for ESL teachers; takes fee in form of percentage of first mo's wages

Positions Available: ESL: 6 positions/yr at various schools in Taiwan (in Taipei and Kaohsiung)

Requirements for Teachers: generally B.A. + 1 yr ESL teaching experience

Salary: varies; approx. US$17,000/yr

Duration: 1 yr; renewable

Benefits: r-t airfare from US for appointee and spouse; furnished housing; health insurance

Academic Calendar: Sep-Jun

Training and Support Services: none

Application Deadline: revolving

Any Special Focus/Affiliation: none; for-profit placement agency

Contact: Recruitment Officer, 4M ELS International, 5761 Buckingham Parkway, Culver City, CA 90230 Tel (800) 468-8978 FAX (213) 410-4688 *or* William Lee, ELS International, Taiwan Language School, #159 Chung King South Rd., Section 2, Taipei, Taiwan   Tel (886-2) 321-7247 FAX (same as tel)

Embassy of the PRC

Applications are placed on file for review by individual Chinese institutions

Positions Available: need teachers of ESL/EFL, English Lit, Linguistics; will arrange placements at various schools in China

Requirements for Teachers: B.A. in any field; M.A. in related field + 2 or more yrs teaching experience for Foreign Expert status; int'l experience preferred

Duration: 1 yr, renewable for 1 yr

Salary: varies

Benefits: housing for appointee and dependents plus other benefits

Academic Calendar: Sep-Jul

Training and Support Services: none

Application Deadline: revolving

Any Special Focus/Affiliation: none

Contact: see list of addresses in Appendix C

Foundation for Scholarly Exchange

Administrative organization for Fulbright exchange program in Taiwan which provides funding to American professors who are lecturers or who are conducting research in Taiwan as well as to visiting artists

Positions Available: up to 6 awards per yr for regular lecturers; 2 research awards and 1 award for visiting artist; plus up to 2 partially-funded lecturing awards to supplement salary of American professors who are invited to teach by an institution on Taiwan; subjects taught by lecturers include, American Literature, Art History, Business Administration, Communications, Environmental Studies, Information Management, Library Science, and Theatre Arts; research topics include classical or contemporary Chinese studies or general research in social/behavioral sciences, the humanities, or the arts related to Taiwan's social and cultural systems; cross-cultural research is encouraged

Requirements for Teachers: Ph.D. + 3 yrs of academic experience; good record of research and publication preferred; an MA/MFA is sufficient for positions in music performance and technical theater; researchers should have 3 yrs of research experience in proposed field of study; fluency in spoken and written Chinese required of those in traditional Chinese Studies

Duration: 10 mos (can be shorter—3-9 mos—for research awards)

Salary: monthly stipend of US$2,304-2,918

Benefits: incidental allowance, int'l travel for grantee and accompanying spouse, tuition allowance for children in grades 1-12; housing provided by host institution for lecturers/researchers performing full-

time teaching as well as a dollar supplement from US$260-$460/mo, based on number of dependents
Contact: Foundation for Scholarly Exchange, 1A Chuan Chow St., Taipei, Taiwan Tel (886-2) 301-1147

FOUNDATION FOR EAST-WEST TRADE DEVELOPMENT
Positions Available: ESL teachers in various Chinese universities
Contact: Director, Foundation for East-West Trade Development, 48 East Main Street, Ramsey, NJ 07446

GRINNELL-NANJING TEACHING PROGRAM
Positions Available: Grinnell arranges teaching posts yearly for 2 of its graduates at a high school in Nanjing
Requirements for Teachers: must be Grinnell grad w/ excellent English abilities, knowledge of US culture, demonstrated interest in Chinese culture
Duration: 1 yr
Salary: stipend for living expenses
Benefits: airfare from US for appointee; housing; insurance
Academic Calendar: Sep-Jul
Training and Support Services: students given orientation before departure, supervised in China; are expected to send 3 reports during yr in China to Grinnell, and to give talk at Grinnell on return
Application Deadline: contact sponsor for info
Any Special Focus/Affiliation: academic
Contact: Grinnell-Nanjing Teaching Program, Office of Off-Campus Study, Grinnell, IA 50112-0810

HONG KONG INTERNATIONAL SCHOOL
Private, co-ed, primary/secondary school, founded in 1966
Positions Available: general: full and part-time positions; ESL: none; administrators: 2 full-time positions
Requirements for Teachers/Administrators/Others: B.A. in education preferred; 5 yrs administrative experience + membership in a Christian church required
Duration: 3 yrs; renewable for 2-3 yrs
Salary: teachers: US$23,000-53,000/acad

yr; administrators: US$60,000-81,000
Benefits: r-t airfare from US for appointee and dependents; housing for appointee and dependents; paid home leave every 2 yrs; health and disability insurance; retirement plan; other
Academic Calendar: Aug-Jun
Training and Support Services: 10-day orientation on-site
Application Deadline: Feb
Any Special Focus/Affiliation: Christian school
Contact: David F. Rittman, Headmaster, Hong Kong International School, 6 and 23 South Bay Close, Repulse Bay, Hong Kong Tel (852-5) 812-2305
FAX (852-5) 812-7037

INTERNATIONAL SCHOOL OF BEIJING
Private co-ed primary school, founded in 1980; current enrollment 350; 50% of faculty US nationals
Positions Available: general: 35 full-time teachers; ESL: 1: administrator: 2 full-time
Requirements for Teachers: B.A. in subject taught + 2 yrs teaching experience + teaching certificate required; language proficiency in Chinese (Mandarin) preferred
Requirements for Administrators/Others: M.A. in administration or related field, + 2 yrs administrative exp, int'l experience required; language proficiency in Chinese (Mandarin) preferred
Duration: 2 yrs; renewable for 1 yr
Salary: teachers: US$17,000-$32,000/ acad yr; administrators: varies
Benefits: r-t airfare from US for appointee only; housing for appointee and spouse; paid home leave every year; health insurance; other
Academic Calendar: Sep-Jun
Training and Support Services: 2-wk orientation on-site
Application Deadline: Jan
Contact: David Eaton, Director; Rod Adam, Principal, Int'l School of Beijing, c/o American Embassy, Beijing PRC or Jiang Tai Rd., Dongzhimenwai, Beijing 100004 Tel (86-1) 523-831 x445; Telex 22701 AMEMB CN

INTERNATIONAL SCHOOLS SERVICES:
a non-profit organization which recruits teachers in all fields for international elementary and secondary schools overseas; administrative positions also available
Requirements for Teachers: General: B.A. in subject; 2 yrs teaching experience in elementary or secondary education; teacher certification preferred but not required
Requirements for Administrators: 2 yrs educational administration experience; previous overseas work experience preferred
Salary: arranged by each host institution
Benefits: arranged by each host institution; however r-t airfare is usually provided for teacher and family
Academic Calendar: determined by host institution
Training and Support Services: for a $50 registration fee ISS keeps candidates applications on file and attempts to locate teaching positions; A $600 placement fee is charged when a candidate accepts a position at a school to which her/his dossier has been supplied by ISS. Some schools pay the candidate's fee or a portion of it. ISS provides no additional services or support once agreement has been reached between teacher and institution
Other: ISS holds 2 int'l recruitment conferences yearly in which representatives from overseas schools meet teachers interested in overseas employment
Contact: International Schools Services, P.O. Box 5910, Princeton, NJ 08543 (609) 452-0990

LECTURESHIP IN AUSTRALIAN STUDIES—CHINA
Australian lecturer in Social Science; preference given to applicants able to teach economics, politics, modern Australian history or international relations.
Eligibility for Teachers: Australian citizen; teaching experience in at least one field of Australian Studies, preferably at the tertiary level; experience in curriculum planning; some knowledge of contemporary China an advantage.
Sites in China: not yet determined, but most likely Beijing or Shanghai
Salary: 1,400Y/mo paid by the State Education Commission of China (SEDC), plus a salary subsidy from the Australian Gov't Dept of Foreign Affairs and Trade
Benefits: housing, teaching-related domestic travel, some medical coverage, local recreation expenses when organized by the place of employment; r-t int'l airfare; 25 k. excess baggage
Academic Yr: early September to mid-July
Application Deadline: December
Contact: The Director, Australia-China Section, Cultural Relations Branch, Dept of Foreign Affairs and Trade, PARKES ACT 2600

THE MORRISON CHRISTIAN ACADEMY
Private, co-ed, primary/secondary school; current enrollment 610; 85% of faculty US national; most of faculty from church-affiliated missions
Positions Available: teachers: 10-18 positions for teachers of all subjects; administrators: none
Requirements for Teachers: B.A. in subject taught required; M.A. preferred; 3 yrs teaching experience + int'l experience preferred
Duration: 3 yrs; renewable
Salary: contact Academy for info
Benefits: r-t airfare from US for appointee and dependents
Academic Calendar: Aug-May
Training and Support Services: on-site orientation
Application Deadline: revolving
Any Special Focus/Affiliation: Christian school
Contact: Arthur L. Westcott, Superintendent, The Morrison Christian Academy, P.O. Box 27-24, Taichung, Taiwan 40098

NATIONAL ACADEMY OF SCIENCES, COMMITTEE ON ECONOMICS EDUCATION AND RESEARCH IN CHINA (CEERC)
CEERC recruits for public professional institutes and univs in the PRC
Positions Available: general: 4 full-time positions for teachers of economics education (macro-/micro- and int'l finance).
Requirements for Teachers: Ph.D. in economics + 4 yrs teaching experience required
Duration: 1 semester; renewable consecu-

tively
Salary: equivalent of appointee's 9-mo univ salary
Benefits: r-t airfare from US for appointee and spouse; housing for appointee and spouse; health and pension benefits equivalent to appointee's 9-mo univ benefits
Academic Calendar: Jan-Aug; Jun-Dec
Training and Support Services: none
Application Deadline: Dec 31
Any Special Focus/Affiliation: academic
Contact: Dr. Todd Johnson, Executive Director, National Academy of Sciences, Committe on Economics Education and Research in China (CEERC), 2101 Constitution Ave. NW, Washington, DC 20418 Tel (202) 334-2718 FAX (202) 334-1774 Telex 4900007565 NRCUI

OBERLIN-SHANSI MEMORIAL ASSOCIATION
Contact: Oberlin-Shansi Memorial Association, Oberlin, OH 44074

PRINCETON-IN-ASIA
Acts as placement agency for recent grads seeking teaching positions in Chinese universities; interns pay $15 (Princeton grads) or $30 (non-Princeton) application fee plus $200 bond (bond returned with interest after completion of contract)
Positions Available: general: 25-40 intern teachers at approx 9 institutions throughout China, including People's Univ in Beijing and Fudan Univ in Shanghai
Requirements for Teachers: young interns (recent college graduates) are recruited primarily from Princeton Univ; must also interview and submit writing samples
Duration: 1 yr; renewable
Salary: 650-800Y/mo RMB (PRC schools); US$384/mo (HK schools)
Benefits: one-way int'l airfare (1-yr contract); r-t int'l airfare (2-yr contract); housing, health insurance, vacation bonus, excursions; terms vary among institutions
Academic Calendar: Sep-Jul
Training and Support Services: interns can take optional TEFL preparation class for $95 fee; provides no support or materials after negotiating contract for intern
Application Deadline: Dec 15

Any Special Focus/Affiliation: academic, for young volunteers
Contact: Robert Pease, Executive Director, Princeton-in-Asia, 224 Palmer Hall, Princeton University, Princeton, NJ 08544 Tel (609) 258-3657 FAX (609) 258-5300 Telex 499-1258 TIGER

PROJECT TRUST
Project Trust is a non-profit program for young volunteers from Scotland
Positions Available: 16 positions teaching ESL at various institutions in China
Requirements for Teachers: UK citizen, in full-time education up to time of departure; must attend selection course on the Isle of Coll in Scotland
Duration: 1 yr; renewable
Salary: similar to local rates
Benefits: r-t airfare from Scotland; health insurance
Academic Calendar: Sep-Jul
Training and Support Services: briefing and training prior to departure; representative in Hong Kong; support visit from UK staff while on site
Application Deadline: Dec 31
Any Special Focus/Affiliation: for young volunteers
Contact: Director Project Trust, Breacachadh Castle, Isle of Coll, Scotland PA78 6TB Tel (087) 93-444 FAX (087 93) 357 Telex 777325-PROJECT 6

SHANGHAI AMERICAN SCHOOL
Private co-ed primary school founded in 1980. Current enrollment 76; 75% of faculty US nationals
Positions Available: general: 6 full-time positions. ESL: 1; administrators: 1 full-time position
Requirements for Teachers: B.A. in education + teaching experience or practical experience required
Requirements for Administrators/ Others: B.A. in education, administration, or business + language proficiency in Chinese (Mandarin) preferred.
Duration: 2 yrs; renewable
Salary: teachers: US$1,400-1,900/mo; administrators: US$1,600 -3,000/mo
Benefits: none

Academic Calendar: Sep-Jun
Application Deadline: Jun
Any Special Focus/Affiliation: academic
Contact: Michael D. Williams, Principal, Shanghai American School, 1469 Huai Hai Zhong Lu, Shanghai, PRC Tel (86-21) 252-1687 FAX 86-21) 433-4122 *or* Shanghai American School, c/o Ameican Consulate General—Shanghai, US Department of State, Washington, DC 20520

SKIDMORE COLLEGE CHINA EXCHANGE PROGRAM

Skidmore is currently expanding program; hopes to soon include other colleges in Shandong Province
Positions Available: general: 4-6 positions/yr teaching Western culture and ESL at Qufu Teachers Univ and the Univ of Petroleum (Dongying)
Requirements for Teachers: B.A. required; Skidmore alums preferred, others considered
Duration: 1 yr; renewable
Salary: 700-800Y/mo, 30% in FEC
Benefits: o-w airfare from US; housing; health insurance; other
Academic Calendar: Sep-Jul
Training and Support Services: orientation in US; teaching materials
Any Special Focus/Affiliation: academic
Contact: Dr. Murray Levith, Director, Skidmore College China Exchange Program, Department of English Studies, Skidmore College, Saratoga Springs, NY 12866 Tel (518) 584-5000

TAIPEI AMERICAN SCHOOL

Private primary/secondary school, founded in 1949; total enrollment 2,125; 85% of faculty US nationals
Positions Available: general: 25-35 full-time positions for teachers of all subjects and special education; ESL: 1-2 full-time positions; administrators less than 1 position/yr
Requirements for Teachers: B.A. + 1-2 yrs full-time primary or secondary experience + teaching certificate required; M.A. + int'l experience preferred.
Requirements for Administrators/Others: M.A. + 3 yrs administrative experience + administrative certificate required,

Ph.D. preferred
Duration: 2 yrs; renewable indefinitely
Salary: teachers: US$27,390-63,675/acad yr; administrators: US$68,772-76,694/calendar yr
Benefits: r-t airfare from US for appointee and dependents; housing for appointee only; paid home leave every 2 yrs; health, life, disability insurance, retirement plan, tuition for children enrolled at this school,
Academic Calendar: Aug-Jun
Training and Support Services: 7-day on-site orientation
Application Deadline: Jan 1
Contact: Human Resources Coordinator, Taipei American School, 800 Chung Shan N. Rd., Section 6, Taipei, Taiwan 11135 Tel (886-2) 873-9900; FAX (886-2) 873-1641

TAMKANG UNIVERSITY, GRADUATE INSTITUTE OF AMERICAN STUDIES

Private co-ed university, founded in 1971; current enrollment 10,000; 50% of GIAS faculty US nationals
Positions Available: general: 4-5 full and part-time positions for teachers of political science, economics, sociology, history, and law; ESL: none
Requirements for Teachers: Ph.D. in subject taught required; teaching experience and language proficiency in Chinese preferred
Duration: 1-2 yrs; renewable
Salary: negotiable
Benefits: one-way airfare from US for appointee only; housing is sometimes provided or univ assists in locating housing
Academic Calendar: Sep-Jun
Training and Support Services: none
Application Deadline: none
Any Special Focus/Affiliation: academic
Contact: Yea-Hung Chen, President, Tamkang University, Graduate Institute of American Studies, Main Campus 151 Ying Chuan Rd, Tamsui, Taipei County Taiwan 25137   Tel (886-2) 393-2517

UNITED BOARD FOR CHRISTIAN HIGHER EDUCATION IN ASIA

UBCHEA also funds various other China-related programs including Overseas Faculty (PRC) Development Program, Asia-

North America Visiting Professors Program (Asia/PRC faculty to teach in North American institutions), and China Studies Programs in other Asian nations
Positions Available: visiting professors: approx 35 positions/yr at various Chinese universities
Requirements for Teachers: usually must have Ph.D. in subject taught and experience as professors in humanities/social sciences subjects taught, be on sabbatical leave or recently retired, and have invitation from the administration of a PRC institution (usually Board-related)
Duration: 1 yr; renewable
Salary: negotiable
Benefits: negotiable; usually limited financial assistance for int'l airfare and possibly a foreign exchange salary supplement to complement benefits provided by PRC institution
Academic Calendar: PRC institution's acad yr, usually Sep-Jul
Application Deadline: Nov 30 for Sep of following yr
Any Special Focus/Affiliation: humanities/social sciences
Contact: David W. Vikner, President, United Board for Christian Higher Education in Asia, 475 Riverside Dr., Rm 1221, New York, NY 10115 Tel (212) 870-3113 FAX (212) 870-2322

U.S.- CHINA PEOPLES FRIENDSHIP ASSOCIATION
USCPFA arranges placements through the Chinese Education Association for International Exchanges for a $30 processing and $7 materials fee, but provides no support or materials after placement
Positions Available: general: places foreign teachers at various institutions in China
Requirements for Teachers: foreign teachers: B.A.; foreign experts: M.A. or higher in English or related field and 2 or more yrs teaching experience
Duration: 1 yr; renewable
Salary: negotiable
Benefits: negotiable
Academic Calendar: Sep-Jul
Training and Support Services: none

Application Deadline: revolving
Contact: Jo Croom, National Coordinator US-China Peoples Friendship Association, Teach-In-China Program, P.O. Box 387, Union City, GA 30291

UNIVERSITY LANGUAGE SERVICES
ULS emphasizes voluntarism for its teachers
Positions Available: general: places ESL teachers at various institutions in China
Requirements for Teachers: must be affiliated with Christian church
Requirements for Administrators/Others: must be affiliated with Christian church
Duration: 1 yr; renewable
Salary: 750Y RMB/mo + 225Y FEC/mo, paid by Chinese institution
Benefits: one-way airfare for appointee; housing; health insurance; domestic travel and excursions
Academic Calendar: Sep-Jul
Training and Support Services: "they gave us 1 notebook and 3 maps"
Any Special Focus/Affiliation: Christian association
Contact: Director, University Language Services, P.O. Box 701984, Tulsa, OK 74170 Tel (918) 495-7045

UNIVERSITY OF TASMANIA CHINA EXCHANGE PROGRAM
Positions Available: places ESL teachers throughout China
Duration: 1 yr; renewable
Salary: 750Y RMB/mo
Benefits: 600Y RMB travel bonus; health insurance
Academic Calendar: Sep-Jul
Training and Support Services: teaching materials provided; no other support provided
Any Special Focus/Affiliation: academic
Contact: Director, University of Tasmania China Exchange Program, University of Tasmania, Hobart, Tasmania 7000

UNIVERSITY OF WASHINGTON INTERNSHIP PROGRAM
Positions Available: places UW Int'l Studies students as English teachers in various institutions in East Asia
Requirements for Teachers: must be UW

Int'l Studies/Int'l Business student
Duration: 1- 2 semesters
Salary: variable, generally from 500-600Y/mo, 30% FEC
Benefits: 400Y RMB travel bonus from Chinese institution
Academic Calendar: Sep-Jul
Training and Support Services: no training or support provided
Any Special Focus/Affiliation: academic
Contact: Director, University of Washington Internship Program, Jackson School of International Studies, DR-O5, Seattle, WA 98105

VOLUNTEERS IN ASIA (VIA)
Contact: Volunteers in Asia (VIA), Stanford University, Palo Alto, CA 94305

WORLDTEACH
WorldTeach places young volunteers in Shanghai for $3,350 fee which includes r-t airfare, health insurance, orientation and training, Chinese language lessons, weekend activities (such as calligraphy, trips to nearby cities, martial arts); financial aid for up to half of program cost available
Positions Available: approx 20 teaching positions for young volunteers in Shanghai (Shanghai Middle School)
Requirements for Teachers: B.A. in any subject + one course in TESOL, or 25 hrs teaching or tutoring experience
Duration: 1 yr; renewable
Salary: small; program emphasizes voluntarism
Benefits: housing and all meals
Training and Support Services: 2-3 wk orientation included in program fee
Application Deadline: Apr 1 (early application recommended)
Any Special Focus/Affiliation: academic, for young volunteers
Contact: Chance Briggs, Desk Officer, China Program, WorldTeach, Harvard Institute for International Development, Harvard University, 1 Eliot Street, Cambridge MA 02138-5705 Tel (617) 495-5527 FAX (617) 495-1239 Telex 275276

YALE-CHINA ASSOCIATION
The Yale-China program is the oldest continuously operating US-China teaching exchange
Positions Available: 10-14 positions for ESL teachers at Changsha Normal School and Hunan Medical College
Requirements for Teachers: must be Yale Univ graduate or recent alumnus
Duration: 1 yr
Salary: contact association for info
Benefits: r-t airfare from US for appointee; housing; insurance; other
Academic Calendar: Aug-Jul
Training and Support Services: 3-wk orientation in US + periodic site visits by Hong Kong director
Application Deadline: contact sponsor for info
Any Special Focus/Affiliation: academic
Contact: Director, Yale-China Association, Yale University, New Haven, CT 06520 Tel (203) 432-0880

YMCA OVERSEAS SERVICE CORPS
Positions Available: association recruits 20- 30 ESL teachers for adults and children at associations throughout Taiwan
Requirements for Teachers: B.A. required in education-related field and fluency in English; TESL training and prior teaching experience preferred
Duration: 1 yr; renewable for 1 yr
Salary: first 6 mos, NT10,000/mo; second 6 mos, NT12,000/mo
Benefits: one-way airfare to US on completion of assignment; housing and meals for appointee provided; reimbursement for half of Mandarin study tuition; health insurance; other
Academic Calendar: Jul-Jul; Oct-Oct
Training and Support Services: none
Application Deadline: Jan 15 for Jul placement and Apr 15 for Oct 1 placement
Any Special Focus/Affiliation: for young volunteers
Contact: YMCA of the USA, International Office for Asia, 909 4th Ave., Seattle, WA 98104 Tel (206) 382-5008

DIRECTORY 3

Sending Organizations for Students

This directory lists organizations which send students to China. The directory is divided by home nation of the sending organization, and listings are alphabetical by name of organization. Please note that each listing is a separate program, and that therefore some of the larger sending organizations have several listings. The authors would like to acknowledge the Institute of International Education's Semester Abroad and Vacation Study Abroad Directories, which provided the basic format for this directory, as well as some of our data. The IIE directories are international, updated yearly, and available from IIE (see listing in Appendix C).

Australian Sending Organizations

As far as student exchanges are concerned there are a variety of programs, some of which are negotiated through universities directly and some through the Commonwealth government. You may want to write the Department of Employment, Education and Training for information regarding nationwide student and teacher-exchange programs. Write:

International Participation Branch
Department of Employment, Education and Training
PO Box 826
Woden A.C.T. 2606
Australia

There are also a variety of teacher exchange programs, most of them organized by individual state Ministries of Education. There are also a few organized through teachers unions. Contact the Ministry of Education in each state/territory for detailed information about such exchanges with their sister states in China. The following is a list of addresses:

OVERSEAS PROGRAMS UNIT
MINISTRY OF EDUCATION
Level 15
Rialto Towers
525 Collins Street
Melbourne, Victoria 3000

OVERSEAS EXCHANGES SECTION
MINISTRY OF EDUCATION
Education Centre
31 Flinders Street
Adelaide, South Australia 5000

OVERSEAS EXCHANGE SECTION
MINISTRY OF EDUCATION
151 Royal Street
East Perth, Western Australia 6000

OVERSEAS EXCHANGE SECTION
DEPARTMENT OF EDUCATION
GPO Box 4821
Darwin, Northern Territory 5794

OVERSEAS EXCHANGES SECTION
DEPARTMENT OF EDUCATION
71 Letitia Street
North Hobart, Tasmania 7000

OVERSEAS EXCHANGES SECTION
DEPARTMENT OF EDUCATION
PO Box 33
North Quay, Queensland 4000

OVERSEAS EXCHANGES SECTION
ACT SCHOOLS AUTHORITY
PO Box 44
Barker Centre, A.C.T. 2604

Other sources of information are:

ASIAN STUDIES COUNCIL
GPO Box 9880
Canberra A.C.T. 2901

CHINA SKILLS TRAINEESHIP
Program Description: gives selected graduates from business related fields the chance to deepen their understanding of China's economic and political systems and to raise their facility in the Chinese language
Site(s) in China: Hopkins-Nanjing Center and Nanjing Univ
Dates: 12 mos for those who are proficient enough in Chinese to attend lectures taught in Chinese; 18 mos for those whose Chinese language skills are not yet sufficient
Eligibility: Australian citizens; excellent academic record; graduates or near-graduates in economics, commerce, business administration, business law, or a related field; min 3 yrs of Mandarin Chinese study.
Subjects Taught: Chinese Economy, Chinese Foreign Trade, Comparative Economics, Chinese Ideology, China and the Pacific Rim
Cost: participants receive a $1,000 monthly stipend, paid tuition, r-t airfare from Australia to China
Contact: Director, Australia China

Council Secretariat, Dept. of Foreign Affairs and Trade, PO Box E393, Queen Victoria Terrace, 2600

AUSTRALIA-CHINA AWARDS
Program Description: Chinese Study awards for scholars of outstanding promise
Site(s) in China: various institutions in China
Eligibility: Australian citizens who are graduates or near graduates of a recognized university or college; min 3 yrs of Chinese language study; preference given to individuals under 35 who demonstrate high academic or professional achievement; students currently receiving other scholarships are not eligible.
Subjects Taught: a course of study within the broad area of China studies, e.g., linguistics, literature, politics, history, philosophy, etc.
Cost: participants will receive a stipend broadly comparable to Australian postgraduate research awards—approximately $10,000 in addition to contribution from the Chinese government; r-t airfare
Housing: dormitory, 2 students per rm
Application Deadline: mid-Dec
Contact: Australian-China Awards, Cultural Dept. of Foreign Affairs and Trade, Canberra 2600, Australia

ENGLISH SCHOOLS FOUNDATION (ESF)
Program Description: operates 9 junior schools and 4 secondary schools for children whose first language is English
Contact: The English Schools Foundation, 43B Stubbs Road, Hong Kong Tel 574-2351 FAX: 838-0957

Hong Kong Sending Organizations

For general information about education in Hong Kong teachers can contact:

Education Department
Lee Gardens, 3/F
Hysan Avenue, Hong Kong   Tel 839-2329

New Zealand Sending Organizations

For information on exchange programs between New Zealand and China, contact:

DEPARTMENT OF EDUCATION (HEAD OFFICE)
55 Lamton Quay
Wellington, New Zealand
Tel (4) 735-544 FAX (4) 499-1327

NORTHERN REGIONAL OFFICE
Giles Avenue
New Market
Auckland, New Zealand
Tel (9) 523-1989 FAX (9) 522-2977

SOUTH AUCKLAND OFFICE
Cnr Grey & Bridge Streets
Private Bag 3011
Hamilton, New Zealand
Tel (71) 383-705 FAX (71) 383-710

CENTRAL REGIONAL OFFICE
Rossmore House
123 Molesworth Street
PO Box 12-135
Wellington, New Zealand
Tel (4) 499-0671 FAX (4) 499-0674

SOUTHERN REGIONAL OFFICE
123 Victoria St.
PO Box 2522
Christchurch, New Zealand
Tel (3) 657-386 FAX (3) 641-631

UNESCO
(in the Head Office of the Department
of Education, address above)
Tel (4) 716-068 FAX (4) 499-1090

TEACHER TRAINEES ASSOCIATION OF NEW ZEALAND
Katie Keyes
Auckland Association
PO Box 11-600
Manners St.
Wellington, New Zealand
Tel (04) 844-806

TEACHERS ASSOCIATION OF NEW ZEALAND, POST PRIMARY
Ruth Chapman, President
Kevin Bunker, General Secretary
PO Box 2119

Wellington, New Zealand
Tel (04) 849-964

ASSOCIATION OF TEACHERS COLLEGE COUNCILS
Prof. I McLaren,
N.V. Close, Secretary
Hamilton Teachers College, Private Bag
Hamilton, New Zealand
Tel (07) 62-859

TEACHERS COLLEGES ASSOCIATION, INC.
John Balstone, President
Wendy Armstrong, National Secretary
PO Box 3044
Wellington, New Zealand
Tel (04) 724-94

ASSOCIATION OF POLYTECHNIC TEACHERS OF NEW ZEALAND
Derek McCormack, President
Lorraine Webber, General Secretary
PO Box 30-159
Lower House
Tel (04) 663-516

Colleges and universities that offer Chinese language training:

THE REGISTRAR
MASSEY UNIVERSITY
Palmerston North, New Zealand
Tel (063) 69-099

THE REGISTRAR
VICTORIA UNIVERSITY
PO Box 600
Wellington 1, New Zealand
Tel (04) 721-000
FAX (04) 499-4601

THE REGISTRAR
UNIVERSITY OF AUCKLAND
Private Bag
Auckland, New Zealand
Tel (09) 737-999
FAX (09) 649-33429

THE REGISTRAR
UNIVERSITY OF CANTERBURY
Christchurch, New Zealand
Tel (03) 667-001

THE REGISTRAR
UNIVERSITY OF WAIKATO
Private Bag 3105
Hamilton, New Zealand
Tel (071) 562-889
FAX (071) 560-135

AUCKAND COLLEGE OF EDUCATION
74 Epsom St. Symonds St.
Private Bag
Epsom, Auckland, New Zealand
Tel (9) 687-009
FAX(9) 689-756

SCHOOL OF SECONDARY EDUCATION
60 Epsom St.
Epsom, Aukland, New Zealand
Tel (9) 686-179

CHRISTCHUCH COLLEGE OF EDUCATION
Dovedale Ave.
PO Box 31065

Christchurch, New Zealand
Tel (3) 348-2059
FAX(3) 348-4311

DUNEDIN COLLEGE OF EDUCATION
Union Street East
N Dunedin, New Zealand
Tel (3) 447-2289

HAMILTON TEACHERS COLLEGE
Hillcrest Road
Hamilton, New Zealand
Tel (71) 62-859

PALMERSTON NORTH COLLEGE OF
EDUCATION
Centennial Drive
Palmerston North, New Zealand
Tel (63) 79-104

WELLINGTON COLLEGE OF EDUCATION
Donald Street
Krori, Wellington, New Zealand,
Tel (4) 763-1699
FAX (4) 767-189

Taiwan Sending Organizations

These organizations are recruitment centers for foreign students. They are not themselves schools. For schools in Taiwan, see listings in Directory 1.

INSTITUTE OF INTERNATIONAL EDUCATION
Foreign Fulbright Program Division,
809 United Nations Plaza, New York,
NY 10017-3580

FOUNDATION FOR SCHOLARLY EXCHANGE
Program Description: administrative
organization (final selection and
placement of 4-6 students/yr) for
Fulbright exchange program sent
through Institute of Int'l Education
Site(s) in China: various institutions in
Taiwan
Dates: Sep-Jun
Eligibility: graduate students; non-
academic professionals in government,
business, or performing arts who have a

bachelor's degree with at least 2 yrs
full-time work experience.
Subjects Taught: students propose a
study plan in the area in which they are
interested
Cost: program provides a monthly
stipend of US$1,382 for ten mos, plus
an incidental allowance; int'l travel and
baggage allowances will also be
provided in the form of a fixed sum for
the grantee; grantee will also be covered
under a group health and accident
insurance policy
Number of Students Sent/Yr Avg: 4-6
Contact: Foundation for Scholarly
Exchange, 1A Chuan Chow St., Taipei,
Taiwan Tel (886-2) 301-1147

FAX (2) 305-8743
OVERSEAS CHINESE STUDY CENTER
Contact: Chiang Chiah-sing, Overseas

Chinese Study Center 2nd fl,
#15 Chi-nan Rd., Section 1, Taipei,
Taiwan Tel (886-2) 341-4175

U.K. Sending Organizations

These sending organizations arrange study programs in China primarily for UK and Commonwealth students.

BRITISH COUNCIL—CHINESE GOVERNMENT SCHOLARSHIPS
Program Description: awards are offered by Chinese government for study in China
Site(s) in China: various institutions throughout China
Dates: Sep-Jul
Eligibility: UK citizen; graduate; sufficient Chinese language for courses taught entirely in Chinese; additionally for researchers: registration for doctorate or post-doctoral research
Cost: students receive a monthly stipend of approx 300 RMB; in addition housing, private medical insurance and r-t airfare from England are provided; scholars may also be eligible for a University China Committee travel grant at Spring Festival; the British Council also has offices in China which can provide student support services
Housing: dormitory accommodation
Application Deadline: early Feb
Number of Students Sent/Yr Avg: up to 23 awards for 10 mos of study and up to 4 awards for 5 of mos research
Other: awards are part of government-to-government agreement
Contact: Overseas Visits and Appointments Department, British Council, 65 Davies Street, London W1Y 2AA Tel (01) 930-8466 FAX (01) 493 5035 Telex 8952201 BRICON G

UNIVERSITY OF CAMBRIDGE
Program Description: Cambridge students enrolled in Chinese Studies program are sent to China during the Michaelmas term of their third yr
Site(s) in China: all universities
Dates: Michaelmas term of third-yr students
Eligibility: Cambridge Chinese Studies students are required to participate in their third yr
Number of Students Sent/Yr Avg: 5-20
Contact: Secretary, Board of Graduate Studies, University of Cambridge, 4 Mill Lane, Cambridge CB2 1RZ

UNIVERSITY OF DURHAM
Program Description: in their second year of East Asian Studies Program, approx 20 Durham students spend a year in China
Site(s) in China: People's University of China, Beijing
Eligibility: must be a Durham student enrolled in East Asian Studies
Credits Granted: equivalent to student's second acad yr
Subjects Taught: all classwork is in Chinese; focus is on developing fluency in spoken and written Chinese
Contact: Registrar, Old Shire Hall, University of Durham, Durham DH1 3HP Tel (091) 374-2000, FAX (091) 374-3740

UNIVERSITY OF EDINBURGH
Program Description: Univ of Edinburgh's second-yr East Asian Studies students are sent to Taiwan
Site(s) in China: Taiwan
Contact: Dept of East Asian Studies, 8 Buccleuch Place, The University of Edinburgh, Edinburgh EH8 9JT Tel (031) 667-1011, ext 6428

THE UNIVERSITY OF LEEDS—DEGREE COURSES IN CHINESE
Program Description: 4-yr degree courses in Chinese or Chinese combined with another subject, involving 1 yr of study in China
Site(s) in China: National Chengchi University, Beijing Normal Univ, Tianjin Normal Univ.
Dates: Sep to Jun of second yr of degree course
Eligibility: completion of first yr of appropriate degree course at the Univ of Leeds
Credits Granted: no specific credits, but the year in China is a requirement for obtaining the degree
Subjects Taught: Chinese language
Application Deadline: entry to UK degree courses is via the University's Central Council on Admissions; enquiries to UCCA at PO Box 28, Cheltenham, Gloucester GL501HY
Number of Students Sent/Yr Avg: 40-50

Contact: Deputy Registrar, The University, Leeds, LS2 9JT

UNIVERSITY OF LONDON SCHOOL OF ORIENTAL AND AFRICAN STUDIES
Contact: Registrar, School of Oriental and African Studies, Center for Asia and Africa, University of London, Thornaugh St., Russell Square, London, WC1H OX6 Tel (071) 637-2388 FAX (071) 436-3844

UNIVERSITY OF OXFORD
Contact: Head Clerk, University Offices, University of Oxford, Wellington Square, Oxford, OX1 2JD

UNIVERSITY OF YORK
This school does not currently send students to China, but is planning to institute a program for third and fourth yr students in Oct, 1992
Contact: Secretary, Department of Language and Linguistic Science, University of York, Heslington, York YO1 5DD Tel (0904) 432650 FAX: (0904) 433433

U.S. and Canadian Sending Organizations

These organizations arrange study programs in China primarily for US and Canadian students

ADVANCED GRADUATE STUDENTS PROGRAM
Program Description: opportunities for graduate students to take graduate level courses and work with Beijing University faculty
Site(s) in China: Beijing University
Dates: fall and/or spring semesters
Eligibility: must have already completed master's degree
Credits Granted: undergrad credit available
Subjects Taught: selected fields
Cost: $350 application and processing fee + $300 placement fee;.tuition paid directly to BeijingUniversity
Housing: Beijing University dorms
Application Deadline: February 15
Contact: Suzanne Fox, University

Programs Dept., CIEE, 205 E. 42nd St., 14th Floor, New York, NY 10017 Tel (212) 661-1414 x 1244

AFS INTERCULTURAL PROGRAMS—CHINESE LANGUAGE AND CULTURAL STUDIES
Program Description: summer introductory program to Chinese culture, run in cooperation with Chinese State Education Commission; part of AFS's Teacher Exchange Project, which invloves 13 countries & has brought 700+ teachers to US, incl 250+ Chinese
Site(s) in China: 2 programs: 1 Hangzhou, 1 Kunming
Dates: 3-6 wks, summer
Eligibility: min age 18, max age 60

Credits Granted: none
Subjects Taught: Chinese Language
(Mandarin: beg), Calligraphy, Cooking,
Drawing, History, Martial Arts
Cost: $3,275 + $50 nonrefundable
application fee, including tuition,
housing, meals, excursions, insurance,
int'l airfare from California
Housing: dorms
Application Deadline: Apr 1
Number of Students Sent/Yr Avg:
approx 40
Other: activities include excursions to
farms, factories, schools, etc.
Contact: Carol Byrne, Chinese
Language and Cultural Studies, AFS
Intercultural Programs, 313 E. 43rd St.,
New York, NY 10017 Tel (800) AFS-
INFO or (212) 949-4242

AMERICAN GRADUATE SCHOOL OF
INTERNATIONAL MANAGEMENT—UIBE/
AGSIM EXCHANGE PROGRAM
Program Description: short-term
program in Management for advanced
students of Chinese at graduate level
Site(s) in China: Beijing (Univ of Int'l
Business and Economics)
Dates: 8 wks, late May-Jul 4 (1 wk
winter course also available)
Eligibility: must be AGSIM student,
graduate level, w/ min 2.5 GPA,
intermediate-level Mandarin
Credits Granted: 3-9 credit hours
graduate
Subjects Taught: Chinese Language
(Mandarin-adv), Business, Economics,
Management
Cost: $350 per credit hours, including
tuition, housing, meals, insurance
Housing: furnished rooms
Application Deadline: Oct 1 for winter;
Mar 1 for summer
Contact: Dean Stephen R. Beaver,
UIBE/AGSIM Exchange Program,
American Graduate School of
International Management, Thunderbird
Campus, Glendale AZ 85306 Tel (602)
978-7133

AMERICAN INSTITUTE FOR FOREIGN STUDIES
(AIFS)—BEIJING LANGUAGES INSTITUTE
INTERNSHIP *[formerly: University of
Florida/American Institute for Foreign
Studies (AIFS), Peking University
Semester]*
Program Description: 1 or 2-semester
program in Chinese language and area
studies
Site(s) in China: Beijing (Beijing
Languages Institute)
Dates: fall semester: Sep 2-Dec 20;
spring semester: Feb 16-Jun 5
Eligibility: must be sophomore or above,
w/ min. 2.5 GPA
Credits Granted: 16 credit hours per
semester undergrad
Subjects Taught: Chinese Language
(Mandarin-beg/int/adv)
Cost: $6,180 per semester;$8,830 per
yr, including tuition, housing, all meals,
int'l airfare, fees, books/materials,
excursions
Housing: dorms
Application Deadline: May 15 for fall;
Oct 15 for spring
Number of Students Sent/Yr Avg: 20
Other: activities include field trips,
excursions
Contact: College Division, American
Institute for Foreign Studies (AIFS)

AMERICAN INSTITUTE FOR FOREIGN STUDY
(AIFS)—CHINESE LANGUAGE
Program Description: summer program
in Chinese language
Site(s) in China: Beijing (Beijing
Language Institute)
Dates: 7 1/2 wks, mid-Jun to mid-Aug
Eligibility: must be undergrad or grad
student or interested faculty
Credits Granted: up to 6 credit hours
undergrad
Subjects Taught: Chinese Language
(Mandarin: beg/int/adv)
Cost: $4,699, including tuition, housing,
meals, int'l airfare, excursions, fees
Housing: dorms
Application Deadline: Apr 15
Number of Students Sent/Yr Avg: 30
Other: activities include 10 days of

program travel
Contact: College Division, American Institute for Foreign Study (AIFS), 102 Greenwich Ave., Greenwich CT 06830 Tel (203) 863-6091 FAX (203) 863-9615

AMERICAN UNIVERSITY—THE AMERICAN UNIVERSITY SEMESTER IN BEIJING
Program Description: 1-semester program in Chinese language/area studies
Site(s) in China: Beijing (Univ of Int'l Business and Economics)
Dates: Sep-Dec
Eligibility: must be second semester sophomore or above, w/ min 2.75 GPA
Credits Granted: 16 credit hours undergrad
Subjects Taught: Chinese Language (Mandarin: beg/int/adv), Economics and Business, History and Civilization
Cost: $9,000 including tuition, housing, extensive field trips outside Beijing, books/materials
Housing: dorms
Application Deadline: 6 mos before start of program
Number of Students Sent/Yr Avg: 22
Other: sponsor accredited in US; activities include field trips, excursions
Contact: Dr. Shaik Ismail, The American University Semester in Beijing, Tenley Campus, The American University, 4400 Massachusetts Ave. NW, Washington DC 20016 Tel (800) 424-2600 FAX (202) 895-4960

BELOIT COLLEGE—FUDAN EXCHANGE PROGRAM
Program Description: 1 or 2-semester program in Chinese language and area studies
Site(s) in China: Shanghai (Fudan Univ)
Dates: Aug-May (1 or 2 terms)
Eligibility: must be college student w/ minimum 1 yr Mandarin
Credits Granted: 16 credit hours per semester undergrad
Subjects Taught: Chinese Language

(Mandarin: beg/int/adv), Chinese Studies
Cost: $15,500 per year, including tuition, housing, all meals, fees
Housing: dorms, sharing rooms with Chinese roommates
Application Deadline: Apr 1
Number of Students Sent/Yr Avg: 6
Other: sponsor accredited in US; activities include excursions, field trips; some scholarships available
Contact: Terance W. Bigalke, Fudan Exchange Program, World Affairs Center, Beloit College, Beloit WI, 53511-5595 Tel (608) 363-2269

BRETHREN COLLEGES ABROAD—DALIAN PROGRAM
Program Description: 1 or 2-semester program in Chinese/American language and culture for Chinese and American students; jointly organized by a consortium of Brethren colleges
Site(s) in China: Dalian (Dalian Institute of Foreign Languages)
Dates: mid-Aug to Jan and/or Feb-Jul
Eligibility: must be sophomore or above
Credits Granted: 23-38 credit hours undergrad per year
Subjects Taught: Chinese Literature, Chinese Language, Chinese Civilization/Culture, Chinese Calligraphy, Chinese Painting
Cost: $7,445 per semester, $12,945 per year, including tuition, housing, all meals, int'l airfare, insurance, fees, excursions
Housing: dorms
Application Deadline: May 1 for fall/ full year; Nov 15 for spring
Number of Students Sent/Yr Avg: 6
Other: sponsor accredited in US; activities include excursions, program travel
Contact: Dr. Allen Deeter, Dalian Program, Brethren Colleges Abroad, 605 College Ave., North Manchester, IN 46962 Tel (219) 982-5238 FAX (219) 982-7755

CALIFORNIA STATE UNIVERSITY—CSU
INTERNATIONAL PROGRAMS IN TAIWAN
 Program Description: 2-semester
program in Chinese culture for
advanced students w/ solid language
background
 Site(s) in China: Taipei, Taiwan
 Dates: Sep-Jun (full period only)
 Eligibility: must be CSU student, junior
or above, w/ min 2.75 GPA (3.0 for
Business program), 2 yrs Mandarin
 Credits Granted: undergrad credit
available
 Subjects Taught: Art History/
Appreciation, Chinese Language
(Mandarin: int/adv), Chinese Studies,
International Business
 Cost: $7,810, including tuition,
housing, all meals, int'l airfare, fees,
excursions, books/materials
 Housing: apartments/homestay
 Application Deadline: Feb 1
 Number of Students Sent/Yr Avg:
varies
 Other: sponsor accredited in US;
activities include excursions, field trips,
program travel; some scholarships
available
 Contact: CSU International Programs
in Taiwan, International Programs,
Office of the Chancellor, California
State University, 400 Golden Shore,
Long Beach CA 90802-4275 Tel(213)
590-5655

CAPE COD COMMUNITY COLLEGE—CHINA
IN PERSPECTIVE
 Program Description: short-term study
tour in China arranged and taught by US
faculty
 Site(s) in China: Beijing
 Dates: summer
 Eligibility: must be min age 18
 Credits Granted: 3 credit hours
undergrad
 Subjects Taught: Chinese Civilization
 Cost: $2,900 from LA, $3,100 from
NYC, including tuition, housing, int'l
airfare, books/materials, fees
 Housing: dormitory, Beijing College of
Economics

 Application Deadline: Feb 1
 Number of Students Sent/Yr Avg: 12
 Contact: Gretchen Farnham, China
Study Tour, Cape Cod Community
College, West Barnstable, MA 02668
Tel (617) 362-2131 x455 FAX (508)
362-8638

CET—CET CHINESE LANGUAGE
PROGRAM, SEMESTER IN HARBIN
 Program Description: fall and spring
programs in Chinese language, includes
China culture course taught by US
faculty
 Site(s) in China: Harbin (Harbin
Institute of Technology)
 Dates: Aug 21-Dec 10
 Eligibility: must be min age 15, max
age 55, w/ min 2 yrs Mandarin
 Credits Granted: undergrad credit
available
 Subjects Taught: Chinese Language
(Mandarin: adv)
 Cost: $4,455, including tuition, housing,
excursions, fees, books/materials
 Housing: dorm rooms shared w/
Chinese students
 Application Deadline: May 15 for fall,
Nov 1 for spring
 Number of Students Sent/Yr Avg: 25
 Other: sponsor accredited in US;
activities include excursions, field trips,
orientation program in Beijing;
curriculum includes a component of
one-on-one instruction
 Contact: Mary Jacob, CET Chinese
Language Program; Semester in Harbin,
CET Academic Programs, 1110
Washington St., Boston, MA 02124 Tel
(800) 225-4262; (617) 296-4262 FAX
(617) 296-6830

CET—CET HARBIN CHINESE LANGUAGE
PROGRAM, SUMMER
 Program Description: summer
program in advanced Chinese language
 Site(s) in China: Harbin (Harbin
Institute of Technology)
 Dates: about 9 1/2 wks, Jun 4-Aug 10
 Eligibility: must be min age 15, max
age 55, w/ min 2 yrs college Mandarin

Credits Granted: undergrad credit available by arrangement
Subjects Taught: Chinese Language (Mandarin: adv)
Cost: $3,500, including tuition, housing, books/materials, excursions, fees
Housing: dorms; share rooms w/ Chinese students
Application Deadline: Mar 15
Number of Students Sent/Yr Avg: 15
Other: activities include excursions, orientation in Beijing; curriculum includes component of one-on-one instruction
Contact: Mary Jacob, CET Harbin Chinese Language Program, Summer Academic Programs, 1110 Washington St., Lower Mills, Boston, MA 02124 Tel(800) 225-4262/(617) 296-0270 FAX (617) 296-683

CET—CET SEMESTER CHINESE LANGUAGE PROGRAM IN BEIJING
Program Description: 1 or 2-semester program in Chinese language, includes Chinese culture course taught by US faculty
Site(s) in China: Beijing (Beijing Foreign Language Normal College)
Dates: Aug 21-Dec 10 and/or Jan 25-May 25
Eligibility: must be min 15 yrs. old, max 55
Credits Granted: undergrad credit available
Subjects Taught: Chinese Language (Mandarin: beg/int/adv)
Cost: about $4,020/semester, including tuition, housing, all meals, fees, excursions, books/materials
Housing: dorms
Application Deadline: May 15 for fall; Nov 15 for spring
Number of Students Sent/Yr Avg: 60
Other: activities include excursions, field trips; program provides on-site Resident Director
Contact: Mary Jacob, CET Semester Chinese Language Program in Beijing, 1110 Washington St., Lower Mills,

Boston, MA 02124 Tel (800) 225-4262/ (617) 296-0270 FAX (617) 296-6830

CET—CET SUMMER CHINESE LANGUAGE PROGRAM IN BEIJING
Program Description: summer program in Chinese language organized by CET in conjunction with Wellesley College; includes courses taught by US faculty
Site(s) in China: Beijing (Foreign Language Normal College)
Dates: Jun 4-Aug 10
Eligibility: must be min age 15, max age 55
Credits Granted: undergrad credit available
Subjects Taught: Chinese Language (Mandarin: beg/int/adv)
Cost: $3,050, including tuition, housing, meals, books/materials/ excursions, fees
Housing: dorms
Application Deadline: Mar 15
Number of Students Sent/Yr Avg: 40
Other: work-study available
Contact: Mary Jacob, CET Summer Chinese Language Program in Beijing, Academic Programs, 1110 Washington St., Lower Mills, Boston, MA 02124 Tel (800) 225-4262/(617) 296-0270 FAX (617) 296-6830

CHINA COOPERATIVE LANGUAGE & STUDY CONSORTIUM/CIEE—SEMESTER CHINA COOPERATIVE LANGUAGE AND STUDY PROGRAM
Program Description: 1 or 2-semester program in Chinese language & culture organized by a consortium of universities in cooperation w/ the Council on International Educational Exchange (CIEE); both 1 & 2 term programs at Beijing & Shanghai campuses; full year only at Nanjing
Site(s) in China: 3 programs: Nanjing (Nanjing Univ); Beijing (Peking Univ); Shanghai (Fudan Univ)
Dates: Aug-Jan and/or Jan-Jun
Eligibility: must be sophomore or above, w/ min 1 yr college Mandarin,

language exam, Chinese area studies course

Credits Granted: 18 credit hours undergrad per semester

Subjects Taught: Chinese Language (Mandarin: int), Chinese Studies, Civilization/Culture, History

Cost: $4,800-$5,750 per semester, including tuition, housing, all meals, int'l airfare, insurance, excursions, fees

Housing: dorms

Application Deadline: Feb 15 for fall; Oct 10 for spring

Other: sponsor accredited in US; activities include excursions, field trips

Contact: Semester China Cooperative Language and Study Program, Academic Programs Department, China Cooperative Language & Study Consortium/CIEE, 205 E. 42nd St., New York, NY 10017 Tel (212) 661-1414 FAX (212) 972-3231

CHINA COOPERATIVE LANGUAGE & STUDY CONSORTIUM/CIEE—SUMMER CHINESE LANGUAGE & STUDY PROGRAMS

Program Description: 2 intensive summer programs in Chinese language organized by a consortium of universities in cooperation w/ the Council on International Educational Exchange (CIEE); see also separate listings for Consortium's semester progs.

Site(s) in China: Shanghai (Fudan Univ); Beijing (Peking Univ)

Dates: 11 weeks, Jun-Aug

Eligibility: must be sophomore or above, w/ min 1 yr college Mandarin, 1 other course in Chinese studies, language test

Credits Granted: 10 credit hours undergrad

Subjects Taught: Chinese Language (Mandarin: int), Chinese Culture

Cost: $4,160 (Fudan program); $4,395 (Beijing program), including tuition, housing, meals, int'l airfare, insurance, fees

Housing: dorms

Application Deadline: Feb 10

Number of Students Sent/Yr Avg: 10-12 per program

Other: activities include excursions, program travel, orientation in Hong Kong

Contact: Summer Chinese Language & Study Programs, Academic Programs China Cooperative Language & Study Consortium/CIEE, 205 E. 42nd St., New York, NY 10017 Tel (212) 661-1414 FAX (212) 972-3231

THE CHINESE UNIVERSITY OF HONG KONG—INTERNATIONAL ASIAN STUDIES PROGRAM

Program Description: multinational/ multidisciplinary program in Asian Studies

Site(s) in China; Hong Kong: Shatin, New Territories (Chinese Univ)

Dates: Aug-Dec and/or Jan-Apr

Eligibility: must be sophomore or above w/ min 3.00 GPA

Credits Granted: 15-18 credit hours undergrad; 15-18 credit hours grad

Subjects Taught: Anthropology, Business/Management, Chinese Language (Cantonese/Mandarin: beg/ int/adv), Economics, Finance, Government, History, Japanese Language, Journalism, Music, Philosophy, Psychology, Religion/ Theology, Sociology

Cost: $4,900 per semester, $7,600 per acad year, including tuition, housing, fees, medical insurance

Housing: dorms with Chinese roommates

Application Deadline: Feb 15 for fall; Oct 1 for spring

Number of Students Sent/Yr Avg: 60

Other: sponsor not accredited in US; activities include excursions; scholarships and work-study available

Contact: Judith M. Collins, International Asian Studies Program, The Chinese University of Hong Kong, PO Box 905A, New Haven, CT 06520 Tel (203) 432-0850 FAX (203) 432-7246

CIEE SEMESTER COOPERATIVE CHINESE BUSINESS AND SOCIETY PROGRAM
Program Description: 1-semester program in business and economics organized by a consortium of colleges and universities through the Council on International Educational Exchange (CIEE); see also separate listing for summer program
Site(s) in China: Beijing (Univ of Int'l Business and Economics)
Dates: Aug-Dec or Feb-May
Eligibility: Must be junior or above (including professionals), w/ 2.75 GPA, 2 yrs Mandarin, language exam, 6 credits in business courses
Credits Granted: 15 credit hours undergrad
Subjects Taught: Business Language, Chinese Language (adv), Civilization/Culture, Economics, History
Cost: $5,900/semester including tuition, housing, all meals, int'l airfare, excursions, insurance, fees
Housing: dorms
Application Deadline: Feb 15 for fall; Oct 10 for spring
Other: sponsor accredited in US; activities include field trips
Contact: Semester Cooperative Chinese Business and Society Program, Academic Programs Dept., CIEE, 205 E. 42nd St., New York, NY 10017 Tel (212) 661-1414 FAX (212) 972-3131

CITY COLLEGE OF SAN FRANCISCO—SEMESTER IN CHINA
Program Description: 1-semester program organized in cooperation w/ CET/Wellesley Chinese Language Training Center.
Site(s) in China: Beijing (Beijing College of Economics)
Dates: Feb 15-May 16
Eligibility: must be min age 17, w/ min 1 semester Mandarin
Credits Granted: 12-15 credit hours undergrad
Subjects Taught: Chinese Language (Mandarin), Chinese Studies

Cost: $3,980 including tuition, housing, airfare, insurance, fees, excursions
Housing: dorms
Application Deadline: Jul 1
Number of Students Sent/Yr Avg: varies
Other: sponsor accredited in US
Contact: Sue Light, Semester in China, International Education, City College of San Francisco, 50 Phelan Ave., San Francisco, CA 94112 Tel (415) 239-3582 FAX (415) 239-3936

CITY COLLEGE OF SAN FRANCISCO—SUMMER STUDY IN CHINA
Program Description: summer study tour arranged and taught by US faculty
Site(s) in China: varies
Dates: 3 weeks, Jun/Jul
Eligibility: must be min age 17, w/ high school diploma
Credits Granted: 3 credit hours undergrad
Subjects Taught: Chinese Civilization, Culture, Literature (in translation)
Cost: $2,500, including tuition, housing, meals, int'l airfare, insurance
Housing: hotels
Application Deadline: May 31
Number of Students Sent/Yr Avg: varies
Contact: Sue Light, Summer Study in China, International Education, City College of San Francisco, Box A71, 50 Phelan Ave., San Francisco, CA 94112 Tel (415) 239-3582 FAX (415) 239-3936

COLLEGE CONSORTIUM FOR INTERNATIONAL STUDIES—(CCIS) SEMESTER IN CHINA
Program Description: 1-semester program in Chinese language and culture organized by a consortium of colleges (CCIS), and Cape Cod Community College. This program has been suspended, but may be instituted again at some time in the future
Contact: Semester in China, College Consortium for International Studies (CCIS), 301 Oxford Valley Rd., Suite 203B, Yardley, PA 19067 Tel (215)

493-4224

**COMMITTEE ON SCHOLARLY COMMUNICA-
TION WITH THE PEOPLE'S REPUBLIC OF
CHINA (CSPRC), NATIONAL ACADEMY OF
SCIENCES, CHINA CONFERENCE TRAVEL
GRANTS PROGRAM**
Program Description: provides
funding for social scientists and
humanists with Ph.D.'s in China Studies
to present results of recent research at
conferences in the PRC
Site(s) in China: varies
Dates: grants offered between Jul and
Dec
Eligibility:Ph.D. in China Studies
Application Deadline: 3 mos before
applicants' research begins
Contact: CSCPRC, National Academy
of Sciences, China Conference Travel
Grants Program, 2101 Constitution
Avenue, Washington, DC 20418

**COMMITTEE ON SCHOLARLY COMMUNICA-
TION WITH THE PEOPLE'S REPUBLIC OF
CHINA (CSPRC), NATIONAL ACADEMY OF
SCIENCES, GRADUATE PROGRAMS**
Program Description: coursework and/
or dissertation research in social
sciences or humanities at a Chinese
university for individuals who are
currently enrolled in graduate programs
Dates: one academic yr, Sep-Jul
Eligibility: currently enrolled in a US
graduate (Ph.D.) program in social
sciences or humanities; min 3 yrs
college-level study of Chinese,
preferably including time in a Chinese
language environment
Subjects Taught: for pursuit of course
work or dissertation research
Cost: contact organization for details of
funding
Application Deadline: mid-Oct
Contact: CSCPRC, National Academy
of Sciences, Research and Graduate
Programs, 2101 Constitution Avenue,
Washington, DC 20418

**COMMITTEE ON SCHOLARLY COMMUNICA-
TION WITH THE PEOPLE'S REPUBLIC OF
CHINA (CSPRC), NATIONAL ACADEMY OF
SCIENCES, RESEARCH PROGRAM**
Program Description: provides support
for in-depth research on China, limited
research in Hong Kong and elsewhere in
East Asia to individuals in social
sciences and humanities
Site(s) in China: varies
Dates: 2 mos to 1 yr, between Jul and
Dec
Eligibility:Ph.D. in social sciences or
humanities
Application Deadline: 3 mos before
applicant's research begins
Contact: CSCPRC, National Academy
of Sciences, Research and Graduate
Programs, 2101 Constitution Avenue,
Washington, DC 20418

**COOPERATIVE INTERNATIONAL BUSINESS &
SOCIETY CONSORTIUM, CIEE CHINESE
BUSINESS AND SOCIETY PROGRAM AT UIBE**
Program Description: intensive
summer program in Business and
Management for advanced students of
Chinese; organized by a consortium of
universities through the Council on
International Educational Exchange
(CIEE); see also separate listing on
Consortium's Beijing semester program
Site(s) in China: Beijing (Univ of Int'l
Business & Economics)
Dates: 9 wks, Jul-Aug
Eligibility: must be junior or above, w/
min 2.75 GPA, 2 yrs Mandarin,
language test; 6 credit hours in
accounting, finance, economics,
management, or organizational behavior
Credits Granted: 8 credit hours
undergrad subjects taught: Chinese
Business Language (Mandarin: adv),
Chinese Business and Society
Cost: $3,700, including tuition,
housing, meals, int'l airfare, excursions,
books/materials
Housing: dorms
Application Deadline: Feb 10
Number of Students Sent/Yr Avg:
varies
Other: activities include excursions,
program travel, orientation in Hong
Kong
Contact: Chinese Business and Society

Program at UIBE, Academic Programs
Department, Cooperative International
Business & Society Consortium, CIEE,
205 E. 42nd St., New York, NY 10017
Tel (212) 972-3231

**COUNCIL ON INTERNATIONAL EDUCATIONAL
EXCHANGE (CIEE)—US -CHINA
EDUCATOR EXCHANGE**
Program Description: reciprocal
summer exchange program for
educators arranged through CIEE and
the Chinese Education Ass'n for Int'l
Exchanges (CEAIE); program includes
visits to secondary schools, universities,
teacher-training institutes, meetings w/
Chinese faculty, students; concludes w/
debriefing in Hong Kong
Site(s) in China: Beijing, Hong Kong,
Nanjing, Shanghai, Xi'an, other cities
Dates: 3 wks, Jun/Jul
Eligibility: must be teacher or other
professional educator, in good health
Credits Granted: none
Subjects Taught: study tour of China's
educational system
Cost: $3,000, including housing, most
meals, int'l airfare from CA, excursions,
fees
Housing: hotels
Application Deadline: Apr 27
Number of Students Sent/Yr Avg: 10-
15
Contact: US -China Educator
Exchange, Council on International
Educational Exchange (CIEE), 205 E.
42nd St., New York, NY 10017
Tel (212) 661-1414 x1209
FAX (212) 972-3231

**COUNCIL ON INTERNATIONAL EDUCATIONAL
EXCHANGE (CIEE)—YOUTH IN CHINA
PROGRAM**
Program Description: summer
program for high school students in
Chinese language and culture; includes
orientation in Hong Kong; program
provides resident US Director; activities
include excursions, field trips, program
travel; scholarships available
Site(s) in China: Xi'an (Xi'an Middle

School), various other sites
Dates: 5 wks, Jun-Jul
Eligibility: must be high school student
Credits Granted: credit available by
arrangement
Subjects Taught: Chinese Language
(Mandarin: beg/int),Culture/Civilization
Cost: write CIEE for info
Housing: dorms
Application Deadline: Jan
Contact: Youth in China Program,
Council on International Educational
Exchange (CIEE), 205 E. 42nd St., New
York, NY 10017 Tel (212) 661-1414
FAX (212) 972-3231

DUKE UNIVERSITY—DUKE-IN-TAIWAN
Program Description: summer
program in Development Issues and
Chinese Society; includes courses
taught by US and foreign faculty
Site(s) in China: Taipei, Taiwan
(Academia Sinica & Nat'l Taiwan Univ)
Dates: 6 wks in summer
Eligibility: must be undergrad student
w/ good academic standing
Credits Granted: 2 credit hours
undergrad
Subjects Taught: East Asian
Development, Modern Chinese Society
Cost: contact sponsor for info
Housing: dorms
Application Deadline: early Feb
Number of Students Sent/Yr Avg: 12
Other: activities include excursions to
industrial parks, urban development
projects; program was suspended from
1989 through 1991, but sponsor plans to
re-offer program in summer 1992
Contact: Dr. Christa Johns, Duke-in-
Taiwan, Summer Session, Duke
University, 121 Allen Bldg., Durham,
NC 27706 Tel (919) 684-2621
FAX (919) 684-3083

**FOUNDATION FOR AMERICAN-CHINESE
CULTURAL EXCHANGES (FACCE)—STUDY
IN CHINA SUMMER PROGRAMS**
Program Description: privately
organized summer Chinese language
programs at 3 sites in China; all 3

programs have on-site US director
Site(s) in China: Shanghai (East China Normal Univ); Nanjing, Changchun
Dates: 8 wks, early Jun-Aug
Eligibility: must be min age 17
Credits Granted: credit available by arrangement
Subjects Taught: Chinese Language (Mandarin: beg/int/adv), Chinese Culture
Cost: $3,298, including tuition, housing, all meals, int'l airfare from San Francisco, books/materials, excursions
Housing: dorms
Application Deadline: Apr 1
Number of Students Sent/Yr Avg: 25
Other: activities include excursions, orientation in China; small class size (max 8); some scholarships available
Contact: Michele Demarest, Study in China Summer Programs, Foundation for American-Chinese Cultural Exchanges (FACCE), 475 Riverside Dr., Suite 245 New York, NY 10115 Tel (212) 870-2525 FAX (212) 870-2125

FOUNDATION FOR AMERICAN-CHINESE CULTURAL EXCHANGES (FACCE)—TRADE AND LAW PROGRAM
Program Description: privately organized summer program in trade & law; faculty includes trade/law specialists, lectures by government officials, lawyers, business execs; 2 wks in Taipei, 2 wks in Shanghai
Site(s) in China: Taipei, Taiwan and Shanghai (Ass'n for International Trade)
Dates: Jun 21-Aug 3
Eligibility: must be student or professional
Credits Granted: none
Subjects Taught: Chinese Trade & Law
Cost: $2,898, including tuition, housing, meals, books/materials, excursions
Housing: dorms
Application Deadline: Apr 1
Number of Students Sent/Yr Avg: 25

Other: activities include excursions; optional travel after program; scholarships available
Contact: Michele Demarest, Trade and Law Program, Foundation for American-Chinese Cultural Exchanges (FACCE), 475 Riverside Dr., Suite 245, New York, NY 10115 Tel (212) 870-2525 FAX (212) 870-2125

FRIENDS WORLD PROGRAM, LONG ISLAND UNIVERSITY, SOUTHAMPTON CHINA PROGRAM
Program Description: 1 or 2-semester program in Chinese language, culture, Agriculture; program prepares students to teach abroad; some religious orientation
Site(s) in China: Hangzhou (Zhejiang Univ)
Dates: Sep-Jan and/or Feb-May
Eligibility: must be sophomore or above, min age 18
Credits Granted: 15 credit hours undergrad per semester; no grad credit available
Subjects Taught: Agriculture, Chinese Language (Mandarin: beg/int/adv), Chinese Studies, Internships, Liberal Arts, Student Teaching
Cost: $6,600 per semester, including tuition, housing, all meals, insurance, fees, books/materials
Housing: apartments
Application Deadline: Jun 1 for fall; Nov 1 for spring
Other: sponsor accredited in US; activities include excursions, field trips, orientation program in both US and Hong Kong; grad students and adults may be accepted as auditors; program provides for individual field study
Contact: Carol Gilbert, Director of Admissions, Long Island University-Southampton, Southampton, NY 11968 Tel (516) 283-4000 FAX (516) 283-4081

GEO VISTA—STUDY TOUR OF CHINA AND INNER MONGOLIA
Program Description: short-term study tour designed for graduate students and

professionals
Site(s) in China: Beijing (Beijing Normal Univ), Inner Mongolia, other sites
Dates: 4 wks in Jul
Eligibility: must be min age 22, max age 65, w/ B.A.or higher degree
Credits Granted: 4 credit hours grad available by arrangement
Subjects Taught: Chinese Language (Mandarin: beg), Chinese Studies (Art, Culture, Education, History, Philosophy)
Cost: $3,790, including tuition, housing, meals, int'l airfare, fees, excursions
Housing: dorms, hotels
Application Deadline: Apr 30
Contact: Jack Miller, Study Tour of China and Inner Mongolia, GEO VISTA, 430 Belmont Ave., Doyleston PA, 18901 Tel (215) 345-0558

GEORGE WASHINGTON UNIVERSITY—
FUDAN UNIVERSITY EXCHANGE PROGRAM
Program Description: 1 or 2-semester program in Chinese Language and East Asian studies
Site(s) in China: Shanghai (Fudan Univ)
Dates: Aug-Jul (1 or 2 terms)
Eligibility: must be GWU student, junior or above, w/ min 3.0 GPA and 1 yr Mandarin
Credits Granted: 30 credit hours undergrad per year; grad credit available; transcripts provided
Subjects Taught: Chinese Language (Mandarin: beg/int/adv), East Asian Studies, Literature
Cost: $14,000 per academic yr, including tuition, housing, fees
Housing: dorms
Application Deadline: Feb 1 for fall; Jul 1 for spring
Number of Students Sent/Yr Avg: 1
Other: sponsor accredited in US; scholarships and financial aid applicable
Contact: Jennifer R. Wright, Fudan University Exchange Program, Study Abroad Office, George Washington University, Elliott School of Interna-

tional Affairs, Washington, DC 20052
Tel (202) 994-6242
FAX (202) 994-0458

GEORGE WASHINGTON UNIVERSITY—
PEKING UNIVERSITY EXCHANGE PROGRAM
Program Description: semester/year abroad program in Mandarin/area studies
Site(s) in China: Beijing (Peking Univ)
Dates: Sep-Jul (may stay fall and/or spring terms)
Eligibility: Must be GWU student, junior or above w/ 3.00 GPA, 1 yr Mandarin
Credits Granted: 30 credit hours undergrad per yr
Subjects Taught: Chinese Language (Mandarin: beg/int/adv), East Asian Studies, Literature
Cost: $14,000/yr includes tuition, housing, fees
Housing: dorms
Application Deadline: Feb 1 for fall; Jul 1 for spring
Number of Students Sent/Yr Avg: 1
Other: sponsor accredited in US; scholarships and financial aid applicable
Contact: Jennifer R. Wright, Peking University Exchange Program, Study Abroad Office, Elliott School of International Affairs, George Washington University, Washington, DC 20052
Tel (202) 994-6242
FAX (202) 994-0458

GOSHEN COLLEGE—STUDY/SERVICE TERM
ABROAD
Program Description: 1-semester program in Chinese area studies with emphasis on service/voluntarism, some religious orientation
Site(s) in China: Chengdu
Dates: Sep to mid-Dec
Eligibility: Goshen students preferred; must be sophomore or above
Credits Granted: 15 credit hours undergrad
Subjects Taught: Field Study, Humanities, Language, Social Studies/Sciences, Sociology

Cost: $6,880, including tuition, housing, all meals, airfare, fees, excursions
Housing: dorms
Application Deadline: 2 terms in advance
Number of Students Sent/Yr Avg: 21
Other: sponsor accredited in US; activities include excursions, field trips; service/volunteerism includes conversational English teaching
Contact: Study/Service Term Abroad, Admissions Office, Goshen College, 1700 S. Main St., Goshen, IN 46526
Tel (800) 348-7422 or (219) 535-7535
FAX (219) 535-7660

HOFSTRA UNIVERSITY—SUMMER IN CHINA
Program Description: summer seminar in Chinese language, business, economics
Site(s) in China: Shanghai (East China Normal Univ)
Dates: about 6 wks, Jul 1-Aug 16
Eligibillty: must be student, teacher, or professional
Credits Granted: 6 credit hours undergrad
Subjects Taught: Chinese Language (Mandarin: beg/int/adv), International Business & Trade (focus on Chinese business & legal procedures)
Cost: $2,790-$4,407, including tuition, housing, meals, int'l airfare, excursions, fees, tour
Housing: dorms, hostels
Application Deadline: Jun 15
Number of Students Sent/Yr Avg: 15-20
Other: activities include program tour in China
Contact: Prof. D. Chiu, Summer in China, Asian Studies, Hofstra University, Hempstead, NY 11550
Tel (516) 463-6797
FAX (516) 472-2251

INDIANA UNIVERSITY—OVERSEAS STUDY PROGRAM IN THE PRC
Program Description: 1-semester program in Chinese language, culture
Site(s) in China: Hangzhou (Hangzhou

Univ)
Dates: Jan-Jun
Eligibility: must be sophomore or above, w/ min 3.0 GPA
Credits Granted: 15 credit hours undergrad
Subjects Taught: Chinese Language, Chinese Studies
Cost: $4,200-$6,800, including tuition, housing, all meals, int'l airfare, insurance, fees, excursions, books/ materials
Housing: dorms
Application Deadline: Oct 1
Number of Students Sent/Yr Avg: varies
Other: sponsor accredited in US; program provides 8 wk orientation in US
Contact: Overseas Study Program in the PRC, Office of Overseas Studies, Indiana University, Franklin Hall 303, Bloomington, IN 47405
Tel (812) 855-9304

INSTITUTE OF CHINA STUDIES—CHINESE LANGUAGE SEMESTER PROGRAM
Program Description: 1 or 2-semester program in Chinese language, area studies, arranged through private exchange; classes include studies in Mandarin together with native students
Site(s) in China: Shanghai (Shanghai Teachers Univ)
Dates: Sep-Jan and/or Mar-Jul
Eligibility: must be min age 15, max age 45
Credits Granted: 12-15 credit hours undergrad per semester; 9-12 grad
Subjects Taught: Chinese Language (Mandarin: beg/int/adv), Chinese Studies
Cost: $3,500 for 3 mos, $4,000 for 5 mos, including tuition, housing, all meals, fees
Housing: dorms
Application Deadline: 2 mos before course begins
Other: sponsor not accredited in US
Contact: Dr. Harry Kiang, Chinese Language Semester Program, Institute

of China Studies, 7341 N. Kolmar St.,
Lincolnwood, IL 60646
Tel (312) 677-0982
FAX (312) 673-2634

INSTITUTE OF CHINA STUDIES—SUMMER CHINESE LANGUAGE AND CULTURAL STUDIES

Program Description: interdisciplinary summer program in Chinese language and culture
Site(s) in China: Shanghai (Shanghai Univ)
Dates: 4-6 wks, Jul/Aug
Eligibility: must be min age 15, max age 45
Credits Granted: undergrad and grad credit available by arrangement
Subjects Taught: Chinese Language (Mandarin: beg/int/adv), Dance, History, Martial Arts, Music, Traditional Medicine
Cost: $2,500 for 4 wks, $3,000 for 6 wks, including tuition, housing, all meals, int'l airfare from West Coast, books/materials, fees, excursions
Housing: dorms
Application Deadline: Apr 30
Number of Students Sent/Yr Avg: varies
Other: some scholarships available
Contact: Dr. Harry Kiang, Summer Chinese Language and Cultural Studies, Institute of China Studies, 7341 N. Kolmar St., Lincolnwood, IL 60646 Tel (312) 677-0982

INTERNATIONAL HONORS PROGRAM
Program Description: around the world study (IHP is an int'l program for honors-level students including short courses in several countries)
Site(s) in China: varies year to year
Dates: academic year
Eligibility: must be college student or older
Credits Granted: 32 credit hours undergrad per yr
Subjects Taught: Global Ecology
Cost: $18,950 (total)
Housing: homestay
Application Deadline: revolving

admissions (spring)
Number of Students Sent/Yr Avg: 25
Other: sponsor accredited
Contact: Joan Tiffany, International Honors Program, 19 Braddock Park, Boston, MA 02116 Tel (617) 267-8612 FAX (617) 451-5160

LOCK HAVEN UNIVERSITY—LOCK HAVEN CHINESE STUDIES PROGRAM
Program Description: 1 or 2-semester program in Chinese language, culture
Site(s) in China: Taichung, Taiwan (Tunghai Univ)
Dates: mid-Sep to Jan and/or late-Feb to Jun
Eligibility: must be sophomore or above, w/ min 3.0 GPA
Credits Granted: undergrad credit available
Subjects Taught: Arts, Chinese Language (Mandarin: beg/int/adv), Chinese Studies, History, Social Studies/Science
Cost: $2,150 per semester, including tuition, housing, fees
Housing: dorms
Application Deadline: Feb for fall; Sep for spring
Other: sponsor accredited in US
Contact: Dean John W. Johnston, Lock Haven Chinese Studies Program, Institute for International Studies, Lock Haven University, Lock Haven, PA 17745 Tel (717) 893-2140 FAX (717) 893-2537

LOCK HAVEN UNIVERSITY—LOCK HAVEN/ BEIJING COLLEGE OF ECONOMICS
Program Description: 1-semester program in Chinese area studies
Site(s) in China: Beijing (Beijing College of Economics)
Dates: Sep-Jan
Eligibility: must be sophomore or above
Credits Granted: 15 credit hours undergrad
Subjects Taught: Chinese Language (Mandarin: beg/int), Civilization/ Culture, History, Social Sciences/ Studies

Cost $3,500 including
tuition, housing, fees
Housing: dorms
Application Deadline: Jan
Other: sponsor accredited in US
Contact: Dean John R. Johnson, Lock
Haven/Beijing College of Economics,
Institute for International Studies, Lock
Haven University, Lock Haven, PA
17745 Tel (717) 893-2140
FAX (717) 893-2537

**LOCK HAVEN UNIVERSITY—LOCK HAVEN/
BEIJING SUMMER EXCHANGE PROGRAM**
Program Description: 3-wk summer
program in beginning Chinese; most
classes taught by US faculty
Site(s) in China: Beijing (Beijing
College of Economics)
Dates: 3 wks, summer
Eligibility: must be sophomore or
above
Credits Granted: 3 credit hours
undergrad
Subjects Taught: Chinese Language
(Mandarin: beg), Chinese Culture,
History
Cost: $2,650, including tuition,
housing, meals, int'l airfare, excursions
Housing: dorms
Application Deadline: Jan 15
Contact: Dean John W. Johnston, Lock
Haven/Beijing Summer Exchange
Program, Institute for International
Studies, Lock Haven University, Lock
Haven PA 17745 Tel (717) 893-2140
FAX (717) 893-2537

**LOCK HAVEN UNIVERSITY—LOCK HAVEN/
CHANGSHA NORMAL EXCHANGE**
Program Description: 1 or 2-semester
program in Chinese language and
culture
Site(s) in China: Changsha (Changsha
Normal Univ)
Dates: Sep-Jan and/or Feb-Jul
Eligibility: must be sophomore or
above
Credits Granted: 15 credit hours
undergrad
Subjects Taught: Chinese Language

(Mandarin: beg/int/adv), Chinese
Studies, Civilization/Culture, Fine Arts,
History, Social Studies/Sciences
Cost: $3,500 per semester, including
tuition, housing, fees
Housing: dorms
Application Deadline: Jan
Other: sponsor accredited in US
Contact: Dean John W. Johnson, Lock
Haven/Changsha Normal Exchange,
Institute for International Studies, Lock
Haven University, Lock Haven, PA
17745 Tel (717) 893-2140
FAX (717) 893-2537

**LOCK HAVEN UNIVERSITY—LOCK HAVEN/
NANJING UNIVERSITY EXCHANGE**
Program Description: 1-semester
program in Chinese language, area
studies
Site(s) in China: Nanjing (Nanjing
Univ)
Dates: Sep-Jan
Eligibility: must be sophomore, junior,
or senior
Credits Granted: 15 credit hours
undergrad
Subjects Taught: Chinese Language
(Mandarin: beg/int), Chinese Studies,
Civilization/Culture, Fine Arts, History,
Social Studies/Sciences
Cost: $3,500, including tuition,
housing, fees, stipend
Housing: dorms
Application Deadline: Jan
Other: sponsor accredited in US
Contact: Dean John W. Johnston, Lock
Haven/Nanjing University Exchange,
Institute for International Studies, Lock
Haven University, Lock Haven, PA
17745 Tel (717) 893-2140
FAX (717) 893-2537

**LOCK HAVEN UNIVERSITY—LOCK HAVEN/
TUNGHAI SUMMER PROGRAM**
Program Description: summer
program in contemporary Chinese
studies
Site(s) in China: Taichung, Taiwan
(Tunghai Univ)
Dates: 5 wks, mid-Jun to Jul
Eligibility: must be sophomore or

above
Credits Granted: undergrad and grad
credit available
Subjects Taught: Contemporary
Chinese Government, Economics,
History, Philosophy, Social Problems
Cost: $1,950, including tuition,
housing, int'l airfare, excursions
Housing: dorms
Application Deadline: Mar
Contact: Dean John W. Johnston, Lock
Haven/Tunghai Summer Program,
Institute for International Studies, Lock
Haven University, Lock Haven, PA
17745 Tel (717) 893-2140
FAX (717) 893-2537

**LOCK HAVEN UNIVERSITY/NATIONAL
COLLEGE OF PHYSICAL EDUCATION &
SPORTS**
Program Description: 1-semester
program in physical education, focusing
on martial arts
Site(s) in China: Taoyuan, Taiwan
Dates: fall or spring semester
Eligibility: must be college student with
outstanding record in physical education
and sports
Credits Granted: 15 credit hours
undergrad
Subjects Taught: Physical Education
Cost: $3,000, including tuition,
housing, all meals, fees
Housing: dorms
Application Deadline: Feb
Other: sponsor accredited in US
Contact: Dean John W. Johnson,
National College of Physical Education
& Sports, Institute for International
Studies, Lock Haven University, Lock
Haven, PA 17745 Tel (717) 893-2140
FAX (717) 893-2537

**MIAMI UNIVERSITY—SUMMER INTENSIVE
CHINESE PROGRAM**
Program Description: summer
program in Chinese language and
literature
Site(s) in China: Shanghai (Fudan
Univ)
Dates: 7 wks, Jun-Jul

Eligibility: must be student or teacher
Credits Granted: 8 credit hours
undergrad, 4 credit hours grad
Subjects Taught: Chinese Language
(Mandarin: beg/int/adv), Chinese
Literature (in English translation)
Cost: approx $2,900, including tuition,
housing, int'l airfare, excursions, fees
(Ohio students pay half of the usual out-
of-state fee)
Housing: dorms
Application Deadline: Feb 28
Other: some scholarships available for
Miami Univ students only; program
moved to Taipei for 1989-1991, will
return to Fudan in 1992; activities
include optional trip to Hong Kong and
tour of China
Contact: Prof. Chiang-Tsu Chow,
Summer Intensive Chinese Program,
Miami University, Oxford, OH 45056
Tel (513) 529-2912

**MICHIGAN STATE UNIVERSITY—CHINESE
LANGUAGE AND CULTURE IN SHANGHAI**
Program Description: summer
program in Chinese language & culture
for advanced students
Site(s) in China: Shanghai
Dates: Jun 23-Aug 10
Eligibility: must be sophomore or
above, w/ min 1 yr college Mandarin;
background in Chinese history, culture
preferred
Credits Granted: 10 credit hours
undergrad
Subjects Taught: Chinese Language
(Mandarin: int/adv), Chinese History/
Culture
Cost: $2,860, including tuition,
housing, some meals, excursions, fees
Housing: dorms
Application Deadline: Apr 23
Other: activities include program travel
in Beijing, Luoyang, Xi'an; some
scholarships available; program
temporarily suspended 1989; planned to
restart 1992
Contact: Dr. Charles Gliozzo, Office of
Overseas Study, Michigan State
University, 108 International Center,

East Lansing, MI 48824-1035
Tel (517) 353-8920
FAX (517) 336-2082

**MICHIGAN STATE UNIVERSITY—FOOD AND
AGRICULTURAL SYSTEMS IN CHINA AND
JAPAN**
Program Description: summer
program in food and agricultural
systems jointly organized by Office of
Int'l Studies and Institutes of Int'l
Agriculture and Water Research
Site(s) in China: Beijing, Harbin,
Chengdu (also Tokyo & Osaka in
Japan)
Dates: Jul 1-Aug 1
Eligibility: must be sophomore or
above, w/ min 1 yr college Mandarin;
background in Chinese history, culture
preferred
Credits Granted: 10 credit hours
undergrad
Subjects Taught: Asian Agricultural
Systems; includes visits with farm
families, lectures by US faculty
Cost: $1,800, including tuition,
housing, some meals, excursions, fees
Housing: dorms, hostels, hotels
Application Deadline: Apr 22
Number of Students Sent/Yr Avg:
new program
Other: activities include trips to Mt.
Fuji, Great Wall, etc.; some scholarships
available
Contact: Dr. Charles Gliozzo, Ofice of
Overseas Study, Michigan State
University, 108 International Center,
East Lansing, MI 48824-1035
Tel (517) 353-8920
FAX (517) 336-2082

**NATIONAL REGISTRATION CENTER FOR
STUDY ABROAD (NRCSA)—STUDY
ABROAD-TAIPEI**
Program Description: NRCSA is a
consortium of 86 universities world-
wide; students can register for study at
any one of these institutions; Taipei
Language Institute is member school,
and students can apply, pay, & receive

US credit through NRCSA
Site(s) in China: Taipei, Shihlin, &
Taichung, Taiwan (Taipei Language
Institute)
Dates: fall and/or spring semesters
Eligibility: must be college student
Credits Granted: credit available by
arrangement
Subjects Taught: Chinese Language
(Mandarin/Taiwanese: beg/int/adv)
Cost: write to NRCSA
Housing: with family
Application Deadline: revolving
admissions
Number of Students Sent/Yr Avg:
6-12
Other: sponsor accredited in US
Contact: Study Abroad-Taipei,
National Registration Center for Study
Abroad (NRCSA) PO Box 1393
Milwaukee WI, 53201
Tel (414) 278-0631

**NORTHERN ILLINOIS UNIVERSITY—ADULT
EDUCATION WORKSHOP IN CHINA**
Program Description: residential
workshop focusing on the theoretical
and practical bases of adult education in
China; organized in cooperation w/
Shanghai 2nd Institute of Education
Site(s) in China: Shanghai, Hangzhou,
Suzhou, Xi'an, Beijing
Dates: 3-1/2 wks, May 15-Jun 9
Eligibility: undergrad or grad student,
w/ good academic standing
Credits Granted: 3-6 credit hours
undergrad; will provide transcript
Subjects Taught: students attend
English-language courses arranged for
group and taught by US faculty
Cost: $3,395, including tuition,
housing, all meals, int'l airfare,
insurance, fees
Housing: dorms and hotels
Application Deadline: Mar 1
Number of Students Sent/Yr Avg: 15
Contact: Northern Illinois University,
Williston Hall 100B, DeKalb, IL 60115
Tel (815) 753-0304 FAX (815) 753-
1488

NORTHERN ILLINOIS UNIVERSITY—CHINA COOPERATIVE LANGUAGE AND STUDY PROGRAM

Program Description: 1 or 2-semester program in Chinese language, area studies

Site(s) in China: Nanjing (Univ of Nanjing)

Dates: Aug to mid-Dec and/or Jan to mid-May

Eligibility: must be sophomore or above, w/ min 2.5 GPA, 1 yr college Chinese, course in area studies; knowledge of Pinyin recommended

Credits Granted: 15 undergrad/semester

Subjects Taught: Chinese Language (Mandarin: int/adv), Chinese Studies

Cost: $5,500 per semester, including tuition, housing, all meals, insurance, fees, excursions, books/materials, lectures, cultural events

Housing: dorms

Application Deadline: Feb 8 for Fall; Oct 3 for spring

Number of Students Sent/Yr Avg: 10

Other: sponsor accredited in US; program developed in cooperation w/ CIEE; activities include travel, excursions, orientation program in Nanjing; qualified students may go from this program on to second semester in Beijing

Contact: Ines DeRomana, Foreign Study Office, Northern Illinois University, Williston Hall 100B, DeKalb, IL 60115-2854 Tel (815) 753-0304 FAX (815) 753-1488

NORTHERN ILLINOIS UNIVERSITY—CHINESE LANGUAGE AND CIVILIZATION PROGRAM

Program Description: 1 or 2-semester program in Chinese language and culture

Site(s) in China: Beijing (Peking Univ)

Dates: Aug to mid-Dec and/or late Jan to mid-May

Eligibility: must be junior or above, w/ min 2.5 GPA, 2 years Chinese language study, working knowledge of Pinyin,

min 1 Chinese area studies course

Credits Granted: 15 credit hours undergrad; will provide transcript

Subjects Taught: Chinese Language (Mandarin: adv), Chinese Studies

Cost: $5,400 per semester, including tuition, housing, all meals, insurance, fees, excursions, books/materials, lectures, cultural events

Housing: dorms

Application Deadline: Feb 8 for fall; Oct 3 for spring

Number of Students Sent/Yr Avg: 15

Other: sponsor accredited in US; program includes 2-day orientation session at Peking Univ in cooperation w/ CIEE, program travel

Contact: Ines DeRomana, Foreign Study Office, Northern Illinois University, Williston Hall 100B, DeKalb, IL 60115 Tel (815) 753-0304 FAX (815) 753-1488

NORTHERN ILLINOIS UNIVERSITY— EDUCATION SEMINAR IN CHINA

Program Description: short-term study tour of China's educational system, focusing on school visits, talks with educators

Site(s) in China: Beijing, Guangzhou, Guilin, Hong Kong, Shanghai

Dates: 4 wks, Jun 21-Jul 19

Eligibility: must be sophomore or above, w/ good academic standing, interest in Chinese education/culture

Credits Granted: 3-6 credit hours undergrad

Subjects Taught: Education in China (special focus on creative new pograms for elementary-postsecondary levels)

Cost: $3,600, including tuition, housing, some meals, int'l airfare from Chicago, excursions, fees, insurance

Housing: hotels

Application Deadline: Apr 1 or until program filled

Contact: Dr. Orville E. Jones, Education Seminar in China, International and Special Programs, Northern Illinois University, Lowden 203, DeKalb, IL 60115 Tel (815) 753-9528

OREGON STATE SYSTEM OF HIGHER
EDUCATION (OSSHE)—OREGON/BEIJING
PROGRAM
Program Description: 1-semester
program in Chinese language
Site(s) in China: Central Institute for
Nationalities (CIN)
Dates: Fall semester, 15 wks
Eligibility: must be sophomore or
above, w/ min 2.75 GPA; prior Chinese
language study not required, but
preference will be given to those with
previous Chinese language study
Credits Granted: equivalent to full yr
of non-intensive language study
Subjects Taught: Chinese Language
(Mandarin beg/int/adv)
Cost: approx $3,500, including tuition,
housing, all meals, fees, excursions,
books/materials
Housing: residence halls
Application Deadline: Feb 15
Other: sponsor accredited in US;
activities include excursions
Contact: Dr. Christine Sproul, Oregon/
Beijing Program, International
Education, Oregon State System of
Higher Education (OSSHE), Snell Hall,
Oregon State University, Corvalis, OR
97331-1642 Tel (503) 737-3006 FAX
(503) 737-3447

OREGON STATE SYSTEM OF HIGHER
EDUCATION (OSSHE)—OREGON/FUJIAN
PROGRAM
Program Description: 1-semester
program in Chinese language, area
studies
Site(s) in China: Fuzhou (Fujian
Teachers Univ)
Dates: Jan   to mid-Jun
Eligibility: must be sophomore or
above, w/ min. 2.75 GPA
Credits Granted: 12 credit hours
undergrad
Subjects Taught: Chinese Language
(Mandarin int/adv), Chinese Studies,
Field Study
Cost: approx $3,500, including tuition,
housing, all meals, fees, excursions,
books/materials

Housing: residence halls
Application Deadline: Oct 1
Number of Students Sent/Yr Avg: 10-
12
Other: sponsor accredited in US;
activities include excursions
Contact: Dr. Christine Sproul, Oregon/
Fujian Program, International
Education, Oregon State System of
Higher Education (OSSHE), Snell Hall,
Oregon State University, Corvalis, OR
97331-1642 Tel (503) 737-3006 FAX
(503) 737-3447

PACIFIC LUTHERAN UNIVERSITY—
COMBINED STUDIES IN CHINESE LANGUAGE/
CULTURE & BASIC SCIENCE
Program Description: 1 or 2-semester
program in Chinese language, including
basic science studies taught in Chinese;
some religious orientation; program
trains students to teach basic science in
China
Site(s) in China: Chengdu (Chengdu
Univ of Science and Technology)
Dates: Sep 1-Jun 25 (1 or 2 semesters)
Eligibility: must be sophomore or
above, w/ good academic standing,
preferably some science background
Credits Granted: undergrad credit
available
Subjects Taught: Chemistry, Chinese
Language (Mandarin: beg/int), Chinese
Studies, Physics
Cost: $13,400 per year, including
tuition, housing, all meals, excursions,
books/materials, local transportation
Housing: dorms
Application Deadline: Mar 2 for fall;
Oct 1 for spring
Other: sponsor accredited in US;
program includes China travel
Contact: Dr. Judith Carr, Combined
Studies in Chinese Language/Culture &
Basic Science, Special Academic
Programs, Pacific Lutheran University,
Tacoma, WA 98447 Tel (206) 535-7296

PACIFIC LUTHERAN UNIVERSITY—TUNGHAI
UNIVERSITY EXCHANGE
Program Description: 2-semester
program in Chinese language and area

studies
Site(s) in China: Taichung, Taiwan
(Tunghai Univ)
Dates: Sep 1-Jun 30 (full period only)
Eligibility: must be PLU srudent,
sophomore or above, w/ min 2.75 GPA
Credits Granted: undergrad credit
available
Subjects Taught: Chinese Language
(Mandarin: beg/int/adv), Civilization/
Culture, Independent Study
Cost: $12,960 includes tuition, housing,
all meals, books/materials
Housing: arranged by program;
residence halls
Application Deadline: Mar 1
Contact: Dr. Judith Carr, Tunghai
University Exchange, Special Academic
Programs, Pacific Lutheran University,
Tacoma, WA 98447 Tel (206) 535-7130

PACIFIC LUTHERAN UNIVERSITY—
ZHONGSHAN UNIVERSITY RECIPROCAL
EXCHANGE
Program Description: full-year
program in Chinese language, area
studies; some religious orientation
Site(s) in China: Guangzhou
(Zhongshan Univ)
Dates: Sep 1-Jun 30 (full period only)
Eligibility: must be PLU student,
sophomore or above, w/ min 2.75 GPA
Credits Granted: undergrad credit
available
Subjects Taught: Chinese Language
(Mandarin: beg/int), Civilization/
Culture, Independent Study
Cost: $12,960, including tuition,
housing, all meals, books/materials
Housing: dorms
Application Deadline: Mar 1
Other: sponsor accredited in US
Contact: Dr. Judith Carr, Zhongshan
University Reciprocal Exchange,
Special Academic Programs, Pacific
Lutheran University, Tacoma, WA
98447 Tel (206) 535-7130

PENNSYLVANIA STATE UNIVERSITY—
GENERAL STUDIES AT NATIONAL TAIWAN
UNIVERSITY
Program Description: 1-semester

program in Chinese language and area
studies (fall semester only)
Site(s) in China: Taipei, Taiwan
(National Taiwan Univ)
Dates: Sep-Dec
Eligibility: PSU juniors and seniors (as
well as occasional students from other
institutions); must have 2.50 GPA; 4
credits of Chinese and a background
course in East Asian Studies required
Credits Granted: 15 credit hours per
semester undergrad
Subjects Taught: Chinese Language
(all levels), Chinese Art History, and a
course on the Literature of Asia
Housing: dorms arranged by program
Application Deadline: 1 year before
program (Nov 1)
Number of Students Sent/Yr Avg: 6-
10
Contact: Michael Laubscher, Director,
Office of Education Abroad Program,
Penn State University, 222 Boucke
Building, University Park, PA 16802
Tel (814) 865-7681 FAX (814) 865-
3336

PORTLAND STATE UNIVERSITY—CHINA:
YESTERDAY AND TODAY
Program Description: 4-wk program
in Chinese language and culture,
organized in cooperation w/ the
American Heritage Ass'n; includes
orientation in US, courses taught by US
faculty
Site(s) in China: Changchun (Jilin Univ
of Technology)
Dates: 4 wks, early Jul/Aug
Eligibility: must be student, teacher, or
professional, min age 18
Credits Granted: 7 credit hours
undergrad; grad unavailable
Subjects Taught: Chinese Language
(Mandarin: beg/int), Chinese Civiliza-
tion/Culture
Cost: $2,950, including tuition,
housing, int'l airfare, excursions, fees
Housing: dorms
Application Deadline: 1 mo before
program starts
Other: activities include excursions

Contact: Steven Harmon, China: Yesterday and Today, Summer Session, Portland State University, PO Box 751, Portland, OR 97207 Tel (503) 464-4081

PORTLAND STATE UNIVERSITY—SUMMER IN ZHENGZHOU
Program Description: summer program in Chinese language & culture
Site(s) in China: Zhengzhou (Zhengzhou Univ)
Dates: Jul 10-Aug 11
Eligibility: must be student or adult
Credits Granted: undergrad credit available
Subjects Taught: Chinese Language (Intensive Mandarin: beg/int/adv), Chinese Art, Calligraphy, Geography, History, Literature
Cost: $1,495, including tuition, housing, some meals, excursions, fees
Housing: dorms
Application Deadline: Jun 1
Contact: Steven W. Harmon, Summer in Zhengzhou, Summer Session Portland State University, PO Box 751, Portland, OR 97207 Tel (503) 464-4081

RESEARCH PROGRAM FOR SCHOLARS
Program Description: research opportunities matched with colleges at Peking Univ
Site(s) in China: Peking Univ, Beijing
Eligibility: already completed Ph.D. in China-related discipline
Cost: $350 application and processing fee + $300 placement fee; tuition paid directly to Peking Univ
Housing: Peking Univ dorms
Application Deadline: Feb 15
Contact: Suzanne Fox, University Programs Dept., CIEE, 205 E. 42nd St., New York, NY 10017 Tel (212) 661-1414 x1244

ST. CLOUD STATE UNIVERSITY STUDY CENTER IN TIANJIN, CHINA
Program Description: 1-semester program for beginning students in Chinese language, area studies
Site(s) in China: Tianjin (Nankai Univ)
Dates: Jan-May

Eligibility: must be college student, min age 18, w/ min 2.25 GPA
Credits Granted: 32 credit hours undergrad
Subjects Taught: Chinese Language (Mandarin: beg), Chinese Studies
Cost: $6,500, including tuition, housing, meals, int'l airfare, fees, excursions
Housing: int'l student dorm
Application Deadline: Sep 15
Number of Students Sent/Yr Avg: 15
Other: sponsor accredited in US; activities include excursions, field trips; work-study available; program provides resident US faculty director
Contact: Study Center in Tianjin, China, Center for International Studies, St. Cloud State University, 720 4th Ave., S. St. Cloud, MN 56301-4498 Tel (612) 255-4287

ST. JOHN'S UNIVERSITY—CHINESE STUDIES PROGRAM
Program Description: 1-semester program in Chinese language/culture; some religious orientation
Site(s) in China: Chongqing (Southwest China Teachers Univ)
Dates: Aug 25-Dec 15
Eligibility: must be sophomore or above, w/ min 2.5 GPA, good academic standing, current enrollment at accredited college
Credits Granted: undergrad credit available
Subjects Taught: Chinese Language (Mandarin: beg/int/adv), Chinese Studies, Martial Arts
Cost: $6,800, including tuition, housing, all meals, int'l airfare, excursions
Housing: apartments
Application Deadline: Mar 1
Other: sponsor accredited in US; activities include field trips
Contact: Chinese Studies Program, Office of International Studies, St. John's University, Collegeville, MN 56321 Tel (612) 363-3612

SCHOOL FOR INTERNATIONAL TRAINING (SIT)—SEMESTER ABROAD-CHINA
  Program Description: 1-semester program in Chinese language/culture w/ emphasis on field study, independent project; includes "home hospitality" match w/Chinese family for visits & weekend homestays, & 2 wk-long study tours, 1 in Chengde, 1 in Qufu; organized in cooperation w/ Chinese-American Education Exchange; SIT also affiliated with Experiment for International Living (EIL) in Brattleboro; EIL occasionally has summer sessions in China, though none planned 1991/1992
  Site(s) in China: Shijiazhuang (Hebei Teachers Univ), Chengde, Qufu
  Dates: fall or spring semester
  Eligibility: must be sophomore or above, w/ min 2.5 GPA, good academic standards; 1 yr college Mandarin recommended
  Credits Granted: 16 credit hours undergrad
  Subjects Taught: Chinese Language (Mandarin: beg/int), Chinese Life/ Culture, History/Politics, Arts/ Humanities, Geography/Economics, Social Anthropology, Field Studies, Independent Project
  Cost: $9,500, including tuition, housing, all meals, int'l airfare, excursions, fees, books/materials, insurance
  Housing: dorms
  Application Deadline: Jun 15 for fall, Nov 15 for spring
  Other: sponsor accredited in US; activities include excursions, program travel, orientation in Beijing, evaluated and supervised 3-wk independent study project
  Contact: Semester Abroad-China, Academic Studies Abroad, School for International Training (SIT), Kipling Road, Brattleboro, VT 05301-0676 Tel (800) 451-4465

SHANGHAI SUMMER LANGUAGE & CULTURE PROGRAM
  Program Description: language and area studies program
  Site(s) in China: Fudan Univ, Shanghai
  Dates: late-Jun to late-Aug
  Eligibility: open to all levels of language training
  Credits Granted: 9
  Subjects Taught: Chinese Society & Culture, Chinese Language
  Cost: $3,100
  Housing: in univ dorms
  Application Deadline: Mar 1
  Other: co-sponsored by California State Univ, Sacramento
  Contact: Suzanne Fox, University Programs Dept., CIEE, 205 E. 42nd St., New York, NY 10017 Tel (212) 661-1414 x 1244 or Monica Freeman, California State University, Sacramento Tel (916) 278-6686

SLIPPERY ROCK UNIVERSITY—SRU/ SHANGHAI INTERNATIONAL STUDIES UNIVERSITY EXCHANGE
  Program Description: 1 or 2-semester program in Chinese language, area studies; includes classes with Chinese students
  Site(s) in China: Shanghai (Shanghai Int'l Studies Univ)
  Dates: Sep-Jun (1 or 2 terms)
  Eligibility: must be sophomore or above, w/ min 2.5 GPA, plus min 1 yr college Chinese
  Credits Granted: 15 credit hours undergrad per semester; will provide transcript
  Subjects Taught: Chinese Language (Mandarin: beg/int/adv), Chinese Studies, Journalism
  Cost: $3,275 per semester PA resident, $4,295 non-resident, including tuition, housing, all meals, insurance, fees
  Housing: dorms
  Application Deadline: Apr 1
  Number of Students Sent/Yr Avg: 4
  Other: sponsor accredited in US
  Contact: Stan Kendziorski, SRU/ Shanghai International Studies, University Exchange, International Studies, Slippery Rock University, Slippery Rock, PA 16057

Tel (412) 794-7425

STANFORD UNIVERSITY—INTER-UNIVERSITY PROGRAM FOR CHINESE LANGUAGE STUDIES IN TAIPEI
Program Description: full academic yr program in Chinese language organized by a consortium of universities; sometimes called "Stanford Center Program"
Site(s) in China: Taipei, Taiwan (National Taiwan Univ)
Dates: Sep-Jun or Sep-Aug
Eligibility: must be student (undergrad or grad), min 2 yrs college Mandarin, good academic standing
Credits Granted: no credit available (but progress reports are available for students to use in gaining credit from their home institutions)
Subjects Taught: Chinese Language (Mandarin: int/adv)
Cost: $2,400 per quarter, including tuition, fees
Housing: students must arrange; sponsor will assist
Application Deadline: Feb 15
Number of Students Sent/Yr Avg: 50
Contact: Inter-University Program for Chinese Language Studies in Taipei, Littlefield Center, Stanford University, Rm 14, 300 Lasuen St., Stanford, CA 94305-5013 Tel (415) 725-2575 FAX (415) 723-9972

SUNY COLLEGE AT CORTLAND—ACADEMIC YEAR/SEMESTER EXCHANGE PROGRAM AT BEIJING
Program Description: 1 or 2-semester program in Chinese language, culture
Site(s) in China: Beijing (Beijing Teachers College, or Beijing Inst of Physical Culture)
Dates: late Aug to mid-Jan and/or mid-Feb to late-Jul
Eligibility: must be junior or above, w/ above-average academic standing, min 1 yr. Mandarin and demonstrated personal maturity
Credits Granted: 14-32 credit hours undergrad; grad credit available
Subjects Taught: Chinese Language (Mandarin), Chinese Studies, Physical Education
Cost: $5,350 per semester, includes housing, all meals, int'l airfare, fees, excursions, books/materials; SUNY tuition not included
Housing: guest house
Application Deadline: Mar 1 for fall, Oct 1 for spring
Number of Students Sent/Yr Avg: 3-4
Other: sponsor accredited in US; program includes some travel
Contact: Dr. John Ogden, Academic Year/Semester Exchange Program at Beijing, International Programs, SUNY College at Cortland, PO Box 2000, Cortland, NY 13045 Tel (607) 753-2209 FAX (607) 753-5999

SUNY COLLEGE AT NEW PALTZ—BEIJING STUDY ABROAD PROGRAM
Program Description: Chinese language and area studies
Site(s) in China: Beijing Univ
Dates: Sep-Jun; semester study also possible
Eligibility: must be junior or above, w/ min 2 yrs college-level Mandarin Chinese
Credits Granted: usual load 12/ semester
Subjects Taught: Mandarin Chinese (int/adv)
Cost: $3,500 for NY residents per semester; non-residents $5,500 per semester; includes tuition, housing, all meals, fees
Housing: dorms
Application Deadline: approx Mar 15
Number of Students Sent/Yr Avg: 3-4
Other: sponsor accredited in US
Contact: College at New Paltz, SUNY Office of International Education, HAB 33, New Paltz, NY 12561 Tel (914) 257-3125 FAX (914) 257-3129

SUNY UNIVERSITY AT ALBANY—CHINA/SUNYA EXCHANGE PROGRAM
Program Description: full-year multinational program in Chinese language

Site(s) in China: Beijing, Nanjing, Shanghai, Tianjin
Dates: Sep 1-Jun 30 (fall/spring/ academic year)
Eligibility: sophomores or above, w/ good academic standing
Credits Granted: 24-30 credit hours undergrad; grad credit available
Subjects Taught: Chinese Language (Mandarin), Chinese Studies, Liberal Arts
Cost: $2,237 per semester (NY resident); $3,912 (non-resident); includes tuition, housing, meals, insurance, fees
Housing: dorms/residence halls
Application Deadline: Feb 15
Number of Students Sent/Yr Avg: 11
Other: sponsor accredited in US
Contact: Dr. Alex M. Shane, China/ SUNYA Exchange Program, LI-84 SUNY University at Albany, International Programs, Albany, NY 12222 Tel (518) 442-3525 FAX (518) 442-3338

UNIVERSITY OF CALIFORNIA—UC
EDUCATION ABROAD PROGRAM IN CHINA
Program Description: 1 or 2-semester multinational, multidisciplinary language and area studies program
Site(s) in China: Beijing (Peking Univ, and Beijing Science and Technology Univ) and Tianjin (Nankai Univ)
Dates: Aug-Jul (1 or 2 terms)
Eligibility: must be UC student, junior yr or above, 3.0 GPA or above w/ min 1 yr college Chinese for semester programs, or 2 yrs college Chinese for academic year program; grad students must have completed 1 yr of grad study at UC
Credits Granted: available for both undergrad and grads
Subjects Taught: Area Studies, Chinese Languages (Mandarin: int/adv), Chinese Studies, Economics, History, Literature, Philosophy, Sociology (academic courses for students fluent in Chinese)
Cost: $4,000-$11,000 estimated min

expenses, includes housing, all meals, int'l airfare, insurance, fees, excursions
Housing: dorms
Application Deadline: Jan 18
Number of Students Sent/Yr Avg: 36
Other: sponsor accredited in US; activities include excursions & field trips; scholarships available
Contact: (Ms.) Randy Arnold, UC Education Abroad Program in China, Education Abroad Program, Information Services, University of California, Santa Barbara, CA 93106 Tel (805) 961-4139

UNIVERSITY OF CALIFORNIA—UC
EDUCATION ABROAD PROGRAM IN HONG
KONG
Program Description: 2-yr program in Chinese language and area studies, full curriculum
Site(s) in China: Hong Kong (Chinese Univ of Hong Kong)
Dates: Jul-Apr
Eligibility: must be UC student, junior or above, w/ min 3.0 GPA; grad students must have completed 1 yr min in UC grad program
Credits Granted: both undergrad and grad available
Subjects Taught: Chinese Language (beg/int/adv), Chinese Studies, full curriculum
Cost: $8,000 estimated min expenses for CA residents, including tuition, housing, all meals, int'l airfare, fees, excursions, books/materials
Housing: dorms, hostels
Application Deadline: Jan 18
Number of Students Sent/Yr Avg: 15
Other: sponsor accredited in US; activities include field trips, excursions, orientation program; some scholarships available
Contact: Randy Arnold, UC Education Abroad Program in Hong Kong, Education Abroad Program, Information Services University of California, Santa Barbara, CA 93106 Tel (805) 961-4139

UNIVERSITY OF CALIFORNIA—UC
EDUCATION ABROAD PROGRAM IN TAIWAN
Program Description: 1-yr program in

Chinese language, area studies and int'l business, art and art history
Site(s) in China: Taipei, Taiwan (National Chengchi Univ)
Dates: Aug-May
Eligibility: UC juniors, seniors, and grad studs only; must have 3.0 GPA; grad students must have already completed 1 yr of grad study; prior study of Mandarin recommended
Credits Granted: undergrad and grad credit available
Subjects Taught: Chinese Language (Mandarin: beg/int/adv), Culture, International Business, Art, and Art History
Cost: $11,000 estimated min expense for tuition, meals, housing, int'l airfare, excursions, books & materials
Housing: dormitories arranged by program
Application Deadline: Jan 18
Number of Students Sent/Yr Avg: 12
Other: some scholarships available
Contact: Randy Arnold, UC Education Abroad, Program in Taiwan, Education Abroad Program, University of California Information Services, Santa Barbara, CA 93106 Tel (805)961-4139

UNIVERSITY OF FLORIDA—ACADEMIC YEAR IN TAIPEI
Program Description: 2-semester program in Chinese languages
Site(s) in China: Taipei, Taiwan (Mandarin Training Center, Taiwan Normal Univ)
Dates: Sep 1-May 31
Eligibility: sophomore or above, 2.5 GPA, and 2 semesters of college Chinese
Credits Granted: 30 undergrad/grad
Subjects Taught: Mandarin Chinese
Cost: $5,000 including tuition, housing, meals, insurance, fees
Housing: arranged by student
Application Deadline: Apr 1 for fall; Nov 1 for spring
Contact: Diana Lopez, Academic Year in Taipei, Center for International Students & Faculty, Exchange

University of Florida, 168 Grinter Hall, Gainesville, FL 32611
Tel (904) 392-4904

UNIVERSITY OF FLORIDA/AMERICAN INSTITUTE FOR FOREIGN STUDIES (AIFS)— PEKING UNIVERSITY SEMESTER
Program Description: full year program in Chinese language and area studies
Site(s) in China: Beijing (Peking Univ)
Dates: Sep 7-Jun 21
Eligibility: must be junior or above, w/ min 2.5 GPA, 1 yr or intensive summer program of Mandarin
Credits Granted: 14 credit hours per semester undergrad
Subjects Taught: Chinese Language (Mandarin: int/adv)
Cost: $5,605 per semester, $10,180 per year, including tuition, housing, all meals, int'l airfare, fees, books/ materials, excursions
Housing: dorms
Application Deadline: May 8 for fall; Oct 9 for spring
Other: sponsor accredited in US; activities include excursions
Contact: Diana P. Lopez, Peking University Semester, Center for International Student and Faculty Exchange, University of Florida/ American Institute for Foreign Studies (AIFS), 168 Grinter Hall, Gainesville, FL 32611 Tel (904) 392-4904

UNIVERSITY OF HAWAII AT MANOA— INDUSTRIALIZATION OF ASIAN COUNTRIES
Contact: Pauline Abe, Industrialization of Asian Countries, Pacific Asia Management Institute, University of Hawaii at Manoa, 2404 Maile Way, C-202, Honolulu, HI 96822 Tel (808) 948-7564

UNIVERSITY OF KANSAS—ACADEMIC YEAR IN TAIWAN
Program Description: full year program in Chinese language, area studies
Site(s) in China: Taipei, Taiwan (National Taiwan Normal Univ)

Dates: Sep 1-May 31 (full period only)
Eligibility: must be junior or above
Credits Granted: 30 credit hours undergrad
Subjects Taught: Chinese Language (Mandarin: int/adv), Civilization/Culture
Cost: $5,500, including tuition, housing, all meals, fees
Housing: dorms
Application Deadline: Feb 16
Other: sponsor accredited in US; sponsor provides summer program in US prior to year abroad; students strongly urged to attend
Contact: Nancy S. Mitchell, Academic Year in Taiwan, Office of Study Abroad, University of Kansas, 203 Lippincott Hall, Lawrence, KS 66045 Tel (913) 864-3742

UNIVERSITY OF KANSAS—STUDY/RESEARCH IN THE PEOPLE'S REPUBLIC OF CHINA
Program Description: full-year multinational program in Chinese language, culture, civilization; w/ provisions for independent study
Site(s) in China: Nanjing, Nankai, Zhengzhou (various univs)
Dates: Aug-Jul (full period only)
Eligibility: Univ of Kansas students only, juniors and above, w/ min 2 yrs college Mandarin
Credits Granted: 12-18 credit hours/semester undergrad; grad credit available
Subjects Taught: Chinese Language (Mandarin: adv), Civilization/Culture, Independent Study
Cost: $5,500 including tuition, housing, all meals, fees
Housing: dorms
Application Deadline: Jan 15
Other: sponsor accredited in US
Contact: Nancy S. Mitchell, Study/Research in the People's Republic of China, Office of Study Abroad, University of Kansas, 203 Lippincott Hall, Lawrence, KS 66045 Tel (913) 864-3742

UNIVERSITY OF LA VERNE—STUDY TOUR TO CHINA AND HONG KONG
Program Description: short semester program in Chinese area studies organized through Wuqi Univ
Site(s) in China: Guangzhou, Hong Kong
Dates: Feb-May
Eligibility: sophomore standing
Credits Granted: 12 credit hours undergrad
Subjects Taught: History, Humanities, Sociology
Cost: $7,200 including tuition, housing, all meals, int'l airfare, fees, excursions
Housing: dorms, hotels, hostels
Application Deadline: May 1
Number of Students Sent/Yr Avg: 12
Other: sponsor accredited in US; activities include lectures, discussions, field trips, program travel
Contact: Dr. John Jang, Study Tour to China and Hong Kong, Department of History/Political Science, University of La Verne, 1950 3rd St., La Verne, CA 91750 Tel (714) 593-3511 x4225

UNIVERSITY OF MASSACHUSETTS AT AMHERST—SHAANXI NORMAL UNIVERSITY EXCHANGE
Program Description: 1 or 2-term program in Chinese language, area studies for advanced students
Site(s) in China: Xi'an (Shaanxi Normal Univ)
Dates: fall and/or spring terms
Eligibility: must be junior or above, w/ 2 yrs Mandarin, good academic standing, current enrollment in degree program
Credits Granted: 30-32 credit hours undergrad per yr
Subjects Taught: Chinese Language (Mandarin: int/adv), Chinese Studies
Cost: $4,000 per semester, $7,000 per yr, including tuition, housing, all meals, fees, excursions
Housing: dorms; share rooms w/ Chinese students
Application Deadline: Feb 15
Other: sponsor accredited in US;

activities include excursions
Contact: Shaanxi Normal University
Exchange, International Programs,
University of Massachusetts at Amherst,
William S. Clark International Center,
Amherst, MA 01003
Tel (413) 545-2710

UNIVERSITY OF MASSACHUSETTS AT
AMHERST—YEAR AT TUNGHAI PROGRAM,
TAIWAN
Program Description: 1 or 2-semester
program in Chinese and general studies
Site(s) in China: Taichung, Taiwan
(Tunghai Univ)
Dates: fall and/or spring terms
Eligibility: must be junior or above, w/
min 3.0 GPA, 2 yrs Mandarin, current
enrollment in degree program
Credits Granted: 30-32 credit hours
undergrad
Subjects Taught: Chinese Language
(Mandarin: beg/int/adv), Chinese
Studies, General Studies
Cost: $4,000 per semester, $7,000 per
yr, including tuition, housing, all meals,
fees, excursions
Housing: dorms; share rooms with local
students
Application Deadline: Feb 15
Other: sponsor accredited in US;
activities include excursions, field trips;
Colorado area students may also apply
for program through University of
Colorado at Boulder, Boulder, CO,
80309-0123, Tel (303) 492-7741
Contact: Year at Tunghai Program,
International Programs, University of
Massachusetts at Amherst, William S.
Clark International Center, Amherst,
MA 01003
Tel (413) 545-2710

UNIVERSITY OF MASSACHUSETTS AT
AMHERST—BEIJING NORMAL UNIVERSITY
EXCHANGE
Program Description: full year
program in Chinese language, area
studies
Site(s) in China: Beijing (Beijing
Normal Univ)
Dates: late Aug-late Jun (full period

only)
Eligibility: must be junior or above, w/
min 3.0 GPA, 2 yrs college Mandarin
Credits Granted: undergrad credit
available; transcript provided
Subjects Taught: Chinese Language
(Mandarin: int/adv), Chinese Studies
Cost: $7,000, including tuition,
housing, all meals, fees, excursions
Housing: dorms
Application Deadline: Feb 15
Other: sponsor accredited in US
Contact: Beijing Normal University
Exchange, International Programs,
University of Massachusetts at Amherst,
William S. Clark International Center,
Amherst, MA 01003
Tel (413) 545-2710

UNIVERSITY OF MASSACHUSETTS AT
AMHERST—BEIJING UNIVERSITY OF
FOREIGN STUDIES EXCHANGE
Program Description: full-year
program in Chinese language
Site(s) in China: Beijing (Beijing Univ
of Foreign Studies)
Dates: Sep-Jun (full period only)
Eligibility: must be junior or above, w/
min 3.0 GPA, 2 yrs college Mandarin,
current enrollment in degree program
Credits Granted: 30 credit hours
undergrad; transcript available
Subjects Taught: Chinese Language
(Mandarin: int/adv), Chinese Studies
Cost: $7,000, including tuition,
housing, all meals, fees, excursions
Housing: dorms (share rooms w/
Chinese students)
Application Deadline: Feb 15
Other: sponsor accredited in US;
activities include excursions
Contact: Beijing University of Foreign
Studies Exchange, International
Programs, University of Massachusetts
at Amherst, William S. Clark Interna-
tional Center, Amherst, MA 01003
Tel (413) 545-2710

UNIVERSITY OF MASSACHUSETTS AT
AMHERST—XI'AN SUMMER PROGRAM
Program Description: summer

program in Chinese history & culture; all classes in English
Site(s) in China: Xi'an
Dates: late Jun-early Aug
Eligibility: must be student, teacher, or professional
Credits Granted: 4 credit hours undergrad
Subjects Taught: Chinese History & Culture
Cost: $3,500, including tuition, housing, all meals, int'l airfare, excursions
Housing: provided
Application Deadline: Mar 31
Other: activities include excursions, extensive program travel in China
Contact: Xi'an Summer Program, International Programs, University of Massachusetts at Amherst, William S. Clark International Center, Amherst, MA 01003 Tel (413) 545-2710

UNIVERSITY OF MASSACHUSETTS AT AMHERST—TUNGHAI SUMMER PROGRAM
Program Description: summer program in Chinese language, literature
Site(s) in China: Taichung, Taiwan (Tunghai Univ)
Dates: 8 wks, Jul-Aug
Eligibility: must be sophomore or above, w/ min B average, 1 yr intensive Mandarin
Credits Granted: 10 credit hours undergrad; no grad credit
Subjects Taught: Chinese Language (Mandarin: beg/int), Chinese Literature
Cost: $1,800, including tuition, housing, meals, excursions, fees
Housing: dorms; share w/ Chinese roommates
Application Deadline: Mar 1
Other: activities include excursions
Contact: Laurel Foster-Moore, Tunghai Summer Program, International Programs, University of Massachusetts, Amherst, Amherst, MA 01003 Tel (413) 545-2710

UNIVERSITY OF MINNESOTA—MINNESOTA/ NANKAI SUMMER CHINESE LANGUAGE INSTITUTE
Program Description: summer intensive language program for int/adv students
Site(s) in China: Tianjin (Nankai Univ)
Dates: about 10 wks, Jun-Aug
Eligibility: must be student, w/ min 1 yr college Mandarin
Credits Granted: 15 credit hours undergrad
Subjects Taught: Chinese Language (Mandarin: int/adv)
Cost: $4,360, including tuition, housing, all meals, int'l airfare, books/ materials, excursions, fees
Housing: dorms
Application Deadline: end of Feb
Other: activities include excursions, optional China travel, cultural activities, (e.g., T'ai-chi, calligraphy)
Contact: Minnesota/Nankai Summer Chinese Language Institute, East Asian Studies, University of Minnesota, 105 Folwell Hall, 9 Pleasant St., Minneapolis, MN 55455 Tel (612) 624-0007

UNIVERSITY OF MINNESOTA, DULUTH— CHINESE LANDSCAPE PAINTING PROGRAMS
Program Description: summer program in Chinese art organized in cooperation with Zhejiang Academy of Fine Arts; includes courses taught by Chinese & US faculty, orientation in Hong Kong & US
Site(s) in China: Hangzhou (Zhejiang Academy of Fine Arts)
Dates: early Jun-mid Aug
Eligibility: must be student or adult; artists and teachers (especially in visual arts & crafts)
Credits Granted: 6 credit hours grad
Subjects Taught: Traditional & Contemporary Chinese Painting, Woodblock Printing
Cost: $4,275, including tuition, housing, all meals, int'l airfare, books/ materials, excursions, fees, insurance

Housing: dorms
Application Deadline: May 31
Number of Students Sent/Yr Avg: 28
Other: activities include excursions in China
Contact: Terry Anderson, Chinese Landscape Painting Programs, Continuing Education and Extension, University of Minnesota, Duluth, 403 Darland Administration Bldg., 10 University Dr., Duluth, MN 55812 Tel (218) 726-8113 FAX (218) 726-6336

UNIVERSITY OF NORTH CAROLINA AT CHAPEL HILL—UNC/BEIJING EXCHANGE PROGRAM
This program is offered through Wake Forest/SASASAAS in China Program (see separate entry)
Contact: Wake Forest Program *or* Judy Tilson, UNC/Beijing Exchange Program, Office of International Programs, University of North Carolina at Chapel Hill, 207 Caldwell Hall, 009A/CB 3130, Chapel Hill, NC 27599-3130 Tel (919) 962-7001

UNIVERSITY OF PENNSYLVANIA—PENN-IN-TAIPEI
Program Description: advanced summer program in Chinese language
Site(s) in China: Taipei, Taiwan (Inter-University Center)
Dates: Jun 5-Aug 11
Eligibility: must be student, w/ ability in elementary Chinese
Credits Granted: 3-4 credit hours undergrad
Subjects Taught: Chinese Language (Mandarin: int/adv), Classical Chinese (beg)
Cost: $2,600, including tuition, housing, meals
Housing: private homes
Application Deadline: Mar 16
Other: activities include orientation program in US
Contact: Dr. Jerome Packard, Penn-in-Taipei, Oriental Studies Department, University of Pennsylvania, 847

Williams Hall, Philadelphia, PA 19104 Tel (215) 898-7466/7470

UNIVERSITY OF WISCONSIN-RIVER FALLS—TAIWAN PROGRAM
Program Description: 1 or 2-semester interdisciplinary program
Site(s) in China: Taipei, Taiwan (National Taiwan Normal Univ, Taiwan Provincial College of Education)
Dates: Sep 1-May 30 (1 or 2 terms)
Eligibility: must be UW-Riv Falls student, junior or above, w/ min 2.75 GPA
Credits Granted: 15 credit hours undergrad per semester
Subjects Taught: Comparative Literature, Education/Teaching, Geography, History, Music, Physical Education, Social Sciences/Studies
Cost: write sponsor for info
Housing: dorms
Application Deadline: 1 semester before program begins
Number of Students Sent/Yr Avg: 2
Other: sponsor accredited in US
Contact: Judy S. Kow, Taiwan Program, International Programs, University of Wisconsin-River Falls, 221 Hathorn Hall, River Falls, WI 54022 Tel (715) 425-4891

UNIVERSITY OF WISCONSIN-STEVENS POINT—SEMESTER IN TAIWAN
Program Description: 1-semester interdisciplinary program; special focus on business
Site(s) in China: Taipei, Taiwan (Soochow Univ)
Dates: spring semester
Eligibility: must be sophomore or above
Credits Granted: 13-17 credit hours undergrad
Subjects Taught: Arts, Business/Management, Chinese Language (Mandarin: beg/int/adv), Fashion, Interior Design, Liberal Arts
Cost: $3,600 for WI residents, including tuition, housing, all meals, int'l airfare, excursions

Housing: dorms
Application Deadline: revolving admissions
Other: sponsor accredited in US; program may be taken on audit basis
Contact: Semester in Taiwan, International Programs, University of Wisconsin-Stevens Point, 2100 Main St., Stevens Point, WI 54481 Tel (715) 346-2717

US-CHINA PEOPLE'S FRIENDSHIP ASSOCIATION—CHINESE LANGUAGE STUDY
Program Description: 6 to 8 wks of intensive Chinese language study; 5 days a wk, 4 hours a day
Site(s) in China: Beijing
Dates: spring, summer and fall
Eligibility: college, pre-college, must be min age 16, max age 60; must be in good health.
Credits Granted: transfer academic credit available through California State University at Sacramento
Subjects Taught: Chinese Language (Mandarin: beg/int/adv)
Cost: $2,200 for spring and fall sessions, approx $2,900 for summer program w/ tour; includes tuition, fees, books/materials, housing, local sightseeing and field trips, cultural performances, int'l airfare
Housing: dorms
Application Deadline: spring, Feb 15; summer, April 15; fall, July 1
Other: sponsor is not US-accredited; sponsor is non-profit organization
Contact: Ruby M. Fong; USCPFA Chinese Language Study, 1175 Volz Drive, Sacramento, CA 95822 Tel (916) 447-3313 or (415) 758-7355 FAX (916) 444-2288

WAKE FOREST CHINA PROGRAM
Program Description: fall-semester program in Chinese language and culture
Site(s) in China: Beijing (Beijing Foreign Languages Normal College)
Dates: fall semester
Eligibility: sophomore or above, 3.0 GPA preferred

Credits Granted: undergrad credit available
Subjects Taught: Chinese Language (Mandarin: beg/int/adv)
Cost: $4,750/semester for tuition, fees and living expenses, + $1,500 int'l airfare
Housing: dorms
Application Deadline: Mar 1
Other: sponsor accredited in US; program includes excursions/field trips; some scholarships available
Contact: Judy Tilson, UNC/Beijing Exchange Program, Office of International Programs, University of North Carolina at Chapel Hill, 207 Caldwell Hall, 009A/CB 3130, Chapel Hill, NC 27599-3130 Tel (919) 962-7001

WESTERN WASHINGTON UNIVERSITY— MONGOLIAN LANGUAGE
Program Description: summer program in Mongolian language
Site(s) in China: Hohhot, Inner Mongolia (Inner Mongolia Univ)
Dates: 8 wks, mid Jun-Aug
Eligibility: students, teachers, adults
Credits Granted: undergrad credit available; no grad credit
Subjects Taught: Mongolian Language (beg/int)
Cost: $2,750, including tuition, housing, all meals, int'l airfare, fees, books/materials, excursions
Housing: dorms, furnished rooms
Application Deadline: Feb 15
Other: activities include program travel to Grasslands
Contact: Prof. Henry G. Schwarz , Mongolian Language, Center for East Asian Studies, Mongolia Program, Western Washington University, Bellingham, WA 98225-9056 Tel (206) 676-3041

WHITWORTH COLLEGE—INTERNATIONAL COOPERATIVE EDUCATION PROGRAM (ICE)
Program Description: TESOL internship, including training, organized by consortium of colleges
Site(s) in China: Jilin (Jilin Teachers College)

Dates: Jul 15-Aug 29
Eligibility: must be student w/ good
English skills and strong interest in
Chinese people and culture
Credits Granted: credit available
Subjects Taught: internship in TESOL,
summer course
Cost: $1,702 + $300 summer tuition,
includes tuition, housing, meals, int'l
airfare, insurance, fees, orientation, pre-
departure kick-off
Housing: dorms
Application Deadline: revolving
Number of Students Sent/Yr Avg: 10
Other: both teaching and tutoring
positions available
Contact: Kathy Cook, International
Cooperative Education Program (ICE),
Center for Int'l and Multicultural
Education, Whitworth College,
Spokane, WA 99251
Tel (509) 466-3232
FAX (509) 466-3221

WHITWORTH COLLEGE—WHITWORTH/
JILIN TEACHERS COLLEGE EXCHANGE
PROGRAM
Program Description: 1 or 2-semester
program in Chinese language and area
studies
Site(s) in China: Jilin (Jilin Teachers
College)
Dates: Aug-Jun (1 or 2 terms)
Eligibility: must be junior or senior
Credits Granted: 15 credit hours
undergrad per semester
Subjects Taught: Chinese Language
(Mandarin: beg/int/adv), Civilization/
Culture
Cost: $7,680 per semester, including
tuition, housing, all meals
Housing: dorms, homestay
Application Deadline: Feb 1 for fall;
Oct 1 for spring
Number of Students Sent/Yr Avg: 2
Other: sponsor accredited in US
Contact: Kathy Cook, Whitworth/Jilin
Teachers College Exchange Program,
Center for International and
Multicultural Education, Whitworth
College, Spokane, WA 99251

Tel (509) 466-3232
FAX (509) 466-3221

WHITWORTH COLLEGE—WHITWORTH/
NANJING UNIVERSITY EXCHANGE PROGRAM
Program Description: 1 or 2-semester
program in Chinese language and
culture
Site(s) in China: Nanjing (Nanjing
Univ)
Dates: Sep-Jun (1 or 2 terms)
Eligibility: must be Whitworth student,
junior or senior year, w/ min 2.5 GPA
and 1 yr of college Mandarin
Credits Granted: 12-15 credit hours
undergrad/semester
Subjects Taught: Chinese Language
(Mandarin: beg/int/adv), Civilization/
Culture
Cost: $7,680 per semester, including
tuition, housing, all meals
Housing: dorms
Application Deadline: Feb 1 for fall;
Oct 1 for spring
Number of Students Sent/Yr Avg: 2
Other: sponsor accredited in US
Contact: Kathy Cook, Whitworth/
Nanjing University Exchange Program,
Center for International & Multicultural
Education, Whitworth College,
Spokane, WA 99251
Tel (509) 466-3232
FAX (509) 466-3221

WORLD COLLEGE WEST—WORLD STUDY
PROGRAM IN CHINA
Program Description: 1 or 2-semester
program combining study in China w/
study in US; Chinese language and area
studies working up to independent
project; program temporarily suspended
1989, but may be reinstituted in a few
years; in addition, the school may offer
some type of China study component to
their "Nepal World Study Program"
Contact: World Study Program in
China, China Study Program, World
College West, 101 S. San Antonio Rd.,
Petaluma, CA 94952
Tel (707) 765-4500 *or* (800) 821-2499

Chinese Language

This appendix includes a pronunciation guide for Chinese in both Pinyin and Wade-Giles; a glossary of Chinese terms of particular interest to students and teachers; a list of Chinese language preparatory programs; and a bibliography of Chinese-language study aids.

I   Pronunciation Guide

(all English phonemes according to standard U.S. English)

Pinyin	Wade Giles	Equivalent English Phoneme
a	a	"o" as in "pot"
b	p	"b" as in "boy"
c	ts	"ts" as in "cats"
d	t	"d" as in "radar"
e	er	no English phoneme; "oe" as in French "oevre"
f	f	"f" as in "father"
g	k	"g" as in "got"
h	h	"h" as in "hot"
i (before n)	i or ih	"i" as in "pin"
i (after sh)	ih	"ur" as in "cur"
i (after other consonants)	i or ee	"ee" as in "week"
j	ch	"j" as in "jump"
k	k'	"k" as in "kite"
l	l	"l" as in "lump"
m	m	"m" as in "mud"
n	n	"n" as in "nut"
o	aw	"o" as in "dog"
p	p'	"p" as in "pig"
q	ch'	"ch" as in "chat"
r	j	"j" as in "jump"
(Chinese has a second "r"-like sound as well with no equivalent English phoneme)		
s	s	"s" as in "sat"
t	t'	"t" as in "toy"
u	eu	"oo" as in "loon"

w	w	"w" as in "wand"
x	hs	"sh" as in "she"
y	io	"y" as in "young"
z	tz	"dz" as in "adze"
ai	i	"y" as in "fly"
ao	au	"ou" as in "loud"
ei	ay or ai	"ay" as in "pay"
ia	ya or ia	"ya" as in "yard"
iao	yao or iao	"eow" as in "meow"
iu	iu	"yo" as in "yo-yo"
ui	uay or uai	"way" as in "sway"
uo	aw	"aw" as in "paw"
ng	ng	"ng" as in "hang"
sh	shr	"shr" as in "shroud"
zh	dz, tz, or dh	no equivalent phoneme; halfway between "dr" as in "drop" and "dz" as in "adze"

II Glossary of Terms for Teachers/Students

Materials and Equipment

blackboard:	heiban	黑板
chalk:	fenbi	粉笔
ditto:	youyin	油印
dittomaster:	youyinji	油印机
marker:	caisebi	彩色笔
notebook:	bijiben	笔记本
overhead projector:	fangyingji	放映机
photocopier:	fuyinji	复印机
photocopy:	fuyin	复印
tape recorder:	luyinji	录音机
slide projector:	huandengji	幻灯机
video/VCR:	luxiang/luxiangji	录相／录相机
white board:	baiban	白板

Classroom Terms

class (academic):	ke	课
class ("class of 1991"):	ban	班
class monitor:	banzhang	班长
department/major:	xi	系
exam:	kaoshi	考试
final exam:	dakao/qimokao	大考／期末考
grades:	fenshu	分数
homework:	gongke	功课
midterm:	qizhongkao	期中考
paper/article:	lunwen/wenzhan	论文／文章
quiz:	ceyan/xiaokao	测验／小考
research paper:	yanjiu baogao	研究报告

School Terms

dean's office:	jaowuchu	教务处
doorkeeper (ogre):	kanmende	看门的
foreign affairs office:	waiban	外办
foreign expert:	waizhuan	外专
foreign teacher:	waijiao	外教
personnel office:	renshichu	人事处
professor:	jiaoshou	教授
assistant professor/lecturer:	fujiaoshou/jangshi	副教授／讲师
president (of school):	xiaozhang	校长
vice president:	fuxiaozhang	副校长
responsible person:	fuzeren	负责人
school shuttle:	banche	班车
service person:	fuwuyuan	服务员
teacher:	laoshi/jiaoshi	老师／教师
work unit:	danwei	单位

Market Terms

Weights and Measures:
(1 jin = .5 kilogram = 1.1 lbs; 1 liang = .1 kilo = .22 lbs)

gongjin (kilo):		公斤
jin:		斤
liang:		两
bang (pound):		磅

Arts and Crafts Store:	gongyimeishudian	工艺美术店
Department Store:	baihuodian	百货店
grain coupon:	liangpiao	粮票
meat rationing coupon:	roupiao	肉票
FEC:	waihuiquan	外汇券
Freemarket:	ziyou shichang	自由市场
Freindship Store:	youyi shangdian	友谊商店
NT$:	taibi	台币
private store:	siying shangdian	私营商店
RMB:	renminbi	人民币
state store:	gongjiadian	公家店
yuan:	yuan	元

Non-Chinese herbs and spices sold in China as herbal medicine

cinnamon:	guipi	桂皮
coriander:	yansui	芫荽
cumin:	xiaohuixiang	小茴香
parsley:	ouqin	欧芹
rosemary:	mishuxiang	迷树香
saffron:	zanghonghua	藏红花
sage:	shuweicao	鼠尾草
thyme:	bailixiang	百里香

III Chinese Language Preparatory Programs

The following schools and institutions have major programs in Chinese language. Starred (*) schools have summer programs as well as semester classes:

UNITED STATES

CALIFORNIA:
City College of San Francisco
Los Angeles City College
Monterey Institute of
    International Studies
Pomona College
San Francisco State University
Scripps College
Stanford University
University of California
    (Berkeley, Los Angeles, San
    Diego, Santa Barbara, Santa
    Cruz)

COLORADO:
University of Colorado
    (Boulder)

CONNECTICUT:
Connecticut College
Yale University*

DISTRICT OF COLUMBIA:
Georgetown University
George Washington University

FLORIDA:
University of Miami

ILLINOIS:
University of Chicago*

INDIANA:
Indiana University
    (Bloomington)

MARYLAND:
University of Maryland
    (College Park)

MASSACHUSETTS:
Harvard University
Tufts University
University of Massachusetts
    (Amherst)
Wellesley College

MICHIGAN:
Michigan State University
Oakland University

MINNESOTA:
St. John's University*
University of Minnesota (Twin
    Cities)

MISSOURI:
Washington University

NEW JERSEY:
Douglass College
Livingston College
Princeton University
Rutgers
The State University of New Jersey
University College (New Brunswick)

NEW YORK:
City College of New York
Cornell University*
Hunter College
Queens College
Skidmore College
St. John's University
State University of New York (Albany,
    Binghamton, Buffalo, Cortland, New
    Paltz, Oswego)
University of Rochester

OHIO:
Oberlin College
Ohio State University (Columbus)
Wittenberg University

OREGON:
University of Oregon (Portland) *

PENNSYLVANIA:
Pennsylvania State
University of Pennsylvania
University of Pittsburgh

UTAH:
Brigham Young University

VERMONT:
School for International Training*
Middlebury College*

WISCONSIN:
Beloit College*
University of Wisconsin (Madison)

CANADA:

BRITISH COLUMBIA:
University of British Columbia (Vancouver)

ONTARIO:
University of Toronto

SASKATCHEWAN:
St. Thomas More College

IV Bibliography for Chinese Language Study:

Business Chinese 500. Beijing Language Institute. San Francisco: China Books & Periodicals, Inc., 1982. Excellent glossary of business terms, with exercises and tape set.

Chinese for Today. Beijing Language Institute. San Francisco: China Books & Periodicals, Inc. 1986. Newest series with simple texts and glossaries.

Chinese in Ten Minutes a Day. Kristine Kershul, ed. Seattle: Bilingual Books, 1988. Surprisingly useful for basic communications.

Practical Chinese Reader. Beijing Language Institute. San Francisco: China Books & Periodicals, Inc. 1986. Good intermediate reading series with glossaries.

Spoken Standard Chinese. Hugh M. Stimson and Parker Po Fei Huang. New Haven, Ct.: Yale Far Eastern Publications, 1976. Good 3-book series each for spoken/written skills.

Strange Stories from a Chinese Studio. Linda Hsia and Roger Yue, eds. New Haven, Ct.: Yale Far Eastern Publications, n.d. Traditional stories in simple Chinese with glossaries and study guide.

DICTIONARIES

A Chinese-English Dictionary and

An English-Chinese Dictionary. Beijing: Commercial Press, 1988. Distributed in the U.S. by China Books & Periodicals, Inc. (San Francisco); very easy to use and remarkably complete dictionaries of modern Chinese arranged in alphabetical order of Pinyin romanization; simplified characters only.

Continental's English-Chinese Dictionary. Hong Kong: Hong Kong Press, n.d. One of the best pocket-sized English-Chinese dictionaries; complex characters only.

Matthew's Chinese-English Dictionary (13th Edition). Taipei: Dunhuang Press, 1975. Too basic for serious study of classical Chinese, Matthew's is still simple enough to use for introductory *wenyan* study or for reading modern literature, but too complex for a purely *baihua* dictionary; complex characters only, organized by alphabetical order of Wade-Giles romanization.

A New Practical Chinese-English Dictionary. Taipei: The Far East Book Company, 1971. A good pocket-sized dictionary of complex characters, organized by radical and stroke order.

Xinhua Zidian. Beijing: Xinhua Press, 1975. Excellent pocket-sized Chinese-Chinese dictionary, with both complex and simplified characters.

Publications on China-Related Topics

FUNDING SOURCES AND OTHER GUIDES

China Bound: A Guide to Academic Life and Work in the PRC. Karen Turner-Gottschang and Linda A. Reed. Washington, D.C.: National Academy Press, 1987. A good handbook for professors and researchers preparing to work or conduct research in China.

Funding for Research, Study, and Travel: The People's Republic of China. Denise Wallen and Karen Cantrell, eds. Phoenix: Oryx Press, 1987. A very complete list of all kinds of grants, scholarships and financial aid available to researchers, organizations, and students going to China. Also included is an index arranged by subject (e.g. International Relations, Calligraphy).

International Institute of Education Publications: *The Learning Traveler; Academic Year Abroad; Teaching Abroad; Vacation Study Abroad; Teaching in China Preparation Series.* For publications write 809 United Nations Plaza, New York, NY 10017 Tel: 212-984-5412

Financial Resources for International Study. Institute of International Education (New York). Princeton, N. J.: Peterson's Guides, 1989.

TOURIST AND BUSINESS GUIDEBOOKS

The China Guidebook. Frederic M. Kaplan. New York: Eurasia Press, 1991.

China, A Travel Survival Kit. Alan Samagalski. Berkeley, Ca.: Lonely Planet Publications, 1991.

China Off the Beaten Track. Brian Schwartz. New York: St. Martin's Press, 1983; Hong Kong: South China Morning Post, 1982.

Tibet: Travel Survival Kit. Michael Buckley. Berkeley, Ca.; South Yarra, Victoria, Australia: Lonely Planet Publications, 1986.

CHINESE ART, LITERATURE, AND PHILOSOPHY

Chinese Art. Daisy Lion-Goldschmidt. New York: Rizzoli, 1980.

A Connoisseur's Guide to Chinese Ceramics. Cecile and Michel Beurdeley. New York: Harper &Row, 1974. Excellent guide to Chinese ceramics through the dynasties.

The Dream of the Red Chamber. Hsueh-Chin Tsao, trans. by Florence and Isabel McHugh. New York: Pantheon, 1958.

My Land and My People. Bstan-dzin-rgya-mtsho, Dalai Lama XIV. New York: McGraw-Hill, 1962.

Outlines of Chinese Symbolism and Art Motives. Charles A. S. Williams. New York: Dover, 1990. A straightforward handbook for understanding Chinese symbolism and art.

A Source Book in Chinese Philosophy. Chan Wing-Tsit. Princeton, N.J.: Princeton University Press, 1964.

Sources of Chinese Tradition. William T. DeBary. New York: Columbia University Press, 1964.

The Story of the Stone. Hsueh-Chin Tsao, trans. by David Hawkes. Middlesex, U.K. Penguin, 1973–1982.

Tao Te Ching: The Classic Book of Integrity and the Way. Lao Tzu, trans. by Victor Mair. New York: Bantam, 1990.

CHINESE HISTORY AND POLITICS

Born Red. Gao Yuan. Stanford, Ca.: Stanford University Press, 1987. A chronicle of the Cultural Revolution.

Broken Portraits: Personal Encounters with Chinese Students. Michael David Kwan. San Francisco: China Books & Periodicals, Inc., 1990. A teacher's intimate account of the thoughts and motives of students in Beijing during the 1989 movement.

China, Alive in the Bitter Sea. Fox Butterfield. New York: Bantam, 1982.

The China Reader. D. Milton, N. Milton, and Franz Schurman. New York: Random House, 1966–1972. A 4-volume history which includes: 1. Imperial China: decline of the last dynasty and the origins of modern China; the 18th and 19th centuries. 2. Republican China: nationalism, war, and the rise of Communism, 1911–1949. 3. Communist China: revolutionary reconstruction and international confrontation;1949– present. 4. People's China: social experimentation, politics, entry onto the world scene, 1966 through 1972.

China Rising: The Meaning of Tiananmen. Lee Feigon. Chicago: I. R. Dee, 1990.

A Daughter of Han; the Autobiography of a Chinese Working Woman. Ida Pruitt, ed. Stanford, Ca.: Stanford University Press, 1967. The autobiography of Ning Lao T'ai-t'ai as told to Pruitt by Ning Lao.

The Death of Woman Wang. Jonathan Spence. New York: Viking Press, 1979.

Fanshen. William Hinton. New York: Vintage, 1966. A documentary of revolution in a Chinese village by an American who served as an agricultural adviser to the Chinese government. See also *Shenfan.*

Making Revolution: The Communist Movement in Eastern and Central China. Yung-Fa Chen. Berkeley, Ca.: University of California Press, 1986.

The Memory Palace of Matteo Ricci. Jonathan Spence. New York: Penguin, 1985.

Monarchs and Ministers: The Grand Council in Mid-Ch'ing China, Beatrice S. Bartlett. Berkeley, Ca.: University of California Press, 1990.

Life and Death in Shanghai. Nien Cheng. New York: Grove, 1986. An account of the experience of an upper-class Chinese woman during the Cultural Revolution. Provides the reader with a good understanding of the nature of the Cultural Revolution.

One Billion: A China Chronicle. Jay and Linda Mathews. New York: Ballantine, 1985.

Popular Protest and Political Culture in Modern China (Learning from 1989). Elizabeth Perry and Jeffrey Wasserstein: Boulder, Co.: Westview Press, 1991.

Red Star Over China. Edgar Snow. New York: Grove Press, 1967. A classic though somewhat naive account of the struggles and accomplishments of Chinese Communism during the early decades of the People's Republic of China.

The Search for Modern China. Jonathan Spence. New York: Norton, 1990.

Seven Years in Tibet. Heinrich Harper, trans. by Richard Graves. New York: Dutton, 1954. An account of an Austrian mountain climber's escape from a British internment camp in India during World War II and his 21-month journey through the Himalayas to safety in the Forbidden City of Lhasa in Tibet.

Shark's Fins and Millet. Ilona Ralf Sues. Boston: Little, Brown, 1944.

Shenfan. William Hinton. New York: Random House, 1983. A post-revolution documentary of the same village covered in *Fanshen.*

Son of the Revolution. Liang Heng and Judith Shapiro. New York: Knopf, 1983.

The Soong Dynasty. Sterling Seagrave. New York: Harper & Row, 1985.

Stilwell and the American Experience in China, 1911–1945. Barbara Tuchman. New York: Bantam, 1972. A fascinating account of American General Stilwell's experience in China.

U.S. Crusade in China. Michael Schaller. New York: Columbia University Press, 1979. Discussion of American policy toward China during World War.

GENERAL

All Under Heaven. Pearl S. Buck. New York: John Day Co., 1973.

China through My Window. Naomi Woronov. Armonk, N.Y.: M. E. Sharpe, 1988. An account of life in China through the eyes of an American teacher.

A Day in the Life of China. David Cohen: San Francisco: Collins, 1985. A book of excellent photographs taken in different places throughout China on exactly the same day.

The Heart of the Dragon. Alasdar Clayre. Boston: Houghton Mifflin, 1985.

In China. Eve Arnold. New York: Knopf, 1980.

Iron and Silk. Mark Salzman. New York: Vintage, 1987.

Spring Moon. Bette Bao Lord. New York: Harper & Row, 1981. A work of fiction that gives a romanticized glimpse of life of affluent Chinese in traditional China.

CULTURAL ADAPTATION AND ADJUSTMENT

The Travelers' Guide to Asian Customs and Manners. Nancy L. Braganti and Elizabeth Devine. New York: St. Martin's Press, 1988.

Teaching China's Lost Generation. Tani E. Barlowe and Donald M. Lowe. San Francisco: China Books & Periodicals, 1987.

Two Years in the Melting Pot. Liu Zongren. San Francisco: China books & Periodicals, Inc., 1988.

MATERIALS FOR TEACHING ORAL AND LISTENING SKILLS

Many of the activities in these books (particularly *Action Plans, Keep Talking,* and *Recipes*) don't require the students to have written material in front of them, making these texts ideal for teachers without easy access to copying facilities.

Action Plans: 80 Student-Centered Language Activities. Marion Macdonald and Sue Rogers-Gordon. Rowley, Mass.: Newbury House, 1984.

Can't Stop Talking: Discussion Problems for Advanced Beginners and Low Intermediates. George Rooks. Rowley, Mass.: Newbury House, 1983.

Great Ideas Listening and Speaking Activities for Students of American English. Leo Jones and Victoria Kimbrough. New York: Cambridge University Press, 1987. (Also buy tape and teacher's manual).

Idiomatic American English: A Step-by-Step Workbook for Learning Everyday American Expressions. Barbara K. Gaines. New York: Kodansha International, 1986. Students love idioms and this book contains about 900 of them (in context), along with exercises.

Keep Talking: Communicative Fluency Activities for Language Teaching. Fredericke Klippel. New York: Cambridge University Press, 1984.

Look Again Pictures: For Language Development and Lifeskills. Judy Winn-Bell Olson. Hayward, Ca.: The Alemany Press, 1984. Contains material that "points out the 8 differences between the top picture and the bottom picture"; good for teaching prepositions, present progressive tense, or simply to make students speak. Overhead transparencies of the illustrations make effective teaching tools.

The Non-Stop Discussion Workbook: Problems for Intermediate and Advanced Students. George Rooks. Rowley, Mass.: Newbury House, 1981.

Recipes for Tired Teachers: Well-Seasoned Activities for the ESOL Classroom. Christopher Sion. Reading, Mass.: Addison-Wesley, 1985.

MATERIALS FOR TEACHING WRITING

From Process to Product: Beginning-Intermediate Writing Skills for Students of ESL. Natalie Lefkowitz. Englewood Cliffs, N.J.: Prentice-Hall, 1988. Takes students through the writing process, from brainstorming to organizing ideas in a logical way. Contains ideas useful for any level, but more appropriate for beginning to intermediate.

Idea Exchange: Writing What You Mean. Linda Lonon-Blanton. Rowley, Mass.: Newbury House, 1988. Contains some of the traditional rhetorical forms (comparison and contrast, classification, etc.) but presents them in an innovative way. There are 2 books: Level 1 for beginning-intermediate and Level 2 for intermediate-advanced.

Practical Guide for Advanced Writers in English as a Second Language. Paul Munsell and Martha Clough. New York: MacMillan,1984. More of a traditional writing text which contains examples of and explanations for all of the major expository writing forms (contrast, classification, etc.).

Writer's Companion. Marcella Frank. Rowley, Mass.: Newbury House, 1983. Small, very useful book which contains an excellent, clear and concise explanation of the most common grammatical mistakes.

China-Related Resource Organizations

Embassies/Consulates/Government Representatives

AUSTRALIA

EMBASSY OF THE PRC
14 Federal Highway
Watson, A.C.T. 2602
(062) 412-446

CONSULATES-GENERAL OF THE PRC IN AUSTRALIA:
539 Elizabeth St.
Surry Hills
Sydney, N.S.W. 2010
(02) 698-7929

75-77 Irving Rd.
Toorak, VIC 3142
(03) 882-0604

TAIWAN
Far Eastern Trading Corporation
P.O. Box 148
World Trade Center
Melbourne, VIC 3005
(03) 611-2988

Far Eastern Trading Corporation,
Sydney Branch
Room 1902, Level 19
MLC Center
King St.
Sydney, N.S.W. 2000
(02) 223-3207

CANADA

EMBASSY OF THE PRC
515 St. Patrick's St.
Ottawa, ONT
KIN 5H3
(613) 234-2706

CONSULATES-GENERAL OF THE PRC IN CANADA:
1296 The Crescent
Vancouver, B.C. V 6H 1T4
(026) 736-3910

240 St. George St.
Toronto, ONT
M5R 2P4
(416) 964-7260

TAIWAN
no Taiwanese government office in Canada

NEW ZEALAND

EMBASSY OF THE PRC
6 Glenmore St.
Wellington
(64-04) 636-5197

TAIWAN
East Asian Trading Center
P.O. Box 10-250

The Terrace
Wellington
(614) 736-474

UK

EMBASSY OF THE PRC
49-51 Portland Pl.
London WIN 3AH
(71) 636-5197

TAIWAN

Free Chinese Center
4th Floor, Dorland House
14-16 Regent St.
London, SWEY 4PH
(071) 930-5767

US

EMBASSY OF THE PRC

2300 Connecticut Ave. NW
Washington, DC 20008
(202) 325-2500

CONSULATES-GENERAL OF THE PRC
IN THE UNITED STATES

Chicago—
104 S. Michigan Ave.
Chicago, IL 60603
(312) 346-0288

Houston—
3417 Montrose Blvd
Houston, TX 77006
(713) 524 0780

Los Angeles—
501 Shatto Pl.
Los Angeles, CA 90020
(213) 380-2507

New York—
520 Twelth Ave.
New York, NY 10036
(212) 868-7410

San Francisco—
1450 Laguna St.
San Francisco, CA 94115
(415) 563-7885

TAIWAN

**Coordination Councils for
North American Affairs:**

Atlanta—
2 Midtown Plaza, Suite 1290
1349 West Peachtree St. NE
Atlanta, GA 30309
(404) 872-0129

Boston—
P.O. Box 775
Boston, MA 02102
(617) 737-2050

Chicago—
20 N. Clark St., 19th Floor
Chicago, IL 60602
(312) 372-1213

District of Columbia—
4201 Wisconsin Ave., NW
Washington, D.C. 20016-2137

Honolulu—
P.O. Box 27165
Honolulu, HI 96827
(808) 595-6347

Houston—
Eleven Greenway Plaza
Suite 2006
Houston, TX 77046
(713) 626-7445

Kansas City—
P.O. Box 413617
Kansas City, MO 64141
(816) 531-1298

Los Angeles—
3731 Wilshire Blvd., Suite 700
Los Angeles, CA 90010
(213) 389-1215

Miami—
The Colonnade
2333 Ponce de Leon Blvd., Suite 610
Coral Gables, FA 33134
(305) 443-8917

New York—
801 2nd Ave., 9th Floor
New York, NY 10017
(212) 697-1250

Seattle—
Suite 2410, Westin Bldg.
2001 6th Ave.
Seattle, WA 98121
(206) 441-4586

Sister-City Programs

US—PRC:

Baltimore, MD (Xiamen)
Boston, MA (Hangzhou)
Boulder, CO (Lhasa)
Charlotte, NC (Baoding)
Chattanooga, TN (Wuxi)
Chicago, IL (Shenyang)
Cincinnati, OH (Liuzhou)
Columbus, OH (Hefei)
Denver, CO (Kunming)
Des Moines, IA (Shijiazhuang)
Erie, PA (Zibo)
Flint, MI (Changchun)
Harrisburg, PA (Luoyang)
Honolulu County, HI (Hainan Island)
Houston, TX (Shenzhen)
Joliet, IL (Liaoyang)
Kansas City, MO (Xi'an)
Long Beach, CA (Qingdao)
Los Angeles, CA (Guangzhou)
Midland, TX (Dongying)
New York, NY (Beijing)
Oakland, CA (Dalian)
Orlando, FA (Guilin)
Philadelphia, PA (Tianjin)
Phoenix, AZ (Chengdu)
Pittsburgh, PA (Wuhan)
Portland, OR (Suzhou)
Sacramento, CA (Jinan)
San Diego, CA (Yantai)
San Francisco, CA (Shanghai)
Seattle, WA (Chongqing)
Spokane, WA (Jilin)
St. Louis, MO (Nanjing)
St. Paul, MN (Changsha)
Tempe, AZ (Zhenjiang)
Titusville, FA (Yueyang)
Toledo, OH (Qinhuangdao)
Tulsa, OK (Beihai)
Washington, D.C. (Beijing)
Wilmington, DE (Ningbo)
Wilmington, NC (Dandong)
Witchita, KS (Kaifeng)

US—TAIWAN

Addison, TX (Panchiao City)
Albuquerque, NM (Hualien City)
Alhambra, CA (Hsinchu County)

Americus, GA (Yungho City)
Atlanta, GA (Taipei)
Austin, TX (Taichung)
Baton Rouge, LA (Taichung)
Beaverton, OR (Hsinchu County)
Bellevue, WA (Hualien City)
Bloomington, IN (Luchou Township)
Brunswick, GA (Ilan County)
Campbell, CA (Keelung City)
Casper, WY (Hsichih Township)
Charleston, IL (Fengshan City)
Cheyenne, WY (Taichung)
Cleveland, OH (Taipei)
Clallam County, WA (Miaoli County)
Colorado Springs, CO (Kaohsiung)
Columbus, OH (Tainan City)
Corpus Christi, TX (Keelung City)
East Orange, NJ (Chiayi County)
Enfield, CT (Chung Li City)
Flagstaff, AZ (Hsintien City)
Grover, CA (Tamsui Township)
Guam (Taipei)
Hawaii County, HI (Hualien County)
Holtville, CA (Chiangchung Hsiang)
Honolulu County, HI (Kaohsiung)
Houston, TX (Taipei)
Indianapolis, IN (Taipei)
Jackson, MS (Chiayi County)
Kansas City, MO (Tainan City)
King County, WA (Kaohsiung County)
Kissimee, FA (Miaoli Township)
Knoxville, TN (Kaohsiung)
Little Rock, AR (Kaohsiung)
Los Angeles, CA (Taipei)
Macon, GA (Kaohsiung)
Mankato, MN (Tamsui Township)
Marshall, TX (Taipei)
Maui County, HI (Pingtung County)
Miami, FA (Kaohsiung)
Mobile, AL (Kaohsiung)
Monterey Park, CA (Yungho City)
Morgantown, WV (Mucha District)
Muncie, IN (Changhua County)
New Haven, CT (Taichung)
Oklahoma City, OK (Taipei)
Orlando, FA (Tainan City)
Pensacola, FA (Kaohsiung)
Phoenix, AZ (Taipei)

Plains, GA (Kaohsiung)
Portland, OR (Kaohsiung)
Prince George's County, MD (Nantou County)
Reno, NV (Taichung)
Richland County, OH (Taipei County)
Salt Lake City, UT (Keelung City)
San Antonio, TX (Kaohsiung)
San Diego, CA (Taichung)
San Francisco, CA (Taipei)

San Gabriel, CA (Changhua City)
San Jose, CA (Tainan City)
Sumter, SC (Fengyuan City)
Tucson, AZ (Taichung)
Tulsa, OK (Kaohsiung)
Wildwood, NJ (Hsinchu County)
Williamsport, PA (Neipu Hsiang, Pingtung City)
Yakima, WA (Keelung City)

China-Related Associations, Organizations, and Foundations

This list reprinted with permission from the National Committee on US-China Relations' China Resource List

(see also listings in Directories 2 & 3 under Sending Organizations: the following have no formal sending programs, but can provide information)

US

AMERICAN BAR ASSOCIATION'S LAW COMMITTEE ON THE PRC
Inernational Programs Coordination Office
750 North Lake Shore Dr.
Chicago, IL 60611

The Asia Society
725 Park Ave.
New York, NY 10021
(212) 288-6400
(regional Asia Societies in: Houston, Los Angeles, and Washington, DC)

THE CHINA COUNCIL OF THE ASIA SOCIETY
725 Park Ave.
New York, NY 10021
(regional China Councils in Athens, GA; Austin, TX; Boulder, CO; Columbus, OH; East Lansing, MI; Milwaukee, WI; Portland, OR; Seattle, WA; St. Louis, MO; St. Paul, MN; Tucson, AZ)

ASSOCIATION FOR ASIAN STUDIES
1 Lane Hall
University of Michigan
Ann Arbor, MI 48109
(313) 665-2490

CENTER FOR CHINESE LEGAL STUDIES
COMMITTEE FOR LEGAL EXCHANGE WITH CHINA
Columbia University School of Law
435 W. 116th St.
New York, NY 10027
(212) 280-3422

CENTER FOR CHINESE RESEARCH MATERIALS
1527 New Hampshire Ave. NW
Washington, DC 20036
(202) 387-7172

CENTER FOR U.S.-CHINA ARTS EXCHANGE
423 W. 118th St., Suite 1E
New York, NY 10027
(212) 280-4648

CHINA INSTITUTE IN AMERICA, INC.
125 E. 65th St.
New York, NY 10021
(212) 744-8181

CHINESE CULTURE FOUNDATION OF SAN FRANCISCO
750 Kearny St.
San Francisco, CA 94108
(415) 986-1822

CHINESE-ENGLISH TRANSLATION
ASSISTANCE GROUP
P.O. Box 400
Kensington, MD 20795
(301) 946-7007

COMMITTEE ON SCHOLARLY COMMUNICATION
WITH THE PRC
National Academy of Sciences
2101 Constitution Ave.
Washington, DC 20410
(202) 334-2718

THE FOUNDATION FOR BOOKS TO CHINA
601 California St.
San Francisco, CA 94108
(415) 765-0664

INSTITUTE OF INTERNATIONAL EDUCATION
809 United Nations Plaza
New York, NY 10017
(212) 883-8200

JOINT COMMITTEE ON CHINESE STUDIES OF
THE SOCIAL RESEARCH COUNCIL AND THE
AMERICAN COUNCIL OF LEARNED SOCIETIES
SOCIAL SCIENCE RESEARCH COUNCIL
605 Third Ave.
New York, NY 10158
(212) 661-0280

MIDWEST CHINA CENTER
308 Gullixson Hall
2481 Como Ave.
St. Paul, MN 66109
(612) 641-3233

NATIONAL COMMITTEE ON
US-CHINA RELATIONS
777 United Nations Plaza
New York, NY 10017
(212) 922-1385

U.S.-CHINA BUSINESS COUNCIL
1818 N St. NW
Washington, DC 20036
(202) 439-6340

WASHINGTON STATE CHINA RELATIONS
COUNCIL
Fourth and Vine Building
2601 Fourth Ave., Suite 330
Seattle, WA 98121
(206) 441-4419

*A list of China-related booksellers, transla-
tion services, university centers, outreach
programs, US government agencies, and
PRC institutions in the US is available from
the National Committee on US-China Relations.*

Key Universities

Anhui Polytechnical University, Anhui

Anhui University, Anhui

Beijing Aerospace University, Beijing Special Zone

Beijing Institute of Post and Telecommunications, Beijing Special Zone

Beijing Transportation University, Beijing Special Zone

Beijing University of Technology, Beijing Special Zone

Beijing University, Beijing Special Zone

Central Academy of Fine Arts, Beijing Special Zone

Central Conservatory of Music, Beijing Special Zone

Central Minorities Institute, Beijing Special Zone

Chengdu Institute of Radio Engineering, Sichuan

Chengdu University of Science and Technology, Chengdu

China University of Science and Technology, Anhui

China University of Geological Science, Hubei

Chinese People's University (Renda), Beijing

Chongqing Institute of Architectural Engineering, Sichuan

Chongqing University, Sichuan

Daqing Petroleum Institute, Heilongjiang

East China Normal University, Shanghai Special Zone

Fudan University, Shanghai Special Zone

Fuzhou University, Fujian

Guangdong Institute of Technology, Guangdong

Guangxi University, Guangxi

Guizhou University, Guizhou

Harbin Institute of Ship and Boat Engineering, Heilongjiang

Harbin Institute of Science and Technology, Heilongjiang

Henan University, Henan

Hunan University of Science and Technology, Hunan

Hunan University, Hunan

Jiangxi University, Jiangxi

Jilin University, Jilin

Jilin University of Science and Technology, Jilin

Lanzhou University, Gansu

Liaoning University, Liaoning

Nanjing Institute of Meteorology, Jiangsu

Nanjing University, Jiangsu

Nankai University, Tianjin Special Zone

Ningxia University, Ningxia

Northeast Institute of Technology, Liaoning

Northwest University, Shaanxi

Quinghua University, Beijing Special Zone

Shandong University, Shandong

Shanghai Foreign Languages Institute, Shanghai Special Zone

Shanghai Institute of Foreign Trade, Shanghai Special Zone

Shanghai Number One College of Medicine,   Shanghai Special Zone

Shanghai Polytechnical University, Shanghai Special Zone

Shanghai Transportation University, Shanghai Special Zone

Shanxi Agricultural University, Shanxi

Shenyang University, Liaoning

Shenzhen University, Guangdong

Sichuan University, Sichuan

South China Agricultural University, Guangdong

South China Institute of Technology, Guangdong

Southwest Institute of Politics and Law, Sichuan

Southwest University, of Transportation, Sichuan

Taiyuan University of Technology, Shanxi

Tianjin University, Tianjin Special Zone

Tibet University, Tibet

Tongji University, Shanghai Special Zone

University of Inner Mongolia, Inner Mongolia

Wuhan University, Hubei

Xi'an Transportation University, Shaanxi

Xiamen University, Fujian

Yunnan University, Yunnan

Zhejiang University, Zhejiang

Zhejiang University of Agriculture, Zhejiang

Zhengzhou University, Henan

Zhongshan University, Guangdong

Index